VISIT US AT

Cyber Crime Investigations

Bridging the Gaps
Between Security Professionals,
Law Enforcement, and Prosecutors

Anthony Reyes New York City Police Department's Computer
Crimes Squad Detective, Retired

Kevin O'Shea

Jim Steele

Jon R. Hansen

Captain Benjamin R. Jean

Thomas Ralph

KEY	SERIAL NUMBER
001	HJIRTCV764
002	PO9873D5FG
003	829KM8NJH2
004	78SPLBBC72
005	CVPLQ6WQ23
006	VBP965T5T5
007	HJJJ863WD3E
008	2987GVTWMK
009	629MP5SDJT
010	IMWQ295T6T

PUBLISHED BY
Syngress Publishing, Inc. ✓
800 Hingham Street
Rockland, MA 02370

Cyber Crime Investigations: Bridging the Gaps
Between, Security Professionals, Law Enforcement, and Prosecutors

Printed in the United States of America
1 2 3 4 5 6 7 8 9 0
ISBN-10: 1-59749-133-0
ISBN-13: 978-1-59749-133-4

Publisher: Amorette Pedersen   Project manager: Gary Byrne
Acquisitions Editor: Andrew Williams   Page Layout and Art: Patricia Lupien
Technical Editor: Anthony Reyes   Copy Editors: Michael McGee, Adrienne Rebello
Cover Designer: Michael Kavish   Indexer: Michael Ferreira

For information on rights, translations, and bulk sales, contact Matt Pedersen, Commercial Sales Director and Rights, at Syngress Publishing; email m.pedersen@syngress.com.

Lead Author and Technical Editor

Anthony Reyes is a retired New York City Police Department Computer Crimes Detective. While employed for the NYPD, he investigated computer intrusions, fraud, identity theft, child exploitation, intellectual property theft, and software piracy.

He was an alternate member of New York Governor George E. Pataki's Cyber-Security Task Force, and he currently serves as President for the High Technology Crime Investigation Association. He is the Education & Training Working Group Chair for the National Institute of Justice's Electronic Crime Partner Initiative. Anthony is also an Associate Editor for the *Journal of Digital Forensic Practice* and an editor for *The International Journal of Forensic Computer Science*.

He is an Adjutant Professor and is the Chief Executive Officer for the Arc Enterprises of New York, Inc. on Wall Street. Anthony has over 20 years of experience in the IT field. He teaches for several government agencies and large corporations in the area of computer crime investigations, electronic discovery, and computer forensics. He also lectures around the world.

Anthony dedicates his chapters to "the breath of his soul": his sons, Richie and Chris, and his mother, Hilda. He would like to thank his family and friends who endured his absence during the writing of this book. He also thanks Kevin O'Shea, Jim Steele, Jon R Hansen, Benjamin R. Jean, Thomas Ralph, Chet Hosmer, Christopher L.T. Brown, Doctor Marcus Rogers, and Paul Cibas for their contributions in making this book happen.

Anthony wrote Chapters 1, 4, and 5.

Contributors

Kevin O'Shea is currently employed as a Homeland Security and Intelligence Specialist in the Justiceworks program at the University of New Hampshire. In this capacity, Mr. O'Shea supports the implementation of tools, technology, and training to assist law enforcement in the investigation of crimes with a cyber component. In one of Kevin's recent projects, he was a technical consultant and developer of a training program for a remote computer-forensics-viewing technology, which is now in use by the state of New Hampshire. He also has developed a computer-crime-investigative curriculum for the New Hampshire Police Standards and Training.

Kevin dedicates his chapters to his family— "his true angels," Leighsa, Fiona, and Mairead, for their patience, love, and encouragement. He would also like to thank Tony Reyes and the other authors of this book (it was a pleasure to work with all of you), as well as the TAG team, Stacy and Andrew, for their unbending support and friendship.

Kevin wrote Chapters 2 and 7; he also cowrote Chapter 6.

James "Jim" Steele (CISSP, MCSE: Security, Security+) has a career rich with experience in the security, computer forensics, network development, and management fields. For over 15 years he has played integral roles regarding project management, systems administration, network administration, and enterprise security management in public safety and mission-critical systems. As a Senior Technical Consultant assigned to the NYPD E-911 Center, he designed and managed implementation of multiple systems for enterprise security; he also performed supporting operations on-site during September 11, 2001, and the blackout of 2003. Jim has also participated in foreign projects such as the development of the London

Metropolitan Police C3i Project, for which he was a member of the Design and Proposal Team. Jim's career as a Technical Consultant also includes time with the University of Pennsylvania and the FDNY. His time working in the diverse network security field and expert knowledge of operating systems and network products and technologies have prepared him for his current position as a Senior Digital Forensics Investigator with a large wireless carrier. His responsibilities include performing workstation, server, PDA, cell phone, and network forensics as well as acting as a liaison to multiple law enforcement agencies, including the United States Secret Service and the FBI. On a daily basis he investigates cases of fraud, employee integrity, and compromised systems. Jim is a member of HTCC, NYECTF, InfraGard, and the HTCIA.

Jim dedicates his chapters to his Mom, Dad, and Stephanie.
Jim wrote Chapter 9.

Jon R. Hansen is Vice-President of Sales and Business Development for AccessData. He is a computer specialist with over 24 years of experience in computer technologies, including network security, computer forensics, large-scale software deployment, and computer training on various hardware and software platforms.

He has been involved with defining and developing policies and techniques for safeguarding computer information, recovering lost or forgotten passwords, and acquiring forensic images. Jon has presented at conferences all over the world, addressing audiences in the United States, Mexico, Brazil, England, Belgium, Italy, The Netherlands, New Zealand, Australia, Singapore, Hong Kong, Korea, Japan, and South Africa.

As the former Microsoft Regional Director for the State of Utah, Jon has represented many companies as a consultant and liaison administrator, including Microsoft, WordPerfect, Lotus Corporation, and Digital Electronic Corporation (DEC).

Jon dedicates his chapters to the "love of his live," his wife, Tammy.
Jon wrote Chapter 10.

Captain Benjamin R. Jean has spent his entire law enforcement career in the State of New Hampshire, starting in 1992 for the Deerfield Police Department. He is currently employed as a Law Enforcement Training Specialist for the New Hampshire Police Standards & Training Council and is Chief of the Training Bureau. Captain Jean teaches classes in various law enforcement topics, including computer crime investigation, and is an active member of the New Hampshire Attorney General's Cyber Crime Initiative. He was recently awarded the 2006 Cyber Crime Innovation Award and holds an Associate's Degree in Criminal Justice from New Hampshire Community Technical College and a Bachelor's Degree in Information Technology from Granite State College.

Benjamin dedicates his chapter to his kids, whom he does everything for, and his wife, who makes it all possible.

Benjamin wrote Chapter 8.

Thomas Ralph graduated *cum laude* from Case Western Reserve University School of Law, where he served as editor on the school's Law Review. In 1998, after serving as legal counsel at MassHighway, Mr. Ralph joined the Middlesex District Attorney's Office, where he performed trial work in the District and Superior Courts. Mr. Ralph became Deputy Chief of the Appeals Bureau, Captain of the Search Warrant Team, and Captain of the Public Records Team. Mr. Ralph has appeared dozens of times in the Massachusetts Appeals Court and Supreme Judicial Court. In 2005, Mr. Ralph became an Assistant Attorney General in the New Hampshire Attorney General's office. His responsibilities there included spearheading the New Hampshire Attorney General's Cybercrime Initiative, an innovative program for processing and handling electronic evidence that has received national recognition, and overseeing complex investigations into the electronic distribution of child pornography.

Tom dedicates his chapter to his beloved father, S. Lester Ralph.
Tom wrote Chapter 3 and cowrote Chapter 6.

Bryan Cunningham (JD, Certified in NSA IAM, Top Secret security clearance) has extensive experience in information security, intelligence, and homeland security matters, both in senior U.S. Government posts and the private sector. Cunningham, now a corporate information and homeland security consultant and Principal at the Denver law firm of Morgan & Cunningham LLC, most recently served as Deputy Legal Adviser to National Security Advisor Condoleezza Rice. At the White House, Cunningham drafted key portions of the Homeland Security Act, and was deeply involved in the formation of the National Strategy to Secure Cyberspace, as well as numerous Presidential Directives and regulations relating to cybersecurity. He is a former senior CIA Officer, federal prosecutor, and founding cochair of the ABA CyberSecurity Privacy Task Force. In January 2005, he was awarded the National Intelligence Medal of Achievement for his work on information issues. Cunningham has been named to the National Academy of Science Committee on Biodefense Analysis and Countermeasures. He is a Senior Counselor at APCO Worldwide Consulting and a member of the Markle Foundation Task Force on National Security in the Information Age. Cunningham counsels corporations on information security programs and other homeland security-related issues and, working with information security consultants, guides and supervises information security assessments and evaluations.

Bryan wrote Appendix A.

Brian Contos has over a decade of real-world security engineering and management expertise developed in some of the most sensitive and mission-critical environments in the world. As ArcSight's CSO he advises government organizations and Global 1,000s on security strategies related to Enterprise Security Management (ESM) solutions while being an evangelist for the ESM space.

Colby DeRodeff (GCIA, GCNA) is a Senior Security Engineer for ArcSight Inc. Colby has been with ArcSight for over five years and has been instrumental in the company's growth. Colby has been a key contributor in the first product deployments, professional services and engineering.

Brian and Colby wrote Appendix B.

Contents

Chapter 1

The Problem at Hand

Midway upon the journey of our life I found myself within a forest dark,
For the straightforward pathway had been lost.
....
I cannot well repeat how there I entered,
So full was I of slumber at the moment
In which I had abandoned the true way

—*Dante Alighieri*
The Divine Comedy—Inferno

Solutions in this chapter:

- **The Gaps in Cyber Crime Law**

- **Unveiling the Myths Behind Cyber Crime**

- **Prioritizing Evidence**

- **Setting the Bar too High**

☑ **Summary**

☑ **Solutions Fast Track**

☑ **Frequently Asked Questions**

Introduction

In the literary classic *The Inferno*, Dante wakes up from a semiconscious state only to find himself lost in the Dark Woods of Error. Uncertain how he came to stray from the *True Way*, Dante attempts to exit the woods and is immediately driven back by three beasts. Dante, faced with despair and having no hope of ever leaving the woods, is visited by the spirit of Virgil. Virgil, a symbol of Human Reason, explains he has been sent to lead Dante from error. Virgil tells him there can be no direct ascent to heaven past the beasts, for the man who would escape them must go a longer and harder way. Virgil offers to guide Dante, but only as far as Human Reason can go (Ciardi, 2001).

As with Dante, I too frequently "strayed from the True Way into the Dark Woods of Error" when investigating cyber crime. Often times, I found myself lost as a result of a lack of available information on how to handle the situations I confronted. Yet other times I wasn't quite sure how I got to the point where I became lost. As a cyber crimes investigator, you've undoubtedly encountered similar situations where there was little or no guidance to aid you in your decision-making process. Often, you find yourself posting "hypothetical" questions to an anonymous list serve, in the hopes that some stranger's answer might ring true. Although you've done your due diligence, sleepless nights accompany you as you contemplate how your decision will come back to haunt you.

We recently witnessed such an event with the Hewlett-Packard Board of Directors scandal. In this case, seasoned investigators within HP and the primary subcontracting company sought clarity on an investigative method they were implementing for an investigation. The investigators asked legal counsel to determine if the technique being used was legal or illegal. Legal counsel determined that the technique fell within a grey area, and did not constitute an illegal act. As a result, the investigators used it and were later arrested. This situation could befall any cyber crimes investigator.

Cyber crime investigations are still a relatively new phenomenon. Methods used by practitioners are still being developed and tested today. While attempts have been made to create a methodology on how to conduct these types of investigations, the techniques can still vary from investigator to investigator, agency to agency, corporation to corporation, and situation to situation. No definitive book exists on cyber crime investigation and computer forensic procedures at this time. Many of the existing methodologies, books, articles, and literature on the topic are based on a variety of research methods, or interpretations on how the author suggests one should proceed. The field of computer forensics is so new that the American Academy of Forensic Sciences is only now beginning to accept it as a discipline under its general section for forensic sciences. I suspect that cyber crime investigations and the computer forensic methodologies are still in their infancy stages and that the definitive manual has yet to be written.

In the following pages and chapters, areas of difficulties, misconceptions, and flaws in the cyber investigative methodology will be discussed in an attempt to bridge the gaps. This book is by no means intended to be the definitive book on cyber crime investigations. Rather, it is designed to be a guide, as Virgil was to Dante, to help you past the "Beasts" and place you back on the road to the True Way. While I anticipate readers of this book to disagree with some of the authors' opinions, it is my hope that it will serve to create a dialogue within our community that addresses the many issues concerning cyber crime investigations. Dante was brought to the light by a guide—a guide that symbolized Human Reason. We, too, can overcome the gaps that separate and isolate the cyber-investigative communities by using this same faculty, our greatest gift.

WARNING

In the Hewlett-Packard case, legal consul did not fully understand the laws relating to such methodologies and technological issues. The lesson for investigators here is don't sit comfortable with an action you've taken because corporate consul told you it was okay to do it. This is especially true within the corporate arena. In the HP case, several investigators were arrested, including legal consul, for their actions.

The Gaps in Cyber Crime Law

When I started my stint as a "Cyber Detective" many cyber crime laws were nonexistent, information on the topic was scarce, and there were only a handful of investigators working these types of cases. Today, cyber crime laws are still poorly worded or simply don't apply to the types of crimes being investigated. Additionally, many cyber crimes laws still vary from state to state. Attempts to address cyber crimes in the law are thwarted by the speed at which technology changes compared to the rate at which laws are created or revised.

In a research report published by the National Institute of Justice in 2001, researchers determined that uniform laws, which kept pace with electronic crimes, were among the top ten critical needs for law enforcement (National Institute of Justice, 2001). It found that laws were often outpaced by the speed of technological change. These gaps in the law were created by the length of time it took for legislation to be created or changed to meet the prosecutorial demands of cyber crimes.

In 2003, I worked a child pornography case that demonstrated the gap between the legal framework and changing technology. In this case, I arrested a suspect who was a known trader in the child pornography industry. He had set up a file server that traded pictures and videos of child porn. This site was responsible for trading child porn with hundreds of users around the world on a daily basis. So the idea was to take over control of the file server and record the activities of the users who logged on. Knowing that I would essentially be recording the live activity of unsuspecting individuals, it was prudent to think I would need a wiretap order from the court. The only problem was that child pornography was not listed as one of the underlying crimes for which you could obtain a wiretap order under the New York State Criminal Procedure Code. Some of the crimes for which wiretapping was allowed at the time included murder, arson, criminal mischief, and falsifying business records—but not child pornography. As a result, we relied on the fact that New York State was a one-party consent state. This allowed me to record my side of the conversation—in this case, the computer activity. However, a problem still arose with the issue of privacy as it pertained to the IP addresses of the individuals logging in. The legal question was whether the unsuspecting users had a reasonable expectation of privacy as it related to their IP address. This issue caused great debates among the legal scholars involved. Nevertheless, we erred on the side of caution and obtained a trap and trace order. This court order allowed us to record the inbound connections of unsuspecting suspects and trace their connection back to their Internet service provider. We then issued subpoenas to identify the connection location and referred the case to the local jurisdiction. In the end, numerous arrests were made and cases where generated around the world. This is an example where the legal framework did not address our situation.

TIP

One-party consent state The wiretap laws differ from state to state, and the # *party consent* refers to the number of parties that must consent to the recording of a conversation in a given state. Two-party states require that both parties consent to the recording of the conversation. Many times you may hear a recording when calling a company informing you that the conversation is going to be recorded. This helps fulfill the consent requirement for states that require both parties to consent. In the case discussed, *one-party consent* means that only one of the conversation's participants needs to agree in order to record the conversation. Traditionally, *one-party consent* applied to only telephone conversations, but in today's world, consent can include the recording of electronic communications.

Trap and trace Trap and trace refers to a court order that allows law enforcement to capture calls to and from a location. Originally, it applied only to telephones but with the advent of computers and Voice over IP, it now encompasses other types of communication methods.

Notes from the Underground...

Warrants

Whenever there is a question of whether or not a warrant should be written, err on the side of caution. Get the warrant; chances are your intuition is right. So remember my little phrase: "when in doubt, write it out."

Even though legal issues identified in the cyber porn example existed back then, little has changed to date. Revisiting the Hewlett-Packard Board of Directors scandal, the investigative techniques included *pretexting and e-mail tracing*. Lawyers, academic scholars, and investigators have raised the issue of whether or not HP's actions during the investigation were in fact illegal. According to news reports, there were no specific federal laws prohibiting HP's use of these investigative techniques (Krazit, 2006). Randal Picker, a professor of commercial law, also stated that he believes the techniques are legal, but that evidence collected from these techniques may not be admissible in a court of law (Picker, 2006).

Getting back to the child porn example from 2003, would it surprise you to know that during the writing of this chapter I perused the New York State Legislature's Web site under the Criminal Procedure Law and still found that none of the laws pertaining to Article 263 (Sexual Performance by a Child) of the Penal Law are listed as designated offenses for which a wiretap order could be granted? Fear not, they at least updated the law to include Identity Theft (New York State, 2006). As you can see, these types of legal issues will continue to be raised as lawmakers and legislators struggle to find ways to respond adequately, and immediately, to change when technology affects the law.

Unveiling the Myths Behind Cyber Crime

Investigating cyber crime can be very intimidating to a technophobe. I recall walking into police stations, prosecutor's offices, and court rooms and seeing the faces of those on duty when I told them I had a crime that involved a computer. Many an expression would transform from a welcoming look to that of abject fear. Maybe the fear comes from the fact that most folks born prior to the year 2000 just weren't exposed to computers. I remember playing with "Lincoln Logs" and a "Barrel of Monkeys" growing up. Today, my nine-year-old son creates his own Web sites, and competes for rank when playing "Call of Duty 3" on his X-Box Live system. My older son, who's only 13, can maneuver quite well in the Linux environment.

I went through great pain in changing from my typewriter to the old Commodore 64 computer in the late 1980s. I experienced similar stress when my police department went from ink fingerprint cards to the live fingerprint scanners. In both instances, I resisted the change until I was finally made to give in. For me, the resistance to change occurred because I thought this technology was too complicated to understand. I also believed I needed special training that required a computer science degree. Either way, I was wrong. Once I embraced computers and high technology I began to understand its use and conceptualize the ramifications of its illegal use.

It's Just Good Ol' Crime

When we remove the veil of mystery surrounding cyber-related crime, an amazing thing happens: we start to remember that a crime has occurred. Unfortunately, when dealing with computer crime investigations, many investigators forget that ultimately the underlying fact is that someone committed a crime. Almost every cyber crime has, at its base, a good-old-fashioned crime attached to it. In a computer tampering case, there is some act of criminal mischief, larceny, or destruction of property. In a cyber stalking case, there is ultimately an underlying harassment. In fact, only a few "True Cyber Crimes" could not exist without the use of a computer. Crimes like web site defacing, Denial-of-Service attacks, worm propagation, and spamming could not occur without a computer being involved. Even though a computer is required to commit these types of crimes, the acts themselves may still be covered under traditional crime definitions. The following is an example of how investigators can "bridge the gap" when relating cyber crime to a traditional crime.

Are You 0wned?

Bridging the Gaps

Real Life Solutions: One of my very first cases was a woman who was being impersonated online by her ex-boyfriend. He created an online user profile using her personal information and her picture on a popular chat site. During his chats, while pretending to be her, he solicited sexual acts from several men and gave her personal contact information to them. This information included her home address. On several of these online chats he described a rape fantasy she wanted to fulfill with the men he was chatting with. When discussing the case with the Prosecutors office, we brainstormed about the charges we would use. There were no identity theft laws in place at that time. So we decided to use traditional charges like: reckless endangerment, aggravated harassment, and impersonation. I have outlined the justification for using these statutes next.

- Reckless endangerment was one of the crimes selected because the males were visiting the victim's home expecting to engage in sexual acts with her. These acts included the rape fantasy that the suspect described during the online chats. The reckless endangerment aspect of this crime was the possibility of some male raping her because of the described rape fantasy the suspect spoke about. Someone could have really raped her.

- Aggravated harassment was another crime we picked due to the amount of phone calls she was receiving day and night that were sexually explicit. In New York, it covered the annoying phone calls the victim was getting.

- The charge of impersonation was chosen because he was pretending to be her. This impersonation included more

Continued

than just saying he was her online to others. It included all of her personal information that the suspect gave out, along with her picture. Today, this would most probably be covered under an identity thief law.

As demonstrated in the preceding case, once an investigator removes the computer aspect of the crime out of the criminality equation (Computer + Crime = Cyber Crime) the investigator will ultimately reveal the underlying crime that has occurred (Crime = Crime).

TIP

Describing cyber crime to a technophobe: When describing your cyber case to nontechnical people, you should always outline the underlying crime. This will help them better understand what has occurred, how the computer facilitated the crime, and remove any fear of the underlying technology.

Desensitizing Traditional Crime

Since its inception, practitioners and scholars alike have attempted to label and categorize cyber crime. While this was done to help society understand how computers and traditional crime co-exist, this labeling creates a disconnect from the underlying crime. Today, terms like child pornographer, dissemination of illegal pornographic material, and identity theft are used to describe several traditional crimes that now occur via the computer. However, in using these terms, we tend to minimize the impact the crime has on society. If we used the term *online solicitation of a minor*, would it have a different connotation than if we had used the term *asking a child for sex*? You bet it does! How about if I told you that John committed the act of cyber stalking? Would it have the same effect if I had stated just the word "stalking"? In these two examples, we remove the element of the crime from its traditional meaning when using cyber terminology. When we use these terms, the underlying crime definition weakens, and the impact or shock value it has on us is reduced.

Another problem we encounter when using cyber terminology is that it tends to infer that the crime is not occurring locally and that the victim is not in immediate danger. The word *cyber* tends to lend itself to an unreal or false and distant location. After all, cyber space is not physically tangible, it's virtual.

Lastly, when we place the act of crime in a separate cyber category, we infer that it only happens when a computer exists. As you know, this is far from the truth. Often, you can clearly prove a crime has been committed even after removing the computer from the cyber crime itself.

As a result of using this terminology I've seen many cases go uninvestigated or unprosecuted because the crime was not viewed as a true crime. To avoid these pitfalls, investigators should attempt to spell out the underlying crime that has been committed when describing a cyber crime to a novice. Explain in detail how the victim was wronged (for instance, fraud was committed, they were sexually exploited, and so on). This will help the novice understand that the computer only helped to facilitate the criminal act. A good practice is to spell out the crime before explaining that a computer was involved.

The Elitist Mentality

I can remember my bosses asking the members in my unit to choose the name we should use to describe ourselves to other members of my department. In every choice, the word *computer* would be included. "The Computer Investigations and Technologies Unit" and "the Computer Crimes Squad" were just some of the choices. Although we used this name to describe our job description, many members in our department took it to mean that we investigated *all* crimes involving computers. To a certain extent, this was true until we began to become overwhelmed with cases and requests. Originally, the unit had the power to take cases that were beyond the technical skills of an investigator. By doing this, we misled the members of our department to believe we were the only ones who could investigate these types of crimes. We used the fact that our technical training was superior to other investigators, so much so that we were referred to by our own boss, respectfully, as "the Propeller Head Unit." The problem was further compounded by the fact that our search warrants and court room testimonies included our *curricula vitae*, outlining our computer investigation history and our training. Fearing that there wouldn't be enough work to justify our existence, we propagated the myth that we should be consulted on all cases relating to computers. I'm sure my agency was not the only one that did this. It was hard to convince superiors why they needed to fund and staff the unit—so we gave them a little push. By engaging in this type of behavior, our unit effectively segregated itself from the rest of our department based on our technological knowledge—real or perceived. In fact, there may have been any number of officers that could have investigated these types of cases.

Prioritizing Evidence

One of the saddest moments of my entire career was when a prosecutor dropped a child rape case because computer evidence was accidentally damaged. In this case, a rapist met a child online and traveled to the victim's home state to engage in sexual intercourse with them. After the child came forward, an investigation was conducted and the suspect was identified. During the arrest and subsequent search of the suspect home, evidence was recovered. This evidence included a computer that contained detailed salacious chats relating to this crime. We turned over the evidence to the prosecuting jurisdictional agency. While in the custody of the prosecuting agency, the computer was turned on and examined without the use of forensic software and a hardware write blocker. Thus, during the pre-trial phase at an evidentiary hearing, the court ruled the computer evidence would not be admissible at trial.

After the loss of this evidence, prosecutors decided not to go forward with the case. They stated that without the computer, the child would have to endure painful cross examination and it would now be difficult to prove the case. While I understood the point the prosecutor was trying to make about the child testifying, I could not understand why they would not go forward. First, with a search warrant, I recovered the actual plane ticket the suspect had used to travel to meet the child. Second, we corroborated most of the child's statements about the rental car, hotel, and other details during our investigation. Many of the following questions came to mind:

- Did the prosecutors rule out testimony from the victim at the start of their investigation? While many prosecutors try to avoid having the victim take the stand, it should never be ruled out as a possibility.

- Was prosecuting this case based solely on the recovery of the computer? If so, their thinking was severely flawed. They could not have possibly known what the outcome of the warrant would be.

- Did the prosecutors think that the chats would eliminate the need for the child to testify? As will be discussed in the "Setting the Bar too High" section of this chapter, computer data was never meant to be self-authenticating. Someone has to introduce those chats, and I would think it should have been the child.

- Did the prosecutors forget that ultimately a child was raped? Not allowing the computer into evidence does not diminish the crime.

Again, repeating the important points of this case, the computer in this case was just a vehicle which allowed the child and the suspect to communicate. The fact that the computer was not allowed into evidence does not diminish the fact that a child was raped. There was other supporting and corroborated evidence to prove the rape had occurred. If you're horrified by this case, you should be. On many occasions I was told by prosecuting agencies that I needed to recover computer evidence in order to proceed, or make an arrest in the case. Although this statement seems outrageous, it is common practice.

Basing the direction of a cyber crime case on whether or not you recover the computer or specific information on the computer in many situations is flawed thinking. Again many crimes committed via the computer will still hold water even if the computer is not recovered. Some examples of crimes that remain intact even after the computer is taken away are fraud, stalking, harassment, endangering the welfare of a minor, and so on. In fact, many crimes are prosecuted even when evidence is not recovered. Homicide investigations provide a perfect example of when this occurs.

In many homicide cases, victims are often found dead with little or no evidence. Through investigative methods, the detective is able to identify and arrest the killer. Many of these arrests occur regardless of whether the murder weapon is found. Often, the detective can still prove the case by finding other physical and circumstantial evidence.

So if we can prosecute other crimes without evidence why not do the same with computer crime? As investigators, we need to stop relying on computer-related evidence to prove our case and get back to good ol' gum shoe detective work. Prosecutors and law enforcement members should always remember that ultimately a crime has been committed and that there are usually other ways to prove the case, even with a lack of computer evidence.

Setting the Bar Too High

As I reflect on the problems I've encountered when investigating cyber crimes, I can't help but think that my predecessors may have set the bar too high when it comes to preserving electronic evidence. Electronic evidence is probably the only evidence that requires investigators to preserve the data exactly as it appeared during the collection phase. Often, the terms bit-stream image and exact duplicate are used when describing how electronic evidence is collected and preserved. Cyber investigators go to great lengths to ensure nothing is changed during the evidence collection and computer forensic process. While this preservation standard is widely accepted in the computer forensics industry, it is seldom applied to other forensic disciplines.

In fact, many forensic methodologies only take samples of items that are later destroyed or altered during the testing phase. Serology and ballistics are just two examples of forensic sciences where this process of destruction occurs. Additionally, it may shock you to know that only 22 states have statutes that compel the preservation of evidence. Furthermore, many of those states allow for the premature destruction of that evidence, which includes DNA according to a report issued by the Innocence Project Corporation (Innocence, 2006). Imagine telling the victim we no longer have the DNA evidence in your case, but we've kept your hard drive's image intact?

NOTE

A chain of custody is the accurate documentation of evidence movement and possession once that item is taken into custody until it is delivered to the court. This documentation helps prevent allegations of evidence tampering. It also proves the evidence was stored in a legally accepted location, and shows the persons in custody and control of the evidence during the forensic testing phase.

A bit-stream image is an exact duplicate of a computer's hard drive in which the drive is copied from one drive to another bit by bit. This image is then authenticated to the original by matching a digital signature which is produced by a mathematical algorithm (usually the MD5 standard) to ensure no changes have occurred. This method has become the de facto standard and is widely accepted by the industry and the legal system.

During my years as a police officer, I was often asked questions about evidence I collected from a crime scene while on trial. These questions would normally occur when the evidence was being introduced to the court for submission into evidence. One of the questions routinely posed to me by prosecutors and defense lawyers alike was whether or not the evidence being produced before the court was a "fair and accurate representation" of how it appeared when I collected it. Many times, this evidence was opened, marked, or changed after I collected it. These changes normally occurred during the testing phase of the item's forensic examination, and long after I released it from my chain of custody. Nevertheless, the court accepted the condition of the evidence as is, and it was later moved into evidence. In contrast, when introducing computer-related evidence to the court, I was always asked if the data being presented was an exact duplicate of its original. Furthermore, I would be asked to demonstrate to the court that the evidence did not change during my examination. This demonstration would consist of showing the matching digital signatures for evidence authentication and validation.

In all my years as a police officer, I was never asked to remove a homicide victim and have the surrounding sidewalk and the adjacent wall marked with splattered blood preserved exactly as is for all time. I surely never brought the victim's body to court and stated that it is exactly as it was when I found it and has not changed! So why would we create such a high standard for electronic evidence? Evidence tampering is the most common explanation I get when debating why such high standards for electronic evidence are needed.

Many of the computer forensic examiners I've spoken to believe that the bit-stream image standard helps defend against allegations of evidence tampering. Although this can be proven scientifically by demonstrating mathematically that no changes have occurred, investigators need to know that allegations of this sort (without a factual basis) are difficult arguments to make in court. In the case of *United States v. Bonallo*, the court stated that just because the possibility of tampering with electronic data exists—because of the ease with which this can occur when dealing with computer evidence— the mere argument of this issue alone is "insufficient evidence to establish untrustworthiness" of the evidence (9th Cir., 1988). Additionally, in *United States v. Whitaker*, the court held that allegations of evidence tampering without any factual basis were not grounds to disallow the evidence into court (7th Cir., 1997). This holds true especially for allegations of tampering that seem farfetched.

Another compelling argument made by my colleagues when defending the bit-stream image is the fact the computer evidence may include hearsay evidence and must meet the *hearsay requirements.* These requirements state that documents containing statements tending to provide proof of the matter they assert must be reliable and trustworthy and authentic in order to be introduced as evidence (Kerr, 2001). The key words here are reliable, trustworthy, and authentic. While clearly the bit-stream image can demonstrate that a document meets all of these criteria, it was never designed to be a self-authenticating methodology for the court.

Ronald L. Rivest authored the RFC1321 on the MD5 MessageDigest Algorithm in which he states that the MD5 does not "specify an Internet standard" and that "The MD5 algorithm is intended for digital signature applications, where a large file must be "compressed" in a secure manner before being encrypted with a private (secret) key under a public-key cryptosystem such as RSA" (Rivest, 1992). Rivest's statement about the purpose of the MD5 algorithm demonstrates it was never designed to be a self-authentication standard for the court. In fact, I have yet to find any U.S. court that specifically requires the sole use of MD5. There are, however, instances where the court has accepted the use of MD5 to establish the hearsay requirements.

By accepting this methodology as gospel, and shifting data authentication from the investigator to technology, we *hinder* the investigator. Is the investigator's testimony less credible than the technological results? Would an officer testifying that he observed this evidence on the screen and then printed the document not suffice? Now do you see the point?

The issue I have with using the bit-stream image as a standard of authentication is that many believe this type of evidence speaks for itself. In the Australian case, *RTA v. Michell*, the New South Wales Supreme Court ruled that speeding camera photos were not sufficient to prove guilt beyond a reasonable doubt because the tickets did not contain the MD5 sum, which is the "required security indicator." What I found extremely disturbing was the following statement made by the Judge: "the photograph may be altered, not (I assume) as the result of any sinister action, but because computer programming is imperfect and the risk of aberrant results needs to be borne in mind" (RTA, 2006). Well, my friends, if computers are imperfect, then why accept the MD5 and not the photo? It came from the same machine. Additionally, the implication here is that MD5 is more reliable than traditional photography. What's next? Will our crime scene photos require MD5 checksums? Anyway, go fight those speeding tickets.

The final point I would like to make is that sometimes cyber investigators have to conduct examinations of live data. The use of encryption, massive hard drive sizes, and the inability to shut down mission-critical servers may leave the investigator with only the option to perform collection or analysis on volatile data. In these instances, the data will be altered by the investigator. Last accessed times, physical memory, and Registry keys are just some of the items that can be changed. As a result of these changes, investigators will have to defend their actions in court. This is because the resulting hash signature from the live machine likely won't match the hash signature created by that investigator once the computer is shut down and the hard drive is then physically imaged.

I pray that this rigid practice will become more flexible to allow evidence that does not always match its hash. Nevertheless, cryptographic algorithms have become the de facto standard for electronic evidence and have deposited today's investigators into a quagmire.

NOTE

The topic of live forensics will be discussed later in greater detail in Chapter 5.

Summary

There are many grey areas in the cyber crime investigative and forensic process. Some of these areas are due to inefficiencies in the law, while others are due to the rapid change of technologies. Additionally, many of these problems are created because we treat cyber crime differently than traditional crimes. Yet other problematic areas are due to the standards we set in place at the inception of this phenomenon we call cyber crime. As our standards, best practices, and methodologies move farther from reality, we must revisit the past and come up with ways to make investigating these crimes less restrictive. Although, many of these practices were great solutions back then, they are no longer a viable option. Our community must ensure that technology does not outpace our capacity to perform investigations. While I do not believe this transition will be easy, I do believe it is necessary. Again, if this chapter angered you or made you think, I've done my job.

Works Referenced

Brown, Christopher L.T., *Computer Evidence Collection & Preservation*, Charles River Media, Inc., 2006.

Carrier, Brian, *File System Forensic Analysis*, Addison-Wesley, 2005.

Ciardi, John, *The Inferno: Dante Alighieri*, Signet Classic, 2001.

Innocence Project Inc., *Preservation of Evidence Fact Sheet*, Benjamin N. Cardozo School of Law, Yeshiva University. Retrieved December 21, 2006 from www.innocenceproject.org/docs/preservation_of_evidence_fact_sheet.pdf (2006).

Kerr, Orin S., *Computer Records and the Federal Rules of Evidence,* The Unites States Department of Justice. Retrieved December 21, 2006 from www.usdoj.gov/criminal/cybercrime/usamarch2001_4.htm (2001).

Krazit, Tom, *FAQ: The HP "pretexting" Scandal,* ZDNet. Retrieved October 20, 2006 from http://news.zdnet.com/2100-9595_22-6113011.html (2006).

National Institute of Justice, *Electronic Crime Needs Assessment for State and Local Law Enforcement,* U.S. Department of Justice: Office of Justice Programs, 2001

New York State Legislature CPL, *Criminal Procedure Law Article 700 §05 Sub 8 "Designated offense" Paragraph (b),* New York State. Retrieved December 12, 2006 from http://public.leginfo.state.ny.us/menugetf.cgi?COMMON-QUERY=LAWS.

Picker, Randy, *In Light of the HP Scandal, Pre-texting,* Picker Typepad. Retrieved October 25, 2006 from http://picker.typepad.com/legal_infrastructure_of_b/2006/09/in_light_of_the.html (2006).

Rivest, Ronald L., *The MD5 Message-Digest Algorithm,* IEFT.org. Retrieved September 16, 2006 from http://tools.ietf.org/html/rfc1321 (1992).

TheNewPaper.com, *Australia: NSW Supreme Court Backs Away from Camera Decision,* TheNewPaper.com. Retrieved December 15, 2006 from www.thenewspaper.com/news/10/1037.asp (3/24/2006).

United States v. Bonallo, 858 F.2d 1427, 1436 (9th Cir. 1988).

United States v. Whitaker, 127 F.3d 595, 602 (7th Cir. 1997).

Solutions Fast Track

The Gaps in Cyber Crime Laws

- ☑ Cyber crime laws do not keep pace with technology.
- ☑ Many laws inadequately cover cyber-related crimes.
- ☑ Traditional laws can often be used to prosecute cyber crimes when the law fails to address a specific type of cyber crime.

Unveiling the Myths Behind Cyber Crime

- ☑ Often, cyber crime has an underlying traditional crime.
- ☑ Computers frequently provide a means to aid in the commission of a traditional crime.
- ☑ Cyber crime terminology can confuse computer novices in making a "traditional" crime connection when a computer is used to help implement the offense.

Prioritizing Evidence

- ☑ Crime committed via computers can often be proven without computer evidence.
- ☑ Computer evidence should not be considered evidence that speaks for itself.
- ☑ Computer evidence should never outweigh the underlying crime.

Setting the Bar Too High

- ☑ Computer forensic standards are too rigid and should be flexible enough to adapt to different situations.
- ☑ Allegations of evidence tampering without proof are hard arguments to make in court.

☑ The MD5 algorithm's initial proposal did not included evidence authentication.

Frequently Asked Questions

The following Frequently Asked Questions, answered by the authors of this book, are designed to both measure your understanding of the concepts presented in this chapter and to assist you with real-life implementation of these concepts. To have your questions about this chapter answered by the author, browse to **www.syngress.com/solutions** and click on the **"Ask the Author"** form.

Q: Is it possible to commit a crime when conducting cyber crime investigations?

A: The answer to this question is a profound yes. Understanding the ramifications of your actions as they relate to the law is an important part of being a cyber crimes investigator. Remember, suspects, employees, and clients still maintain all the legal rights and protections afforded them per the United States Constitution. Reading e-mails, intercepting communication, searching and copying computer data may land you in hot water if you do not have the proper permissions, or authority to do so. When in doubt, confer with different legal, technical, and adminstrative sources.

Q: How much training do I need to become a cyber crimes investigator?

A: Because of the rapid rate of technological change, investigators must constantly update their skills and attend ongoing educational programs to keep on the cutting edge. Although a fair amount of training is required, you don't necessarily need a Masters degree in computer science to be a competent and skilled cyber crime investigator.

Q: What should I do if a cyber crime is not covered by a written law?

A: When a crime committed via a computer is not defined by written law, you should seek the advice of the prosecuting attorney. Many times, cyber crimes fall within the legal definitions of crimes such as theft of service, criminal mischief, or eavesdropping.

Q: What should I do if the judge or prosecutor does not understand the treminology behind the cyber crime I am describing to them.

A: Try to outline the crime in its traditional form. This may help them understand.

Q: Does not finding computer evidence in a cyber crime case automaticlly weaken my case?

A: No. Computer crimes often leave evidence that can be found thru good ol' fashioned investigative work.

Chapter 2

"Computer Crime" Discussed

Solutions in this chapter:

- Examining "Computer Crime" Definitions
- Dissecting "Computer Crime"
- Using Clear Language to Bridge the Gaps

☑ Summary

☑ Solutions Fast Track

☑ Frequently Asked Questions

Introduction

What image comes to mind when one hears the term *computer crime*? What about the term *cyber crime*? One may think of pimply-faced teenage hackers locked up in a dark bedroom littered with diet soda cans, accessing top-secret files on super-secret government computers. Others may think of a creepy old man, hiding behind a keyboard in his attempts to lure children into an illicit rendezvous. Still others may see the Nigerian e-mail scammer, or the auction fraudster, or the identity thief. The important point here is that the term computer crime has different connotations depending on the situation, the person, and their individual frame of reference. If the investigation of computer crime didn't require the involvement of many different communities—from law enforcement to private security, and from prosecutors to network administrators—the definitional issue would not be a problem. However, computer crime is, by its very nature, not restricted by conventional or physical borders. Many different communities all have a part to play in the investigation of computer crime. Understanding the definitions, and more importantly the connotations, of the words we speak are critical in bridging the gaps between these disparate communities,

That is not to say the term computer crime is not without its definitions. Several authors have provided solid attempts to place delineating boxes around computer crime, cyber crime, Internet crime, and so on. In the pages that follow, we will take a closer look at the existing definitions—first to educate the reader on the complexity of the definitional issues, and then to show how the use of a broad term like computer crime can alienate people that aren't as familiar with how computers are used as an instrument of criminality. After we examine the definitional and usage issues, we will discuss a new way to describe computer crime, one that is more direct and more easily grasped by both fans of technology (*technophiles*) and those afraid of it (*technophobes*).

Examining "Computer Crime" Definitions

Donn Parker is generally cited as the author that presented the first definitional categories for computer crime. Parker's three works (dating from 1976,

1983, and 1998) follow the story of the development and progression of computer crime.

TIP

Donn Parker's *Crime by Computer* from 1976 is a must-read for anyone new to the computer crime arena. The book is completely compelling since it takes a look at computer crimes in a pre-World Wide Web, low-bandwidth world—and also includes an ATM withdrawal scheme and stolen source code from a publicly available time-sharing computer system! The historical perspective provided by Parker's case studies may be the missing piece needed by newer investigators who did not grow up in a world without an Internet.

Parker clearly favors the term *computer abuse* as a higher-level definition and describes it as "…any incident involving an intentional act where a victim suffered or could have suffered a loss, and a perpetrator made or could have made a gain and is associated with computers" (Parker, 1976). Parker further goes on to describe the ways in which computers play a role in computer abuse:

1. The computer is the object, or the data in the computer are the objects, of the act.
2. The computer creates a unique environment or unique form of assets.
3. The computer is the instrument or the tool of the act.
4. The computer represents a symbol used for intimidation or deception.

These categories have proved to be broad enough to encompass both the computer abuses described by Parker in 1976 as well as the modern computer crimes we see today. Parker's categories served as a foundational framework in which computer crime could be comprehended by a society that had yet to come to understand how computers would be used outside of a NASA control room. Today, we still wrestle with framing our discussions of "computer abuse" in a way that the general public can understand.

Eoghan Casey cites Parker's definition in his book *Digital Evidence and Computer Crime* and primarily defaults to Parker's definitional categories; however, Casey's book is more focused on the issue of digital evidence and he correctly notes that Parker's definition omits the role of computers as a source and/or storehouse of digital evidence. Specifically, the situation would arise when the computer merely holds evidence of a crime but is not in any way used as a tool or instrument of the crime. Casey provides the example of e-mails examined in the Microsoft anti-trust case—a few of them contained incriminating evidence but did not play an active role in the commission of the crime. Setting the definitional framework appears to be a necessary evil that must be discussed before moving on to more interesting topics since Casey builds upon Parker's definition but also notes that defining computer crime is problematic.

Robert Taylor also notes the problematic nature of attempting to define computer crime in the book *Digital Crime and Digital Terrorism*, in which they state "Defining computer crime sufficiently is a daunting and difficult task." Taylor and company expand on Parker's definitions and present four categories of computer crime:

- **The computer as a target** The attack seeks to deny the legitimate users or owners of the system access to their data or computers. A Denial-of-Service (a.k.a., DOS or DDOS) attack or a virus that renders the computer inoperable would be examples of this category.

- **The computer as an instrument of the crime** The computer is used to gain some other criminal objective. For example, a thief may use a computer to steal personal information.

- **The computer as incidental to a crime** The computer is not the primary instrument of the crime; it simply facilitates it. Money laundering and the trading of child pornography would be examples of this category.

- **Crimes associated with the prevalence of computers** This includes crimes against the computer industry, such as intellectual property theft and software piracy.

Here in Taylor's definition, we see that the focus remains on the technology, but the definitional categories have been more clearly outlined. Clearly, the expansion of personal computing from the late 1970s to the early 2000s brought with it a completely new spectrum of crime—one that would have been unimaginable to Parker in 1976. Taylor tweaks Parker's definition to be inclusive of "new" computer crimes.

Majid Yar presents an argument that supports the proposition that computer crime / cyber crime are ill-defined and problematic terms: "A primary problem for the analysis of cyber crime is the absence of a consistent current definition, even amongst those law enforcement agencies charged with tackling it." Yar cites Furnell in stating that "One commonplace approach is to distinguish between 'computer-assisted crimes' (those crimes that pre-date the Internet but take on a new life in cyberspace, e.g., fraud, theft, money laundering, sexual harassment, hate speech, pornography) and "computer focused crimes" (those crimes that have emerged in tandem with the establishment of the Internet and could not exist apart from it—e.g., hacking, viral attacks, Web site defacement)." Yar further expands upon his point by citing Wall: "…[cyber crime] has no specific referent in law, yet it has come to enjoy considerable currency in political, criminal justice, media, public, and academic discourse. Consequently, the term might best be seen to signify a range of illicit activities whose common denominator is the central role played by networks of information and communication technology (ICT) in their commission."

Based on the preceding statement, Yar presents Wall's four legal categories for cyber crime:

- **Cyber-trespass** Crossing boundaries into other people's property and/or causing damage—for example, hacking, defacement, and viruses.

- **Cyber-deceptions and thefts** Stealing (money, property)—for instance, credit card fraud and intellectual property violations (a.k.a., "piracy").

- **Cyber-pornography** Activities that breach laws regarding obscenity and decency.

- **Cyber-violence** Doing psychological harm to, or inciting physical harm against others, thereby breaching laws pertaining to the protection of the person—for example, hate speech and stalking.

The categories presented by Yar and Wall are, like Parker's and Taylor's definitions, sufficiently broad to cover most crimes that involve a computer. Both Parker and Taylor place the technology—in this case, the computer—at the center of the definitional categories, whereas Wall flips the definition around to be focused on the class of criminal infraction. Wall's definition is important because it signals the beginning of a paradigm shift away from the focus on technology to a focus on the criminal act. This shift in focus is representative of the increased acceptance that computers are an integral part of our society and that a move has been made toward more personal crimes, as opposed to attacks against the technology.

Marjorie Britz, in her book *Computer Forensics and Cyber Crime: An Introduction*, provides a well-researched history of computer crime, which is well beyond the scope of this work. She states that computer crime is "…traditionally defined as any criminal act committed via computer," and also provides a definition of computer-related crime "…as any criminal act in which a computer is involved, usually peripherally." Britz provides a definition of cyber crime as "… traditionally encompass[ing] abuses and misuses of computer systems which result in direct and/or concomitant losses." For example, Britz states that the "…the theft of millions of dollars via computer hacking is most properly denoted as cybercrime." She also highlights the definitional issues with computer crime, computer-related crime, and cyber crime when she remarks that "…a variety of definitions [for these terms] exist, and that such variations have resulted in confusion among legislators and investigators alike."

Thomas and Loader describe cyber crime as "…computer-mediated activities which are either illegal or considered illicit by certain parties and which can be conducted through global electronic networks" (*Cybercrime*, Routledge, 2000). This definition could be interpreted as overly broad, but the authors provide a good list of examples—including network break-ins, industrial espionage, and software piracy—to frame their discussions of cyber crime within the book. I have to admit to getting a slight chuckle from the authors' reference to the ubiquitous use of the prefix "cyber" in a book title to boost sales—I will contend that in this current title we elevated "cyber" from a lowly prefix status to a higher ranking as an adjective.

The U.S. government is not absent from this definitional quagmire. The Computer Crime and Intellectual Property Section (CCIPS) Web site is titled *Cybercrime.gov*, yet text on this Web site uses the terms *computer-related crime* and *Internet-related crime* interchangeably. Unfortunately, the CCIPS Web site does not provide a definition for cyber crime, computer crime, or Internet-related crime that would be helpful in this discussion.

TIP

Although the U.S. Department of Justice's Web site (www.cyber-crime.gov) does not provide the definition(s) the author was looking for, it does provide a number of very valuable resources—particularly the cyberethics page—available at www.usdoj.gov/criminal/cybercrime and www.usdoj.gov/criminal/cybercrime/cyberethics.htm.

Considering the power of a binding legal definition, we turn to the legislature to settle the true definition of computer crime—more specifically, the United States Code. The law with the most relevance to this discussion is the 18 USC 1030: the Computer Fraud and Abuse Act.

The federal government passed the Computer Fraud and Abuse Act (CFAA) in 1986 (amended 1994, 1996, and in 2001) in response to the perceived threat of an army of hackers breaking into government computers to steal state secrets. During its conception, CFAA was designed to include only government computers that stored secret information, but it has expanded to also encompass computers within the financial sector. The CFAA is primarily focused on "access" to computer systems by unauthorized persons, or persons that have exceeded their authorized access permissions. Both of these situations are usually grouped under the term *unauthorized access*. The CFAA details the different situations in which unauthorized access could occur, which unauthorized accesses are considered criminal, and the related punishments for these crimes.

Security Alert...

The CFAA

The CFAA covers unauthorized access to:

Sensitive governmental information; national security and foreign relations information

Records of a financial institution or card issuer

A department of the U.S. government

Any protected computer involved in interstate or foreign commerce

Any protected computer, with the intent to defraud and which causes $5,000+ in damages—or would have caused damages or bodily harm if an unsuccessful attempt was successful

Other issues addressed in the CFAA include password trafficking and any extortion demands related to a threat to damage a protected computer. Although, the CFAA does not specifically identify every scenario in which computers could be used, the punishments listed do offer some guidance as to how these offenses could affect the government, a business, or an individual. For example, the CFAA addresses the following:

The offense was committed for purposes of commercial advantage or private financial gain.

The offense was committed in furtherance of any criminal or tortuous act in violation of the Constitution or laws of the United States or of any state.

The value of the information obtained exceeds $5,000.

For example, unauthorized access to protected governmental computers that contain sensitive information would be covered under this act.

The CFAA does provide a definition for computer: (1) the term *computer* means an electronic, magnetic, optical, electrochemical, or other high speed data processing device performing logical, arithmetic, or storage functions, and includes any data storage facility or communications facility directly related to or operating in conjunction with such a device, but such a term does not include an automated typewriter or typesetter, a portable hand held calculator, or other similar device." This definition is very broad—and appropriately so. It is apparent that the crafters of the language of the code were very aware of the changing state of technology and were careful not to limit the language to existing technology. The act does not substantially cover any definitions for computer crime, cyber crime, and so on, and the overarching broadness of the definition of computer, and the caveats at the end of the definition, open the door for "what-if" scenarios that plague most every broad-based technology definition.

The name Computer Fraud and Abuse Act might lead one to believe that the CFAA covers a broad range of computer frauds and abuses. To the contrary, the CFAA is primarily focused on defining and criminalizing unauthorized access to protected computers—one very narrow sliver of all the possible "computer frauds" and "computer abuses" that exist. For example, the CFAA criminalizes the manipulation of financial data on a computer that is part of the financial sector, but would not be applicable to the manipulation of financial data on your personal computer.

It is clear that the CFAA has a very specific purpose—to criminalize unauthorized access to protected computers—and is drafted to specifically criminalize that act. Although the theft or manipulation of financial records or sensitive documents would be covered under numerous existing, non-digital, traditional laws, discerning if information has been copied after unauthorized access has occurred is problematic at best. Obtaining access to unauthorized information requires a willful desire to do so, and such access needs to remain criminalized, regardless of the ability to prove theft or manipulation.

The Evolution of Computer Crime

The term *computer crime* is poorly defined, its definitions are not widely accepted, and the existing definitions may address very different topics related to the use of high technology in criminal activities. Few other terms in criminal justice have such a broad definition base, particularly when contrasted against other terms such as "homicide" and "assault," both of which are fairly narrowly defined in both a legal sense and within informal conversation.

Why is it then that we still hold computer crime and cyber crime as terms to delineate a particular subset of crime and/or class of investigation? Are these terms used merely as terms of convenience with those already in-the-know? Do people that use these terms—from investigators to the media—really understand the scope of crimes and investigations the terms encompass?

The answer may lie with how the field of computer crime investigations evolved. For a long time, computer crime investigations were separate from other criminal investigations and only those with specialized knowledge could truly understand the mysteries of packets, IMs, and e-mails (oh my!). Those without the specialized knowledge were reluctant to even take a report, let alone follow up on an investigation that involved a computer. These computer crimes were immediately forwarded to the computer crime investigator and/or task force—often without any regard to the actual crime that occurred.

One explanation for this behavior lies in the history of the development and use of high-technology. When computers were new and novel—in this case, *novel* means *expensive*—there were limited ways in which they could be used, often dictated by the limited class of people or businesses that could afford them. As would be expected, there were correspondingly limited manners in which computers could be used to assist in criminal endeavors. The primordial definition of computer crime was fairly narrow and focused on crimes against computers, such as phone phreaking, virus creation/propagation, and hacking of government computers. Because there were fewer people with a personal presence on the Internet, there were fewer opportunities for interpersonal crimes.

The development of personal computers in the early 1980s, the creation of the World Wide Web in the 1990s, and the explosion of social networking sites in the early 2000s created an unprecedented opportunity for people to construct a personal presence on the Internet. Computer crime in 2006 is a much broader and more complicated term than it was 20, 10, and even 5 years ago. Many computer crimes of *today* simply didn't exist *yesterday*. No longer is computer crime relegated to attacks against a college LAN or telephone infrastructure. Instead, people with a personal presence online are now the target of criminals using high-technology via the Internet.

Issues with Definitions

Generally, the authors discussed earlier in this chapter note a significant definitional issue with the terms computer crime and cyber crime. This problem does not lay with an inability to somehow draw boundaries around what crimes would be included under computer crime, cyber crime, and so on. The problem rests with the global nature of these types of crimes—in other words, as soon as limits are placed around the term to make it relevant to a particular audience, you make broad assumptions based on the specific audience, and the importance of the term is diluted. We saw this earlier in Parker's initial attempt to draw a box around computer crime. Parker put forth a rather comprehensive definition of computer crime. Casey questioned the base assumptions of the definition and noted that Parker's definition was vulnerable to "what-if" questions related to the computer used as a store of evidence. In this way, we see how definitions of very broad topics are difficult to construct—and in this case may be inappropriate.

Dissecting "Computer Crime"

The first issue in attempting to define computer crime comes in examining the phrase itself. The *Oxford English Dictionary* (www.oed.com) defines a computer as an automatic electronic device for performing mathematical or logical operations—a much broader definition than even the definition provided in the CFAA—and defines crime as an act punishable by law. Therefore, a "computer crime" is an act that is punishable by law using an automatic electronic device that performs mathematical or logical operations. It is actually painful to attempt to draft a broader definition of the term. However, just as we discussed earlier, every attempt to narrow down the definition of computer crime will necessarily make broad assumptions, and once these assumptions are challenged, the definition is weakened. For example, one assumption in the provided definition is that the device is a high-tech device. What if a drug dealer uses a 50¢ calculator or an electronic scale in the course of his criminal activity? These are surely electronic devices that perform mathematical operations. Could this be considered a true computer crime? Another assumption is that the crime occurs electronically. What if the "device that performs logical operations" is a hard drive, and I decide to beat someone about the head and shoulders with it. Is this a computer crime? You get the point. Whenever the definition is challenged with a "What if…" scenario it can't support, the definition is undermined.

Linguistic Confusion

Looking at the phrase *computer crime* through a linguistic lens, we can demonstrate the issue at hand. Let's take a look at a sample statement: "I'm a computer crime investigator." Because computer crime is ill-defined and includes broad categories of both technology and crime, the people I'm speaking to may not comprehend exactly what I do. In this instance, the person I'm communicating with must have prior knowledge of my particular focus within the computer crime arena, or they must ask for clarification. If we look at the situation from another point of view—let's say I was a child pornography investigator—I might assume that all computer crime investigators do the same work I do.

In 1975, a linguist named Paul Grice published work regarding the analysis of conversation. He proposed that being a good communicator is based on a number of principles or *maxims.* Making ambiguous or obscure statements violates one of Grice's conversational maxims (see "Logic and Conversation" in *Speech Acts*, 1975). Each speaker's turn in a conversational exchange should provide all the information that the other party requires to move the conversation along. When conversational maxims are violated, the other party in the conversation stops listening to the actual content of the speaker's statements, and begins wondering why the maxim was violated. If we apply this principle to the preceding example, when I use the term computer crime, you stop listening and instead begin to wonder what that term means to you. While we'd like to believe that people will ask for clarification of things they don't understand; but in reality, they won't be listening, they'll be wondering why you didn't just offer that information in the first place and they won't ask for clarification.

Jargon

The specific jargon developed by technophiles includes terms with broad definitions used in a very specific manner. Within a group of computer technicians, there would be little confusion when discussing the wireless network—it would be clear they were addressing that the data network exists in their particular area. An outsider would not be able to determine they were talking about an IP data network as opposed to a cellular phone network. The fact that "wireless" has so many different definitions makes the word itself meaningless—the user's intended meaning for the word must be derived from the context of its usage. What can be purchased in a store named "Wireless everything"? Cordless phones? Cellular phones? Bluetooth keyboards? 802.x-compatible hard-drive enclosures? We would all figure it out as soon as we saw the massive "Wireless Everything" billboard with a giant cell phone, but until we were able to put the term in context, the name would be of little value.

Here the broad term "wireless" has a different connotation based on the context or frame of reference in which it is used. This is not a problem if everyone is familiar with the frame of reference, but what happens when the group of insiders tries to communicate with an outsider? The communication breaks down.

In February of 2003, the White House released Homeland Security Presidential Directive #5 (HSPD-5) on the subject of Managing Domestic Incidents. This directive called for the creation of the National Incident Management System, which was released in March of 2004. One of the most striking recommendations within NIMS, and its closely integrated Incident Command System, is the use of plain language for all emergency responders. During the development of NIMS/ICS, it was identified that the use of "10-codes" and other agency specific abbreviations was counter-productive—and sometimes fatal—because emergency response agencies that responded from another jurisdiction would not be able to understand the local jurisdiction's private codes. In an emergency response situation, hearing a "10-12" for one officer may mean "all clear," but in his neighboring mutual-aid community, "10-12" may mean "officer down."

NIMS/ICS has begun to turn the tide so that all communications are in plain language to reduce any possible confusion. Obviously, this would not be needed if agencies never had to work together. Each agency could create its very own private community, with specific in-group language that serves as a distancing mechanism and a barrier to entry into their private community. But the world has changed—it is now a much smaller place than it once was. Those responding to emergencies in the physical world are beginning to realize they need help from their neighbors—neighbors that may come from thousands of miles away.

Although the physical response community is just now coming to grips with their new inter-jurisdictional missions under NIMS, those that have been operating in the virtual world have known nothing else but an inter-jurisdictional universe. The cyber crime community has always known that their job was based on easy information exchange in a land where physical jurisdictions have little meaning. Why is it then that the cyber crime community is fully entrenched in its use of jargon?

In-Group and Out-Group

Human group dynamics is sometimes explained using the terms *in-group* and *out-group*. People naturally group with other people similar to themselves, and people within this group tend to be protective and supportive of the group and its members. There does not need to be a specific out-group; anyone that is not in the in-group is, by default, in the out-group. This concept has been applied to a whole range of human interaction, from prejudicial behavior to cooperative farming. In the context of our discussion here, we find it natural that some people are drawn to technology and others are naturally afraid of technology. Those that embrace technology have created their own in-group, and a new in-group exists for each level of knowledge. Linux and Mac users have created their own in-groups—each Windows or network certification, such as MCSE or CCNA, in essence creates its own in-group. Each of these in-groups creates their own language—similar to how an older sister may use pig-Latin with her friends to keep a younger brother from listening in—and part of the barrier to entering these groups is the in-group-specific language. The presence of technology-related in-groups and out-groups provides an opportunity for technophobes to distance themselves from technology and allows for the technophiles to hoard technical knowledge.

Even though there may be little technology involved in a computer crime, the fact that technology is central to the term allows technophobes to distance themselves from anything related to technology. This distancing often takes the form of case referrals—the technophobes' excuse being that the case involves computers and therefore the computer specialist needs to handle it.

Conversely, the use of "computer" or "cyber" leads one to believe that only "cyber" investigators with considerable skill and knowledge are capable of solving the crime; that investigating computer crime is a complicated matter, to be handled only by highly intelligent, specially trained individuals, who look good in white lab coats. By keeping the secrets of computer investigation and computer forensics as just that, secrets, computer investigators and forensic personnel never have to answer for the magical work that happens behind the green curtain. We see the manifestation of the technology in-groups in the way that in-group members will often hoard knowledge and purposefully attempt to alienate and subjugate others in an attempt to keep their competitive edge.

NOTE

As a reality check, I discussed the technology in-group/out-group with Capt. Benjamin Jean from the NH Police Standards and Training Council who specializes in teaching technology to police cadets and officers. Capt. Jean had this effect pegged as the "right-click-effect." Often, context-sensitive menus within software programs can only be found by using the right-click button. In essence, those "in-the-know" or in the in-group, will look for menus by using the right-click button. The classic example of this is the often maddening endeavor to modify the formatting of charts within Microsoft Excel—the x and y axes, chart type, data source, colors, and so on are accessed through right-click menus that change depending on where your cursor is located on the chart.

The in-group consists of those that are aware of the power of the right-click, while the out-group consists of everyone else that searches through the toolbars and menus looking for the correct command. One function of the in-group is to protect its image as having an advantage over nonmembers, but the truth is there is often very little difference between the technological knowledge of the in-group and the out-group.

Saturday Night Live captured the essence of the technophile who uses his knowledge to alienate others from technology in the character Nick Burns in the skit "Nick Burns, Your Company's Computer Guy" (complete with the "He'll fix your computer and make fun of you!" musical ditty). Nick Burns uses his knowledge of computer support and specific computer terminology to ridicule his co-workers, assert control in a situation, and elevate his status. In one exchange, a coworker is having a problem printing from a given computer:

Nick: Just scroll to your chooser.

Worker: That thing that you pull down?

Nick: <sarcastic> That thing you pull down? Ya. If you mean Apple File, yes, do that.

Worker: I didn't know what it was called!

Nick: Obviously!

Nick finishes this exchange with an impatient and rude "MOVE!" when he is tired of attempting to explain this apparently so-easy-a-monkey-could-do-it operation, and then takes over the keyboard to fix the printing problem. This example, specifically the worker's exasperated outburst of "I didn't know what it was called!" highlights how the words we use dramatically effect the manner in which people will feel included, part of the in-group of those in-the-know, or excluded as part of the out-group. Nick treats his co-worker as if the fellow is stupid because he is unable to perform a given function on the computer, and because he doesn't know the specific "lingo" of the in-group.

Using Clear Language to Bridge the Gaps

Returning to the focus of this book—bridging gaps between disparate communities—we can clearly see there are a number of private communities that (1) are all protecting their specific information, (2) are all fearful the other groups will discover there is no specialized knowledge attainable by only a few (that is, no process so complicated that only a few could learn it), and (3) are all fearful that the out-group will pull the curtain back and find that the mighty Oz is nothing more than a normal man with a few interesting, high-tech gadgets.

The problem does not lie in the fact that people create in-groups and out-groups; human nature dictates that people of similar knowledge and experience will naturally cluster together. Knowledge is power, and people will find a way to gain status through the use of their knowledge. Neither of these issues would be a problem if the following points were not a basic assumption in our current and future world:

- There are bad people doing bad things facilitated by the use of computers and high-technology—often people are hurt financially, emotionally, and physically.

- We, the collective cyber-crime investigative community—academia, law enforcement, prosecutors, private sector, security professionals—must work together to prevent, mitigate, investigate and prosecute crimes committed using computers and high-technology.

We've discussed how the use of "cyber crime" and "computer crime" is problematic. Many of us use these phrases as a term of convenience within our in-group—and truthfully I don't expect that to change—but we must realize that when we use these terms in a casual manner, others that are not as familiar with the term will feel alienated as part of the out-group. As was highlighted under the National Incident Management System document, localized and proprietary language is a hindrance to response—and nowhere is cooperation across jurisdictions more common than in the investigation of computer crime. You may want to prove you are smarter than your co-worker, but will you gain their respect by alienating them? You may want to prove to the presiding judge you are a computer whiz, but will the use of complicated jargon impress her or turn her against you? Will your boss be supportive of you when he learns the process you described in complicated terms really involves a simple right-click?

In the final analysis, alienating other members of the greater investigative, prosecutor, and research community serves no positive purpose. The specialized knowledge to work through the cyber component of a crime often is not highly technical or unteachable. We are in the position to begin a revolution. A revolution where the technology out-group is assimilated by the decision to cease the use of in-group lingo, by the patient plain-speaking teaching of technology, and by the inclusion of others so we may all leverage technology in catching the bad guys.

A New Outlook on "Computer Crime"

I do not plan to offer yet another attempt to place definitional boundaries around computer crime or "cyber" anything. Doing so would only further complicate an already complicated and convoluted lexicon—a lexicon that may be too far corrupted to attempt to correct. Other scholarly fields—psychology, for example—maintain a long definitional history and their lexicon has developed and evolved slowly, primarily through peer-reviewed journals.

The definition I propose is a move away from jargon, away from proprietary and exclusionary in-group speech. The purpose is to correct the focus of the discussion away from cyber crime, making the proposition that from this point forward many traditional crimes will have a cyber, computer, or high-technology component. Currently, computer crime places the focus on the technology used to commit the crime. This is akin to calling all violent crimes and property crimes committed to secure money for drugs as "drug crimes." Although drugs are a significant factor in many crimes, calling a burglary/murder a "drug crime" certainly has the effect of minimizing the importance of a murder. Additionally, as discussed previously, using "drug crime" as a big bucket of crime types provides the listener with no details as to what crime actually occurred.

I propose that we place the crime committed as the central point in the phrase and add a qualifier that a computer or high-technology component was involved—for instance, "Crimes with a cyber-component" or "crimes with a high-technology component." Here I suggest using "crime with a cyber component" for crimes involving computers or computer networks, and "crime with a high-technology component" for crimes involving other high-tech devices.

NOTE

For this book, I use the *cyber* prefix to refer to computers and networks, and the *high-technology* prefix to reference high-technology devices such as cell phones, PDAs, and so on.

In this sense, "online child solicitation" becomes "solicitation of a child with a cyber-component," and "online auction fraud" becomes "fraud with a cyber-component." A computer in use by a drug operation to track drug sales would be "possession with intent to distribute with a cyber component." Placing the focus on the crime corrects years of misappropriated focus on the technology used in the crime.

The terms computer crime and cyber crime will never disappear. For one, they are already burned into our collective consciousness and will continue to be found in the media and legislation, and will persist in rolling off the tongues of countless investigators, prosecutors, and academia, myself included. But addressing "crimes with a cyber component" as opposed to "cyber-crime," and so on, comes closer to solving the definitional issues, the misuse of jargon, and the exclusivity issues described earlier. In a law enforcement setting, it places the criminal offense as the central point of the phrase, where the crime should be the central focus—not the technology.

In order to bridge the gaps between disparate communities, we need to speak in simple, clear terms that allow for greater cooperation. Some investigators or prosecutors might not believe they have all the necessary skills to work a cyber crime, but most would believe they could work a theft case. If we remove the focus on technology and delete the jargon, we will empower others to join the fight against those that commit crimes with a cyber component.

Summary

Defining cyber crime appears to be a necessary evil within the community of people involved in researching, investigating, and prosecuting their occurrence. Why we endeavor to define the term is not clear. Perhaps it is because the term held specific meaning years ago when there were fewer ways in which computer technology could be involved in criminal activity—and by hanging on to the term we are magically transported to the good ol' days. Maybe the media has used "cyber crime" as a term of convenience and now the term sits within the collective consciousness of the public, even though the public may feel the catchiness of the term but not understand the depth and breadth of the activities involved. Several scholars and authors have attempted to place definitional boundaries around the term cyber crime, but its meaning has grown as the range of criminal activity facilitated by computer was inevitably lumped under the cyber crime heading.

Groups within the cyber crime community continue to use the term, again mainly out of convenience. Normally, the use of such a term with a broad definition would require that additional clarification be provided, but often the groups understand the intended connotation and no clarification is given. Those that do not have the frame of reference to understand the intended connotation will not understand the specific "in-group" jargon and will feel alienated. If the investigation of "cyber crime" did not require the cooperation of many disparate communities, the definitional and jargon issues would not be a problem. However, cyber crime by its very nature crosses jurisdictions and business sectors, and the successful investigation of it requires the cooperation and assistance of many parties.

In order to bridge the gaps that exist between the cyber investigative communities, we need to first address the manner in which we communicate. The use of specific jargon or in-group language can alienate the very people needed in a successful investigation. In this chapter, I propose a move away from proprietary and technology-focused speech and suggest a return to plain speech that can be inclusive of all interested parties. Cyber crime is better discussed as a "crime with a cyber component" for crimes involving computers or computer networks, and "crime with a high-technology component" for crimes involving other high-tech devices. The term cyber crime is sexier and makes a better sound bite for the news, so I don't expect the use of "cyber crime" as a term of convenience to diminish. What I do hope for is that the use of "crime with a cyber component" will help an investigator work with a prosecutor, help a security professional work with an officer, or help a prosecutor work with a judge and jury and bridge the gaps that keep us apart.

Works Referenced

Books and Journals

Bloombecker, Buck. *Spectacular Computer Crimes: What They Are and How They Cost American Business Half a Billion Dollars a Year!* Homewood, IL: Dow Jones-Irwin, 1990.

Brewer, Marilynn. "The Psychology of Prejudice: Ingroup Love or Outgroup Hate?" *Journal of Social Issues*, Volume 55, Number 3, 429–444, 1999.

Britz, Marjorie. *Computer Forensics and Cyber Crime: An Introduction.* Upper Saddle River, NJ: Pearson, Prentice Hall, 2004.

Casey, Eoghan *et al. Digital Evidence and Computer Crime; Second ed.* San Diego, CA: Elsevier Academic Press, 2004.

Grice, Paul H. "Logic and conversation." In Cole, P. and J.L. Morgan, eds., *Speech Acts.* New York: Academic Press, 1975.

Parker, Donn. *Crime by Computer.* New York, NY: Charles Scribner's Sons, 1976.

Taylor, Robert W. *et al. Digital Crime and Digital Terrorism.* Upper Saddle River, N.J.: Pearson, Prentice Hall, 2006.

Thomas, Douglas and Brian Loader. "Introduction—Cybercrime: Law Enforcement, Security and Surveillance in the Information Age." In D. Thomas and B. Loader, eds., *Cybercrime: Law Enforcement, Security and Surveillance in the Information Age.* London: Routledge, 2000.

United States Department of Homeland Security. *2004 National Incident Management System.* Washington, DC: US DHS.

Wall, David. "Cybercrimes and the Internet." In Wall, D., ed., *Crime and the Internet.* London: Routledge, 2001.

Yar, Majid. "The Novelty of Cybercrime: An Assessment in Light of Routine Activity Theory." *European Journal of Criminology*, Volume 2 (4), 407–427, 1477–3708. Thousand Oaks, CA: SAGE Publications, 2005.

Legislation and Executive Orders

Computer Fraud and Abuse Act. 18 USC 1030. Available at www.cyber-crime.gov/1030_new.html (12/8/06).

Homeland Security Presidential Directive / HSPD-5: Management of Domestic Incidents. The White House. February 28, 2003. Available at www.whitehouse.gov/news/releases/2003/02/20030228-9.html (1/7/07).

Solutions Fast Track

Examining "Computer Crime" Definitions

- ☑ Several authors have provided solid definitions for computer crime and cyber crime. Early definitions focused on the manner in which computers were used in the criminal infraction. The definition appears to have evolved to place the focus on the class of criminal infraction.

- ☑ Computer crime and cyber crime are broadly defined, but the definition may have been more applicable when first constructed because of the limited availability of computers. The definition has expanded to include almost all crimes that involve a computer.

- ☑ Definitional issues exist with the terms "cyber crime" and "computer crime." They encompass such a broad topic that the intended meaning is diluted.

Dissecting "Computer Crime"

- ☑ The use of technology jargon may alienate technophobes—and "cyber crime" is technology jargon.

- ☑ The focus on the technology in the phrase "computer crime" and "cyber crime" allows technophobes to distance themselves from criminal cases that involve technology. Conversely, the focus on the technology allows technophiles to hoard knowledge and alienate those with less technical knowledge.

Using Clear Language to Bridge the Gaps

- ☑ People do bad things—often facilitated by the use of computers and high-technology.

- ☑ The investigation of "cyber crimes" often involves many disparate communities, including academia, law enforcement, prosecutors, private sector, and security professionals. The successful investigation of "cyber crimes" involves significant cooperation between these different communities.

- ☑ Alienating the people you depend on for cooperation and assistance is foolish at best. Lack of similar jargon or technical prowess should not be confused with limited intellect.

- ☑ It should be proposed that we move away from focusing on the technology when describing cyber crime and instead focus on the criminal act and note how the technology played a role. "Cyber crime" then becomes "crime with a cyber component."

Frequently Asked Questions

The following Frequently Asked Questions, answered by the authors of this book, are designed to both measure your understanding of the concepts presented in this chapter and to assist you with real-life implementation of these concepts. To have your questions about this chapter answered by the author, browse to **www.syngress.com/solutions** and click on the **"Ask the Author"** form.

Q: Should we cite specific technology in computer crime laws and legislation?

A: The legal framework is necessarily delayed in addressing new technologies; therefore, I believe it is counter productive to constantly invent "new" terminology or "new" crimes, and then attempt to create legislation to criminalize the misuse of the technology. Because the legal framework will never catch up with technology, we are, by default, creating unenforceable laws by specifically defining the specific technology in the law.

For example, some people define theft narrowly, stating it relates to depriving someone of the use of an item. This clearly is a myopic viewpoint that ignores whole categories of criminal theft, including intellectual property theft, espionage, and so on, where the theft of the information—regardless of whether actual physical items were involved—is still clearly a form of theft. Does the law need to specifically state how the information was stolen—even if "stolen" could include copying of the information? Of course not. As soon as the law gets enacted (which may take years) the technology has moved on, and the language that makes a specific act illegal is now nonsense. For example, the law may prohibit taking pictures of classified materials with a camera-phone. In two years, we may be seeing an explosion of sunglass cameras or nose-ring cameras. It is more important that the law outline the legal issues regarding ownership, due care of property, and malicious intent, and leave the specific methods out of the discussion.

Earlier work on this topic leads me to believe that the legal framework did need to be adjusted for the changing technology. Since that time, I've seen the technology change radically—with little alteration in the overall legal system. The viewpoint I have now is based more on the legal system's inability to be nimble than it is on suggesting the absolute best course of action. Would it be best to have a law passed that addresses each possible high-tech component to each traditional crime? Absolutely! But change will not come about by suggesting unreasonable goals. If the legal system is simply unable to specifically address these types of crimes, this community must accept this fact and find a way to either maximize the existing laws or seek to pass less specific laws that may cover a wider breadth of criminal activity that has a cyber or high-technology component.

Q: "Crime with a cyber component" doesn't exactly roll off the tongue... Do you really expect me to use this phrase all the time instead of "cyber crime"?

A: Yes... and no. I do not expect the use of "cyber crime" as a term of convenience to diminish. However, I do suggest you think about the people you speak to, and determine if their frame of reference matches yours. For example, if you are a private security professional, and the other person is an investigator who primarily investigates crimes against children, you can be relatively sure your two definitions of "cyber crime" will be very different. In cases such as this one, where the frame of reference is different, I highly recommend taking a step back, focusing on the crime, and then discussing how technology was involved—for example, "Theft of IP assets, and the thief used a computer to gain access to our information."

Chapter 3

Preparing for Prosecution and Testifying

Solutions in this chapter:

- **Common Misconceptions**
- **Chain of Custody**
- **Keys to Effective Testimony**
- **Differences between Civil and Criminal Cases**

☑ **Summary**

☑ **Solutions Fast Track**

☑ **Frequently Asked Questions**

Introduction

Well over 90 percent of cases will be resolved prior to trial either through a pretrial motion or plea bargain. Nonetheless, cyber crime investigators should approach every case with an eye toward trial. It is important for investigators to maintain this mindset because the strength of a case ultimately is determined by the weight of the evidence and the defendant's perception of the prosecutor's ability to effectively present the evidence to the trier of fact. In order to effectively testify and present evidence, investigators must understand not only the basic mechanics of testifying but also the "big picture" of what the case is about and where their testimony will fit in to the case as a whole.

This chapter will start with some common misconceptions about an investigator's role at trial. Then, we will offer some basic guidance on how best to present yourself as an effective witness. Finally, we will explore some of the "big picture" issues to help investigators understand how their testimony will fit in to the case as a whole.

Notes from the Underground...

Pretrial Motions and Plea

Cases involving the forensic analysis of digital evidence frequently rise or fall on pretrial motions to suppress. In these motions, the issue for the court to decide is the legality of the search. If, for example, investigators relied upon consent rather than obtaining a search warrant authorizing the examination of the digital evidence, defense attorneys are likely to challenge the legality of the consent. If, on the other hand, investigators obtained a search warrant, defense attorneys may claim that the warrant was invalid either for technical reasons or because there was insufficient probable cause to believe that evidence relating to a crime would be found upon the computer. Pretrial motions are frequently the most important part of a case: if the government wins the pretrial motion and the court holds that the evidence will be admissible

Continued

at trial, in most cases defense attorneys will enter into a plea bargain to avoid trial. On the other hand, if the evidence is suppressed, prosecutors may not be able to proceed any further with the case. Cyber crime investigators, therefore, should treat testifying at a pretrial motion every bit as seriously as testifying at a trial.

Common Misconceptions

Perhaps because the evidence in most cyber crime is so powerful, or perhaps because defense attorneys and prosecutors are simply reluctant to delve into the intricacies of forensic electronics, the vast majority of cyber crime cases are resolved without the necessity of the investigator ever having to testify. As a result of the rarity in which cyber investigators are called upon to testify, misconceptions among cyber investigators about testifying in these types of cases abound. Some of the more common misconceptions are addressed next.

The Level of Expertise Necessary to Testify as a Cyber Crime Investigator

Cyber crime investigators are primarily *percipient witnesses*. This means that although the analysis of a computer might have involved complex technical issues, the basic purpose for which the investigator's testimony is offered is to describe what the investigator saw and did, rather than to offer complex technical information about computers or forensic software. Although cyber crime investigators frequently use high-tech tools like forensic software to find evidence, ultimately their testimony is not different in kind from that of a police officer who used a complex pair of binoculars to find evidence. A police officer using such binoculars to witness a drug transaction would not be expected to be an expert in binoculars and optics in order to testify at trial concerning what he saw. Similarly, a cyber crime investigator who used a complex computer program to discover child pornography on a suspect's computer would not have to be an expert computer programmer to describe what the investigator discovered through the use of the program. Although cyber crime investigators must be generally familiar with computers and the forensic software that they used to perform their investigation, there is no need in order for a cyber crime investigator to testify to be a computer expert with qualifications such as an advanced degree in computer science.

> **NOTE**
>
> An expert witness is a witness who possesses specialized knowledge that an ordinary juror would not likely possess.
>
> A percipient witness is a witness who testifies about what he "perceived" (e.g., what he saw, did, or heard).

The Requirements for Establishing a Foundation for the Admissibility of Digital Evidence

A related misconception among investigators is the testimony that they will be required to offer at trial in order to establish the admissibility of the electronic evidence that the investigator discovered. Investigators worry that they will be asked to describe and explain the inner workings of either the computer that they used to analyze digital evidence or the program that was running on the computer that allowed them to discover the files on the suspect's media storage device. Or, investigators worry about how they can establish that they did not either intentionally or inadvertently create the evidence with the investigator's computer. Furthermore, investigators worry that in order to prove that they did not create the evidence, they will need to be able to explain to a jury how computers work. Finally, investigators worry about whether they will need to be knowledgeable about the computer program, how it is written, the reliability of the algorithms that the computer program uses, and whether it is capable of somehow "making up" files. *Fortunately, these worries are unfounded.*

In order for the government to establish a proper foundation for the admissibility of evidence derived from a search conducted by a cyber crime investigator who used a computer to uncover electronic evidence, the prosecutor need only ask a series of basic questions about the tools and techniques that the investigator used to gather the evidence. For example, perhaps the single most common subject that investigators are called upon to testify about at trial is which files were found in the defendant's storage media. In order to establish a foundation for the investigator's discovery of the files in such a case, the government need only establish two things:

- The government would have to establish that the computer file was in fact a file that was located on the defendant's hard drive rather than somebody else's hard drive. This is frequently referred to as "chain of custody" evidence, and we will discuss it later.

- The government must show that the file that was allegedly discovered upon the suspect's media storage device originated there and was not somehow placed there or created by the investigator's computerized black box.

NOTE

Keep in mind that defense counsel may not bother to challenge the foundation. If so, this issue becomes moot. There are a variety of reasons why defense counsel wouldn't bother to challenge the foundation. First, they may view it as a waste of time, since in almost every case the judge is going to allow the evidence to come in. Second, defense counsel may not understand the technical issues involved in authenticating computer evidence, and may choose therefore to focus on different issues.

Although the establishment of a solid foundation sounds like a tricky issue, the reality is much more mundane. None of the questions that are necessary to establish the proper foundation are technical in nature. A line of questions like the following should be enough to establish a proper foundation that the computer used by an investigator to perform a forensic examination was reliable:

Q: What type of a computer did you use to perform your forensic examination of the suspect's hard drive?

A: I used a Dell Technica Model 6700.

Q: And have you used that computer to perform examinations in the past?

A: I have.

Q: Approximately how many times?

A: Forty to 50 times.

Q: And to your knowledge, did the computer appear to function normally at all times?

A: Yes.

NOTE

The line of questioning as shown could continue in greater depth, including questions like whether, when, where, and why the computer may have been serviced. However, these questions illustrate the simple type of questions that a prosecutor would ask to show that the computer appeared to be functioning normally.

Questions like the following would establish a proper foundation to show that the results generated from the computer program were reliable:

Q: What computer program did you run on the Dell Technica Model 6700 to forensically analyze the suspect's hard drive?

A: "Forensic Tool Kit," which is also known as "FTK."

Q: And to your knowledge, is this program commonly used in the law enforcement community to perform forensic examinations on hard drives?

A: It is.

Q: And are you aware of any errors or issues concerning the accuracy or reliability of the program?

A: I am not.

Q: Have you used the program in the past?

A: Yes.

Q: Approximately how many times?

A: Forty to fifty times.

Q: Have you encountered any problems with the accuracy or reliability of the program?

A: No.

Although the defense might try to argue that you are not a computer scientist and you have no way of knowing for a fact that the results of your search are reliable, such arguments would go to the weight (or believability) of the evidence and would not prevent the finder of fact from considering the evidence. As a practical matter, once the judge admits the evidence based on simple foundation questions like those shown here, the finder of fact is likely to trust the results generated by the computer.

NOTE

The weight of the evidence is the value that the jury may choose to place upon the evidence.

The Limitations on an Expert Witness's Expertise

Sometimes cyber crime investigators are qualified by courts to testify as experts because of specialized knowledge that they possess. Courts qualify witnesses to testify as experts only in limited areas, and an investigator should not suggest that they know more than they actually do. For example, although an investigator may be qualified by the court to testify as an expert in the use of FTK to search media storage devices, this qualification would not make the investigator an all around computer expert.

There is something exhilarating about being declared an expert, and witnesses who are qualified as experts can easily get carried away with it. If you hold yourself out as an all-around computer expert, you are begging defense counsel to ask you about computer chip design or the intricacies of HTML programming. Jurors like plainspoken witnesses who testify in simple terms about what they said and did. Don't let the technical tools that you may have used to discover evidence confuse the jury: you are simply there to tell them what you did and what you saw.

Chain of Custody

In order for any evidence to be admitted at trial, the *proponent*, or the party offering the evidence to the court, must authenticate the evidence. That, is the proponent must establish that the evidence actually is what it purports to be. What this means as a practical matter can best be explained by way of example. In a murder case in which the defendant was stabbed to death, a bloody knife might be powerful evidence. On the other hand, unless the bloody knife was actually the one that was found at the scene of the crime, then the evidence is entirely irrelevant and useless for the jury to consider.

In this type of a case, how is the evidence authenticated? The answer is simple: The first investigator who discovered the knife would testify that the knife being offered into evidence by the prosecutor is the same one that was found at the murder scene, in the same condition as when it was discovered. If the investigator couldn't remember exactly what the knife looked like at the scene, the investigator could refresh his memory by looking at a photograph of the knife at the scene. Any type of evidence that is unique and readily identifiable may be authenticated in this way.

Some types of evidence, however, are trickier to authenticate. For example, in a case in which investigators discovered three ounces of cocaine in a shoebox at the defendant's house, how could an investigator honestly say at trial that the bag of nondescript white powder that the prosecutor wants to offer into evidence is actually the cocaine that the investigator discovered in the defendant's house? In legal terms, how can the proponent of the evidence authenticate that the evidence is what it purports to be? In these types of cases, investigators usually must resort to authenticating the evidence by establishing the "chain of custody" of the evidence.

Any investigator who has testified frequently in drug cases is familiar with how the process of establishing chain of custody works. First, the investigator explains how and where he found the cocaine. Then, he explains that he put the cocaine into a sealed evidence bag marked with his name, initials, or other distinctive mark. Next, the investigator explains that the bag was then transferred to the evidence room. Finally, the investigator explains that the bag that was received from the evidence room prior to trial seems to be the same bag that he found at the scene of the crime. The evidence is authenticated, therefore, because the chain of custody can be established, all the way from the defendant's house to the courtroom.

In cyber crime cases, investigators and prosecutors frequently use the wrong procedure for authenticating digital evidence. They use a chain of custody authentication procedure rather than the much simpler procedure of having the investigator say how he can tell by comparing hash values (even without knowing the chain of custody) that the digital files being offered into evidence are the same files that were discovered in the defendant's possession. For example, in many investigations, hard drives or other storage media are seized, placed in sealed evidence bags like drugs, and then transferred somewhere for forensic analysis. Later, when the prosecutor attempts to introduce the files into evidence at trial, defense counsel may attack the authenticity of the digital evidence by suggesting that the files were not actually on the hard drive when it was at the defendant's house, but were somehow placed on it during the forensic examination process. The confusion stems from an attempt to authenticate the files through a chain of custody technique (like one that would be used in a drug case), rather than simply having the investigator authenticate the evidence by comparing the hash value of the file being offered into evidence with the hash value of the file seized from the defendant.

In order to avoid this, investigators should adopt procedures in which all relevant files and the entire hard drive or other storage media themselves, are hashed as soon as possible. A record that can be referred to at trial should then be made of the relevant hash values. As a legal matter, recording hash values of seized digital evidence is no different than photographing a homicide scene so that an investigator can later testify that the knife that the prosecutor is trying to offer into evidence is the same one that was present at the homicide scene. By simply comparing the two hash values, the evidence will be authenticated and admissible, and nobody will ever have to worry about the chain of custody.

Keys to Effective Testimony

Law enforcement investigators are accustomed to testifying in routine criminal matters. Testifying as a cyber crime investigator calls upon the same basic skills that an investigator would use in testifying about an assault and battery investigation, but it also requires additional knowledge and preparation. First, we will examine the unique issues involved in testifying as a cyber investigator, and then we will review some of the fundamentals of effective testimony that apply to all trials.

The First Step: Gauging the Prosecutor's Level of Expertise

In a cyber crime investigation, unlike an "ordinary" criminal matter, the first step in preparing to testify is to evaluate the prosecutor's level of technical expertise. This is essential because a cyber crime prosecution, like all other criminal cases, is a team effort between the investigator and the prosecutor. If the prosecutor doesn't understand how and where the investigator found the evidence or the prosecutor does not understand the significance of the evidence, the prosecutor will not be able to effectively elicit testimony from the investigator. If your testimony is not presented effectively, the finder of fact will be confused, and the defense attorney will be able to exploit that confusion to create doubt in the jury's mind—this is to be avoided.

It is the prosecutor's job to present the evidence that the cyber crime investigator discovered in a manner that will be comprehensible and persuasive to an untrained juror. In order to do this, the prosecutor must understand the evidence well enough to explain it to somebody else and to effectively anticipate the attacks that defense counsel is likely to make on the credibility of the evidence. Prosecutors, like the public at large, have widely differing levels of knowledge about computers. If you are fortunate enough to have a prosecutor with extensive knowledge and experience in cyber crime, you will be able to immediately get down to case specifics when you meet with the prosecutor; describing the evidence that you found, where you found it, and discussing likely attacks by defense counsel. If, on the other hand, you have a prosecutor who does not have significant technical expertise or background in cyber crime prosecutions, you must be prepared to educate the prosecutor so that the prosecutor can help you to testify effectively.

> **NOTE**
>
> In order to work effectively together as a team, cyber crime investigators and prosecutors must be able to "speak the same language." Prosecutors must have a good general understanding of basic computer terminology as well as a working knowledge of the forensic tools that cyber crime investigators use to do their jobs. Cyber crime investigators, on the other hand, must understand how they will present what they did during their investigation in the form of testimony in court. Whenever possible, therefore, it makes sense for cyber crime investigators to conduct joint training with prosecutors so that they can later work together effectively as a team.

The Next Step: Discussing the Case with the Prosecutor

You should always discuss your testimony with the prosecutor prior to testifying, preferably in person. Even when the prosecutor has not reached out to talk with you about the case, the cyber crime investigator, as a professional, should always attempt to discuss the case with the prosecutor before testifying. A pretrial conversation is critical to ensure that the investigator is thoroughly prepared to testify. With that said, it should be understood that prosecutors are incredibly overworked and harried professionals. It is not unusual, for example, for a prosecutor in a large urban district to carry a caseload of 300 or more cases. As a practical matter, what that means is that prosecutors must constantly struggle to send out subpoenas, review files, and prepare documents in an effort to stay ahead of the constant tide of hearings and trials. Therefore, in many cases the burden must fall upon the cyber crime investigator to contact the prosecutor.

During your discussion with the prosecutor, you should, at a minimum, review your report with the prosecutor, ensure that the prosecutor is clear about what the report contains, and answer any questions that the prosecutor may have. Additionally, you should inquire who the defense attorney is, and the areas that the prosecutor feels that the defense attorney is going to focus on with you. In larger, more complex cases, it is good practice to actually do a dry run of your proposed testimony with the prosecutor.

You should also understand from the prosecutor what the defendant's defense is likely to be. For example, in a child pornography possession case, the focus of your testimony will be significantly different depending on whether the defendant is claiming that "somebody else put it on my computer," "a virus, Trojan horse, or other malware put it on my computer," or "the picture is that of a virtual child not a real child." As we will discuss later, understanding these "big picture" ideas will help you focus your preparation on the issues that are in dispute and will make you a more effective witness.

Gauging the Defense

The defense bar, like the prosecution, has widely varying levels of technical expertise with computers. Some defense attorneys have developed expertise in defending cases involving computers and digital evidence. Technically adept defense attorneys are more likely to closely question you on the protocols that you employed and whether those protocols are industry best practices.

Most defense attorneys, however, do not have such an expertise. Defense attorneys without technical expertise are likely to focus on different issues when defending the case, such as whether the search was lawful or whether the defendant was actually the person who put the evidence on the computer. To the extent that such an attorney does attempt to attack the computer forensics, the most common approach is to argue that your "black box" simply cannot be trusted because it is so darned complicated that neither you nor anybody else really understands how it works.

The best defense to an attack like this is to work with the prosecutor to ensure that you can explain in simple, nontechnical terms what you did and how you found the evidence. One useful technique is to practice explaining to lay people like your spouse, parents, neighbors, or friends, what it is that you do. To the extent that you can demystify what you do, you will be a better, more effective witness.

Reviewing Reports

If an investigator does nothing else to prepare to testify, the one thing that the investigator must do is to review his or her report shortly before testifying. Reviewing the report doesn't mean just reading it over; it means reading the report over closely at least five or six times. One of the most frustrating things from the vantage point of a prosecutor is watching defense counsel attack an investigator on the details of the investigator's report when the investigator's knowledge of the report is clearly hazy because he or she wrote the report a long time ago and did not properly review the report before trial. In almost all cases, most of the defense attorney's cross-examination of the investigator will be based upon the investigator's report. Investigators have a huge advantage when testifying: they know almost exactly what most of the defense attorney's questions are going to be based upon. Use this to your advantage.

Presenting Yourself as an Effective Witness

The key ingredients in presenting yourself as an effective witness are the same in cyber crime cases as they are in all cases. First, keep in mind that there is no one right or wrong way to testify—everybody that testifies is going to have a different style. As long as your style of testimony is likely to be credible to a jury, your style of testimony is just fine. As part of your conversation with the prosecutor, get advice from the prosecutor about testifying effectively. Different lawyers are going to focus on different things, and regardless of how many times you have testified, there is always something that you can learn about doing it better.

The most basic general rule about testifying is to listen to the question carefully and to answer the question to the best of your ability. After the question is asked, pause for a second to gather your thoughts before answering. This serves two purposes: First, simply blurting out an answer is the best way to get into trouble. Second, a pause provides the attorneys with an opportunity to object. If you don't know the answer to a question or you can't fairly answer the question as asked, just say so.

Direct Examination

On direct examination, you ideally want to develop a rapport with the prosecutor. Once again, listen carefully to the prosecutor's questions and answer them to the best of your ability. You should answer the prosecutor's questions *fully*. In an ideal direct examination, the prosecutor's role is almost unnoticeable. What the prosecutor is striving to do on direct examination is to ask open-ended questions that allow you to tell your story in a comfortable and complete manner that is as close to a narrative as possible. It doesn't always end up this way, but that is what the prosecutor is striving to do.

Most prosecutors suggest that you direct your answer to the finder of fact (either the judge or jury as appropriate). Sometimes, however, this can seem a bit contrived. If you aren't sure about this, ask the prosecutor.

Finally, keep in mind that you are going to be nervous. Testifying is an inherently stressful thing, and if you aren't somewhat nervous, you simply don't appreciate the significance of what you are doing. With that said, try to keep things in perspective: your sole job is to answer specific questions truthfully.

Cross Examination

The cardinal rule about testifying on cross-examination is not to volunteer information that was not asked. As a witness, your role is simply to respond to the questions that are asked of you. On cross-examination, defense counsel will ask you closed questions like, "Isn't it true that you didn't write that in your report?" Or "you didn't photograph the computer screen before you started to work on the computer, did you?" There is an almost irresistible temptation for investigators either to try to justify what they did or to play "gotcha" by offering information that wasn't asked. Resist the temptation. The prosecutor will get a chance to clarify anything on redirect examination that is important. If you volunteer information, you are simply going to open up additional areas for defense counsel to inquire about, possibly areas that defense counsel would not have delved into otherwise.

Keep in mind that the defense counsel is not your enemy. You should treat defense counsel's questions to you as an opportunity to educate the finder of fact about what you observed and did. If you allow defense counsel to bait you into squabbling about things in front of the finder of fact, your credibility will inevitably suffer even if you think that you got the better of the argument. Don't try to one up defense counsel by showing off your technical knowledge.

Understanding the Big Picture

Testifying effectively requires not only following the basic rules just described, it also involves understanding how your testimony fits into the big picture of the trial as a whole. Attorneys call this big picture the *theory of the case*. For example, in a child pornography case, the defense attorney's theory of the case might be that there were many people with access to the computer, and the government really can't establish that the defendant is responsible for the child pornography on the computer. Another defense might be that although the defendant may have put the images on the computer, the images weren't of real children. The prosecutor's theory of the case is usually as simple as "the defendant intentionally committed x crime." Sometimes the prosecutor will also use the defendant's apparent motive as a theme to tie the case together.

NOTE

Defense attorneys are legally entitled to present alternative defenses, for example, I didn't send the e-mail, but even if I did, it wasn't threatening. Although presenting alternative defenses is not at all unusual, it is generally recognized that at some point having too many different theories of defense becomes confusing to the jury and is ineffective.

In order to testify effectively, you should understand the theory of the case that the prosecutor and defense counsel are relying upon. As an investigator, it is easy to develop "tunnel vision" so that you see only your piece in the jigsaw puzzle, rather than the jigsaw puzzle as a whole. If you develop a broad understanding of the case as an investigator, you will be able to assist the prosecutor in identifying the testimony you could offer that would be helpful for the trier of fact to understand the issues that are really in dispute. Moreover, you will be able to better anticipate the questions that the defense attorney is going to ask you.

An example might be helpful: If the issue in a case is the defendant's sanity, most defense attorneys aren't going to quibble with the protocol that the cyber investigator followed while searching the defendant's computer. If the cyber investigator understands that the theory of the defendant's case is that the defendant is insane, the cyber investigator, working with the prosecutor, could effectively tailor his testimony to address the issue of sanity. The cyber investigator might testify, for example, about how the defendant organized his files (suggesting that the defendant was rational) or how the defendant hid or destroyed certain files (suggesting rationality and consciousness of guilt on the defendant's part). This sort of high level understanding of the case should be the ultimate goal of a cyber crime investigator.

Differences between Civil and Criminal Cases

Investigators need not concern themselves with legal issues like the differences in the burden of proof between civil and criminal proceedings. The major difference between civil and criminal proceedings from the perspective of an investigator is simply the much broader scope of discovery in civil cases than in criminal cases. In civil cases, the parties are permitted to serve detailed questions and requests for production of documents upon one another before trial. Moreover, the parties may depose or question witnesses under oath. During the course of such depositions, the scope of questions is extremely broad. The general rule is that lawyers can ask you anything that is either relevant or likely to lead to the discovery of relevant evidence. In practice, this means that the questioning is wide-open, and there will be few—if any— objections to the questions that are asked of you. The principles for testifying effectively on cross-examination that were just described are equally applicable to testifying during a deposition.

Summary

By preparing thoroughly before testifying and working effectively with prose-cutors, cyber crime investigators can be extraordinarily effective witnesses. Testifying in cyber crime cases calls upon all of the same skills that testifying in any other matter requires. Additionally, in cyber crime cases, it is essential to learn to effectively talk in lay terms about what the investigator did and what the investigator found. Finally, in cyber crime cases investigators have to assess the technical expertise of both the prosecutor and the defense counsel in order to effectively present evidence on direct examination and anticipate attacks by defense counsel. The ultimate goal as a cyber crime investigator is to understand the theory of the case, and apply that knowledge to effectively guide the investigation and present evidence in court.

Solutions Fast Track

Common Misconceptions

☑ The level of expertise necessary to testify as a cyber crime investigator.

☑ The requirements for establishing a foundation for the admissibility of digital evidence.

☑ The limitations on an expert witness's expertise.

Chain of Custody

☑ In order for any evidence to be admitted at trial, the proponent, or the party offering the evidence to the court, must authenticate the evidence.

☑ In cyber crime cases, investigators and prosecutors frequently use the wrong procedure for authenticating digital evidence. They use a chain of custody authentication procedure rather than the much simpler procedure of having the investigator say how he can tell by comparing hash values (even without knowing the chain of custody) that the digital files being offered into evidence are the same files that were discovered in the defendant's possession.

☑ In many investigations, hard drives or other storage media are seized, placed in sealed evidence bags like drugs, and then transferred somewhere for forensic analysis. Later, when the prosecutor attempts to introduce the files into evidence at trial, defense counsel may attack the authenticity of the digital evidence by suggesting that the files were not actually on the hard drive when it was at the defendant's house, but were somehow placed on it during the forensic examination process.

Keys to Effective Testimony

☑ Discuss the case with the prosecutor before testifying.

☑ Prepare for testifying by thoroughly reviewing your report shortly before testifying.

☑ On cross-examination, listen to the question, pause, and then answer the question truthfully without volunteering additional information.

Differences between Civil and Criminal Cases

☑ The scope of discovery in civil cases is much broader than it is in criminal cases. Expect to be deposed in a civil case and expect to have to answer far more questions at a civil deposition than you would in a criminal proceeding.

Frequently Asked Questions

The following Frequently Asked Questions, answered by the authors of this book, are designed to both measure your understanding of the concepts presented in this chapter and to assist you with real-life implementation of these concepts. To have your questions about this chapter answered by the author, browse to **www.syngress.com/solutions** and click on the **"Ask the Author"** form.

Q: Do I need to have a computer science degree in order to testify about the computer investigation I conducted?

A: The answer to this question is no. Again you will be testifying as a percipient witness.

Q: As a prosecutor, should I attend computer training, or rely solely on the officer's knowledge base?

A: If you, as a prosecutor, are going to be prosecuting computer-related cases on a regular basis, then the answer is clearly yes, get the additional training. The answer is also yes even if you do not anticipate doing these types of cases. Knowledge is power and it can't hurt to learn about the technology involved.

Q: Should I prepare my cyber crimes case differently then my civil computer case?

A: No. Many cases that start out civil in nature may eventually turn into a criminal matter. As such you should also conduct your investigation as if it was a criminal matter.

Chapter 4

Cyber Investigative Roles

Solutions in this chapter:

- **Understanding Your Role as a Cyber Crime Investigator**
- **The Role of Law Enforcement Officers**
- **The Role of the Prosecuting Attorney**

☑ **Summary**

☑ **Solutions Fast Track**

☑ **Frequently Asked Questions**

Introduction

In the Hewlett-Packard case, I can't help thinking of how HP could have prevented its pretexting scandal. Clearly, the practice of corporate America as it relates to reporting incidents is at fault here. It is not uncommon for companies to handle criminal incidents in-house, electing not to seek help from outside agencies. This reluctance is due to the fear that reporting the incident will result in negative media exposure, which could lead to a loss of customers, a loss of customer confidence, and ultimately a loss of profits. This holds true even for companies that are required by law to report criminal incidents.

As a cyber crime detective, I was contacted on numerous occasions by companies looking to get help with a criminal case long after their investigation had commenced. In many of these cases, the company was required by law to report the incident immediately, but did not. By the time the cases got to me, they had clearly spun out of control. At this stage of the investigation, my role in their eyes was more of a cleanup crew than someone out to catch the suspect. As a result of involving law enforcement late in the investigation, crucial evidence was lost, suspects got off, and reputations were damaged. These companies played Vegas odds with full disclosure and ultimately rolled craps.

In the Hewlett-Packard case, board members were leaking corporate information outside of the company's board room. HP, as a publicly traded company, had a financial responsibility to protect its confidential business information. Additionally, according to business ethicist Kirk Hanson, they were obligated to investigate these leaks under the Sarbanes-Oxley Act (Mullins, 2006). Where I believe HP strayed *"from the True Way in to the Dark Woods of Error"* is when it decided to investigate this potential criminal case on its own. If HP had contacted the appropriate regulatory agencies from the beginning, it might have been able to find the leak without the use of pretexting and e-mail tracing software. Investigating agencies could have obtained search warrants and possibly a wiretap court order, and HP would have been able to obtain the information legally, sparing them embarrassment, and avoiding the ruin of those individuals who thought they were just doing their job.

Often, the decision to investigate cases in-house is made at an executive level. This has been relayed to me on many occasions when interviewing employees of companies as I investigated cyber crime incidents. They followed the instructions of their superiors even if the activities were illegal. Many employees I talked to believed they had a right to engage in these activities based on their conversations with corporate consul and/or their superiors. Others explained they just did what they were told because they feared being fired. In almost every case, it boiled down to individuals not understanding their roles in the criminal justice process.

I remember an incident where company employees decided to handle a criminal case on their own, acting on the advice of their corporate counsel in the handling of a criminal matter. The offense: their CFO had been spotted viewing child porn at work. In this case, the system administrator uncovered some network traffic that gave a hint of wrongdoing. Knowing that evidence would be required to prove this allegation, he began capturing traffic from his firewall. The system administrator was able to lasso content both in text and graphics form. Once he amassed his proof, he approached the Human Resources manager and informed him of what had transpired. The HR manager then approached the CEO and informed him of what was going on. After several days, the person from HR contacted the CEO and asked if he had resolved the issue, but the CEO stated he would need to consult with legal counsel. After a few more days of hounding the CEO, the HR manager attended a meeting with the system administrator, the CEO, and legal counsel. At the meeting, legal counsel advised the system administrator to clean the computer and block the CFO from connecting to the Internet at the firewall. Fearing the loss of his job, the system administrator did what legal counsel recommended. Uneasy with the corporate counsel's decision, the HR manager contacted me and informed me of what happened. Needless to say, once I responded, the trouble the company faced was now twofold.

These incidents are not unique to corporations. Law enforcement and prosecuting agencies can also find themselves defending their actions in court when this invisible line is crossed. Issues of unlawful search and seizure, entrapment, and false arrest are just some of the problems that can result from failing to stay within defined roles.

I believe that the preceding case could have been prevented had the investigators and lawyers acted within their defined roles. Each one of us plays an intricate role in the war on cyber crime—from the private sector investigator to the law enforcement officer to, ultimately, the prosecutor. The ideal flow of events should start when the private sector discovers the crime, which should then be reported to the law enforcement officer who investigates the crime. If a perpetrator is eventually found, the prosecutor should prosecute them. This process aids in the overall checks and balances of cyber crime investigations. It is a chain that should not be broken.

WARNING

When investigating crimes for your corporation, be aware that ultimately you can be charged with a crime, regardless of corporate counsel's advice, if you engage in illegal activities.

Additionally, cyber crime investigators from one sector need to be aware of the needs of other sectors in order to avoid confusions and reduce tensions. During my investigations, I found that the different sectors fail to reach out to one another for help because of the belief that the other sector lacks the understanding of that sector's needs and concerns. What may be important to one sector may not be necessarily important to another. This causes immediate gaps between the two sectors when working together. Errors from one sector can have detrimental effects on the other. The most important aspect of all is for these different sectors to understand how each role interacts with the other. In the pages that follow, I will address areas within each sector that can become problematic and cause harm to the overall process.

Understanding Your Role as a Cyber Crime Investigator

With great power comes great responsibility.

—Uncle Ben to Peter Parker in Spider-Man

Corporate investigators are afforded a number of powers, many of which supersede those of law enforcement. Eavesdroping, recording network traffic, and reading e-mails are just a few of the powers corporations can wield over their employees, whereas law enforcement requires a court order to engage in many of these types of activities. As a corporate investigator, you must understand how and when to invoke these powers, and how to avoid the pitfalls of using them. In doing so, you can keep from trampling on someone's rights, and avoid the possibility of yourself becoming liable, or even worse, arrested.

Understanding Employees Rights: Employee Monitoring

In a survey done by the American Management Association (AMA), it found that almost 75 percent of companies monitor their employee's activities (American Management Association, 2001). Additionally, it reported that such monitoring had doubled since 1997. Among the items monitored were e-mails, computer files, and telephone calls. Reasons for monitoring an employee's communications vary. Some employers engage in this behavior to protect their trade secrets, others to monitor misconduct. The list is long and varied. Although the Electronic Communications Privacy Act (ECPA) routinely prohibits the intentional interception of communications, it is rarely applied to corporations. The courts have routinely upheld a company's right to protect its interests over their employees individual right to privacy.

In *Smyth v. The Pillsbury Company*, Pillsbury had assured its employees that their e-mails would remain confidential and privileged. It further assured them that no e-mail would be intercepted or used as grounds for termination or reprimands. Nevertheless, Pillsbury later fired Smyth for sending out inappropriate e-mails. Smyth sued on the grounds that Pillsbury violated its "*public policy which precludes an employer from terminating an employee in violation of the employee's right to privacy as embodied in Pennsylvania common law*" (*Smyth v. The Pillsbury Company*, 1996). In its decision, the court stated there was no reasonable expectation of privacy for Smyth's e-mail even though Pillsbury made assurances that e-mails would not be intercepted by management. Moreover, once Smyth sent his message over the e-mail system used by the entire company, all reasonable expectations of privacy were lost.

Although, the Smyth case has literally granted companies the unlimited right to monitor its employees, as an investigator you should be aware that employees still maintain their constitutional protections, and so you must exercise care when monitoring e-mails or computer files. According to Jean A. Musiker, an attorney of labor and employment law, employers have constraints when it comes to an employee's right to privacy. She refers to *Bratt v. International Business Machines, Corp.* 392 Mass. 508 (1984) where the Massachusetts Supreme Court found that the state's privacy statute (Mass. G.L. c. 214, §1B) did apply to the workplace and does offer protection regarding an employee's right to privacy (Musiker, 1998). She also points out that in order for employers to violate the privacy statute, they must meet the balance test. Musiker quotes the court in *O'Connor v. Police Commissioner of Boston* [408 Mass. 324, 330 (1990)], where the court ruled that in order to violate the statue the "interference with privacy must be both *unreasonable* and *substantial or serious*" (Musiker, 1998). Musiker further quotes *Cort v. Bristol Meyers* [385 Mass. 300, 307 (1982)], which found that employees were protected from companies that monitored their workers purely for personal reasons. Jean also points out that an employee's position within a company may be a factor when applying the balance test. She refers to the Massachusetts case of *Webster v. Motorola, Inc.* [418 Mass. 425 (1994)] when making this point. In this case, the court suggested that employees in upper-level management positions had a lesser expectation of privacy than those of lower positions within the company.

The point that I'm trying to make here is that IT investigators must use caution when dealing with the privacy of employees. IT security personnel should not automatically assume they have the right to violate the privacy of employees. Furthermore, companies should be aware that the actions of their IT investigator on behalf of the company will not remove them from total civil and criminal liability. In a Scottsdale, Arizona case, a police officer was granted $300,000 after the police department fired him from the force for sending an inappropriate e-mail to a co-worker (Spykerman, 2007). The co-worker was a close friend of the officer, and found the e-mail amusing. Nevertheless, the police department fired him, but later lost the case.

The bottom line here is that if you determine a crime is being committed, get law enforcement involved. They may be able to remove the risk of injury to yourself or your company by pursuing appropriate legal action.

Notes from the Underground…

The Electronic Communications Privacy Act

The Electronic Communications Privacy Act was passed in 1986 and governs how and when electronic communications can be intercepted. It also provides definitions as to what an electronic communication is, and describes penalties for violating the Act's provisions. Although very little in this statue applies to corporations, it behooves you to read it to obtain a better understanding of the law.

Understanding Law Enforcement Concerns

As a law enforcement officer, one of my biggest fears when contacting a company in regards to a cyber crime investigation is that the systems administrator or IT personnel are the persons committing the crime, which often has been the case. Statistics show most crimes that occur within a corporation are usually committed by its employees (Secret Service *et al.*, 2002). As such, I was always leery of company employees before ruling them out as a potential suspect. What the corporate IT staff needs to know is that law enforcement officers have a duty to investigate the crimes. They can not tip their hat to the potential perpetrator. As a result, IT personnel, as well as company employees, will usually experience the following until the law enforcement official rules them out as a possible suspect:

- Law enforcement will provide you with the smallest amount of information possible.

- Sometimes officers will allow you to believe they are investigating a different crime than the one you suspect.

- On occasion, law enforcement may ask you for unnecessary documents in order to throw you off track from what they are investigating.

In light of the preceding circumstances, you should not take this personally. They are only doing their job. Once an officer has gained confidence in you and ruled you out as a suspect, he will usually provide you with a little more detail. However, do not expect him to pour his heart out to you and go over every aspect of the case. There are two reasons for not doing this. One, he does not want you to be coached on the case since it would appear to a judge or jury that the two of you conspired to frame the suspect. Second, by law he can not instruct you on what to do since it may make you an "*agent of the government.*"

Agent of the Government

IT personnel are routinely contacted by law enforcement. This contact can range from providing subscriber information to allowing officers to forensically image a computer system. Many times the IT investigator plays an intricate part in the investigation. A relationship between the police officer and the investigator is established, and together they help to solve the crime. Although the IT investigator may want to continue assisting the law enforcement official in the investigation once it has been turned over, often his role will automatically become reduced. This reduction in the investigative role is not because the officer dislikes or distrusts the IT investigator (he has already been vetted from being a suspect), but because the police officer must ensure that the company's personnel do not become an agent of the government.

In theory, a person acts as an agent of the police when his or her actions are directed at the behest of a law enforcement official. The courts have held that in order for a private citizen to be an agent of the government, two conditions must exist (11th Cir. 2003). First, the person must have acted with the intent to help law enforcement. Second, the government must know about the person's activities and either acquiesced in, or encouraged, them. Routinely, defendants argue that their rights have been violated when it comes to search and seizures that are conducted by civilians at the request of a law enforcement agency. Instances where a defendant can prove that a law enforcement agency used a civilian to investigate someone will usually result in the dismissal of the criminal case.

A case that addressed this very issue was *United States v. Jarrett*. In *Jarrett*, law enforcement officers utilized information from a Turkish hacker who on two occasions obtained information on child molesters (Fourth Cir. 2003). The hacker, referred to by the district court as the Unknownuser, utilized a Trojan horse program to gain access to the unsuspecting child molesters' computer systems. William Adderson Jarrett was arrested after the Unknownuser used a Trojan horse program to recover images of child pornography from Jarrett's computer and reported him to the police. During his trial, Jarrett asked the court to suppress the evidence obtained by Unknownuser from being used against him since it violated his constitutional rights. The district court denied his motion and allowed the evidence into the proceedings. Jarrett later adopted a plea of guilty and during his sentencing motioned again for the district court to suppress the evidence based on new e-mail evidence that was not disclosed during the trial. The e-mail communications were between the Unknownuser and an FBI agent. During the e-mail conversations, which occurred after Jarrett's arrest, the agent engaged in what the district court deemed to be a "proverbial wink and a nod." The e-mail contained the following message:

> I can not ask you to search out cases such as the ones you have sent to us. That would make you an agent of the federal government and make how you obtain your information illegal and we could not use it against the men in the pictures you send. But if you should happen across such pictures as the ones you have sent to us and wish us to look into the matter, please feel free to send them to us. We may have lots of questions and have to e-mail you with the questions. But as long as you are not 'hacking' at our request, we can take the pictures and identify the men and take them to court. We also have no desire to charge you with hacking. You are not a U.S. citizen and are not bound by our laws.
>
> —*United States v. Jarrett*, Fourth Cir.

The district court further stated that the relationship between the agent and the hacker was that of a pen pal–like relationship, and that the agent never instructed the hacker to stop his illegal activity in obtaining the evidence. Additionally, the district court felt that the government and Unknownuser had "expressed their consent to an agency relationship." Although the district court reversed the plea of guilty, the United States Court of Appeals later would reverse the district court's decision. Ironically, the appellate court cited *United States v. Steiger*, which was the first case that involved the Unknownuser, in reversing the district court's decision. This decision to reverse was based partly on the fact that the e-mails occurred after Jarrett's arrest, and because the government failed to meet the two conditional requirements of the agency. I believe the outcome would have been different had no e-mails occurred before Jarrett's arrest.

NOTE

A Trojan horse in the computer sense refers to a software program containing malicious computer code. The name Trojan horse comes from the Trojan War military tactic where the Greeks hid soldiers in a wooden horse and then offered it to the city of Troy as a gift, thus secretly gaining entrance to the city and eventually laying siege to it.

Providing the Foundation

One of the most important things an IT security investigator can provide in any case is information. No one understands your network setup better than you. Also, you know the technology involved within your organization. Many times law enforcement officers will not have experience with many of the devices or systems they will come upon. It is here that you play your second biggest role after detection. Imparting your knowledge of the system setup and how it works will help the law enforcement officer better understand how the crime was committed. Point out what types of security and monitoring devices you may have at your locations. Take the time to explain where all the log files are, and what they show. Become the technical teacher and help bridge the gap between technology and law enforcement. You will find this very satisfying.

The Role of Law Enforcement Officers

Cyber crime police officers should be cognizant of the concerns of corporations. Often, this lack of understanding leads to tension and standoffs between the two.

Understanding Corporate Concerns

I remember sending a subpoena to a company, and receiving a phone call several days later. The owner of this small ISP asked me how important the information was I was seeking since it would take some work to sift through all of his logs. My immediate response was, "it was important enough for me to write a subpoena for it." He then proceeded to ask me information about the type of case I was investigating. We established earlier in this chapter that I don't trust until I vet a possible suspect, so I told him I could not disclose the type of case I was working on to him. The owner then responded by saying that if he was not informed about the type of case I was working on, he would just respond to my subpoena by saying he did not have any log files. (Can you see where this is going?) I then informed him that he had just admitted to me that he did in fact have log files, and that I am directing him to preserve them while I apply for a search warrant. Furthermore, I told him that if any files were deleted I would seek to have him arrested for tampering with evidence. Prior to hanging up the phone, I told him that the search warrant would include all computers, routers, switches, and so on where I believed evidence would be found. A short time later, as I was on the phone with the District Attorney, he called me back. At that point, we both agreed the conversation had spun out of control, and we worked together to minimize the information I needed.

After our initial headbutt, I discovered he was a one-man operation, and that he was unsure how to retrieve the logs. I wish he had told me that upfront since I would have worked with him to get the logs I needed.

Shutting Down and Seizing Systems

I remember getting a call to respond to a company whose server was being illegally accessed by remote. The owner of this company stated that numerous files were deleted, and that he believed the computer had a *remote access Trojan*.

I immediately invoked my forensics best practices and proceeded to shut down the server. At that point, I was literally tackled by the owner who stated that the server was a production server and could not be taken down. I needed an alternate plan. I didn't want to victimize the victim by shutting down his company. So I called the District Attorney and informed him of the facts. Based on my conversation with the DA, I was able to generate a list of items I'd need to prove the case, and proceeded to image only the things I required. If you're wondering why I didn't just mount the drive and image it with a network tool, it was because the server was 300 terabytes in size. In the end I was able to understand the company's needs and avoid causing additional harm to them. We will discuss the issue of network forensics further in the next chapter.

NOTE

A remote access Trojan is a program that allows hackers to gain illegal access.

Protecting Confidential and Privileged Information

In another case, I responded to a law office where an employee had been arrested for viewing child pornography. The log files clearly showed that the IP connections had originated from this employee's office. Once there, I asked for consent to take the computer. I could have applied for a search warrant but I expected that the law firm would cooperate. Well, wouldn't you know that the law firm began to take the position that I could not have the computer because it contained legally privileged and confidential information? I knew this was about to get ugly. Imagine me explaining to the law firm that I would be able to get a search warrant and seize all the computers in their company. After all, this was no E-Discovery case. Additionally, I explained that getting a search warrant and returning to their office in the middle of the day with a bunch of police officers in raid jackets just might be of interest to their NBC-TV neighbors. So we struck a deal. They agreed to give me the computer, and several floppy disks and CD-ROMs, if I agreed not to view the computer's contents until I received a signed search warrant. They also wanted to be present when I reviewed the CD-ROMs and floppy disks so I could quickly return these items to them if they did not contain child porn. So, to avoid becoming famous in the *United States v. Anthony Reyes* case, I obliged them and we worked it out. In this case, I understood the law firm's need to protect its confidential and privileged information and worked with them to find a solution.

Avoiding Media

Going back to my media comment, companies hate being mentioned for data breaches and cyber investigations on the five o'clock news. As a cyber investigator, you should attempt to avoid thrusting a company into the limelight for your two minutes of fame. I found that once I showed a company that I could investigate a cyber crime and make an arrest quietly, that company would feel comfortable contacting me on future cases. Also, it's bad business to have a company come to you with a case, provide you with assistance, and then hold a press conference on how the company screwed up. In this scenario, you victimize the company twice, and may harm their reputation with their clients. So, whenever possible, refrain from attracting media attention to a company that has already been a victim.

Understanding Corporate Practices

Understanding a company's corporate practices is an important step toward easing tensions between the public and private sectors. Often, law enforcement gets frustrated when a company fails to turn over documents requested via subpoena, or when a company's retention policy is at odds with an officer's needs.

What law enforcement needs to understand is that respecting an employee's privacy as it relates to providing personal information outside of the company, is a serious and important task of any company. While information may easily be circulated within a company, providing it to outside entities may require the investigator to consult with corporate consul. This may also require more time and possibly additional paperwork in order to secure the information. Don't get frustrated if corporate consul requests an additional subpoena and or search warrant.

Secondly, officers need to understand that maintaining log files can be a daunting task for many companies. So, retaining these files for long periods of time may not always be an option. You should attempt to communicate to the company what type of data you're looking for and work with them in minimizing your request. Trust me on this one: requests for large data sets are usually met with resistance, even with the existence of a subpoena. You'll get better cooperation from the company if you work with them, as opposed to threaten them with a search warrant.

Providing the Foundation

As a cyber crime officer, your job should be to lay the foundation of how the crime was committed, and how the computer aided in the commission of this crime. You should also attempt to explain the techniques, methodologies, and technologies, to prosecutors, judges, and juries in simple terms. This will help you removed the veil of mystery behind the technology and aid in helping build the case against the suspect.

The Role of the Prosecuting Attorney

Understanding your role as a prosecutor will better serve the overall legal process when it comes time for prosecution.

Providing Guidance

Your goal should always be that of a legal advisor and not of an investigator. Oftentimes, prosecutors become personally involved with a case and jeopardize the process, as well as their immunity. Additionally, you should act as a bridge between the information gap of technology and the judge or jury. It will be your job to remove the mask behind the technology presented in the case, and ease the fears of the technophobes.

Avoiding Loss of Immunity

Prosecutors are afforded special privileges when acting on behalf of the court. One of the most important privileges they possess is that of *immunity*. This immunity shields them from both criminal and civil liability when acting in their official capacity and performing related duties. However, when a prosecutor engages in conduct that is beyond the scope of their responsibilities, they may place themselves in harm's way. The reason I raise this issue is because I have seen many attorneys become emotionally involved in a case and dance close to the line of trouble. Although it is extremely rare and difficult to prove a prosecutor has lost their immunity, it is not impossible.

NOTE

Prosecutors are afforded *absolute immunity* from liability for their actions when their prosecutorial activities are directly associated with their judicial responsibilities during the criminal process. This entitles them to absolute immunity from any action for damages.

Prosecutors are afforded the privilege of *qualified immunity* from liability for damages due to their actions when performing official discretionary functions, as long as their conduct does not violate any clearly defined statutory or constitutional rights that a reasonable person would have known.

In *Richards v. NYC*, Samantha Richards was accused of killing her live-in boyfriend Gersham O'Connor. The police, along with the District Attorneys, conducted the investigation. The investigators interviewed Richard's two daughters, ages four and five, who implicated their mother as the killer. Based on the interviews, Ms. Richards was subsequently arrested. During Richards' trial, it was discovered that her daughters never witnessed the shooting and that their statements were based on the interview tactics of the police and prosecutors. Richards brought suit against the District Attorneys involved and alleged that they "*supervised, assisted,* and *gave advice* to the police [throughout] the course of their investigation; *acted and conspired* with them in that investigation; *decided whether there was probable cause to arrest the plaintiff*; and/or *knew or should have known* that the police *conducted the investigation in disregard*" of her civil and constitutional rights (Southern District of New York, 1998). The court found that the District Attorneys were not fully immune to civil penalties, citing *Barbera v. Smith* and *Burns v. Reed*. The court wrote the following statement in its opinion:

> Absolute immunity is not available . . . when a prosecutor undertakes conduct that is beyond the scope of his litigation-related duties. (*Barbera v. Smith*, 836 F.2d 96, 100 [2d Cir. 1987])

Thus, when a prosecutor supervises, conducts, or assists in the investigation of a crime, or gives advice as to the existence of probable cause to make a warrantless arrest—that is, when he performs functions normally associated with a police investigation—he loses his absolute protection from liability. (See *Burns v. Reed*, 500 U.S. 478, 493, 114 L. Ed. 2d 547, 111 S. Ct. 1934 [1991])

> We do not believe... that advising the police in the investigative phase of a criminal case is so intimately associated with the judicial phase of the criminal process... that it qualifies for absolute immunity. (Southern District of New York, 1998)

As you can see, performing tasks outside of your prescribed role may put you at risk of liability.

Providing the Foundation

As in the other roles described previously, your job, in addition to prosecuting the case, should be to explain the offense to judges and juries in order to aid them in understanding how computers and technology can be used to commit crimes. Your duty is to also provide guidance as it relates to prosecution, and not the total investigation.

Summary

The preceding examples provided are just some of the issues that can be encountered when investigating cyber crime. Again, the roles of each type of investigator should always remain defined, and lines should never be crossed. Also, each sector should come to understand the concerns of the other to avoid confusion and misunderstandings. We should work together to find solutions rather than isolate ourselves from other sectors because of a lack of understanding. Try joining a group that provides an exchange of ideas between all sectors. One such organization is The High Technology Crime Investigation Association (www.HTCIA.org), which is designed to encourage, promote, and aid in the voluntary exchange of data, information, experience, ideas, and knowledge about methods, processes, and techniques relating to investigations and security in advanced technologies. It was where I was able to get help with a great number of my cases when I was in law enforcement, and has helped me even to this day.

Solutions Fast Track

Understanding Your Role as a Cyber Crime Investigator

- ☑ It is possible to violate the law when conducting cyber crime investigations.

- ☑ Cyber crime investigators should be aware that their actions, on behalf of their company, may not absolve them of criminal or civil liability if their actions are illegal.

- ☑ Corporations should involve law enforcement in the beginning of a criminal investigation.

- ☑ Corporate consul should consult a prosecutor prior to taking actions in a criminal matter.

- ☑ Corporate investigators should always be cognizant of employee's rights when conducting investigations.

☑ As a corporate investigator, you may not be privy to much of the information when visited by a law enforcement officer.

☑ Be cognizant that your actions can be construed as acting as an agent of law enforcement.

The Role of Law Enforcement Officers

☑ Understand that companies may have privileged and confidential information on the computers you are seizing.

☑ It is a wise practice to avoid victimizing your victim further by parading your case before the media.

☑ It is important to understand the data retention policies and subpoena process of a company prior to requesting their assistance.

The Role of the Prosecuting Attorney

☑ One of the primary functions of a prosecutor is to provide guidance and direction as it relates to the law during an investigation.

☑ Prosecutors should avoid directing law enforcement when investigating a case since it may cause the loss of immunity.

☑ As a prosecutor, you explain to the judge and jury how technology was used to commit a crime.

Frequently Asked Questions

The following Frequently Asked Questions, answered by the authors of this book, are designed to both measure your understanding of the concepts presented in this chapter and to assist you with real-life implementation of these concepts. To have your questions about this chapter answered by the author, browse to **www.syngress.com/solutions** and click on the **"Ask the Author"** form.

Q: Is it possible to commit a crime when conducting a cyber crime investigation?

A: The answer to this question is a profound yes. Understanding the ramifications of your actions as they relate to the law is an important part of being a cyber crimes investigator. Remember that suspects, employees, and clients still maintain all the legal rights and protections afforded them by the U.S. Constitution. Reading e-mails, intercepting communications, and searching and copying computer data may land you in hot water if you do not have the proper permissions or authority to do so. When in doubt, confer with different legal, technical, and adminstrative sources.

Q: Can I monitor my employees e-mails and Internet activity ?

A: Yes, but do so with caution. I recommend you have a clearly defined policy that informs your employees they will be monitored.

Q: Will I be acting as an agent of law enforcement if I collect evidence of a crime prior to calling the police?

A: No. Again, in order to become an agent, two conditions must exsist. First, the person must have acted with the intent to help law enforcement. Second, the government must know about the person's activities and either acquiesced in, or encouraged, them. If you conduct this activity prior to contacting them, then you need not worry.

Q: How long will an ISP retain data?

A: This all depends on the ISP policy. Some ISPs retain data longer than others. The key is to contact several of the ISPs you deal with and ask them how long they retain data. You may also want to ask them about the necessary legal documents they require to retrieve such information.

Works Referenced

AMANET. "American Companies Increase Use of Electronic Monitoring: AMA Calls on Employers to Raise Level of Dialogue with Employees." AMANET.org. Retrieved December 19, 2006 from www.amanet.org/research/specials/elecmont.htm (2000).

Barbera v. Smith, 836 F.2d 96, 100 (2d Cir. 1987).

Burns v. Reed, 500 U.S. 478, 493, 114 L. Ed. 2d 547, 111 S. Ct. 1934 (1991).

Gahtan, Alan. "Monitoring Employee Communications." Gahtan.com. Retrieved November 16, 2006, from www.gahtan.com/alan/articles/monitor.htm (1997).

Muskier, Jean A. "E-Privacy Balancing Employer's Interests and Employee's Rights in the High Tech Workplace – A Review of Massachusetts Law." Srbc.com. Retrieved from http://srbc.com/publications_eprivacy.html on October 25, 1998.

Mullins, Robert. "Analysis: Corporate Leak Probes Walk a Fine Line." *IDG News Service*. Retrieved December 21, 2006, from www.macworld.com/news/2006/10/02/leakanalysis/index.php (2006).

Richards v. City of New York. U.S. Dist. LEXIS 13675, Southern District of New York, 1998.

Smith v. The Pillsbury Company, No. 95-5712 (E.D. Pa. 1996).

Spykerman, Mike. "Is E-mail Monitoring Legal?" *Redearthsoftware.com*. Retrieved December 14, 2006 from www.redearthsoftware.com/email-monitoring-article.htm.

United States v. Jarrett, 338 F.3d 339, 343–344 (4th Cir. 2003).

United States v. Steiger, 318 F.3d 1039, 1044 (11th Cir. 2003).

Secret Service, CERT. "Comprehensive Report Analyzing Insider Threats to Banking and Finance Sector." secretservice.gov. Retrieved on November 12, 2006 from www.secretservice.gov/press/pub1804.pdf (2002).

Chapter 5

Incident Response: Live Forensics and Investigations

Solutions in this chapter:

- Postmortem versus Live Forensics
- Today's Live Methods
- Case Study: Live versus Postmortem
- Computer Analysis for the Hacker Defender Program
- Network Analysis

☑ Summary
☑ Solutions Fast Track
☑ Frequently Asked Questions

Introduction

To pull or not to pull the plug, that is the question. Today, cyber crime investigators are faced with the grueling task of deciding whether shutting down a computer system is the most efficient and effective method to gather potential electronic evidence. Traditionally, computer forensics experts agreed that shutting the computer system down in order to preserve evidence and eliminate the potential changing of information is best practice prior to examination. I remember having the phrases "shut it down," and "don't change anything" beaten into my brain during the numerous trainings I've attended throughout the years. However, one of the fundamental misconceptions with this philosophy is that computer forensics is the same as physical forensics. I would argue that they are not the same, given that computer forensics technology changes faster than traditional forensics disciplines like ballistics, serology, and fingerprint analysis. The second misconception is that we always collect everything at a physical crime scene. In a physical forensics environment, we commonly photograph the physical crime scene and take "reasonable" precautions to ensure the evidence is not disturbed. The truth is, in many cases, we only collect samples from a physical crime scene.

Nevertheless, we have accepted this methodology as best practice, and have backed ourselves into a litigation corner. The evolution of technology has put us face to face with the harsh reality that it is sometimes more advantageous to perform "Live" analysis than a "Postmortem" one. The problem is that live analysis often changes evidence by writing to the hard drive. File time stamps, Registry keys, swap files, and memory are just some of the items that can be affected when conducting analysis on a live computer system. Often, once the live analyst is done, the resulting MD5 hash will not match the hash collected prior to the live collection.

Postmortmem versus Live Forensics

Why should we even consider conducting live investigations as a valid forensic methodology? The reason is we have to! In the pages that follow, I will discuss the need to move away from traditional methods of computer forensics and toward a live forensics model.

TIP

Postmortem and live forensics are both great evidence gathering techniques. However, in cases where you can only conduct a postmortem forensics, the need to look at other systems within the environment is strengthened. This expansion of your scope to include other systems on the network will give you a better understanding of how the target system acted within its native environment.

Evolution of the Enterprise

Technology has evolved in such a way that conducting live investigations is really the only option you have under certain circumstances. In the days of old, computer networks were simple. In today's world, the evolution of the enterprise network work makes it difficult for system administrators, IT security personal, and the like to be at more than one location. Managing IT resources at a single site can be a daunting task. Now think of the larger corporate network schema. Many companies have multiple computers at a single location. Additionally, those corporations may also have several locations in a city, country, or continent. What would happen to our resources if we had to respond to every site and pull the computer off the network to conduct a forensic analysis for every suspected compliance issue, security breach, or compromised host? This would be even worse if after all the effort, time, and resources, we conclude that none of the aforementioned even occurred. Sound familiar? It should, because it happens every day in the cyber world. Triage is a common practice when diagnosing problems within a network. It is our first reaction, and we don't necessarily assume we are under attack, or that our systems have been compromised. In a live forensic environment, IT security personnel could log on remotely, view running processes, dump physical memory, and make an educated guess as to whether or not the computer should be imaged remotely, or be physically removed from the network for further analysis. In this scenario, the investigator, using live forensics techniques, doesn't have to physically respond to the location to address the issue until they are satisfied with their initial inquiry. This methodology will help conserve resources.

Evolution of Storage

Now back to pulling the pull. Once upon a time there was a server. This server was about 630 terabytes (TB) in size. It was responsible for handling the day-to-day operations of Company X, which traded stocks for its clients 24 hours a day. This server was believed to be compromised because of some unusual traffic detected within the log files of the firewall. This scenario presents us with the following issues. Problem 1: How are we going to fit this 630TB image into our 250GB USB2 external drive? Problem 2: How long would it take to image a drive that size? Problem 3: The machine cannot be shut down because the company would suffer a financial loss. In addition to all these issues, we must remember to make a bit-stream image, which was discussed earlier in Chapter 1. Let's discuss the preceding problems one at a time.

Problem 1: It's not possible. You will need a bigger drive.

Problem 2: The data resides on a substantially large server (630TB). Imaging the entire server is not practical, even though best practices dictate we should. Here is one of the reasons why: 630TB is equal to 6,926,923,254,988,880 bytes. 630 x 1,099,511,627,776 (1 Terabyte) = 6,926,923,254,988,880 bytes. See Table 5.1 to determine the byte sizes used in this scenario.

Table 5.1 Byte Conversion Chart

Drive Size	Numerical Representation	2 to the Following Power
1 kilobyte	1,024	10
1 megabyte	1,048,576	20
1 gigabyte	1,073,741,824	30
1 terabyte	1,099,511,627,776	40
1 petabyte	1,125,899,906,842,624	50
1 exabyte	1,152,921,504,606,840,000	60

Let's assume you use the ICS Image MASSter Solo-3 IT, which states it can duplicate hard drives at a rate of 3 GB a minute.

- Divide 6926923254988880 / 3221225472 (3 gigabytes) = 2150400 total minutes

- Divide 2150400 minutes /60 minutes (1 hour) = 35840 total hours

- Divide 35840 total hours / 24 hours (1 day) = 1493 total days

- Divide 1493 days / 365 day (1 year) = over 4 years to image the entire drive.

As you can see from the preceding bullets, imaging the entire one-to-one drive is not practical. Even if you imaged the data, by utilizing additional resources, the analysis of such a large volume could prove just as prohibitive. The difference in conducting an analysis on such a large volume, as compared to specific data objects and/or smaller storage systems, (using a detective's analogy) would be equivalent to interviewing every person who lives on a block where a homicide has occurred (reasonable), versus interviewing everyone who lives in the city of the homicide victim (not reasonable).

Notes from the Underground...

Using Compression

If you're thinking that the use of compression could solve the preceding problems, you would be mistaken. Compression increases the time it takes to image the server's hard drive because the compression algorithm needs to examine and remove the redundant items prior to compressing them. Additionally, it would still be impossible to compress the larger hard drive into the smaller USB external drive.

Problem 3: Shutting down the server is also not an option since the most obvious side effect would be the economic harm Company X would experience as a result. Many systems in existence today are mission critical, such as those supporting health care, transportation, and so on, and they couldn't be shut down without causing detrimental effects.

Encrypted File Systems

The use of encryption has increased during the last few years. Its increased use presents a unique problem to investigators when conducting postmortem analysis. When encryption is applied to a data object, the contents of that object are illegible. Encryption, by default, is designed to obfuscate, and sometimes compress, the contents of the data object it encrypts. Once encrypted, the object's contents are hidden and are pretty much impossible to interpret. Encryption is applied to these data objects in one of three ways. The first implementation is file level encryption, in which individual files are encrypted. Figure 5.1 shows the contents of an encrypted file.

Figure 5.1 File Contents When the File Is Encrypted Using AccessData's FTK Imager

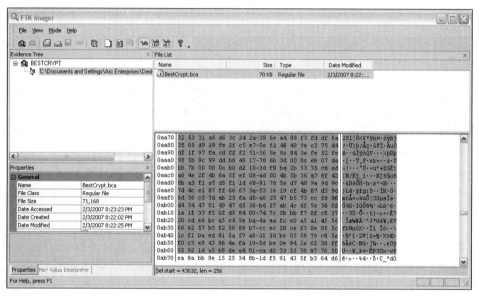

In order for an examiner to perform a postmortem analysis, he must first decrypt the file. Figure 5.2 shows a decrypted file. This could prove extremely difficult if the investigator does not have access to the encrypted file's password. No password may result in having to use a password cracking program. This decrypting process may prove useless if the password is too large, or the file is encrypted with a strong encryption algorithm and implementation.

Figure 5.2 File Contents When the File Is Not Encrypted Using AccessData's FTK Imager

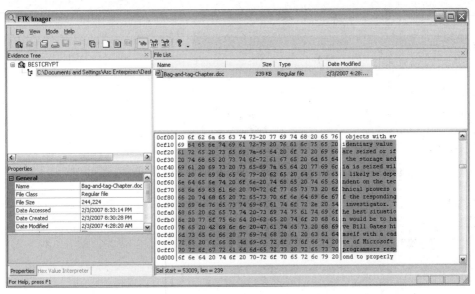

The second method used when applying encryption is volume level encryption. In this case, a volume within the hard disk is encrypted. Figure 5.3 shows an encrypted volume.

Figure 5.3 A BestCrypt Encrypted Volume

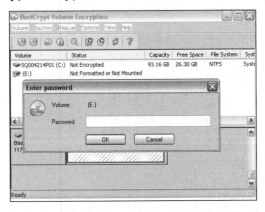

The third method used when encrypting a data object is whole disk encryption. This is when the entire hard drive is in encrypted. Figure 5.4 offers a forensic image of a fully encrypted disk. As you can see, its contents are illegible, and are of little value to a forensic examiner.

Figure 5.4 A Forensic Image of an Encrypted Hard Drive Using AccessData's FTK Imager

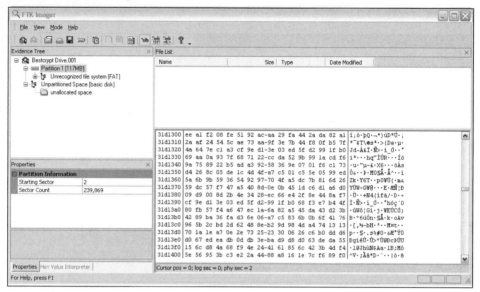

When conducting postmortem forensic analysis against the first two methods, investigators often hope to find artifacts of an encrypted file in its decrypted state that may be left in allocated or unallocated space. These artifacts are sometimes created once the document has been opened, or when the plug has been pulled while the file is still displayed on the screen. While this is a valid premise, recovery of these artifacts may not always be successful. Moreover, performing a proper shutdown may further decrease your chances of finding such evidence. In Figure 5.5, you will notice that the program BestCrypt offers to open the file in a temporary folder, and then securely delete the file when the program is closed.

When you use live forensics, the chances are significantly greater to view the contents of the encrypted file. If the document is open, it will most likely be loaded into physical memory. In a live forensic environment, the investigator could image the physical memory of the computer system and glean useful information about what files and programs the suspect may be currently using. So, before pulling the plug, it may be worth our while to examine the contents of the physical memory. Figure 5.6 shows one example of how we could image physical memory by using a network forensics tool.

Figure 5.5 A File-Cleaning Operation Offered by BestCrypt

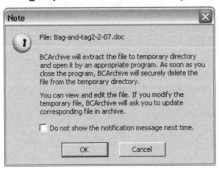

Figure 5.6 The Technologies Pathways' ProDiscover IR Imaging Screen

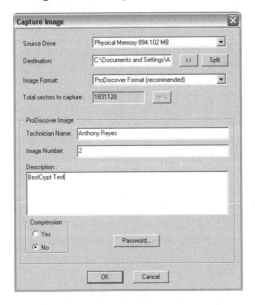

Once the image has been created, we can examine its contents. In Figure 5.7, you will notice the contents of the encrypted file are displayed in a readable format in the lower right-hand pane. Recovery of this information is because the file has been unencrypted by the user who is currently working with the document. Additionally, in Figure 5.8 you can see the BestCrypt program is running in physical memory. This information is also displayed in the lower right-hand pane.

Figure 5.7 An Unencrypted Document in Memory Using Technologies Pathways' ProDiscover IR

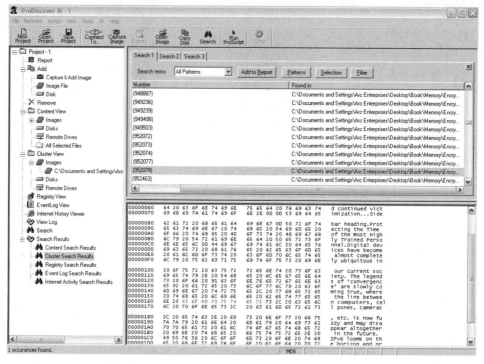

Figure 5.8 A View of Physical Memory Contents Using Technologies Pathways' ProDiscover IR. Note that the BestCrypt Process Is Running.

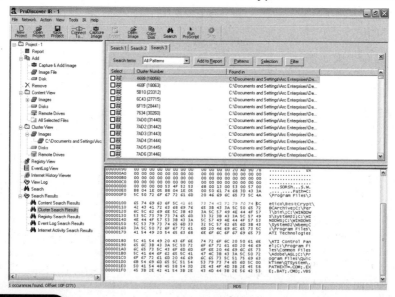

In the case of whole disk encryption, a forensic examiner using live forensics techniques would be able to view the content of the drive when it is mounted by the suspect. Simply put, because the drive is presently being used, it is unencrypted. Figure 5.9 demonstrates our ability to view the mounted drive's contents in its unencrypted state.

Figure 5.9 An Encrypted Hard Drive's Contents When Mounted Live with a Forensics Tool Like Technologies Pathways' ProDiscover

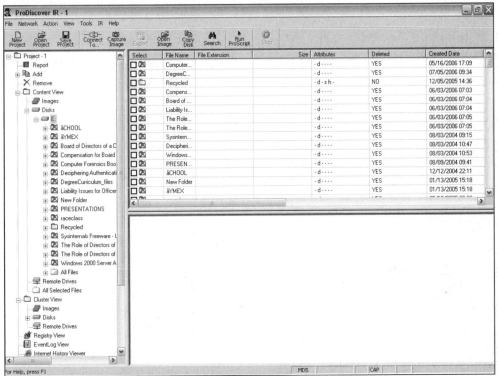

As you can see from the preceding examples, encryption presents a variety of problems for the traditional forensics examiner. With live investigative techniques, however, we can overcome these problems and obstacles.

Today's Live Methods

Several software companies presently manufacture network forensic and investigative software. Guidance Software, Technologies Pathways, Wetstone Technologies, ASR Data, E-fense, and E Trust by CA are just some of the companies that produce this forensic and incident response software. These manufacturers use a variety of methods to conduct live investigations. The first method employed is the Pre-Deployed Agent model, where special software is pre-installed on a computer system prior to an incident. It is usually hidden from the end user and is invoked once it is connected to remotely. The second method currently in use is the Direct Connect model. In this model, the target computer is directly connected to by a remote machine and the software is pushed into memory. The connection remains active until the remote machine is disconnected. A third method is the On Demand Connection model, where the computer connects to the target machine and pushes the software into memory for a specific task. Once the task issued by the remote machine is completed, the connection is immediately torn down. Finally, some software developers use a boot disk or an investigative CD-ROM. During a live analysis, a disk is loaded to the live machine and a virtual session is initiated with a set of examination tools. Figure 5.10 shows a boot disk that allows you to conduct live forensics, as well as investigations.

Figure 5.10 The E-fense's HELIX Incident Response, Electronic Discovery, and Computer Forensics Boot Disk

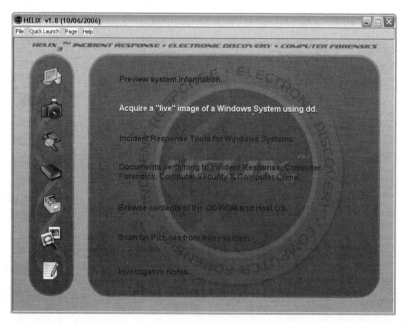

Case Study: Live versus Postmortem

Live investigations allow investigators to capture volatile information that would not normally be present in a postmortem investigation. This information can consist of running processes, event logs, network information, registered drivers, and registered services. Why is this important to us, you ask? Let's take a look at the case of running services and how this could be extremely important us.

Running services tell us the types of services that may be running on a computer. These services run at a much higher priority than processes, and many users are unaware that these services actually exist. Given their high priority and lack of attention by the typical end user, they are a common target for hackers. By conducting a live investigation, we are able to see the state of these services, which could prove crucial to our investigation. For example, a hacker could turn off the service for McShield, which is a McAfee Antivirus service, and then later come back and infest the machine with malicious software.

You might argue in the case of registered drivers that you could get a list of the drivers in a postmortem investigation. This is true; however, if you are at a crime scene and you conduct a live investigation, you might be able to see a driver for a digital camera. So you know to look for that camera in your surrounding area. But if you left the location, and then returned later to find that camera driver, you could only hope that the camera is still there when you make it back. As shown in the previous example, seeing registered drivers gives investigators knowledge of the peripherals of a suspect machine. Figure 5.11 illustrates some of the volatile information you can obtain about a systems state.

Viewing running processes with the associated open network ports is one of the most important features of analyzing the system state. To peek into a system and correctly assess what processes are running and what ports they may be using is critical when trying to perform an investigative triage. Figure 5.12 offers a detailed look at the running processes of a target machine under investigation.

Figure 5.11 An Example of Live System Information You Can Obtain Using Wetstone's LiveWire

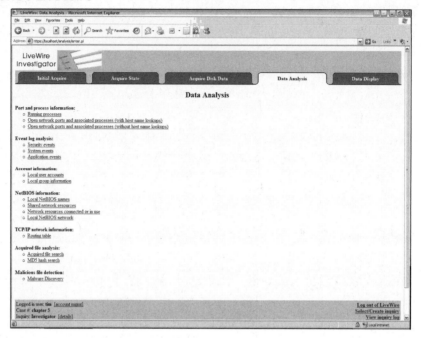

Figure 5.12 A View of Running Processes Using Wetstone's LiveWire

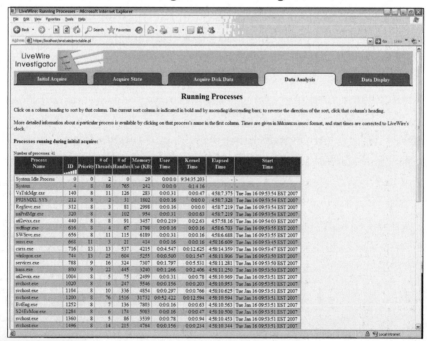

Notice how we can see not only the process's name in Figure 5.12 but also the priority, the number of threads, number of handles, memory usage, and uptime. Again, you might ask why all of this is important. Well, if you are trying to assess what someone is currently doing, or even what they have done in the past, this information is critical. In addition, in the world of memory resident executables, analyzing the current process list is vital.

In a postmortem investigation, physical memory (RAM) is potentially the most important piece of evidence that is lost. However, this crucial piece of evidence is easily captured using live forensic and investigative tools, allowing the entire contents of RAM to be captured locally and even remotely. In Figure 5.13, we can see the contents of a memory dump and can conduct a search for the word keylogger in memory.

Figure 5.13 A Keyword Search for the Term Keylogger in a Memory Dump Using Wetstone's LiveWire

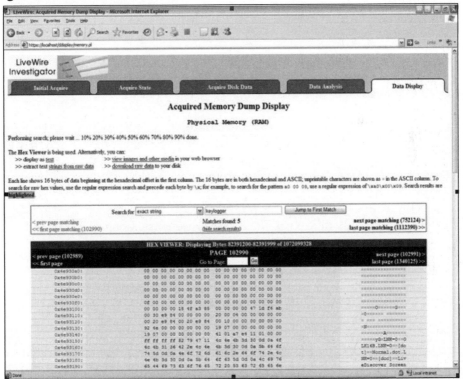

The raw data contents of the memory provide a vast amount of information that could have been lost if the machine was powered down for a post-mortem investigation. Memory contains evidence ranging from user accounts, passwords, unsaved document content, and malicious software.

Terminology Alert...

Malicious Software

Malicious software is a term describing a broad range of tools. However, memory-resident malicious software generally is seen with rootkits, Trojan horses, worms, and keyloggers. The following example contains a detailed explanation on how some memory-resident malicious software work.

Computer Analysis for the Hacker Defender Program

Hacker Defender is a popular rootkit that is capable of hiding processes, files, and even open ports. By default, when Hacker Defender is executed, it hides every file containing the prefix "hxdef." As a result, the file "hxdef100.ini," which is part of Hacker Defender, is hidden as soon as Hacker Defender executes. This file is then hidden from all users and even Windows Explorer itself. However, the file still exists in physical memory. Using live investigation techniques, you can take a memory snapshot and identify the file "hxdef100.ini" stored in RAM (see Figure 5.14). This same method can be used to reveal any file or process that Hacker Defender hides (see Figure 5.15). During a postmortem investigation, any files or processes hidden by Hacker Defender may not be accessible to the investigator. Figures 5.14 and 5.15 show evidence of the Hacker Defender program in the physical memory of a computer.

Figure 5.14 Hacker Defender in Psychical Memory Using Wetstone's LiveWire

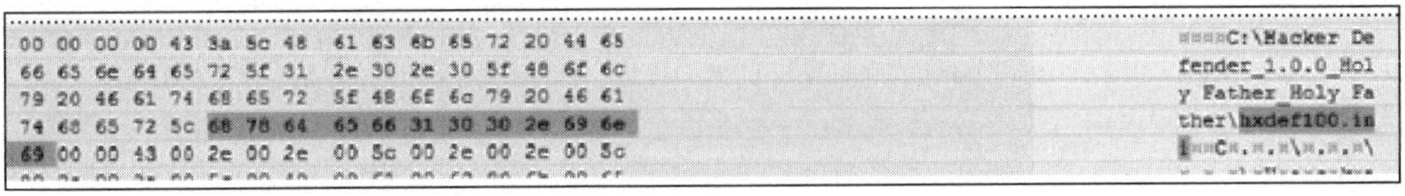

Figure 5.15 Another View of Hacker Defender in Psychical Memory Using Wetstone's LiveWire

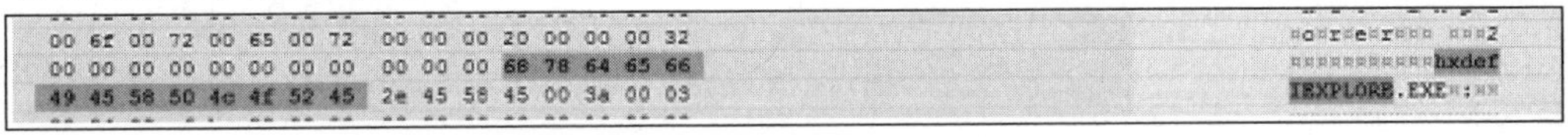

As stated earlier, investigating a computer's system state is an important part of any investigation. It could help glean valuable information in a case and reduce the risk of missing data that could prove critical to your investigation.

Network Analysis

Often overlooked in live investigations is the environment in which the target computer resides. Data obtained from firewall laws, routers, intrusion detection systems, and so on are equally important to an examiner in obtaining the big picture. In the Hacker Defender case presented earlier, a defense attorney may argue that his client's machine was compromised and could not have committed the crime. A review of the firewall logs may show that the Hacker Defender activity from this computer was blocked, making this argument about the rootkit a moot point. As a live investigator, you should try to gain as much information about the network activity as possible. You might want to install a packet sniffer—with the appropriate permission, of course—and conduct a packet analysis of the traffic. Using this technique, you could determine if someone is connected to the box before conducting an analysis on the target machine. So remember, you may find additional evidence beyond the computer you are examining. Look for it.

Summary

As we move forward, computer forensics as we now know it will change dramatically. The release of Microsoft's Vista will enable users to fully encrypt their hard drives. The use of virtual machines and virtual server farms are becoming more commonplace. Internet-based application servers will be harder for forensic examiners to physically collect. Additionally, Internet-based applications may generate diskless workstations, leaving the only evidence in physical memory. Finally, software vendors are starting to deploy a larger amount of software that securely deletes data because of identity-theft concerns. Because of these changes, and as I have pointed out in the examples in this chapter, I surmise that traditional forensics will become more impractical, and live investigations will become a necessity rather than a luxury. Traditional methodologies are becoming somewhat obsolete. The need to adopt a new way of conducting these types of investigations is essential. While we have shied away from touching the computer in order to prevent any changes, it is now obvious that there are times when an examiner must interact with a live computer in order to retrieve vital data. Under the circumstances described earlier, you should be able to provide a reasonable explanation to any judge or jury as to why live forensics was used in place of traditional methods. However, should none of these circumstances exist, it may be best just to pull the plug.

Special Thanks

I would like to give thanks to my colleagues Christopher L. T. Brown and Chet Hosmer for their help with this chapter. Their wisdom and insight into incident response and network forensic issues were invaluable.

References

Brown, Christopher L.T. *Computer Evidence Collection & Preservation*. Massachusetts: Charles River Media, Inc., 2006.

Chirillo, John. *Hack Attacks Revealed*. New York, John Wiley & Sons, Inc., 2001.

Mandia, Kevin et al. *Incident Response: Investigating Computer Crime.* California: Osborne/McGraw-Hill, 2001.

McClure, Stuart *et al. Hacking Exposed: Network Security Secrets & Solutions.* California: Osborne/McGraw-Hill, 2001.

Szor, Peter. *The Art of Computer Virus Research and Defense.* New Jersey: Addison-Wesley, 2005.

Solutions Fast Track

Postmortem versus Live Forensics

- ☑ In a live investigation, a system administrator can conduct an analysis remotely.
- ☑ Imaging large volumes can be a daunting task.
- ☑ Live forensics can be used to obtain data when encryption is in use.
- ☑ Capturing the contents of memory may provide you with the "missing link."

Today's Live Methods

- ☑ A Pre-Deployed Agent is software that is installed onto the computer prior to an incident.
- ☑ A boot disk can be used to contact live investigations.

Case Study: Live versus Postmortem

- ☑ Live investigations allow investigators to capture volatile information that would not normally be present in a postmortem investigation. This information can consist of running processes, event logs, network information, registered drivers, and registered services.
- ☑ Running services tell us the types of services that may be running on a computer. These services run at a much higher priority than

processes, and many users are unaware that these services actually exist.

☑ Viewing running processes with the associated open network ports is one of the most important features of analyzing the system state. To peek into a system and correctly assess what processes are running and what ports they may be using is critical when trying to perform an investigative triage.

Computer Analysis for the Hacker Defender Program

☑ Hacker Defender hides files from the user.

☑ Rootkit artifacts can sometimes be found in physical memory.

Network Analysis

☑ You should look for evidence beyond the target computer.

☑ Understanding the network where the system resides can help you when conducting a live investigation.

Frequently Asked Questions

The following Frequently Asked Questions, answered by the authors of this book, are designed to both measure your understanding of the concepts presented in this chapter and to assist you with real-life implementation of these concepts. To have your questions about this chapter answered by the author, browse to **www.syngress.com/solutions** and click on the **"Ask the Author"** form.

Q: Can I view encrypted data in a live environment without having the password?

A: The answer is yes, provided that the drive or file is unencrypted on the suspect's machine.

Q: Can I view hidden processes like rootkits on a live computer?

A: Using special software, you can view hidden processes and files on a live computer.

Q: If I cannot image the entire drive, can I just copy the files I need?

A: Yes, you can copy the files you need using live forensic software to ensure you have the entire copy. Also, take notes when doing this since you may have to testify later about why you chose this method and what, if anything, you changed.

Chapter 6

Legal Issues of Intercepting WiFi Transmissions

Solutions in this chapter:

- WiFi Technology
- Understanding WiFi RF
- Scanning RF
- Eavesdropping on WiFi
- Fourth Amendment Expectation of Privacy in WLANs

☑ Summary

☑ Solutions Fast Track

☑ Frequently Asked Questions

Introduction

WiFi—an acronym for wireless fidelity (wireless)—encompasses a number of standards that enable computers and other devices to connect wirelessly to local area networks. The proliferation of WiFi devices is a success story in standards development and represents a market that generates over $750 million per quarter in sales worldwide (Infonetics Research). Most computer systems, particularly laptops, are shipped with WiFi-compliant hardware and software as a standard feature. For example, even the least expensive laptop available at Wal-Mart is WiFi equipped. Further, the equipment necessary to set up your own WAN—with existing computers and existing Internet service—can be obtained for less than $100.

A number of organizations have chosen to make WiFi access freely available to any who would wish to connect. Dartmouth College offers free WiFi over its entire campus; Panera Bread and many CompUSA stores throughout the nation offer free WiFi access; Bradley International Airport in Connecticut and Ft. Lauderdale Airport in Florida provides free WiFi access. WiFi is a technology that is far from being in use only by the technologically advanced early adopters, and it is now clearly mainstream in its adoption and use.

TIP

The list of locations that provide free WiFi is several hundred entries long. The full list is available at: www.wififreespot.com/.

In this chapter, we will attempt to highlight the technology behind the WiFi explosion and how various federal laws may or may not apply to eavesdropping on WiFi communications.

WiFi Technology

WiFi fits in a family of standards developed under the IEEE (I-triple-E) or The Institute of Electrical and Electronics Engineers. The IEEE is a standards body that developed the 802 family of standards. These standards describe a framework—physical media and the working characteristics—that would enable two or more devices to communicate within a network. Most notable of these standards is the 802.3 standard, the specification for Ethernet. The Ethernet standard describes a method of physical communication in a local area network (LAN). A wide majority of computer networks now employ Ethernet as their communication standard; almost every computer sold includes an Ethernet jack for connecting to an Ethernet network. The success of the 802.3 standard is quite likely responsible for the massive proliferation of computing networks in businesses, schools, and government facilities.

A similar explosion in growth and success is occurring with the 802.11 standard from IEEE. The 802.11 standard is a family of specifications for wireless local area networks (WLANs). Similar to the 802.3 standard, it specifies the method of physical communication between devices on the network—but where the 802.3 standard addresses communication over a physical link through cabling, the 802.11 standard addresses communication between devices over infrared and radio frequency (RF) transmissions. Although the use of infrared has been beneficial in some instances—short range wireless printing for example—its use has been dwarfed by the use of radio frequency transmissions.

In order to connect to a WLAN, each device on a WiFi network must possess a wireless card, or an 802.11 complaint radio transceiver. Some computers may have a built-in wireless card, whereas others may need to attach one through a PCMCIA or a USB interface. Within this wireless card is a transceiver tuned to a particular frequency, a frequency dictated by the 802.11 standard. Another device called an access point serves as the bridge between the devices on the wireless network and the wired local area network. The network owner configures the access point, and options for authentication and security are available—most security features are disabled by default. The access point and the wireless card in a computer (or other device) communicate with one another to transfer both data and network management information over the chosen radio frequency.

NOTE

WiFi is addressed by the IEEE as being only attributable to the 802.11b standard—however, in practice, and in this chapter, 802.11a, 802.11b, and 802.11g standards, as well as associated devices, are all considered WiFi. Information on the IEEE 802 standard can be found on the IEEE Web site at www.ieee.org/about/802std.

Authentication and Privacy in the 802.11 Standard

It is important to note that within the 802.11 standard, both authentication (who is allowed to connect to the network) and privacy (who is allowed to view information off the network) are both addressed. However, users of WiFi devices rarely take the necessary steps to properly configure their WiFi network. Wireless networks are different than a physical-wired network. To join a physical network, one must have physical access to the network in order to connect to it. Therefore, physical security plays a significant role in authenticating users in physical network. Wireless networks, on the other hand, do not stay neatly contained within the walls of a building—who's allowed on a WLAN is handled through *authentication*.

Authentication is defined in the 802 standard as "The service used to establish the identity of one station as a member of the set of stations authorized to associate with another station." (ANSI/IEEE Std 802.11, 1999 Edition (R2003)) Therefore, there must be a way to limit access to any particular WLAN—and indeed there is. One manner is to limit access through MAC address authentication. In this process, the access point holds a list of authorized MAC addresses. Network interface cards with MAC addresses on the authorized list will be allowed to connect to the WLAN. If you're not on the list, the access point won't let you in.

NOTE

Media access control (MAC) addresses are *unique* numbers associated with each network interface card, including wireless network interface cards—unique is a relative term here as a number of software utilities exist to change the MAC address of a network interface card.

Encryption is another method used to control authentication. WLANs can be set up to use a number of encryption schemes, WEP and WPA being the two most common. Encryption controls authentication by limiting the decryption of WLAN signals. Authorized users must possess the appropriate secret *key* to decrypt the signal—and in fact must have the proper credentials even to connect to the access point at all.

One would assume that equipment by default would enable either MAC access control or one of the encryption schemes to help the user manage authentication. However, this is not the case. Most access points' default configuration falls under what the 802.11 standard calls Open System Authentication. In this scheme any device that requests authentication can receive authentication and be added to the WLAN. Even though more secure manners exist for authentication—MAC filtering and encryption—open system authentication is described as default setting for 802.11 devices in the 802.11 standard.

Privacy

In a wired LAN, privacy is controlled by the routing of information. Routers and switches on a LAN control the flow of information so that devices on a LAN get only data sent through their cable that is specifically addressed to them or is broadcast data addressed to all devices. Therefore eavesdropping on a wired network can be very difficult, usually requiring some level of physical access to the network and/or direct access to the device of interest. For example, if someone were to listen to data traffic on the cable anywhere between computer X and the network switch, the eavesdropper would be able to view only traffic specifically sent to computer X.

Within a WLAN, data is sent to all devices attached to the WLAN over RF transmissions—data is not limited to traveling in specific cables to a particular computer. Since the RF can't be contained, a much higher level of access to data intended for any of the machines in a WLAN can be achieved without physical access to the network. Additionally, the radio waves from the access points will often exceed the limits of the room or building where they are installed and intended for use. The 802.11 standard directly addresses this issue with rather strong language for a technology standard:

> Any IEEE 802.11-compliant [station] may hear all like-[physical] IEEE 802.11 traffic that is within range. Thus the connection of a single wireless link (without privacy) to an existing wired LAN may seriously degrade the security level of the wired LAN....To bring the functionality of the wireless LAN up to the level implicit in wired LAN design, IEEE 802.11 provides the ability to encrypt the contents of messages. This functionality is provided by the privacy service.... IEEE 802.11 specifies an optional privacy algorithm, WEP that is designed to satisfy the goal of wired LAN "equivalent" privacy. The algorithm is not designed for ultimate security but rather to be "at least as secure as a wire...." If the privacy service is not invoked, all messages shall be sent unencrypted.

As noted earlier in the authentication discussion, a method to keep all information private is built into the standard. Most access points are equipped with a number of encryption schemes that would allow the user to encrypt the data between the access point and the wireless card in their computer. The most common encryption schemes are WEP and WPA. However, as is the case with the open system authentication, the default privacy setting is open with all information being sent in clear text. Important to note is that the standard states that any 802.11 compliant station/device may hear all 802.11 traffic within range.

Notes from the Underground...

WEP

WEP is an acronym for Wired Equivalency Protocol. The inside joke is that the E in WEP doesn't stand for encryption; although WEP uses an encryption algorithm to encrypt the data, the particular algorithm

Continued

doesn't mesh well with how WiFi networks are set up and used. For example, all users on a WEP'd WiFi network share the same network key and the passage of traffic is readily observable. Without a detailed cryptography discussion, the moral of the story is that the WEP key can be obtained by listening to network traffic. Depending on the number of users and amount of network traffic, the key may be able to be determined in as little as a few minutes. WEP isn't dead; it still has its uses. First, when WEP is enabled, unauthorized users cannot accidentally connect to your access point; so this at least keeps the neighbor from hogging your pipe to download music. Second, it sends a message to (ethical) wardrivers and hotspotters that you would prefer them not to use your access point. Lastly, it still takes a dedicated effort—however easy the effort may be with the tools available to crack WEP—to listen to your network traffic to obtain the network key. Whoever does crack your WEP has a dedicated intention to do so.

WPA (and WPA2) is an acronym for WiFi Protected Access. WPA uses the same algorithm as WEP, but the implementation of the particular algorithm has been improved to drastically limit, and all but eliminate, the possibility of an attacker being able to determine the key through passive monitoring. Users of WPA can be much more secure about the confidentiality of their data.

Understanding WiFi RF

The FCC regulates the ownership of the RF spectrum. If the FCC issues a license to a particular person or organization, the FCC must closely regulate the output wattage of the licensee and the licensee's neighbors to ensure that there is no interference on either licensee's area of coverage. To illustrate this point, we can examine the cellular industry. Each cellular carrier obtained the rights to particular frequencies in particular geographic areas allocated for use by cell phone communications. No other carrier can use a licensed frequency within the geographic area of the licensee—particularly if the licensee's transmissions are interfered with.

NOTE

The 802.11 family of standards is broken down into a number of more specific standards. The most familiar standard is the 802.11b standard, which operates in the 2.40GHz to 2.4835GHz band—colloquially known as 2.4gig. 802.11g also works within this frequency band, but uses a different protocol to achieve a greater throughput of information; 54 Mbits per second compared with 802.11b's 11 Mbits per second. A third commonly available 802.11 standard is 802.11a, which operates in the 5.725GHz to 5.850GHz (5GHz) frequency band and provides for a 54 Mbits per second throughput.

What makes the 802.11 so available and so ubiquitous is its use of an unlicensed portion of the radio frequency spectrum set aside for industrial, scientific, and medical (ISM) use. Users of the unlicensed ISM band do not need to purchase rights or ownership of a particular frequency: "Persons operating ISM equipment shall not be deemed to have any vested or recognizable right to the continued use of any given frequency, by virtue of any prior equipment authorization and/or compliance with the applicable rules." (47CFR18.111(a)) Instead, the unlicensed bands are open to all as long as certain conditions are met. These conditions include limiting the output wattage, and all devices using this band must not cause interference with other devices on the band. It is crucial to note that WiFi devices are not the only devices using the ISM band. Cordless phones, remote car starters, baby monitors all use this small section of unlicensed spectrum. Most importantly, there is no license holder that can prohibit others from trespassing on their spectrum holdings. In summary, it is generally accepted that the ISM bands are open to the general public.

Scanning RF

The airwaves are full of signals in a variety of frequencies; television broadcasts, emergency services radio dispatches, FM radios, pagers, and cellular telephones are just a few of these signals. We are all technically always receiving these signals whenever the energy hits our bodies, but in order to make sense of the signals, we need special equipment to decode or interpret the signal. To make sense of a broadcast television signal, for example, we need a television. Generally speaking, a device designed to be tunable to a wide variety of frequencies for the intent of listening in on any communications is called a scanner. There are scanners that focus on voice communications—a fire/police scanner for example would enable someone to listen in on the communications of their local emergency services. There are scanners that focus on video feeds—for example there is a specialized scanner that attempts to listen in on security cameras that send their images to the main security panel via a radio link.

Some of these types of communication use more complicated protocols, or specific codified languages, that enable two or more electronic devices to communicate with one another. Digital protocols are demonstrative of this in that the analog signal (a sine wave) is modulated to form approximately-square peaks and valleys that represent 1's and 0's of a digital message. One who eavesdrops on a digital message may be able to pick up sounds on the given frequency, but the human ear would not be able to make sense of the garbled series of tones. Many police transmissions are now digitally encoded, and often encrypted, as a mitigating measure against scanning and eavesdropping.

Prior to 1992, it was legal to purchase scanning equipment capable of listening in on cellular phone conversations. In 1992, Public Law 102–556, the Telephone Disclosure and Dispute Resolution Act, was passed, amending the Communications Act of 1934. The act, which is codified at 47 U.S.C. § 302a(d), prohibits the authorization, manufacture, and import of scanning equipment capable of:

(A) Receiving transmissions in the frequencies allocated to the domestic cellular radio telecommunications service,

(B) Readily being altered by the user to receive transmissions in such frequencies, or

(C) Being equipped with decoders that convert digital cellular transmissions to analog voice audio.

Given that Congress chose to regulate cellular monitoring equipment there now appears to be a reasonable expectation of privacy by users of cellular phones that their conversations will not be readily susceptible to monitoring by the general public. Further, the cellular carriers themselves enhanced cell phone users' expectation of privacy by phasing-in protocols that cause cellular phones to hop around a group of frequencies, thus making scanning of any one particular cellular phone or phone call very difficult. Therefore, any electronic monitoring of cellular telephone conversations without appropriate legal authorization would constitute an unconstitutional search in violation of the Fourth amendment (see Fourth amendment discussion later).

> **NOTE**
>
> Although 802.11x uses two protocols, Frequency Hopping Spread Spectrum (FHSS) and Direct Sequence Spread Spectrum (DSSS) that both hop around among different frequencies, no special equipment is needed to track the data transfer. The hardware and software in the wireless card and packet capture software can continually collect data emitting from a particular access point.

However, as was discussed in the Authentication and Privacy sections of this document, 802.11x does not *by default* employ any specific protocols designed to secure communications between parties. Where the Telephone Disclosure and Dispute Resolution Act restricted the scanning of cellular communications through criminalizing the sale or purchase of equipment that could intercept cellular communications, the equipment needed to scan or eavesdrop on WiFi transmission is not illegal to own—in fact it is the same equipment needed to connect to any wireless network, which is clearly not illegal to own. Further, the ISM band on which 802.11x communicates is not protected by a specific law highlighting its frequency; but there is a case to be made that some existing laws do provide eavesdropping prohibitions.

Eavesdropping on WiFi

The knowledge and skill required to eavesdrop on WiFi transmissions is not prohibitive, and the technology, both hardware and software, is readily available. A number of software products are available that both find and listen in on WiFi transmissions. For the most part, these software packages are completely legitimate network analyzers used by network administrators to debug networks and to find access points that have been installed illegitimately on the network.

Every communication over the WAN that is not encrypted can be grabbed from the airwaves and viewed. MAC authentication applies only to devices that wish to connect to the network—limiting who connects to a network does keep the overall network safer, particularly the information on other devices on the network, but does nothing to prevent people from intercepting unencrypted transmissions. Transmissions must have some level of encryption as a guard against any 802.11-equipped device from viewing the contents of the transmission.

Legal Framework

To best understand the legality of WiFi eavesdropping, we must look at how existing laws relate to WiFi technology. As we shall see, federal statutes relating to the interception of various types of electronic communications do not appear to govern the interception of WiFi transmissions.

The Electronic Communications Privacy Act (ECPA)

Although WiFi transmissions fall within the meaning of electronic communications as defined in the ECPA, unless the signals transmitted by WiFi devices are encrypted, they are accessible to the general public. Therefore, ECPA does not govern the interception of nonencrypted WiFi signals that are not sent by a common carrier.

WiFi transmissions would fall within the meaning of "electronic communications" under the ECPA. The ECPA prohibits the interception of any electronic communications, regardless of the physical media of transport (U.S.C. 18 § 2510). The ECPA defines electronic communication as "…any transfer of signs, signals, writing, images, sounds, data, or intelligence of any nature transmitted in whole or in part by a wire, radio, electromagnetic, photoelectronic or photo-optical system that affects interstate or foreign commerce…" Courts have historically adopted a broad definition of what constitutes interstate commerce. Therefore the use of WLANs to transmit data, particularly if connected to the Internet, would be considered "electronic communications" within the meaning of the ECPA.

A computer trespasser is defined as a person who accesses a protected computer without authorization and thus, has no reasonable expectation of privacy in any communication transmitted to, through, or from the protected computer (U.S.C. 18 § 2510). It is interesting to note, as with the CFAA, that this definition makes no provisions for wireless eavesdroppers where no access is required. Anyone who "Intentionally intercepts, endeavors to intercept, or procures any other person to intercept or endeavor to intercept, any wire, oral, or electronic communication;" is in violation of the ECPA (U.S.C. 18 § 2511 (1)(a)).

Although WiFi transmissions fall within the ECPA's definition of electronic communications, the ECPA excludes electronic communications that are readily accessible to the general public from the ambit of the statute. Many of the attributes of typical WiFi transmissions make them readily accessible to the general public. Therefore, the ECPA does not appear to govern most WiFi transmissions.

First, WiFi transmissions are not scrambled or encrypted. The default setting for 802.11 standard is open system authentication with no encryption. Therefore, in a default setting with no encryption enabled, 802.11 WiFi networks do not meet these criteria. Next, WiFi transmissions are not transmitted using modulation techniques whose essential parameters have been withheld from the public with the intention of preserving the privacy of such communication. The 802.11 standard is a public standard. Further, the hardware and software required are neither controlled nor restricted items and the hardware in fact often is included as a standard feature of many computers.

In fact, the only applicability of the ECPA to WiFi transmissions is to those transmissions that are transmitted over a communication system provided by a common carrier. A common carrier is a company that provides communication service for hire to the public. Some common carriers operate WiFi networks and would be protected under the ECPA. However, when the WiFi network in question is operated by a private citizen or other entity not involved in providing communication service, the ECPA does not apply. *See Andersen Consulting LLP v. UOP*, 991 F. Supp. 1041 (N.D. Ill. 1998) (defendant did not provide electronic communication service to the public and therefore could not be sued under the ECPA).

Telecommunications Act

The Telecommunications Act also does not appear to govern WiFi intercep-tions because WiFi communications can be available to the general public. The Telecommunications Act states: "No person not being authorized by the sender shall intercept any radio communication and divulge or publish the existence, contents, substance, purport, effect, or meaning of such intercepted communication to any person. . . . *This section shall not apply to the receiving, divulging, publishing, or utilizing the contents of any radio communication which is transmitted by any station for the use of the general public…*" 47 U.S.C. § 605 (emphasis added).

Computer Fraud and Abuse Act

The Computer Fraud and Abuse Act (CFAA) does not appear to apply to the intercept of WiFi signals as the Act is focused primarily on accessing (Kern, 2004) computer systems. Although there does not appear to be any case law directly on point, passively monitoring a WiFi communication would not seem to involve accessing the person's computer as the term is generally understood. The first six major statutory violations are centered on unautho-rized access to a computer system, and the seventh concerns making threats of damage against a protected system (the following items are paraphrased for brevity):

1. Intentional access to a computer with sensitive government information.

2. Intentional access to a computer, without authorization or exceeds authorized access and obtains financial information from a financial institution or card issuer, any U.S. government files, or information from protected computer related to interstate or foreign commerce.

3. Intentionally, without authorization, accesses any nonpublic computer of a department or agency of the United States.

4. Knowingly and with intent to defraud, accesses a protected computer without authorization, or exceeds authorized access, in order to commit or further a fraud

5. Accesses to a protected computer and knowingly disseminates malicious code or causes damage, reckless or otherwise, or attempted access that would have caused loss of $5000 or more, physical harm, modification of medical treatment, a threat to public safety, or damage to a government system.

6. Knowingly, and with intent to defraud, traffics in any password or similar information through which a computer may be accessed without authorization, if—

   (A) Such trafficking affects interstate or foreign commerce; or

   (B) Such computer is used by or for the Government of the United States.

7. With intent to extort any money or other thing of value, any person who transmits any communication containing any threat to cause damage to a protected computer.

Eavesdropping on WiFi can be done in a passive manner with no outgoing data emitting from the eavesdropping computer. No connection to an access point is required to capture data carried on the radio frequency transmissions. Therefore each section of the CFAA that mentions access (items 1-6) would specifically exclude WiFi eavesdropping.

NOTE

A significant ethical and legal debate exists for those that engage in wardriving—a practice of geographically locating open wireless access points—and for those that unabashedly use open wireless access points to access resources on the Internet. Some of the software programs used for locating and listening to wireless access points will attempt to connect with the access point. This often incidental connection, however benign it might be, could technically constitute an unauthorized access as described in 18 U.S.C. 1030, even if no network resources were used, the network was not accessed, and no eavesdropping was conducted.

Fourth Amendment Expectation of Privacy in WLANs

Although Congress has chosen not to prohibit the interception of WiFi traffic via statute, cyber crime investigators, as law enforcement officers, still are prohibited by the Fourth Amendment from engaging in unreasonable searches. The constitutional protection against unreasonable searches extends only to those areas in which the subject of the search has exhibited an actual (subjective) expectation of privacy and that expectation is one that society is prepared to recognize as "reasonable" (*Katz v. United States*, 389 U.S. 347, 361 (1967)). Although an individual has a constitutionally-protected expectation of privacy in his home, "[w]hat a person knowingly exposes to the public, even in his own home or office, is not a subject of Fourth Amendment protection" (*Katz*, 389 U.S. at 351). "The Fourth Amendment protection of the home has never been extended to require law enforcement officers to shield their eyes when passing by a home on public thoroughfares" (*California v. Ciraolo*, 476 U.S. 207, 213 (1986)). "Nor does the mere fact that an individual has taken measures to restrict some views of his activities preclude an officer's observations from a public vantage point where he has a right to be and which renders the activities clearly visible" *Id*. (citing *United States v. Knotts*, 460 U.S. 276, 282 (1983)).

The question becomes, then, whether an expectation of privacy in electronic communications transmitted via WiFi would be reasonable, in a Fourth Amendment sense. Although this issue has not been decided yet, the better view appears to be that such an expectation of privacy would not be reasonable in a Fourth Amendment sense. It is a basic function of WiFi transmissions that, at the option of the WiFi user, they may be encrypted and therefore effectively shielded from public view. Therefore, if a user chose not to shield his WiFi transmissions from public view through the built-in encryption—specifically specified in the WiFi standard—courts would likely conclude that the WiFi user had foregone any reasonable expectation of privacy (see *United States v. Granderson*, 182 F. Supp. 2d 315, 321–22 (2001) defendant had no reasonable expectation of privacy when conducting drug activities behind a boarded-up window that had a slot between the boards since the defendant easily could have shielded his activities from public view by taking simple and obvious steps).

Summary

WiFi, as defined by the 802.11 standard, is clearly a technology that is empowering millions to break free from the bounds of a wired infrastructure. The convenience and personal freedom afforded by a wireless connection has fueled the enthusiasm for home networking and has cut the cost of employing networks in underfunded organizations like churches and schools. However, there is a cost in the loss of privacy of data transmitted across the wireless network if users do not take steps to encrypt the transmissions.

The 802.11 standard clearly articulates that additional privacy measures, primarily authentication measures such as MAC filtering and encryption, are needed to prohibit any other 802.11 equipped device from connecting to the wireless access point. The 802.11 standard further articulates that encryption such as WEP and WPA must be used to protect the privacy of data on the WLAN; however, the default in the setting—and the resulting default setting on most wireless devices—has the privacy/encryption feature disabled. Out-of-the-box, the device is vulnerable to eavesdropping and additional actions usually are required of the new owner to enable the security features.

But one would think that eavesdropping on electronic communications would be decidedly illegal. Under the currently-existing federal statutes discussed earlier, this does not appear to be the case. The Electronic Communications Privacy Act , 18 U.S.C. 2510, does not appear to govern most WiFi communications not owned by a communications carrier, because the communications are "readily accessible to the general public" unless security measures were taken to secure otherwise wide open communication.

After reviewing the applicable laws, we see that the WiFi is positioned at a confluence of a number of technical and legal issues that make the situation rather unique. The 802.11 communications standard allows for wide-open, unencrypted data communications; over an unlicensed frequency band; for which the technology to intercept the communications is not only readily available, but often unavoidable; and for which common carrier involvement is rare. It does not appear that WiFi interception are specifically addressed by the laws presented earlier—and even where WiFi interception might technically fall within the ambit of a statute, WiFi transmissions seem to be implicitly excluded elsewhere.

For example, 47 U.S.C. 605 clearly states: "No person not being authorized by the sender shall intercept any radio communication and divulge or publish the existence, contents, substance, purport, effect, or meaning of such intercepted communication to any person." But, as discussed earlier, the statute does not apply to communications that are transmitted by any station for the use of the general public. Similarly, the Computer Fraud and Abuse Act, 18 U.S.C. § 1030, is primarily concerned with "accessing" a "system" without proper authorization. However, eavesdropping on WiFi requires no connection or access to a computer system. Since the common understanding of the term "access" suggests a two-way communication, a hand-shake, or some level of mutual interaction, then passive monitoring would not be a form of access. Since WiFi communications are available to the general public, most WiFi signals are lawfully open to interception under the applicable federal statutes discussed previously.

Notes from the Underground...

Access versus Passive Listening

The CFAA places a significant amount of weight on the access to a computer system. Access could be construed in two ways—each having a significant impact on the CFAA's applicability to many wireless issues. If access were to be construed in the broadest sense of the term to include any type of access to information on a system, the CFAA might be applicable to WiFi eavesdropping. If, however, access was construed to mean situations where information is exchanged between a computer and a human (logging in at a terminal) or between two computers (negotiating a cyber-handshake to begin the exchange of information), then access may have less applicability to WiFi eavesdropping. Based on the era in which the CFAA was written, it could be argued that the intent of the law was to prevent hacking, where a user maliciously exceeds his or her authorization level or level of privilege. When construed in this context, the CFAA would not govern passive monitoring of electronic communications where no escalation of privileges—nor any two-way interaction at all—is needed to gain access to the information.

Regardless of the legality of WiFi eavesdropping, the public should be advised that the 802.11 family of standards places network authentication and information privacy in the hands of the network owner. Steps beyond the default install must be taken to ensure the privacy of your data and the security of your network. It is not clear that WiFi users would have any legal recourse if somebody eavesdropped on communications that the user had implicitly invited the world to listen to by leaving the door wide open.

Works Cited

47 U.S.C: Communication Act of 1934

47CFR18.111(a); Title 47—Telecommunication Chapter I, Federal Communications Commission, Part 18 Industrial, Scientific, And Medical Equipment, Subpart A General Information, Sec. 18.111 General operating conditions, (a)

Kern, Benjamin D. 2004. Whacking, Joyriding and War-Driving: Roaming Use of Wi-Fi and the Law. *Santa Clara Computer and High Technology Law Journal.*

Infonetics Research's quarterly market share service, available at www.beerfiles.com.au/content/view/1334/0/

Solutions Fast Track

WiFi Technology

☑ WiFi is a colloquial term referring to a wireless communication technology described in the IEEE's 802.11 body of standards.

☑ WiFi covers both infrared and RF as mediums for communication—but most WiFi devices operate in the 2.4GHz or 5GHz RF bands.

☑ WiFi access points use an open system architecture as their default settings—therefore additional measures such as encryption must be configured to control network access, authentication, and privacy.

Understanding WiFi RF

☑ 802.11 WiFi networks use an unlicensed band of the RF spectrum set aside for industrial, scientific and medical (ISM) use.

☑ The ISM band generally is considered open to the general public.

Scanning RF

☑ Scanning is a well-documented practice of listening to RF transmissions.

☑ A specific piece of legislation made the manufacture and sale of equipment to monitor cellular communications illegal.

☑ There is no legislation that criminalizes the manufacture, sale, or possession of equipment to monitor or intercept WiFi—in fact the same equipment used to connect to a WiFi network is used to monitor traffic on a WiFi network.

Eavesdropping on WiFi

☑ A legal framework exists around the legality of both wiretaps and unlawfully accessing computer systems—including the Telecommunications Act, The Computer Fraud and Abuse Act, and the Electronic Communications Privacy Act.

☑ Applicable federal statutes do not appear to govern eavesdropping on private WiFi communications.

Fourth Amendment Expectation of Privacy in WLANs

☑ Although Congress has chosen not to prohibit the interception of WiFi traffic via statute, cyber crime investigators, as law enforcement officers, are still prohibited by the Fourth Amendment from engaging in unreasonable searches.

Frequently Asked Questions

The following Frequently Asked Questions, answered by the authors of this book, are designed to both measure your understanding of the concepts presented in this chapter and to assist you with real-life implementation of these concepts. To have your questions about this chapter answered by the author, browse to **www.syngress.com/solutions** and click on the **"Ask the Author"** form.

Q: Can I use my neighbor's wireless to surf the Internet?

A: There appears to be some applicability within ECPA related to surfing your neighbor's wireless network. In order to be connected to the Internet, you have to associate with the access point—or connect to the WiFi network. Where there appears to be some uncertainty regarding how ECPA view access, it may be hard to argue that *connecting* to the network isn't a form of access. Second, there is an ethical argument about connecting to the network without the permission of the owner. Although it could be argued that the neighbor's act in leaving the access point open is an implicit invitation to you for some level of access to their network; such an argument appears a bit strained. Perhaps the network owner was fully aware of the issues related to open wireless networks and wanted to share the love by sharing his bandwidth with the world; but in fact in all likelihood the network owner had no idea that other users were accessing the network, and he would not have been happy about such actions. Lastly, as a user, I do not recommend connecting to unknown open networks because the owner of the network has the ability to capture and view all of my data going through his network. I may assume that the network owner is of a lower technological level because their network was left wide open, but maybe the network owner put the access point out there just so that people would connect to it. I am extremely wary of connecting to unknown open networks when I'm at a hotel or coffee shop.

Q: Are you stating in this article that we have the green-light to go and start intercepting WiFi signals?

A: No. Sorry. The point of this chapter was to show how federal statutes that govern the interception of other types of electronic communications do not squarely address WiFi technology. Further, and perhaps more important, it appears that many state wiretap laws would criminalize the interception of WiFi signals. So although the discussion here shows that the federal statutes discussed here may not address WiFi eavesdropping, the interception of WiFi may be criminalized by your State's wiretap or other laws. You should consult with your local prosecutor before attempting to eavesdrop on WiFi signals.

Chapter 7

Seizure of Digital Information

Solutions in this chapter:

- **Defining Digital Evidence**

- **Digital Evidence Seizure Methodology**

- **Factors Limiting the Wholesale Seizure of Hardware**

- **Other Options for Seizing Digital Evidence**

- **Common Threads within Digital Evidence Seizure**

- **Determining the Most Appropriate Seizure Method**

☑ **Summary**

☑ **Solutions Fast Track**

☑ **Frequently Asked Questions**

Introduction

Computers and digital devices are employed by the majority of people in the U.S. for myriad business and personal uses. Because of the wide acceptance of computers in our daily lives, it is reasonable to conclude that people will use a computer to assist them in the commission of crimes, record aspects of crimes on a computer, and use computers to store the fruits of their crimes or contraband.

Any of the computers involved in the situations just discussed will likely contain upwards of hundreds of thousands of pieces of information stored in a digital format, including operating system files, program files, user documents, and file fragments in drive free space. While the challenge for the laboratory examiner is to find the relevant *data objects* on a hard drive or other media, a greater challenge exists for the on-scene responders and investigators: How can the information be collected from the scene and brought to a location where it can be examined? Does all the hardware on-scene need to be seized as evidence, or will an exact copy of the information serve the purposes of an investigation? Are there other seizure options to be considered?

Notes from the Underground...

Data Objects

Throughout this chapter, the term "data object" will be used frequently to discuss information found on a storage device or a piece of storage media (SWGDE, 2000). The digital information on a piece of media is nothing more than a long string of 1s and 0s recorded on either magnetic, solid-state, or optical media. Hard drives and floppy disks are examples of magnetic media; USB thumb drives and flash memory cards are examples of solid-state media; and CDs and DVDs are types of optical media. Any number of digital devices, including computers, cell phones, and iPods, will have operating systems and programs that arrange the 1s and 0s into a particular order to create images, documents, spreadsheets, music, and so on. For the purposes of our discussion, each of these discrete arrangements of information that

Continued

are logically organized into something meaningful will be called a *data object*. The choice to use the term "data object" instead of the more frequently used term "file" is based on the fact that not all organized digital information comes in the form of a file. Information attached to a file such as a file header and metadata are not technically separate files, but can be culled out from the file as separate data objects. Other types of information found on storage media are not files, but fragments of files left by the constant write and overwrite of information caused by the deletion of existing files and the creation of new files. For example, a certain amount of an old file may be left behind when a new file is overwritten in the same space—so-called file slack space. Still other types of informational fragments may include files and commands temporarily stored in the swap file or within the RAM itself. For these reasons, I believe it is more appropriate to call these organized pieces of information "data objects."

What we consider to be evidence has a dramatic effect on how we view the electronic crime scene. The current model of digital evidence seizure is focused on physical hardware, which is appropriate in most situations. However, as we move forward from this point in time, factors such as the size of media and full-disk encryption will impact the ability to seize all the hardware on-scene for later analysis at a forensics laboratory. Other options besides wholesale hardware seizure—RAM recovery, on-scene imaging of hard drives, and imaging of select files—need to become part of the basic toolkit of on-scene responders.

But the acceptance of other options for digital evidence seizure will not be a spontaneous event. The legal framework, the established workflows of existing computer forensic best practices, and the fear of the unknown will all play a part in determining how quickly the digital evidence seizure methodologies are adjusted to accept other options besides wholesale hardware seizure. The community of people that respond to, investigate, and prosecute crimes that have a digital evidence component is a very diverse population with different frames of reference and different technical understanding. If one group decides to unilaterally implement a change in practices or policy, the ripple effect is felt across the entire system—which is what makes *bridging the gaps* such an important part of considering and implementing any change resulting from advances in technology. As the author and a member of the greater crime-with-a-cyber-component-community, I hope this work serves to create discussion between the disparate communities on the appropriateness of both the familiar and innovative methods to seize digital evidence.

To these ends, I have organized the following pages to guide the reader through a number of topics relating to both the existing method of digital seizure and the innovative options available for on-scene responders. First, we will examine some of the framework surrounding the legal view of evidence, then we will address how the current digital evidence seizure methodology evolved, and afterward we'll take a look at each of the seizure steps individually. This work is not intended to be a step-by-step guide for digital evidence seizure, but many of the current best practices are examined, and some common pitfalls are discussed. Following the discussion of the current method of seizure, we will explore some of the reasons why the wholesale seizure of hardware on-scene may become problematic in the future. Finally, we will discuss a number of options available for seizure of information, including the on-scene preview of information, the seizure of data held in the computer's RAM, on-scene imaging of entire hard drives, and the on-scene imaging of specific data objects.

WARNING

In the sections that follow, we will primarily be discussing criminal procedures, as I would hope that the civil procedures would follow the guidelines set forth by the criminal side of the house. Many civil procedures often turn into criminal events, and vice versa, so it's probably wise to be working each case as if it were destined for criminal court. Further, most of my work has been as a bridge between the technical community and that of law enforcement—and it is from this viewpoint that the chapter is written.

Obviously, criminals may actually steal a computer or other device directly—but the focus of this chapter is not on the physical theft of hardware. Instead, we target how information held within the storage medium can be processed into evidence.

Here, I will colloquially refer to computers and hard drives when discussing digital information. I do realize many types of digital devices and media contain data, but it is often too cumbersome to individually point out each item or specify each situation.

This chapter focuses more specifically on the seizure of digital evidence when that evidence relates to a static event, such as receiving a harassing e-mail or seizing a computer that contains child pornography. An analysis and discussion of recovering information and evidence from a more dynamic event, such as a Denial-of-Service attack or a network intrusion are included in Chapter 5. Although much of what is discussed in the following sections still apply to network forensics, please note that I am purposely minimizing the points that apply to it.

Finally, I am not a lawyer, nor do I play one on TV. The intent of this chapter is to provide investigators, prosecutors and private sector personnel with options and discussion topics related to the collection of digital evidence. **Any conclusions or recommendations in this chapter that may resemble legal advice should be vetted through legal counsel. Always check with your local jurisdiction, local prosecutors, and local forensics laboratory as to their preferred method(s) of digital evidence collection.**

Defining Digital Evidence

Black's Law Dictionary—the Bible for legal definitions—provides several definitions for *evidence* (Nolan, 1990). One of the definitions reads "Testimony, writings, or material objects offered in proof of an alleged fact or proposition." I have to say it is rather refreshing to have a generally straightforward and concise legal definition; generally, I don't equate straightforward and concise with legal…well… anything. The definition does provide a good launching point for our discussions on how digital information is viewed in the criminal justice system.

Black's definition of evidence as applied to digital evidence can be viewed in two ways. First, we can examine the computer itself as the evidence. This is clearly the case when the computer is the actual instrument of the crime, such as when the physical parts of the computer are used to commit a crime—for example, I hit you over the head with a keyboard. Colloquially, most law enforcement investigators and prosecutors will call the computer itself evidence even in cases where information on the computer relates to a given crime. As one investigator told me: "Everything seized at a crime scene is evidence until someone tells me it's not." In this sense, when the computer itself is seized at a crime scene or through a warrant, it is considered by many to be evidence.

Building on the view of the computer as evidence, many assert that the information on the computer requires the original computer to view the contents. In other words, the original computer—along the lines of how the best evidence rule requires the "original" whenever possible—may have an impact on how the information on the computer was actually viewed by the suspect. This is a valid viewpoint because many forensic software packages will not provide a view that is exactly as the suspect would have seen it. Too many different programs may show a given file, image, movie, or e-mail in a particular manner. The computer forensic analysis programs will often use a generic viewer capable of displaying any number of different formats. For example, Access Data's FTK has a generic format in which all e-mails would be displayed regardless of the program in which they were created. The generic format provides all the same information that would have been shown in the original e-mail, but it clearly is shown in a very different format than what the suspect would have seen. An e-mail viewed through the AOL e-mail program will include all the banners, advertisements, and formatting that make up the AOL look and feel or "user experience." The e-mail itself will contain a number of standard fields, such as the e-mail header and the body of the message. The AOL program places these fields in a particular "package." However, that same e-mail viewed in FTK, though containing the same content, would lack the AOL packaging. In court, the examiner may be asked "Is this exactly what the suspect saw?" and the obvious answer is "No—but…" And it is within this "but…" that the court may suggest that the evidence—the complete computer and information as a unified package—be brought forth in front of the court.

A second way to view *Black's* definition is that the information, or *data objects*, contained on the digital storage medium are the "testimony, writings, or material objects" offered in proof of an alleged fact. This viewpoint makes the computer nothing more than a device that is used to access the information, and the components of the computer that store digital information nothing more than mere physical containers that house information—similar to a file cabinet or briefcase. Arguments can be made that only the desired information can be seized as evidence. The ramifications of this change in focus from hardware-as-evidence to information-as-evidence are far reaching.

If we do propose there is a distinction between the data objects and the physical container, we need to examine the legal framework within which we operate and seize information to determine if it is permissible to seize either the physical hardware or the information, or both. Rule 41 of the Federal Rules of Criminal Procedure (FRCP), titled "Search and Seizure" provides a definition for property, stating that "'Property' includes documents, books, papers, any other tangible objects, and information" (FRCP, Rule 41(a)(2)(A)). Within this definition is our first inclination that, in fact, the legal system views both storage containers and information as property. When we move forward in the FRCP into the discussions on seizure, we see that persons or property are subject to search or seizure and that a warrant may be issued for any of the following: (1) evidence of a crime; (2) contraband, fruits of crime, or other items illegally possessed; (3) property designed for use, intended for use, or used in committing a crime; or (4) a person to be arrested, or a person who is unlawfully restrained (FRCP, Rule 41[c]).

TIP

A number of legal documents will prove helpful in the coming discussions. The *Federal Rules of Evidence* (FRE) addresses the manner in which evidence can be presented in a federal court. *The Federal Rules of Criminal Procedure* (FRCP) provides the guidance for bringing an accused through the process of arrest and trial. The Computer Crime and Intellectual Property Section within the Criminal Division of the United States Department of Justice publishes a document titled *Searching and Seizing Computers and Obtaining Electronic Evidence in Criminal Investigations* (Manual). The Manual provides a very thorough review of a number of issues related to working with digital evidence—particularly as it relates to federal case law. Obviously, the depth of the information contained in the FRE, FRCP, and the Manual is well beyond the scope of this chapter, but I recommend that anyone interested in this field become familiar with these documents. Absent from the following discussions is talk of state law. Although many states will retain the ability for their own courts to be the "final say" regarding procedural or evidentiary matters, many states have adopted rules very similar to the FRE and FRCP.

Of interest to our discussion here is that property includes information, and that search and seizure is authorized, with a warrant, for property that is evidence of a crime. The next logical conclusion being that warrants can be issued for information that is evidence of a crime—but do the courts interpret using specific files or data objects as evidence, or should the focus be on the physical storage devices? Here, we consult the United States Department of Justice's Computer Crime and Intellectual Property Section's document titled *Searching and Seizing Computers and Obtaining Electronic Evidence in Criminal Investigations* (Manual):

> The most important decision agents must make when describing the property in the warrant is whether the sizable property according to Rule 41 is the computer hardware itself, or merely the information that the hardware contains (pg. 61). ...if the probable cause relates in whole or in part to information stored on the computer, the warrant should focus on the content of the relevant files rather than on the storage devices which may happen to contain them." The Manual references *United States v. Gawrysiak* (972 F. Supp. 853, 860 [D.N.J. 1997], aff'd, 178 F.3d 1281 [3d Cir. 1999]) which upheld the seizure of "...records [that] include information and/or data stored in the form of magnetic or electronic coding on computer media . . . which constitute evidence" of enumerated federal crimes (Manual, pg. 62). ...The physical equipment merely stores the information that the agents have probable cause to seize. Although the agents may need to seize the equipment in order to obtain the files it contains and computer files do not exist separate from some storage medium, the better practice is to describe the information rather than the equipment in the warrant itself (pg. 65)...

The guidance from the Manual is that the Rules on Criminal Procedure, and the interpretation of the same in the courts, points to the difference between the information held in data objects and the physical container (hard drive, flash media) in/on which the data resides. This provides some positive reinforcement to those that make the claim that the data itself is the evidence and that the computer or storage device is merely a vessel.

The preceding discussions regarding the computer as the evidence versus the data as the evidence has a dramatic effect on how we "seize" or "collect" evidence both at the scene and in the forensics laboratory. If your viewpoint is that the computer is the evidence, then your seizure methodology will be focused on the collection of the computer itself at the scene of the crime. If your viewpoint is that the information is the evidence, then you may be more inclined to attempt to locate and retrieve the information-as-evidence, with less care as to the eventual fate of the hardware. Further, you may be more inclined to call your "computer forensic" efforts simple "evidence collection" and remove the requirement for expert classification at trial. The important point here is that there are options to be considered, examined, and discussed within the community—options that have the ability to significantly change the entire approach to computer seizure and analysis.

Digital Evidence Seizure Methodology

The proliferation of personal computers changed how computers were involved in criminal issues. In the past, computers were often used primarily as the attack platform or target of the attack—now the more personal use of computes creates a situation where the computer is the storehouse of evidence relating to almost every type of crime imaginable. The result is that more computers are involved in some manner in crime and that more computers need to be examined for information of evidentiary value. But before they can be examined, they must be seized.

Previously, the highly trained computer specialist would attend to each seizure personally; however, the proliferation of computers and their use in criminal endeavors made personal attention to each case impractical. In some areas of the country, one specialist may serve an entire region. It is clearly unreasonable to believe that one specialist will be able to perform each seizure and complete the examination of the digital evidence for every crime with a cyber component. To fill this apparent gap in need versus capability, state and local law enforcement agents have become involved in recovering digital evidence from a crime scene where a computer is directly involved. Not only are state and local investigators faced with dealing with a new type of crime, but they are also asked to perform the seizures of digital evidence.

The on-scene responders/investigators often know very little about computers and often have not been instructed on how to "properly" seize digital information. Existing seizure protocols for physical items are used, resulting in a focus on the seizure of the computer hardware—sometimes the entire computer, including the monitor, printers, keyboard, and so on are seized and packaged for delivery to the lab. Over time, it became accepted to use the seizure methods focused on the seizure of the *physical hardware* for the seizure of *digital information*. Let's take a look at the flow of a general seizure of a personal computer.

TIP

A number of other authors have nicely addressed the larger digital investigative model. Most notably, Carrier and Spafford present a "digital crime scene" model that exists within the physical crime scene (Carrier, 2003). Generally, these models present a complete framework for digital investigations, from incident response preparation right through to the examination and analysis of the seized information. Although this holistic viewpoint may be relevant to the administrator responsible for the entire operation, these models hold less applicability to the actual on-scene seizure of the relevant information, which is the focus of this chapter.

The current manner of seizure of computer hardware expects that the on-scene responder has a general knowledge about computers—to the level of "THIS is a keyboard, THIS is a mouse, THERE is no 'any' key," and so on. Better yet, the responder should have basic training on digital evidence collection, or, at the very minimum, be able to consult a guide on best practices, such as the *USSS Best Practices Guide* (USSS, 2006) or the *NIJ First Responder's Guide* (NIJ, 2001). Next, the responder would arrive at the scene, secure the scene physically, and begin to assess how the digital evidence is involved. The responder would take steps to secure the digital crime scene, which may include inspecting the devices for physical booby-traps and isolating the devices from any networks. The responder then seizes as many physical containers—physical media including hard drives, CDs, DVDs—as necessary to ensure the seized items reasonably include the information with probative value. The seizure of the hardware/physical containers involves labeling all wires connected to the computer or devices, and photographing the scene—paying specific attention to the labeled connectors. The physical items are seized, documented, packaged, and prepared for transport to an offsite facility for examination. At the offsite facility, possibly the local police agency or a state/regional forensic laboratory, the seized physical containers are examined for data objects with evidentiary value. If found, these data objects are usually included in a forensic findings report and are printed out or copied to other media and then provided to the investigator and prosecutors. Figure 7.1 outlines the steps of the traditional method for seizing computer hardware.

Figure 7.1 Traditional Seizure Methodology

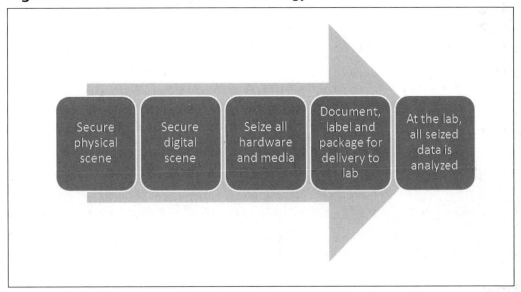

That sounds pretty straightforward, doesn't it? For the most part, the preceding reflects the general process that the wide majority of law enforcement agencies follow when it comes to the seizure of digital evidence. As you can see, the general methodology reflects a focus on the seizure of the physical items. Further, the preceding model shows that a division exists between the investigators / on-scene responders and the forensic laboratory/examiners.

Seizure Methodology in Depth

Unfortunately, current seizure methodology does not adequately prepare our investigators to respond to scenes that are more complicated than a single machine sitting alone in a bare room. The fact is that the world is a messy place. Our responders need to understand that they need to have a methodology in place that allows them to work through more complicated scenes, such as finding dozens of computers or dozens of pieces of removable media or hundreds of CDs. *The steps presented in Figure 7.2 are representative of current seizure methodology, but the steps have been crafted to provide a higher level guidance about approaching nonstandard seizure scenes.* Specifically, the "Seize All Hardware and Media" step shown in Figure 7.1 has been replaced by a series of three steps that help guide the responder through identifying all the digital media on-scene, minimizing the crime scene through prioritization, and then seizing the hardware and media that have the highest probability of containing the relevant evidence.

Figure 7.2 Seizure Methodology Featuring Minimization

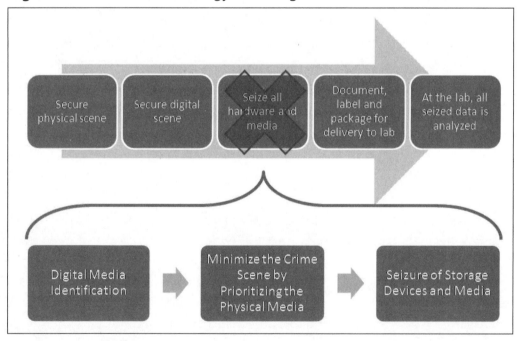

We begin our seizure methodology at the scene, where a warrant for digital evidence is being served. It is assumed in the following that the scene has been physically secured, and the responder has a safe working environment. It is also assumed that the responder has a properly drafted warrant that identifies the information to be seized and outlines that an offsite examination of the media may be required if the situation makes the on-scene seizure infeasible.

Step 1: Digital Media Identification

The first step is to begin to canvas the scene in an attempt to locate the digital media that you believe has the highest probability of containing the evidentiary information described in the warrant. If the suspect has one computer sitting in his bedroom and another in a box in the attic, I'd bet my money that the information I'm after is the one in his bedroom. Taking a step beyond the simple situations, one needs to also consider removable media such as flash drives and CDs or DVDs. Flash drives are often held as personal file cabinets and may contain information of a personal nature. Look for flash drives on key chains, watches, in cameras, and just about anywhere—flash media can be unbelievably small. Another strategy is to look for media that contains backups of files from on-scene computer(s). If the information is important, you can be sure it will be backed up somewhere.

Where can digital media be found? The answer is pretty much anywhere. Locating very small, but very large storage media could be a significant issue when conducting a search. Be sure to balance the perceived technical expertise of the suspect versus the type of crime versus where you expect to find the relevant information. For example, it is fairly well documented that obsessive collectors of child pornography will gather tens-of-thousands of pictures of children being victimized. In this type of case, it would be most logical to be looking for a hard-drive or optical disks, given the amount of storage required. At this point in time, obtaining such large amounts of storage on flash media would be difficult, however. On the other hand, the same collector may be accused of taking pictures of children being victimized, and in this case the search should definitely focus on small flash media–type storage cards that could be used in a digital camera and/or be used to store and hide coveted images.

Documentation is part of every step, so this won't be the last time you see it mentioned. Nevertheless, it's worth mentioning here as a reminder. While conducting the search for digital media, it may be appropriate to narrate your movements into a voice recorder and to photograph the found media in place before moving it.

Step 2: Minimizing the Crime Scene by Prioritizing the Physical Media

After all the digital media is identified, an effort must be made to determine which storage devices or pieces of media have the highest probability of containing the information described in the warrant. Why? Because at some point it time, it will be impractical to seize all the digital devices, removable media, and storage media at a crime scene. At the current time, it may be possible to walk into a residence and only find one computer and maybe a few CDs. In this situation, the minimization of the physical media is all but done for you—you have in front of you only a few pieces of media that may contain the informational evidence. But technology is enabling homeowners to easily build rather complicated networks that may include wireless storage devices, multiple operating systems, shared Internet connections, integration with traditional entertainment media, and integration with home appliances and devices. Downloadable and burnable movies and music are generally an accepted technology, greatly increasing the amount of optical media found in homes. Based on the availability of technology, on-scene responders will be faced with multiple computers, storage devices, and dozens to hundreds of pieces of media—all adding up to terabytes of information.

The responder must make some tough decisions about where she believes the information will most likely be found. One suggestion is to prepare a prioritized ranking to help decide which storage devices and pieces of media should be seized for offsite review. The prioritized ranking is also critical in deciding which devices or pieces of media are previewed on-scene—one of the options we'll be discussing later in this chapter.

Step 3: Seizure of Storage Devices and Media

The seizure itself is rather straightforward. After the scene is secured and it is determined that the hardware must be seized, the investigator begins by labeling all the connections/wires attached to the computer. Be meticulous in the labeling of wires and thorough in your documentation. It's a good practice to label both the end of a cable and place a matching label where the cable connects—for instance, label a Monitor's VGA Cable B^1 and label the computer's VGA port as B^1'; label the monitor's power cable plug as B^2 and label the wall outlet as B^2'. Photograph as many relevant objects and seizure steps as you see fit—digital photos are basically free and can be burned to disk and added to the case file. Don't forget to remove the sticky labels from the power outlets once they have been photographed.

After the computer has been labeled, documented, and photographed, disassemble the components and prepare the computer case for shipment. Best practices state that an unformatted floppy disk should be placed in the floppy drive with a piece of evidence tape sticking out like a flag. The presence of the disk in the floppy drive may prevent an accidental boot to the hard drive—but the new trend from computer and laptop manufacturers is to omit the standard floppy drives entirely, so this recommendation may be deprecated over time. Other options available to prevent an accidental boot are to unplug the power to the hard drive in a desktop machine and remove the battery from a laptop. Some recommend placing evidence tape over the external drives, including the floppy drive and any CD/DVD drives. When transporting, be careful not to drop, or otherwise jar or shock, the computer, as this may result in damage to the hard drive and possibly the motherboard. When transporting, keep the storage devices away from heat and strong magnetic fields, such as high-powered radios and big trunk-thumping subwoofers.

WARNING

Regardless of what hardware seizure methodology is written here or contained in any of the other published guides, always check with the laboratory or department that is going to process the seized hardware. Most have preferred methods for hardware seizure and transportation.

To Pull the Plug or Not to Pull the Plug, That Is the Question

I always wondered where the phrase *pull the plug* originated. I can picture a stressed out, overworked computer forensic technician on the phone with an on-scene responder, attempting to guide them through a proper shutdown and then a controlled boot process—prompting the following exchange:

Responder: It says to hit any key.

Forensic Tech: Uh-huh.

Responder: Hang on…. Um… where is the any key?

Forensic Tech: You've got to be kidding me…. Just pull the @#$@#% plug, wrap it in tape, and bring it to me!

Since that first hypothetical exchange—which still gives me a chuckle when I think about it—the mantra from the forensic community has been to pull the plug from the back of the machine, regardless of the state of the machine—on, off, writing to the drives, or anything else. *I have no doubt that, across the board, the simplest most teachable method of seizure that will generally preserve most of the data and evidence is to pull the plug from the back of the machine.* Pulling the plug and prepping it for transfer to an examination lab is the only option that is reasonably teachable in a few hours to first responders of any skill level. But, surely, we need to be able to do something other than pull the plug. We cannot possibly make advances in this field if we limit all officers and agents to a methodology based on the lowest common denominator.

The most pressing issue relating to *pull-the-plug* is that some operating systems (OSes) really like to be shut down properly. Rapid power loss in some OSes can actually corrupt the operating system's kernel or the central module of the system. UNIX, Linux, and Macintosh operating systems are the most vulnerable, but some Windows-based OSes, such as a Windows 2000 server, should be shut down properly. Moore (2005) presents a good review of the proper shutdown method (shutdown versus pull-the-plug) for different operating systems based on the operating system's ability to recover from rapid power loss.

Obviously, if you intend to shut down the machine properly, you must determine the OS. To determine the OS and to initiate a proper shut down sequence, you need to manipulate the computer's mouse and/or keyboard, but manipulating the mouse/keyboard will change data on the suspect's machine. You say "But I'm not allowed to change data on the suspect's machine!" That may be the guidance given, but it is more appropriate to take the position: "I will do the most appropriate and reasonable actions during seizure to ensure I retain as much of the relevant information as possible. Here is the documentation of my actions." The focus here is on reasonableness and the documentation of actions. Also, it is important to key-in on the retention of the *relevant information,* which includes the information of potential evidentiary value and should not include the Registry changes made to indicate that a shutdown occurred. Simply put, moving the mouse to determine the OS and starting a shutdown sequence did not place 5,000 images of child pornography on the computer's hard drive. However, pulling the plug on a Linux system may actually impact the ability to recover those same images.

There is no one correct answer to the pull-the-plug question. If you have the skill and knowledge to determine the operating system of the suspect computer and you determine that the operating system and other data could be damaged by pulling the plug, then shut the machine down properly. Document your actions and explain clearly and knowledgeably how you prevented damage to the computer, and possibly to the evidentiary information, by following a shutdown procedure. Show how your actions preserved the evidence, as opposed to corrupting it. If you have the skill and document the steps you followed, you have solid footing on which to defend your actions. If you do not possess such skill, or if the more advanced techniques are not working in a given situation or on a particular piece of hardware, then by all means, pull the plug.

Factors Limiting the Wholesale Seizure of Hardware

Earlier we contrasted the historic seizure context versus the current context and discussed how the historic context placed a focus on the on-scene seizure of data objects, as compared with the current situation where the focus of the on-scene activities is to seize all the physical containers. The question I pose to you is this: Are we heading in the right direction by focusing on the seizure of the physical hardware (the container items) rather than focusing on the seizure of the relevant information (data objects)?

Earlier seizures of digital evidence focused on data objects because it was impractical to attempt to image an entire server, based on the high costs of storage media. I suggest we are heading toward a similar impracticality—although this time our inability to seize *all* the information is based on a number of different factors, including massively large storage arrays, whole disk encryption, the abundance of non-evidentiary information on media and related privacy concerns, and the time involved in laboratory forensic analysis. At some point in the future, the process by which we image entire pieces of media for forensic analysis will become obsolete (Hosmer, 2006).

I suggest we make the distinction that there other options beyond whole-sale seizure available to our responders. We need to train our responders to have the ability to perform on-scene data preview, full data-image, and imaging of only the relevant data objects. Further, we need to begin to change the wholesale seizure paradigm now—for all responders not just the specialists—before we are faced with a greater volume of cases we are ill prepared to address.

Size of Media

Storage devices are getting big—very big. Now, at the end of 2006, it is quite common for a single hard drive to contain 100 gigabytes of information—roughly equivalent to a library floor of academic journals. It is very achievable for the home user, both technologically and financially, to put together a 2-terabyte storage array—an array that could house the complete works within an entire academic research library (SIMS, 2003). Storage is relatively cheap, and people are taking advantage of the extra space by storing music, movies, and creating mirrored backups (RAID 1 arrays). Anthony reyes provides an excellent example in Chapter 5, "Incident Response: Live Forensics and Investigations," where he discusses exactly how long it would take to image a multi-hundred terabyte server—based on today's latest technology, the imaging duration would be measured in years. The typical crime that involves a computer won't include a multi-hundred terabyte server, but showing up at a crime scene with a 200-gigabyte destination drive and finding a 1.5-terabyte RAID will certainly have a negative impact on your ability to create an on-scene image of the data.

What exactly happens when the full 1.5 TB RAID and 200 DVDs are seized and brought back to the forensic laboratory for analysis. Do you actually have the hardware and software to acquire and process that much data? If the laboratory is not a regional or state lab, but a small laboratory set up at the local agency, the answer might be yes—but processing the case might use the entire budget set aside for target drives for the entire year for that one case. Once the data is examined, does the jurisdiction or local policy dictate that the imaged data be archived? At some point, the ability to seize and process *everything* will exceed the budget set aside for the purchase of forensic processing computers, target drives, and archival media and will also exceed the time available for forensic examiners to process the case.

Disk Encryption

A number of encryption programs exist now that provide whole disk encryption, a common one being PGP from pgp.com. These types of encryption programs encrypt all the data on the hard drive and are generally transparent to the user; meaning that one password in the startup sequence "unlocks" the contents for viewing and editing. Of course, looming on the horizon is the Windows Vista operating system, purported to incorporate BitLocker Drive Encryption tied to the Trusted Platform Module cryptographic chip in the higher-end versions of the operating system.

Whole disk encryption has some serious implications for law enforcement when performing seizures. First, if a whole disk encryption is enabled on a running computer, and the computer is shut down or the power is removed, there is a very good chance that the data on the drives will be unrecoverable without the proper key. Responders may need to determine if a whole disk encryption program is enabled before shutting down / pulling-the-plug on a computer during seizure. If one is present, bringing the computer back to the lab for analysis may be futile. One of the best chances to retrieve the evidentiary information is when the machine is running and the user has access to the files. Second, the implementation of the TPM chip may lock the drive so the data may only become available on a specific machine. This would prevent an image of the drive from being booted in another computer or viewed with a computer forensics program. The use of disk encryption is forcing law enforcement to have other data seizure options available beyond the seizure of physical hardware.

Privacy Concerns

Personal computers often contain myriad information about a person's life, including financial, medical, and other personal information, information related to their job (such as work products), and even information owned by several people, possibly a spouse, family member, or roommate. It's unclear how the criminal and civil courts would view a challenge from an impacted third party regarding the seizure of a common computer. However, if that third party maintained a blog or Web site, their information may be protected from seizure under the Privacy Protection Act (PPA) (42 U.S.C. § 2000aa). The PPA was specifically developed to provide journalists with protection from warrants issued to obtain information about sources or people addressed in their publications. The PPA reads "…it shall be unlawful for a government officer or employee, in connection with the investigation or prosecution of a criminal offense, to search for or seize any work product materials possessed by a person reasonably believed to have a purpose to disseminate to the public a newspaper, book, broadcast, or other similar form of public communication." The PPA may not protect the person that possesses the information if that person is suspected of committing the criminal offenses to which the materials are related. Simply put, if you committed a crime and you have publishable information related to that crime on your computer, that information most likely will not be protected under the PPA. However, the PPA may protect the interests of a third party that uses or stores data on a computer, and may possibly protect the information of the accused if the information does not relate to the crime being investigated.

The potential situations of co-mingled evidentiary data and publishable materials, each owned by a separate person do sound unlikely if you only consider a single computer. But what if you consider a network addressable storage device located in a home network? For example, let's say that such a storage device exists at the scene of a seizure. Every member of the household stores information on the device, and little Susie's unposted blog entries on her life-as-a-brainy-15-year-old-girl are located on the storage device commingled with the information described in the warrant. Although you may seize the storage device, you may also be involved with other court proceedings related to the violation of the PPA—civil, and possibly criminal, proceedings where you are the defendant!

The Secret Service ran across a similar situation in the case of *Steve Jackson Games, Inc. v. Secret Service* (*Steve Jackson Games, Inc. v. Secret Service*, 816 F. Supp. 432 [W.D. Tex. 1993]). The Secret Service seized two computers from the company, believing that the company's system administrator had stored evidence of a crime on company computers. The day after seizure, the Secret Service learned that the computers contained materials intended for publication; materials that belonged to the company. Regardless, the Secret Service did not return the computers until several months had passed. The district court ruled that the Secret Service had in fact violated the PPA and awarded Steve Jackson Games $50,000 in damages and $250,000 in attorney's fees. The story of this raid goes well beyond the short summary provided here. The raid and the trial play a significant role in hacker mythology and also played a part in the formation of the Electronic Frontier Foundation (Sterling, 1994). Nonetheless, the moral of the story is that the Secret Service was not prepared to seize the specific information described in the warrant when they learned of the to-be-published materials present on the seized hardware. It's not known how the Secret Service would have changed their seizure methodology if they knew about the publishable materials before they served the warrant—but, for example, if they didn't have the capability of solely seizing the relevant data objects, the Secret Service might have had no other option but to seize the hardware. This example goes to show that having other seizure options available may be a critical skill that determines the success of an investigation.

Delays Related to Laboratory Analysis

If investigators of crimes involving a computer rely completely and absolutely on their computer forensic laboratory for the processing of their seized hardware in search of evidence, they are at the mercy of the timing dictated by the laboratory. From my experience, a computer forensic laboratory can process anywhere from 30 to 60 cases per examiner per year; possibly more depending on the types of cases they work and their equipment, but considering most forensic laboratories are government agencies, I doubt they are operating year after year on the most current computers available. To make matters worse, the increase in the size of storage media has far outpaced the increases in processor power. The same $500 that could afford a 100MB drive in 1991 can now put a 750GB drive in your pocket. Compare that to a 50-MHz Intel from 1991, next to a 3-GHz processor in today's fastest computers, and you'll see that the cost effectiveness of hard drives grew 125 times faster than that of processors from 1991 to the present (Gilder, 2006). Depending on the backlog at the laboratory, investigators can be faced with waiting up to—and over—a year for the results of their examination to be returned from the lab.

I am unable to specifically quantify how delays in the forensic examination are impacting investigations and prosecutions, but I can offer my opinion that delays in the processing of digital evidence are one of the most significant impediments in investigations and prosecutions that have a digital-evidence nexus. Given the opportunity to perform an on-scene seizure of the relevant information versus being forced to wait one year for the results from the laboratory, the choice will be clear for many investigators. However, there are difficulties and challenges in seizing the information on-scene—but these challenges must be weighed against the time delay in receiving the processed evidence.

One investigator I interviewed about this type of situation described a child pornography possession case where there was a chance that the accused possessor was also creating and distributing images of child sexual abuse. Unfortunately, the investigator had no means to preview the digital information on-scene, nor back at the department, nor did the investigator have the ability to perform a digital information analysis in-house. The computer was sent off to a computer forensics laboratory, where it sat in the queue behind other just-as-important cases. Because the information could not be reviewed, the investigator had no evidence to substantiate the drafting of an arrest warrant for either the possession of child pornography or the child sexual abuse.

In such cases, any delay caused by a backlog at a forensics laboratory not only impacts an investigation, but also has a direct effect on a (potential) victim and continued victimization.

Protecting the Time of the Most Highly Trained Personnel

Digital devices have become almost completely ubiquitous in our current society. The legends of "convergence" are slowly coming true, where the line between computers, cell pones, cameras, and so on is now fuzzy and may disappear altogether in the future. IPv6 looms on the horizon and promises to equip every device, from cars to toasters, with an IP address. How do we find the time to train our law enforcement community in an entirely new set of skills? What is the balance between knowing enough and making a specialist out of everyone?

Determining whether the individual data objects with evidentiary value are seized or the storage media is seized will likely depend on the technical prowess of the responding investigator. The best situation would be to have a team of highly trained digital evidence seizure specialists respond and then properly prepare a Windows computer for seizure. The reality is that there will never be enough computer specialists to respond to every crime scene—let alone a "team" of them—to seize every piece of information or computer involved either directly or peripherally in a crime.

Looking forward, we can anticipate that the number of computers and other electronic devices requiring seizure and examination to surely increase. Clearly, from all accounts of the situation, the current methodology has its flaws. Delays in the examination of seized digital media are frustrating investigators and are impacting prosecutions. Although we clearly need more computer forensic specialists, do we have the resources—specifically the personnel, time, and money—to train and equip enough specialists to meet the current demand for seizures and exams? What about future demands? From what I have observed, I don't believe we have anywhere near the number of qualified personnel to address the current issues, let alone what the future will hold. Nor do I believe that the existing infrastructure can support the required increase in the number of computer forensic examiners or specialists. Most agencies fight for the addition of a single position—so I'm doubtful that the system will suddenly change and begin hiring scores of new personnel.

The situation comes down to a simple law of economics: productivity will only be increased by adding more people or making existing people more efficient. We don't really have the ability to throw more people at the problem, so the only option is to do more with the people we have. As it pertains to cyber crimes and crimes with a high-technology component, this means we cannot continue to rely on computer specialists for every aspect of an investigation that involves a computer. Every law enforcement agent, from on-scene responders to detectives performing investigations, now have a duty to begin to pick up the slack that has created the conflict between the large—and growing—number of crimes with a high-technology component and the relatively small number of specialists available to work these types of cases. We need to consider the computer specialists and the computer forensic laboratories as a finite resource, and any constructive work performed in the field by patrol officers or detectives reduces the strain on the forensic system. *With this view, the most valued resource is the time of the highest-trained individuals* (see Figure 7.3).

The general scenario of protecting the time of the most highly trained individuals so that they may focus on the most important issues is not a new concept. Those trained in hazardous material response work under a pyramid-like distribution of knowledge; the wide base of the pyramid consists of awareness-level trained people, while the small tip of the pyramid consists of highly trained specialists. Not only are these training levels generally accepted within the hazardous material response community, but they are codified in 29 CFR 1910.120(q)(6). The training code establishes the general level of knowledge, the hours of required training, and what can be expected from responders that have achieved each of the training levels. Because the different training levels are clearly defined, each responder on-scene understands their role and, more importantly, the role of other responders. Those with awareness-level training are taught to basically recognize that something bad has happened, call for help and watch from a distance with binoculars. Operations-level training prepares responders to respond in a defensive fashion, without attempting to stop the release. Technician-level responders are trained to attempt to stop hazardous material release, and specialist-level responders usually have specific knowledge pertaining to a particular chemical. At each level, the responder receives more training to be better pre-pared when responding to a scene.

At the current time, it would not be practical to attempt to regulate or codify the training requirements or duties of those involved in digital evidence seizure, but it is important to recognize that people of different training levels will likely approach seizure in different ways.

The seizure methodology that is developed for the knowledge level of the non-technical responder is in direct conflict with the best possible seizure scenario. Any seizure methodology adopted by an agency must be fluid enough to allow a minimally trained responder and a highly trained responder to both seize the digital information in the manner most applicable to their knowledge level.

Figure 7.3 Digital Evidence Seizure

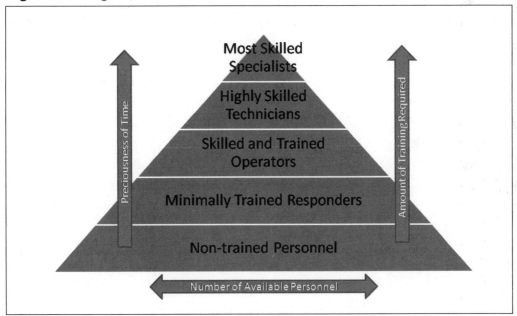

The Concept of the First Responder

Who exactly is the "First Responder" referenced in numerous digital evidence seizure guidelines and reports? Is the first responder simply the person that happens to be on-scene first? If yes, then the first responder could be any line officer. If every first responder needs to be trained to seize digital evidence, and we acknowledge that the seizure methodology will be necessarily fluid based on the responder's technical knowledge, you begin to see the problems involved with designing one particular training for first responders.

A second issue is the number of hours of training that could be allotted for first responder training. Will the administration of an organization allow their personnel to take a half-day course on digital evidence seizure? Probably. Realistically, though, what could you cover in four hours of instruction? I would guess the limit would be the recognition of digital evidence. So, would a two- or three-day training be sufficient to cover the recognition of digital evidence plus the seizure of digital information? Possibly, but would the people attending that training still be considered first responders or would the additional training necessitate they become specialists in this area? I am doubtful an agency's administration would agree to send every line officer to a three-day training to be first responders.

We are clearly caught in a catch-22. All line officers need to be able to seize digital evidence, but the first responder–level of training may not fully equip the officers to seize the evidence. The level of training required to more completely understand the digital evidence seizure process may involve multiple days of training, and multiple days of training on a single topic will most likely not be provided to all line officers. Unfortunately, it is not as simple as identifying one cadet in the academy that will specialize in investigating crimes with a cyber component, and putting this cadet through weeks of specialized training. The ubiquity of computers and digital evidence make the training of one single person insignificant—everyone's expertise needs to be raised to allow the specialists to focus on more technically challenging crimes.

There will be no clear-cut answer to this dilemma, but a number of factors could help mitigate the issue. First, law enforcement officers need more training in general computer skills. During a law enforcement officer's daily work, which is more likely? Arrest a suspect, be involved in a shooting, or spend some time working at a computer? The answer is a no-brainer—computers are an integral part of the law enforcement landscape and most officers cannot go a day without having some level of mission-critical interaction with a computer. However, the general level of computer knowledge among law enforcement personnel is low, and use of a computer is rarely a focus of academy setting. Providing law enforcement with basic, fundamental computer skills would not only impact their views toward digital evidence, but would also positively impact their daily work activities.

Second, all law enforcement personnel should receive basic awareness–level training on digital evidence. Awareness-level training need only cover the basics of a computer and where digital evidence may be stored. It is important for all officers to recognize that storage media, particularly flash-based media, may be no larger than a postage stamp, yet possibly contain several gigabytes of information. Understanding that many seemingly single-purpose devices, such as cell phones or mp3 players, may contain other types of information—for example, documents may be stored on an mp3 player—will have important investigative implications far beyond simple search and seizure concerns. Perhaps the next time a drug dealer is arrested with a PSP, you may want to search him for a small flash media card—as a dealer, his contact list might be accessed from the flash card on the PSP. Until a more uniform level of basic knowledge and awareness is reached among law enforcement, it is hard to speculate how the increased awareness will benefit investigations. But as the saying goes, you miss 100 percent of the shots you don't take, and more appropriately, you miss 100 percent of the evidence you don't look for.

Third, any seizure methodology developed and/or adopted by an agency must be fluid to allow for seizures to be conducted by both minimally trained individuals as well as highly trained specialists. Do you want to put your specialist on the spot when he breaks protocol to perform a function that is technically more appropriate? Conversely, do you want the specialist to be on-scene at every warrant service, arrest, or vehicle search? There must be options within the methodology that allow each officer to act reasonably according to his or her skill level.

Other Options for Seizing Digital Evidence

The wholesale seizure of the physical storage device/media is arguably the most common form of seizure practiced by law enforcement responders today. The question remains, are there other options besides the seizure of physical devices that are available to responders? If yes, are these methods of seizure within the reach of anyone but the most technical of responders?

For a long time, up to and including today, many in the forensics community place little faith in the ability of responders on-scene to deal appropriately with the computers they may encounter. The direction was simply "Don't touch the keyboard. Pull the plug and send everything to the lab." In many cases, the forensics side of the house is correct to protect against the possible corruption or destruction of data by taking this hard-line approach—particularly based on the technology of yesterday—but at what cost? Although the computer forensics community might have intended to do the most good by promulgating the pull-the-plug mantra, we need to examine how disempowering the on-scene responders may affect the overall forensic process, from seizure through analysis to investigation and ultimately prosecution.

The latest *Search and Seizure of Computers and Obtaining Digital Evidence* (Manual), published by the Department of Justice supports the proposition that the seizure of digital evidence should be an incremental process, based both on the situation and the training level of the responder. The Manual describes an incremental approach as a search strategy (pg. 221) for the seizure of digital evidence from a functioning company where the wholesale seizure of all the computers from the company would be impractical.

The Manual provides the following steps in its incremental approach:

1. After arriving on-scene, Agents will attempt to identify a systems administrator or similar person who would be willing to assist law enforcement in identifying, copying and/or printing out copies of the relevant files or data objects defined in the warrant.

2. If there are no company employees available to assist the Agent, the Agent will ask a computer expert to attempt to locate the computer files described in the warrant and will attempt to make electronic copies of those files. It is assumed that if the Agent is an expert, he/she would be able to proceed with the retrieval of the evidence.

3. If the Agent or expert are unable to retrieve the files, or if the onsite search proves infeasible for technical reasons, then the next option is

to create an image of those parts of the computer that are likely to store the information described in the warrant.

4. If imaging proves impractical or impossible for technical reasons, then the Agent is to seize those components and storage media that the Agent reasonably believes includes the information described in the warrant.

The Manual has a focus on Federal law enforcement and the incremental search strategy is described in the context of responding to a functioning business where evidence of a crime may reside on the business's systems—hence, the focus in the Manual on gaining assistance from the business's systems administrator. Even though, realistically, you are not going to ask the suspect for help in retrieving the files of interest, there is good reason to expand this incremental search strategy to the search and seizure of digital information that resides on non-business systems. First, many home users set up networks similar to what would be present in a small business. Second, the amount of storage on a home network may exceed the amount of storage used for business purposes, as home users are more likely to possess large music and movie files. Lastly, current and impending technologies such as whole disk encryption make the offsite analysis of storage media impractical, if not impossible. A mechanism must be developed now that enables responders to pull evidence off of a running system before these types of systems are in widespread use. Otherwise, we may be changing the paradigm a few years too late.

Although the change in focus from hardware-as-evidence to information-as-evidence may be a radical departure from how many people currently view digital evidence, it is not exactly a new viewpoint. In fact, the change to a focus on the information as evidence may be a renaissance of sorts; the computer crime investigators of yesterday knew nothing other than the retrieval of relevant information from servers and networks. Much of the investigation of computer crime in a historic context related to examining events that occurred within a network infrastructure. In his book from the pre-World-Wide-Web year of 1990, *Spectacular Computer Crimes*, Buck Bloombecker discusses numerous computer crimes, most of which involve attacks on the network infrastructure (virus, worm) or schemes that were enabled by the presence of a network infrastructure, such as stealing unauthorized computer time or manipulating the wire transfer system to steal bank funds.

As was discussed in Chapter 2, "'Computer Crime' Discussed," crimes with a cyber component changed dramatically following the personal computing revolution, which was hand-in-hand with the rise of the World Wide Web. Prior to the 1990s, few people with personal computers used them solely for personal purposes. Prior to the 2000s, few people were providing personal information about themselves for the world to view. So it's not surprising that when we take a look backward, we see that the investigation of cyber crime involved incident response tasks, like pulling logs and records off of servers and other infrastructure-level digital devices, and less often concerned the seizure of a personal computer. Wholesale duplication of servers was impractical, storage costs were high, and so it was cost prohibitive to attempt to pull together the necessary equipment to image the entire server. Although the investigators of the time were breaking new ground, they knew enough to document their actions, make best efforts not to change the data objects with evidentiary value, and image the relevant data objects so they could be printed or referred to at a later date. Responders to network intrusion events were faced with no other option but to seize the relevant data objects—which is still the case today.

Responding to a Victim of a Crime Where Digital Evidence Is Involved

There is an old saying that all politics are local politics. Although I'm not quite convinced of the particular weight of that adage, I do believe that all crime is local crime. The Internet may have created a global community, but crime, even crimes committed over the Internet, will be reported to a local agency. It is imperative that local agencies have the ability to field a complaint regarding a crime with a cyber component and be able to respond appropriately. I have heard horror stories where complaints of e-mail harassment, auction fraud, and other crimes with a cyber component were just ignored by a local agency. Yes, a statement was taken and a report prepared, but no follow-up investigation was conducted. Worse, I have heard of agencies telling victims that the investigation of their complaint involved the seizure of their machine for forensic analysis, and that the analysis might take over a year to complete. I think it's pretty obvious why the complaint was dropped.

The unfortunate part of the situation is that the responding officer (or local agency) places an improper focus on the technology and loses sight of the crime that occurred. Often, the technology used is secondary and of little relevance. It could be quite possible that harassing statements in an e-mail might be coming from someone the victim already knew. If the harassment occurred through some other non-seizeable, non-virtual means (for example, spray paint on a car), the officer would most likely follow up with a knock-and-talk with the suspect. The follow-up on the e-mail harassment should use the same logic. Does the investigation need to be focused on tracing an e-mail to its source when you already have a good idea as to who sent the e-mail? It is important that investigators do not switch off their investigative skills because a computer is involved.

When you are responding to a victim, the focus must be on having the victim provide the law enforcement officer with something that substantiates their complaint—a print-out of the harassing e-mail with full header information, a cut-and-paste printout of the IM conversation where their child was sexually solicited, or a screen-print of a disturbing Web page. Any information that can be provided by the victim to a responding officer will increase efficiencies in the entire investigative process. The officer will be able to read the e-mail header and get preservation orders out to the ISPs; the detectives will be able to begin working the case, rather than securing another statement from the victim; and the computer forensics system won't be burdened by yet another machine requiring examination—particularly for data objects that could have reasonably been obtained on-scene.

Cases occur where the victim's computer must be seized. Harassments in e-mail or chat (when logging) that violate a protective order may have to be seized, depending on the situation. If a spouse or roommate finds child pornography on a computer, the computer should be seized since it contains contraband. But barring these unavoidable circumstances, the seizure of victim computers is often unnecessary and contributes to the logjam at the digital forensic laboratories.

When communicating with a victim, be sure you let them know to not delete anything on their system until their complaint has gone through the entire process. Also be quite sure to document the steps the victim took to provide you with the substantiating evidence. If you had to assist the victim in any way—maybe you showed them how to see full headers on an e-mail, for example—make sure those actions appear in the documentation. Make a note of the system time on the computer, and verify that the evidence contains a time and date stamp, and that the time and date make sense to the victim. Lastly, be responsive to the victim's needs. Many crimes with a cyber component—particularly frauds and thefts—will have an international component that makes the apprehension of a suspect and reimbursement to the victim nearly impossible. Be sympathetic and provide the victim with any resources that can assist them in dealing with banks, credit card companies, and creditors, such as a properly written police report. They have already been victimized; don't let your actions lead to a prolonging of the victimization.

Seizure Example

Here we will examine an example of a digital seizure to help explore the options available to on-scene responders. Let's start by saying that Sally receives a harassing e-mail from an anonymous sender. She believes it is a former co-worker named Sam, who has harassed Sally using non-computer-based methods before. The officer follows the guidance discussed in the "Responding to a Victim of a Crime Where Digital Evidence Is Involved" section and instructs Sally to print off a copy of the e-mail showing the full header information. Sally prints off the e-mail as substantiating proof to back up her complaint, and the officer leaves the scene with a statement from Sally and a copy of the harassing e-mail.

You notice that Sally was not told that her computer would need to be seized and held for a year—which would, in effect, cause Sally to drop her criminal complaint and also drop her opinion of the police. Instead, the officer leaves the victim scene with a statement, and some level of proof to back up the complaint, which allows the investigation to proceed without undue hardship to the victim.

The investigator then uses the information contained in the e-mail header to contact the e-mail provider, legal paperwork is sent to the provider looking for the account holder's information, and finally the e-mail is traced back to Sam's Internet service provider (ISP) account. We now have a general confirmation that the e-mail was sent from a computer connected to Sam's ISP account—although this could be any number of computers at Sam's house and possibly even be a neighbor using Sam's wireless access.

The investigator drafts a search warrant affidavit looking specifically for the information that is relevant to this case—specifically a preserved copy of the sent e-mail. The investigator is careful to focus the search warrant on the information to be seized, and does not focus on the containers or storage media in which the information may reside. The investigator further notes that an incremental approach will be used, which dictates that onsite seizures will occur when possible, but that factors yet to be determined may necessitate that all digital storage devices and media that may reasonably contain the sought after evidence may be seized for offsite review.

The investigator serves the warrant and finds a single computer at Sam's home. The system is on and, according to the suspect, has a Windows XP operating system. Based on the suspect's assertion that the computer is password-protected, and he has not given the password out to anyone, it is reasonable to believe that the computer is used solely by its owner. At this point, the on-scene investigator is staring at a glowing monitor with a happy desktop picture of calming fields and clouds, but the investigator is now faced with a few tough decisions. The computer appears to be running Windows XP, which corroborates the suspect's statement. Windows XP can survive a rapid power loss, so pulling the plug is an option, but pulling the plug means that the entire computer would need to be brought back to the computer forensics laboratory for examination. The investigator knows that the backlog at the computer forensics laboratory is approaching six months—way too long to determine if the suspect is stalking the victim. In six months, the stalking could escalate if there is no police intervention (depending on the type of stalker), and the victim could be physically assaulted. Further, the investigator knows that Windows XP is equipped with the Windows Encrypted File System, a seldom-used folder and file encryption system that, if enabled, would make the recovery of the information on the system very difficult without the suspect's cooperation.

The investigator thinks of other options at his disposal. The investigator could use a software preview tool in an attempt to locate the information stated in the warrant. In this case, Sam uses Microsoft Outlook as his local e-mail client, and a .pst file containing all the Outlook-related folders would exist on the system. This .pst should contain an e-mail in the sent items folder that matches the e-mail received by the victim. If the investigator had reason to believe there was information stored in the RAM that would be relevant to the case, the investigator could dump the RAM for later analysis. This might be the scenario if the investigator notices a draft of another e-mail currently on the screen. If the e-mail is found in the .pst during a preview, the entire drive could be imaged, or just the .pst could be imaged if the investigator has reason to believe that imaging the entire drive would be difficult.

In this example, maybe the investigator would decide to pull-the-plug and deliver it to the lab. Maybe the investigator believes there is enough evidence based on the victim's complaint to have the suspect come to the station for a talk about what is going on. But maybe the investigator's hair on the back of his neck rises up when talking to the suspect and the investigator gets a gut reaction about the level of urgency regarding the case. Maybe the on-scene preview and securing the .pst provides the investigator with enough evidence to take the suspect into custody. The important point is that without additional options to review the digital data, the investigator's hands are tied.

In line with the incremental approach described in the Manual, the investigator may have other options available besides wholesale seizure, such as:

- Previewing information on-scene
- Obtaining information from a running computer
- On-scene seizure of information through the complete imaging of the media
- On-scene seizure of information through the imaging of a specific data object

In the next section, we take a look at the preceding options and discuss how each fits into the larger picture of responding to and investigating crimes with digital evidence.

Previewing On-Scene Information to Determine the Presence and Location of Evidentiary Data Objects

The on-scene responder must make conclusions about where the information described in the warrant is most likely to be present on the storage device or media. In the case of a CD or DVD, the preview is much less complicated, as the chances of inadvertently writing to a piece of optical media are much lower than if they were working with magnetic-based media. With a CD or a DVD, the responder could use a forensics laptop running any number of computer forensic tools to quickly acquire and examine the contents of a CD or DVD for review. A similar process could be conducted for flash-based media, although a greater level of care may need to be taken to ensure the media is not changed. Here, flexibility is once again a critical characteristic. Previewing a few pieces of optical media on-scene may be appropriate, but greater numbers of media may need to be taken off-scene for review at the laboratory.

Technology exists that enables responders to preview the data on the storage media in an effort to locate the information described in the warrant. These "forensic preview software" packages, now in their infancy, are becoming more accepted within the community that investigates crimes involving a computer. The most common preview software packages come on CD and are essentially a Linux operating system that runs completely in the RAM and does not require any resources from the hard drive(s). Several of these disks are in current use by law enforcement, including Knoppix, Helix, and Spada. Several controlled boots will need to be performed to ensure the correct changes are made to the BIOS to direct the computer to boot from the CD. Although best practices should be determined locally, I recommend that the power to all the hard drives in desktop computers be disconnected and that laptop hard drives be removed while controlled boots are conducted to determine how to change the boot sequence in the BIOS. Further information on using controlled boots to examine and change BIOS and CMOS information can be found in the seizure procedures in the publication *Forensic Examination of Digital Evidence: A Guide for Law Enforcement* (NIJ, 2004).

Once the system is booted to the forensic preview software, the computer's hard drives can be mounted, or made available, in Linux as read-only. Once mounted, the preview software will provide the responder with an interface to either search for the desired information through keyword searches, or the responder can navigate through the directory tree in an attempt to locate a given file or directory. If the information described in the warrant is located during a preview, the responder may choose to image the specific data object, file, or folder where the information is located. The responder may also choose to seize the entire hard drive, now that the preview has provided him with a greater level of comfort that this particular "container" includes the desired information.

Over time, these forensic preview software packages will continue to evolve and develop as the problems with wholesale seizure become more evident and the need to focus the seizure of individual data objects from a digital crime scene becomes more apparent. It is hoped that the evolution of these tools will include the addition of features and special characteristics that make a tool "law enforcement specific." The lack of law enforcement specific features, such as intuitive interfaces, audit trail recordkeeping, and the production of evidence-quality data, are often an impediment to the adoption of commercial software by the law enforcement community (ISTS, 2004).

Obtaining Information from a Running Computer

If the investigator encounters a computer that is running, and the investigator believes there is information of evidentiary value stored in the computer's active memory, or RAM, there are options available that allow for the RAM to be recovered. For example, let's examine a situation where an investigator shows up on-scene at a location where a suspect has been chatting online with a minor or undercover officer. When the officers arrive at the scene, the suspect quickly closes the chat window. By default, many chat programs do not keep a log of the chat sessions and almost all of the actual chat activity happens in a portion of the program running in the computer's RAM. Without being able to obtain a *dump*, or download of the RAM, there would be little chance to obtain any information from the suspect's computer about the chat session that just occurred. Chatting is not the only type of data that would be held in RAM. Passwords, unsaved documents, unsaved drafts of e-mails, IM conversations, and so on could all be held in the RAM, and in no other place on the computer. The investigator needs to make a decision if the information described in the warrant would reasonably be found in the RAM of the computer. If the warrant describes information related to proof of embezzlement, there may be little reason to believe that the data held in the RAM would be relevant to the case. That is not to say that it isn't possible—but the responder needs to go through the process of determining the locations that have the highest probability of containing the information described in the warrant. Even if the suspect had worked on a relevant file and remnants of the same existed in the RAM, it would be logical to conclude that the file would be saved onto more permanent media, such as the hard drive. On the other hand, if the warrant detailed information related to inappropriate chat or instant messaging sessions, the RAM of the running computer would be the primary, and most likely the only, location where the information described in the warrant could exist. In this case, the use of a program such as Helix to "dump" the RAM to the responder's storage device would be a very high priority (Shipley, 2006).

Be careful about what you wish for, however, as the RAM dump could include several gigabytes of semi-random information. Pieces of documents, Registry keys, API calls, and a whole host of other garbage will be interwoven into a gigantic text file. Minimization still is a factor even when the RAM has been identified as being one of the locations where relevant data could exist—if the data might reside elsewhere, it may be more productive to go that route than to attempt to carve it from the RAM dump.

SEARCH, a national law enforcement training organization, recently published a primer on the collection of evidence from a running computer, which involves using preview software to obtain the contents of the RAM from a running machine before seizure (Shipley, 2006). SEARCH's article represents a departure from the norm in that the article recognizes that changes to the computer operating system will occur when a USB drive is inserted into the machine in order to receive the contents of the RAM. However, the important point highlighted by the SEARCH article is that the changes are known, explainable, and do not affect any information that has evidentiary value. "Hold on," you say, "moving the mouse and/or inserting a USB device will change the information on the suspect's drive, and that is strictly forbidden!" In response, I say that there are many in the investigative and legal communities that see little issue with a law enforcement agent performing operations that changed data on a suspect's hard drive or other media—as long as the agent acted in a reasonable manner and documented their actions appropriately. The firm and absolute stance that data cannot be changed needs to be examined to determine if our cases have been negatively affected by the promulgation of bad advice.

Imaging Information On-Scene

Imaging of an entire hard drive on-scene is fairly common among the more technically savvy digital crime scene responders—even more so for private sector investigators that often face cases where the hard drives need to be examined, but the business in question is not comfortable with letting the original drive out of their possession. In both of these cases, the analysis of the imaged drive usually occurs back at the laboratory. Rarely do you hear of a drive being both imaged and previewed on-scene—although such a process may actually address a number of concerns about the use of preview software to review the information on a drive while on-scene—specifically, performing a preview of the evidence on the original drive.

While the acquisition of an image of a drive on-scene may be fairly common among the more technically skilled, usually for corporate crimes, we find there is little use of this technique by less skilled personnel for low-level crimes. However, there are a number of good reasons to perform imaging on-scene for most computer crimes. First, as mentioned earlier, previews of the evidence can be performed on the imaged copy with less worry about the investigator inadvertently damaging information on the original hard drive. Second, in those instances where outside concerns prevent the seizure of the physical media, such as PPA concerns, third-party data, and multiple users of the computer, the imaging of the hard drive provides another option for the on-scene investigators.

Terminology Alert...

Imaging versus Copying and Hashes

It is important that the data on the suspect's hard drive be imaged to the destination drive/device rather than just copied. The process of imaging creates a bit-stream copy—or an exact copy of the 1s and 0s—of the information being copied. The regular copy function within the operating system will attempt to write the file according to its logical programming—meaning that the file being written to the drive could be spread across numerous clusters on the target drive. The point of imaging the data is that an exact replica of the data as it appears on the source drive is created on the destination drive—specifically the exact order of the bits (the 1s and 0s) on the drive—hence, the term *bit stream copy*. Because imaging preserves the exact order of the bits from the original to the copy, hash functions are able to be run against the entire chunk of the source drive, which is then imaged and compared against the exact replica created on the destination drive. Image hashing allows the responder to mathematically prove that the data that exists on the source drive is exactly the same on the destination drive. Some claim that a few of the hash algorithms (like the MD5 hash algorithm) have been cracked. This is technically true; however, the circumstances for collisions—two different files that generate the same MD5 hash—were specifically created to prove that collisions can occur. The chances of an MD5 hash collision occurring during the comparison of a source drive and an improperly imaged drive would be unbelievably small. I would feel very confident that a hash match between two files/images that are supposed to match to be proof that the two files/images are in fact an exact copy. I feel even stronger about the validity of the next generation of hash algorithms, including SHA1, SHA-256, or SHA-512.

Imaging Finite Data Objects On-Scene

In the current law enforcement climate, there is little discussion of the seizure of particular pieces of information. Generally, the entire computer is seized—

and the seized computer is usually called "evidence." The data contained within the computer are reviewed at a later date for any files or other pieces of information that can help prove or disprove a given premise. From an outsider's perspective, it would appear as if the seizure of the entire computer is the preferred method of obtaining the evidentiary information, but we've established that imaging on-scene is fairly well accepted within the digital investigative community. So, are there other options that include the seizure of a finite number of data objects as evidence?

If we can image the entire hard drive on-scene, there is an argument that we can image sections of it. We routinely ask companies and ISPs to do just that when we ask them to preserve evidence of a crime—rarely do we seize the ISP's servers, nor do we ask them to provide an image of the entire server so a computer forensics exam can be performed. Are there reasons why we can't use the same logic when responding to a suspect? The larger question is whether this type of seizure is appropriate. Are there circumstances when a finite amount of information is needed to prove guilt, and the seizure of the original hard drive is not an option? This discussion is very similar to the previous discussion regarding imaging the entire drive on-scene in situations where the physical media cannot be seized. There may also be situations where a finite piece of information would suffice to move the case forward. In these situations, the seizure of a finite number of data objects may be a viable option for responders.

In our case example discussed earlier, where Sam is accused of stalking Sally, let's assume that an arrest warrant hinged on the presence of the harassing e-mail on Sam's computer. If the preview of the computer showed that the e-mail in question existed on Sam's computer, and the investigator had the ability to image the .pst file that contained the e-mail, the investigator could take Sam into custody at this time and have all the evidence needed to wrap up the case. There would be no need to add yet another machine to the computer forensic backlog, and the investigation could be wrapped up immediately, rather than having to wait weeks to months for a completed forensic review.

NOTE

The focus on the seizure of data objects discussed within the other options section does not transfer well to the seizure of computers suspected of containing child pornography. It is strongly recommended that guidance on the seizure of computers containing child pornography be obtained from the Internet Crimes Against Children (ICAC) Task Forces. This network of 46+ law enforcement agencies specializes in the investigation and prosecution of crimes against children facilitated by computer. Additional information about ICAC can be found at www.icactraining.org.

I can hear you yelling "WAIT! What if I think he might have child pornography on his computer?" Good question. If the warrant for the case specifies that the investigator can search for and seize the sent e-mail in question, then it would be hard to justify why the investigator spent all day looking through the suspect's vacation pictures for possible images of child pornography. A warrant for the seizure of a given piece of information that results in the seizure of a computer, or other digital storage device, does not give the law enforcement agent carte blanche to look through every file on the computer. As it relates to the child pornography question, if the investigator believes there is evidence of child pornography on the computer, the investigator is better off obtaining a warrant for the suspected child pornography rather than to search for evidence of one crime under the pretenses of another crime.

That is not to say there aren't instances when you may stumble across evidence of a different crime when reviewing digital information. Should the occasion arise when you are looking for one type of information under a specific warrant, and inadvertently find evidence of another crime, the legal guidance is that you should immediately stop the review and obtain a second warrant to search for evidence of the second crime. It is theoretically possible that you could finish examining the computer under the first warrant, and not specifically search for items pertaining to the newly discovered crime. However, that strategy is not recommended.

But do we have the tools necessary to enable us to copy-off only the relevant data objects? Can this be done within a reasonable time frame? From a technologist's viewpoint, the technology is often more flexible than the legal framework within which the technology operates. The current technology allows us to search very rapidly through thousands of pages of information for keywords, a feat that would be all but impossible with paper records. But much of the specialized computer forensic tools are designed to be used in a forensic laboratory environment and not for on-scene response. These powerful forensic tools often require a fair amount of time to analyze and process the information on a target drive. Often, these laboratory examinations involve tools that may take hours to complete a given function, and the review of information often involves hours of pouring through documents and graphics. If we consider that "time" is one of the most limiting factors when conducting on-scene analysis, there is definitely a conflict between the best technical analysis that could be performed and the time frame in which a reasonable on-scene analysis should be completed.

The seizure of data objects from large servers while in the course of investigating network intrusion cases is fairly common and accepted, but it is difficult to tell if the seizure of data objects will become more common in the everyday investigator's response toolkit. Although there appears to be a general legal and technological framework within which data object seizure can occur, it is still difficult to swallow the fact that the original evidence will be left behind. The use of this technique on business computers and networks follows the argument that the business is a disinterested third party, and that if relevant data is missed, the investigator can go back and retrieve additional information because the business has no desire to interfere with the investigation. But would a spouse or roommate constitute a disinterested third party with regards to data on their computer? Can we develop tools that give the investigator a greater level of comfort regarding the thoroughness of the on-scene previewing/review? These questions, and others that will spring from discussions like this, will shape the way in which this technique, and the other options presented earlier, become accepted or rejected by the digital evidence response community.

Use of Tools for Digital Evidence Collection

Where the computer forensics of yesterday relied on vary basic tools that allowed manual manipulation of the seized data objects, we have since developed tools that assist in the acquisition, organization, and examination of the data. Both the ubiquity of electronic information and the sheer volume of seized digital information have necessitated the use of tools to assist in the investigative process. Hardware and software write blockers and hard-drive duplication devices have reduced the chances of damaging the information on source drives. Tools beyond simple hex editors and command-line scripts were developed to assist the examiner in performing keyword searches, sorting data objects by file type and category, and scouring the source disk for file remnants in file slack space and drive free space. Tools like Autopsy Browser, SMART, iLook, Encase, and Forensic Toolkit are dramatic departures from manual command-line searching and have had a significant impact on the efficiency in which large volumes of data are examined. These tools have also increased the accessibility of digital evidence to those outside of the closed circle of highly trained forensic examiners.

The way in which digital information is analyzed has changed over the years—obviously driven by the ever-increasing amount of information stored digitally. But other changes have been driven by the increase in our knowledge of how to work with digital evidence—most notably in the development of tools to assist in different phases of the investigative and forensic process. The use of software and hardware tools by on-scene responders can begin to address how we work toward achieving a greater level of data object seizure. Current tools, such as ImageMasster and Helix, begin to enable an on-scene responder to image an entire drive and to seize the contents of the RAM. Other tools in this domain provide some capacity to preview the contents of a suspect drive and to image only the necessary information, as has been the case for years in the incident response disciplines.

Some will argue that no one should use a tool if they cannot explain exactly what the tool is doing. In the computer forensics realm, this often translates to "no one should use a tool if they cannot perform, by hand, the operations that the tool is performing." There is a fair amount of disagreement on this position. The law enforcement community commonly uses tools where they can explain the basic principal, but not the exact manner in which the tool is accomplishing its task. For example, when an officer is trained on the use of the radar gun, she is taught the principals of the Doppler Effect and how the tool records the very precise timings between the sending of a radar impulse and the receipt of the reflected radar energy. The officer would also be shown how the unit is tested and calibrated to ensure reliability. In this way, the officer understands generally how the tool works—it is not reasonable to instruct them on how to construct the device, nor should the officer be required to manually calculate how the speed of a vehicle is determined from recorded radar signals in order to be a proficient operator of the tool.

That is not to say that we should be able to use any tool without accountability. Tools that are used in the seizure or analysis of digital evidence must be tested. This testing is commonly performed by the organization using the tool—since the tool must be tested within the parameters of the agency's protocols—but larger tool verification efforts are underway at the National Institute for Standards and Technology (NIST). NIST has created tool testing specifications for disk imaging tools, physical and software write blockers, and deleted file recovery programs. A number of products have been tested under this program, and the results look very promising. Almost all of the programs or devices tested actually work as purported. That's not to say there are not issues with the NIST program. Technology changes faster than the standards development and tool testing processes, and the overall number of standards developed through the NIST program has been, unfortunately, small.

However, placing tools at the disposal of the greater law enforcement community has some significant impacts related to the overall model that we follow when working with digital evidence: If we are able to train officers/investigators on the proper use of a given tool, and the tool has passed muster through testing under a given protocol, whether at their local agency or at the NIST, then the officer/investigator is empowered to take an active role in the recovery of digital evidence and in the investigation on the whole.

It is clear that we do not have all the answers to the technological hurdles worked out, but the technology is often not the limited factor, as was discussed earlier. Understanding that the technology will forever be changing and advancing, the legal community must begin to play an active role in providing the technologists with direction and boundaries. The technologists need to heed the legal guidance, examine how future issues will affect law enforcement, and begin designing tools that will provide a critical edge to the good guys.

Common Threads within Digital Evidence Seizure

The landscape of potential seizure environments is complicated and variations are nearly infinite. The level of knowledge of the on-scene responders includes a wide range of skills and abilities. Because the seizure process will be greatly impacted by the particular hardware and software arrangements and knowledge of the on-scene responder, it is not possible to present one correct way to seize digital evidence, unfortunately. What does exist is a continuum of methods mapped against the complexity of the scene versus the skill of the responders.

There are, however, basic threads that tie any seizure process together. The first thread is that you must be able to explain what steps you took to arrive at a particular destination. It does not matter if you come out of a building with a floppy disk or an entire network, you should be able to replicate each step in the process. If you were presented with an exact replica of the scene, you should be able to refer to your notes and do everything exactly the same from arriving on-scene, to collecting the evidence, to walking out the door. In order to achieve this level of enlightenment, there are two sub-threads: (1) Document everything—and I mean everything. Have one person process the scene while the other one writes down every single, mind-numbing step. The documentation should be as complete as practically possible. If one is working alone in the seizure process, consider using a voice recorder and narrate each step for later transcription. The exact steps taken in the process become doubly important if and when the target computer is manipulated in any way—for instance, moving the mouse to deactivate the screen-saver, or initiating a shutdown sequence. (2) Confucius is attributed to saying: "To know that you know what you know, and that you do not know what you do not know, that is true knowledge." Translated for relevance for the second sub-thread here, it means that if you don't know what you are doing (or worse, what you just did…), or aren't really comfortable with determining the next steps, *stop*, and revert to a less technical seizure method, or seek assistance from someone more qualified. Your knowledge will be judged by your ability to know what you don't know—when to stop—over the knowledge you do possess.

The second thread is that you should seek the seizure method that best minimizes the digital crime scene. If you can reasonably come up with an "area"—meaning drive, directory, file, and so on—where you believe the evidence will be located, it makes the most sense to look in that specific location for the digital evidence. Limiting or minimizing the crime scene has different implications based on whether the search for digital evidence is occurring on-scene, at the station, or back at the forensic laboratory. On-scene, minimization may include excluding professionally produced and labeled CDs from the seizure. Minimization may also include the use of software tools to preview the contents of a computer for a specific data object. Offsite minimization efforts may include searching only certain keywords or examining only a given file type. Even given our ability to search for and find most anything on a computer, we must remember that not every fact is relevant, and analyses that are 100-percent comprehensive do not exist. At the heart of minimization is the ability to know when to stop while looking for digital evidence.

The third thread is that whatever is seized as having potential evidentiary value must be authenticated by the court before it can be admitted into the case. The ability for the court to authenticate the evidence is a significant issue related to digital evidence. Authentication is governed by the Federal Rules of Evidence Rule 901 (28 U.S.C.), which states "The requirement of authentication or identification as a condition precedent to admissibility is satisfied by evidence sufficient to support a finding that the matter in question is what its proponent claims." The salient point of the definition for our discussions is that digital evidence can be authenticated by providing evidence that shows that it is in fact what it is purported to be. I realize that is a bit of cyclical logic—so let's break down the authentication process further for clarification.

Evidence presented to the court can be authenticated a number of ways, including the identification of distinctive characteristics or by merely what type of evidence it is, as is the case for public records. Evidence may also be authenticated by way of testimony to the fact that the matter in question is what it is claimed to be. Courts have upheld the authentication of documents based on testimony (U.S. v. Long, C.A.8 [Minn.] 1988, 857 F.2d 436, habeas corpus denied 928 F.2d 245, certiorari denied 112 S.Ct. 98, 502 U.S. 828, 116 L.Ed.2d 69).

However, in the past, computer forensics has relied less on the testimony of those performing the on-scene seizure and more on the testimony of the computer forensic technician. Where the on-scene responder would be able to testify as to where the hardware was located before seizure, the computer forensic technician would take the position to defend their laboratory techniques. The computer forensics community chose to address the authentication issue by creating exact duplicates of the seized digital information and proving mathematically that the copied information was an exact copy of the seized information—and the courts have supported the position that a duplicate of the information can be submitted in lieu of the original when it can be proved that the duplicate is the same extant as the original (U.S. v. Stephenson, C.A.5 [Tex.] 1989, 887 F.2d 57, certiorari denied 110 S.Ct. 1151, 493 U.S. 1086, 107 L.Ed.2d 1054).

As it relates to our options for seizure discussed earlier, there are two salient points for discussion. The first is that the seized data—whether from a RAM dump or as a result of the creation of an image of the drive or file—may be authenticated by the testimony of the investigator that retrieved the evidence from the suspect machine. If the case involved a child pornography photograph, and the investigator saw the photograph during a preview, the investigator may be able to assert that the recovered photograph is the same photograph he saw during a preview. The second point is that the creation and matching of mathematical hashes provides a very high level of proof that the recovered data is an exact copy of the original. Although the best evidence rule states that the original should be provided whenever possible, *U.S. v. Stephenson*, noted earlier, shows that an exact duplicate is satisfactory when circumstances limit the production of the original evidence in court. Hard drives, the most commonly encountered type of storage media, are mechanical devices, and all mechanical devices will fail at some point—perhaps after days, months, or decades—but they will fail. By working off of a copy of the seized drive, and presenting the same in court, the investigator is reducing the chances of completely losing all of the data on the seized drive. Taking steps to reduce the complete loss of the digital information relating to the case is but one of the reasons to justify the use of exact copies over the original data.

The final thread is the admissibility of the evidence. The admissibility of evidence is based on the authentication, and the authentication is based on the proof that the seized object is materially unchanged—proof that can be accomplished by showing a complete chain of custody (*U. S. v. Zink*, C.A.10 [Colo.] 1980, 612 F.2d 511). For digital evidence, the proof that the data is what it purports to be and is unchanged has been accomplished by both testimony and use of the cryptographic hash algorithms. Similar to how the forensic laboratory technician uses the hash function to show that the entire seized drive was copied accurately, the on-scene responder can refer to their detailed notes to testify as to the location of the seized information and show that the hash functions proved that the integrity of the data was not compromised during imaging.

Determining the Most Appropriate Seizure Method

Clearly, there will be cases where the most appropriate action is to seize all the physical hardware at a suspect's location. Perhaps it is the only option that the minimally trained responder has at their disposal. Maybe the forensic preview software didn't support the graphics card for the computer. It's possible that additional keyword searches need to be performed or items need to be carved from drive free space, and both would be better performed in a controlled laboratory environment. There are any number of reasons why the on-scene responder will choose to seize the physical container, and that's ok! The important point is that the most appropriate method of seizure is chosen to match the responder's skill level, and that it appropriately addresses the type of crime.

The minimization stage may provide the investigator with the places—computers, storage media, and so on—that have the highest probability of containing the desired information. A preview on-scene may verify that the information exists. In cases of child pornography possession, the on-scene preview may allow the investigator to take the suspect into custody right at that moment—or at least have some very frank discussions about the material found on the computer. The case may be provided to a prosecutor with just the previewed images, and discussions of sentences and pleas can occur immediately, instead of having to wait for a complete forensics examination. If the case is referred to trial, the full forensic analysis of the seized computer can be conducted at that time. On the other hand, maybe a full examination of the data should be conducted to determine if the suspect has produced any new images of child pornography—information that is critical in determining if an active victimization is occurring and is critical to the overall fight against this type of crime. *This simple scenario shows how the incremental approach and the seizure options discussed earlier are needed so as to even begin to get a foothold on crimes with a cyber component, but that circumstances may force investigators to throw out the incremental approach in favor of a complete examination.*

There are a few other key points relating to physical seizure. The first is that the entire computer will be needed by the laboratory to determine the system time and other settings related to the motherboard. If you plan on only seizing the hard drive, imaging the hard drive on-scene, or only imaging relevant information, follow the methodology outlined by NIJ in the *Forensic Examination of Digital Evidence* (NIJ, 2004) to use controlled boots to record the system time versus a trusted time source.

The second key point is that there are many computers and laptops that do not allow for easy access to the hard drives—which would make any attempts to image on-scene impractical and, as a result, require seizure of the hardware. For example, some laptop designs require the majority of the laptop to be disassembled to gain access to the hard drive. I strongly recommend that the disassembly of laptops or other hardware take place in a controlled laboratory or shop environment—there are just way too many little pieces and screws, often with unusual head designs, to be attempting a disassembly on-scene. In these cases, the physical seizure of the computer itself may be required even if you came prepared to image on-scene.

The third key point is that there may be other nondigital evidence that could reside with the physical computer. Items such as sticky notes can be found stuck to a monitor; passwords or Web addresses can be written in pencil or marker on the computer enclosure; or items may be taped to the bottom of a keyboard or hidden inside the computer itself. I remember one story of a criminal that hid his marijuana stash inside the computer; the wife asserted that he had child pornography on the computer and the computer examiner—and wife—were amazed when bags of marijuana were found inside the computer enclosure.

One last note: Don't turn off the investigative part of your brain while conducting the seizure. Use all the investigative techniques you learned in the academy and employ during the execution of physical search warrants. You will get much further in the case if you use information from one source (computer/suspect) to gain more information from the other source (suspect/computer)—but remember that Miranda rights may be applicable when having discussions with the suspect.

Summary

There is no doubt that the investigators of tomorrow will be faced with more digital information present in greater numbers and types of devices. Seizing the relevant evidentiary information is, and will continue to be, a critical step in the overall computer forensics process. The current view that the physical hardware is the evidence has now been joined by a different view that the information can be regarded as evidence—whether the hardware or information is viewed as evidence has a dramatic effect on how we "seize" or "collect" evidence both at the scene and in the forensics laboratory.

A number of factors may limit the continued wholesale seizure of the physical hardware. The storage size of the suspect's computer hard drive or storage network may exceed an investigator's ability to take everything back to the forensics laboratory. Full disk encryption, now released as part of the Windows Vista operating system, may foil an investigator's ability to recover any data without the proper encryption key. Further, concerns over commingled and third-party data, covered by the Privacy Protection Act, may impact the ability of an investigator to seize more data than specified in the warrant. Lastly, the increasing amount of seized digital evidence is having an effect on the ability of many of the computer forensics laboratories to complete forensic analyses in a timely manner. Both investigations and prosecutions may be suffering because of delays in the processing of digital evidence.

While the existing seizure methodology is focused on the seizure of hardware, investigators need to be able to select the most appropriate option for seizure according to the situation and their level of technical expertise. There are other seizure options that could be considered by the digital evidence response community. On-site previews using Linux- or Windows-based bootable CDs allow an investigator to review the contents of a suspect's computer in a relatively forensically sound manner. Techniques exist to dump the RAM of a suspect's computer to attempt to recover any information that may be stored in RAM but not written to disk, such as passwords, chat sessions, and unsaved documents. Imaging on-scene is yet another option available to investigators. Full disk imaging—where a complete bit-by-bit copy of a hard drive is created on a black drive—is more common and is currently used by a fair number of investigators. Less common is the imaging of select data objects that have evidentiary value. While still controversial, there appears to be a legal and technological framework that makes the imaging of data objects a viable option.

Clearly, there will always be more digital evidence than we can process within our existing organizational and governmental structures. Having more trained examiners in the field does not always equate to more trained examiners in the understaffed laboratories or out in the field. The *time* of the most highly trained personnel is one of our most precious resources. There is no possible way that the limited number of specialists can process electronic evidence at every scene. Not only would they not be able to cover every scene, the laboratory work would undoubtedly suffer. In order to protect the time of the most highly trained and specialized people, those with less technical knowledge need to receive some level of training that allows them to perform a number of duties normally performed by the specialist. In this way, knowledge and high-technology investigative skills are pushed-down to all levels of responder. That is not to say that *training for first responder* isn't plagued with problems—the knowledge required to properly deploy advanced tools often exceeds the amount of time allotted for such training. We're caught in a catch-22: all line officers need to be able to seize digital evidence, but the first responder level of training may not fully equip the officers to seize the evidence, and the level of training required to more completely understand the digital evidence seizure process may involve multiple days of training, and multiple days of training on a single topic will most likely not be provided to all line officers.

The level of training will affect the responder's use of technology, and the technology encountered will dictate whether the responder's level of training is appropriate in a given situation. There will be cases where the most appropriate action is to seize all the physical hardware at a suspect location. Perhaps it is the only option that the minimally trained responder has at their disposal, or maybe the technology encountered is so complex that none of the responders know exactly how to handle the seizure.

As it stands now, the forensic collection and analysis system works—sometimes tenuously, and frequently at a snail's pace—however, we will undoubtedly continue to face more change: change coming in the way of new devices, higher levels of inter-connectivity, and the ever-increasing amounts of data storage requiring examination. Will the existing manner in which we go about seizing and examining digital information be sufficient in five years? Ten years? Are there changes we can institute now in the way we address digital evidence that will better position us to face the coming changes?

I hope throughout this chapter that I made myself clear that I am not advocating any one seizure methodology over another—the critical take-away point is that we need to provide our responders with options to choose the appropriate seizure method based on their level of technical skill and the situation at hand. I have found in my work with law enforcement in New Hampshire, as well as throughout the nation, that crimes that involve a computer closely map to crimes that do not involve a computer—all of it part of the migration of traditional crime into the digital medium. If we expect our law enforcement agents to be responsive to traditional crimes with a high-technology component, we must provide them with the appropriate tools and procedures to enable them to actually investigate and close a case. Asking investigators to send each and every case that involves a computer to a forensic laboratory for review is not a sustainable option. If we don't "push down" technical knowledge to investigators and line officers, the specialists will quickly become overwhelmed and investigations will grind to a halt—a situation that has already begun to occur across the country.

The volume of computer forensic exams is only one factor that is driving us toward changing our approach to digital evidence seizure. As outlined in the previous pages, whole disk encryption, personal data and Privacy Protection Act concerns, and massively large storage arrays are all playing a part in the move to minimize the amount of information seized from a suspect machine. The landscape is quickly changing, and designing solutions to problems of today will not prepare us for the challenges of tomorrow. It is hoped that the change in focus away from the wholesale seizure of digital storage devices and media, in the appropriate situations, will better prepare our law enforcement agents and private sector investigators for the new technologies and coming legal concerns that the future holds.

Works Cited

Association of Chief Police Officers and National High Tech Crime Unit. 2004. Good Practice Guide for Computer based Electronic Evidence, Version 3.0. Available on the Internet at www.acpo.police.uk/asp/policies/Data/gpg_computer_based_evidence_v3.pdf (12/2006).

Bloombecker, Buck. *Spectacular Computer Crimes: What They Are and How They Cost American Business Half a Billion Dollars a Year.* 1990. Homewood, IL: Dow-Jones Irwin.

Carrier, B. and E. Spafford. "Getting Physical with the Digital Investigation Process." *International Journal of Digital Evidence.* Volume 2, Issue 2, 2003. Available at www.ijde.org (12/2006).

Computer Crime and Intellectual Property Section (CCIPS), Criminal Division. "Searching and Seizing Computers and Obtaining Electronic Evidence in Criminal Investigations." United States Department of Justice. Washington, DC. 2002.

Gilder, G. "The Information Factories." *Wired Magazine.* Volume 14, Number 10, 2006.

ISTS. "Law Enforcement Tools and Technologies for Investigating Cyber Attacks: Gap Analysis Report." Institute for Security Technology Studies, Dartmouth College. Hanover, NH. 2004.

ISTS. "Law Enforcement Tools and Technologies for Investigating Cyber Attacks: A National Research and Development Agenda." Institute for Security Technology Studies, Dartmouth College. Hanover, NH. 2004.

Meyers, M. and Rogers, M. "Computer Forensics: The Need for Standardization and Certification." *International Journal of Digital Evidence.* Volume 3, Issue 2, 2004. Available at www.ijde.org (12/2006).

Moore, Robert. *Cybercrime: Investigating High-Technology Computer Crime.* Anderson Publishing, LexisNexis Group. 2005.

National Institute of Justice (NIJ). *Forensic Examination of Digital Evidence: A Guide for Law Enforcement*. Office of Justice Programs, U.S. Department of Justice, Washington, DC. 2004.

National Institute of Justice. *Electronic Crime Scene Investigation: A Guide for First Responders*. Office of Justice Programs. U.S. Department of Justice. NIJ Guide Series. Washington, DC. 2001.

National Security Agency Information Assurance Solutions Technical Directors. *Information Assurance Technical Framework*, Release 3.1. 2002. Available at www.iatf.net/framework_docs/version-3_1/index.cfm.

Nolan, Joseph R. and Jacqueline Nolan-Haley. *Black's Law Dictionary*, Sixth ed. St. Paul, MN: West Publishing Company. 1990.

School of Information Management Systems (SIMS). "How Much Information?" University of California Berkeley. 2003. Available on the Internet at www2.sims.berkeley.edu/research/projects/how-much-info-2003.

Shipley, T. and H. Reeve. *Collecting Evidence from a Running Computer: A Technical and Legal Primer for the Justice Community*. SEARCH, The National Consortium for Justice Information and Statistics. Sacramento, CA. 2006. Available on the Internet at www.search.org/files/pdf/CollectEvidenceRunComputer.pdf (12/06).

"Scientific Working Group on Digital Evidence (SWGDE) and International Organization on Digital Evidence. Digital Evidence Standards and Principles." *Forensic Science Communications*. Volume 2, Number 2, 2000. Federal Bureau of Investigation. U.S. Department of Justice. Washington, DC.

Sterling, Bruce. "Hacker Crackdown." *Project Gutenburg*. Champaign, IL. 1992. Available on the Web at www.gutenberg.org/etext/101.

Technical Working Group for Electronic Crime Scene Investigation, Office of Justice Programs. *Electronic Crime Scene Investigation: A Guide for First Responders*. U.S. Department of Justice, National Institute of Justice. NIJ Guide series, NCJ 187736. Washington, DC. 2001.

United States Secret Service (USSS). "Best Practices for Seizing Electronic Evidence." 2006. Available on the Internet at www.secret-service.gov/electronic_evidence.shtml (12/2006).

United States Department of Justice. *Federal Guidelines for Searching and Seizing Computers*. United States Department of Justice. Washington, DC. 1994.

Federal Rules of Evidence (FRE) are available at judiciary.house.gov/media/pdfs/printers/108th/evid2004.pdf.

Federal Rules of Criminal Procedure (FRCP) are available at judiciary.house.gov/media/pdfs/printers/108th/crim2004.pdf.

Additional Relevant Resources

Daubert v. Merrell Dow Pharmaceuticals, Inc., 509 US, 579 (1993).

Noblett, M., M. Pollit, and L. Presley. "Recovering and Examining Computer Forensic Evidence." *October Forensic Science Communications*. Volume 2, Number 4, 2000. Federal Bureau of Investigation. U.S. Department of Justice. Washington, DC.

Duerr, T., N. Beser, and G. Staisiunas. "Information Assurance Applied to Authentication of Digital Evidence." *Forensic Science Communications*. Volume 6, Number 4, 2004. Federal Bureau of Investigation. U.S. Department of Justice. Washington, DC.

Brown, C. and E. Kenneally. "Risk Sensitive Digital Evidence Collection." *Digital Investigation*. Volume 2, Issue 2, 2005. Elsevier Ltd. Available on the Internet at www.sciencedirect.com/science/journal/17422876.

Brenner, S.W. and B.A. Frederiksen. "Computer Searches and Seizures: Some Unresolved Issues." *Michigan Telecommunications Technical Law Review*. Volume 8, Number 39, 2002.

Joint Administrative Office/Department of Justice Working Group on Electronic Technology in the Criminal Justice System. "Report and Recommendations." 2003. Available on the Internet at www.fjc.gov/public/pdf.nsf/lookup/CompInDr.pdf/$file/CompInDr .pdf (12/06).

Wright, T. *The Field Guide for Investigating Computer Crime: Parts 1–8. 2000–2001.* Available on the Internet at www.securityfocus.com/ infocus/1244 (12/2006).

Solutions Fast Track

Defining Digital Evidence

- ☑ The term *data objects* is used in this chapter to refer to discrete arrangements of digital information logically organized into something meaningful.

- ☑ Digital evidence can be viewed as either the physical hardware or media that contains the relevant data objects or the data object itself.

- ☑ How the evidence is viewed—the physical container versus the information itself—impacts the method of seizure.

Digital Evidence Seizure Methodology

- ☑ The current seizure methodology employed by many law enforcement agencies focuses on the seizure of physical hardware.

- ☑ A revised methodology should provide high-level guidance about approaching non-standard crime scenes such as digital media identification, minimizing the crime scene by prioritizing the physical media, and the seizure of storage devices and media.

- ☑ Whether to pull the plug or shut down properly is a difficult problem facing this community. The answer lies in the technical ability of the responder versus the complexity of the situation.

Factors Limiting Wholesale Seizure of Hardware

☑ Several factors may limit our future ability to seize all the physical hardware. These factors include the size of media, disk encryption, privacy concerns, and delay related to laboratory analysis.

Other Options for Seizing Digital Evidence

☑ Based on factors that may limit future hardware seizure, we must educate our responders now about the other seizure options available.

☑ These seizure options include preview of information on-scene, obtaining information from a running computer, imaging information on-scene, and the imaging of finite data objects on-scene.

Common Threads within Digital Evidence Seizure

☑ A number of common threads tie all seizure methods together.

☑ Responders must be able to explain the steps taken during seizure. Documentation and knowing limitations are key.

☑ The seizure method should include minimization efforts.

☑ Any items seized must be able to be authenticated in court.

☑ Seized items must be admissible in court.

Determining the Most Appropriate Seizure Method

☑ The most appropriate seizure method will be based upon the knowledge and training of the responder, as compared with the type of crime and the complexity of the crime scene.

☑ The incremental approach and the seizure options discussed herein are needed in the fight against crimes involving digital evidence—however, there will be circumstances that force investigators to seize and analyze all hardware.

Frequently Asked Questions

The following Frequently Asked Questions, answered by the authors of this book, are designed to both measure your understanding of the concepts presented in this chapter and to assist you with real-life implementation of these concepts. To have your questions about this chapter answered by the author, browse to **www.syngress.com/solutions** and click on the **"Ask the Author"** form.

Q: What is your opinion on the certification of personnel? Can't we fix all the problems regarding experts and admissibility of evidence once personnel are certified?

A: Certification of personnel is, in my opinion, counterproductive. One of the more commonly seen certifications is vendor certification. These trainings are generally useful as long as the training certified that they attended training, not that they are certified in the use of a tool. Another option is to obtain a certification through an independent certifying body. A number of these types of organizations exist and they do provide a means by which people can advertise their level of knowledge and skill, which is rather handy when reaching out for assistance across jurisdictional boundaries, as often occurs while investigating crimes with a cyber component. However, it is highly unlikely that the court system will give carte-blanche acceptance to a particular certification. If you were to testify as an expert, your certifications may assist you in passing muster as an expert witness, but the certification won't be an automatic bye onto the stand.

Some last thoughts on certifications: Let's assume for a minute that Congress took up this issue and passed a law requiring that all computer forensic examiners must be a Certified Forensics Guru. As soon as the first person achieves the certification, it means that everyone else, by default, is not certified. Forensics personnel would need to spend time working on obtaining the certification, time that should be spent on existing cases. Finally, how would such an overarching certification affect onsite acquisition, live-forensic previews, and the seizure of digital evidence? Although there may be some benefits to such a certification, the negatives, particularly related to empowering all law enforcement to play a role in investigating crimes with a cyber component, appear to outweigh the potential positive affects.

Q: Is the seizure of data objects or evidence preview relevant when a computer or other device is actually stolen?

A: In the instance where the digital device was actually stolen, or generally when the hardware or media represent the instrumentality or fruits of a crime, then it is again appropriate, without question, to seize the physical hardware or media. In these cases, the hardware or storage media may itself be the "evidence" and *there may not necessarily be a need to examine data objects on the computer or device* (CCIPS, 2001). These types of seizures show why it is important to understand exactly how the computer was used in committing the criminal act. It is important to remember that not all crimes that involve a computer will necessarily involve digital evidence. What is worse is that many of these seized devices are needlessly processed by an overtaxed computer forensic system. As discussed earlier, remember to keep computers and digital devices in perspective, and look to use digital evidence only when appropriate.

Chapter 8

Conducting Cyber Investigations

Solutions in the chapter:

- **Demystifying Computer/Cyber Crime**
- **Understanding IP Addresses**
- **The Explosion of Networking**
- **The Explosion of Wireless Networks**
- **Interpersonal Communication**

☑ **Summary**

☑ **Solutions Fast Track**

☑ **Frequently Asked Questions**

Introduction

We often fear most what we don't understand. That could be said about computers and the investigation of computer crimes. Many investigators cringe at the mention of a computer and seek to offload any computer-related crime to the "computer crime guy" in their office. Although computers have been around for a few decades, they've finally reached levels where it is feasible to expect that everyone has access to a computer. The computer is no longer a "nice to have," it is a "must have." Those who don't own their own computers can walk into a public library or cyber cafe to gain access to a computer. Similarly, access to the Internet is becoming ubiquitous through connections provided by libraries, coffee shops, computer stores, and even fast food restaurants. This explosion of computer technology and acceptance has opened up a whole new world of opportunity to the criminal element that constantly looks for new ways to exploit people through time proven scams and tactics. As computers become more deeply integrated within society, it is likely that a computer or similar type device will play a role in criminal activity. A basic understanding of computers is all that investigators will need to learn that *computer crime* is just plain old crime packaged up in a shiny new wrapper.

Demystifying Computer/Cyber Crime

Computers start to play a role in crime in situations where the capabilities of the computer allow a person to commit that crime or store information related to the crime. An e-mail phishing scam is a common example where the bad guy generates a fictitious e-mail for the sole purpose of enticing people to a spoofed site where they are conned into entering sensitive personal information. That sensitive information is then available to the bad guy in order to perpetrate an Identity Theft. In another example, a suspect might use the computer to scan and generate fake bank checks, or create fake identification. In both of these cases the crime required the inherent capabilities of the computer for its commission.

WARNING

!

The mere presence of a computer does not make a crime a computer crime. We must be careful not to hastily label a crime a "computer crime" just because a computer was involved. What if the new laptop I purchased was stolen from my vehicle while I was in the convenience store getting milk? This would not be a computer crime just because a computer was involved, but a theft. How about an office fight where an employee strikes another with the keyboard of their computer—should we call out the Forensic team? Absolutely not (well, maybe, if the assault resulted in a homicide). The computer in and of itself is not important, it is just merely an object like many others in our lives.

Since computers are so pervasive, it is an absolute necessity that investigators learn how to investigate crimes that involve a computer. The basic design of computers—including vast amounts of storage and meticulous file timestamping—can make them a wealth of evidence as traces of the crime can often be retrieved by an experienced investigator. This does not mean that every investigator needs to become an expert in computer technology, but there are basic concepts and methods that must be learned in order to develop old school leads. *The key is to gain at least some basic computer knowledge and skills to put you ahead of the average computer user; skills that allow you to apply traditional policing skills and procedures to the case.*

The crimes that are being committed haven't changed, just the manner in which they're being committed. Think about it. Back before the Internet, the telephone, the telegraph, and the Pony Express, if a person wanted to threaten to kill someone, it was likely they would have to physically place themselves in proximity to the person and speak that threat. As services and technologies developed, new ways emerged through which a person could commit that same threatening act. They could send a letter, a telegram, or even better, make a phone call. Now we can send an e-mail or instant message (IM). Same crime; same underlying elements and facts to be proven. The only change is the manner of delivery. The key to a successful investigation of a computer crime is the development and follow-up of case leads. Although many leads will dead end, it is the one that continues to develop into further leads that can end up solving your case. Many believe that investigations involving computers are above their capabilities, but that is often not the case. By learning and adapting some basic computer knowledge and skills, today's investigator can react to new technologies and still develop workable old school leads.

NOTE

IM stands for instant message. Instant messaging is another way for people to communicate with each other by computer in real time. A chat session is established between two or more computers using compatible applications through which written messages and files can be transmitted back and forth. The unique challenge of instant messages is that their content is not often recorded by service providers or the applications facilitating the chat. Once the IM session closes, the contents tend to be lost. This is not always the case as users can turn on chat logging, but by default most chat applications do not record sessions.

Throughout this chapter, critical skills will be discussed that prepare an investigator to deal with computer crime investigations. By developing a basic understanding of key concepts and learning to apply basic computer skills, an investigator can learn how to proceed with computer crime cases much in the same way as traditional cases. Issues such as IP Addresses, Networks, Wireless Devices, and Interpersonal Communication will be discussed with the sole purpose of providing the investigator with a basic understanding of each topic area and the skills that can be employed to yield workable physical leads. Many of these skills will build the foundation of computer crime investigations not only today, but well into the future as these technologies expand and become more complex.

Notes from the Underground...

"Application Stupid"

Even though computers have been in our society for quite some time, it is still arguable that many within the population are not highly skilled with them. With the prevalence of computers today, it becomes increasingly important for computer and software companies to develop systems and applications that are "user friendly." These user friendly devices and systems are intended to make people's lives easier. People, being creatures of habit, are often quick to embrace any solution that will allow them to work less. This has facilitated the rapid acceptance and integration of complicated systems into everyday life.

In the quest to make applications and operating systems easier for the end user, programmers have had to develop very advanced and complicated programs. There is a direct correlation between the ease of use by the end user compared to the complexity of the underlying code that is required for the application to run. Many operating systems today are so advanced compared to their earlier versions that little interaction is required of the end user to install new programs or add peripherals. The system itself is able to identify new devices or programs, load the necessary supporting drivers, and set parameters to make the new device or program function. All this is done for the benefit of the end user, who is no longer required to have a fundamental understanding about how the computer and/or its software functions.

A large majority of people are what I call "application stupid"; the process of using a computer or application is so simplified that the user is not required to possess any enhanced level of computer skill or knowledge. The user is able to operate the computer, sometimes at a fairly high level, without having any understanding about what is going on in the background. Application stupidity can provide an opportunity to the investigator to obtain traces of information or evidence that has been left behind as a result of the complexity of the application or operating system versus the rudimentary skill of the user. For example, a suspect creates a file on their computer that is incriminating in nature, they delete it, and then they empty their recycle bin. They believe that the file no longer exists—which is not the case. Their

Continued

limited knowledge about how operating systems handle deleted files has created an opportunity for the investigator to retrieve the deleted file.

The simpler the program is to the end user, the more complex the coding; the more complex the coding, the more likely that fragments of information will be left behind. The theory of application stupidity is likely to become more pervasive as the complexity of operating systems and programs increase to keep pace with a growing user base that demands simplicity.

Understanding IP Addresses

All law enforcement investigators need to understand the basics of IP addressing in order to trace users of the Internet to a physical location. Just as a phone number that shows up on a caller id box from a threatening phone call can provide investigators with a specific starting location for their investigations, an IP address can provide that same type of lead. By understanding what IP addresses are, how they're assigned, and who has control over them, an investigator can develop workable case leads.

IP addresses provide a connection point through which communication can occur between two computers. Without getting into too much detail about them, it is important that you understand how to identify an IP address when you see one. These addresses are made up of four 8-bit numbers divided by a ".", much like this one: 155.212.56.73. Currently the Internet operates under the IPv4 (Internet Protocol Version 4) standard. In IPv4 there are approximately 4 billion IP addresses available for use over the Internet. That number will be expanding in the near future to about 16 billion times that number when transition is made to IPv6.

During the birth and initial development of today's Internet, IP addresses primarily were assigned to computers in order for them to pass network traffic over the Internet. Computers were physically very large, extremely expensive, and pretty much limited to the organizations that controlled the primary networks that were part of the primordial Internet. During this time, an IP address most likely could be traced back to a specific computer. There are a limited number of large organizations that own and control most of the

IP Addresses available with IPv4. Therefore, if an investigator has been able to ascertain the IP address of an illegal communication, they will also be able to determine which organization owns the network space within which that address is contained. That information in and of itself will often not be enough since many of these organizations sublease blocks of the IP Addresses they own to smaller companies, such as Internet Service Providers (ISP). It will be the investigative follow-up with the ISP that is likely to provide the best results. Using an analogy, we can think about IP addresses much like phone numbers, where the major corporations are states and ISPs are towns or calling districts. If an investigator was following up on a case involving a phone number, the area code would narrow the search down only to a particular state, and the remaining numbers would identify a particular account.

Remember that for Internet traffic to occur, an external IP address must be available to the device. Access to an external IP address is provided by an ISP. ISPs sublease blocks of IP addresses from one or more of the larger corporations that control address space and in return they will in essence sublease one of those addresses to the individual customer. This connection to the Internet is most often done through a modem. Modems came in varying configurations such as dial up, cable, and DSL. Depending on at what point in time you began using the Internet, you may already be familiar with these devices. The older of the three listed is the dial-up modem that required the use of a telephone line. When users wanted to connect to the Internet, they would plug the modem installed in their computer to their phone line and then dial one of the access numbers provided by the ISP. The dial-up modem is the slowest of the available devices that can make the transfer of large files a painful process. Therefore when dealing with cases that require large file transfers such as child pornography, it is less likely that a dial-up connection would be used. A distinct advantage of the dial-up modem, though, is the portability since the connection can be made on any phone line by dialing an appropriate access number and providing valid account information.

More common today is Internet service provided through TV cable or through DSL (Digital Subscriber Line); both of these services provide higher connection speeds making the transfer of large files relatively easy. When a consumer contacts an ISP about Internet access, typically they are assigned an installation date when a technician comes to the residence to connect the necessary wiring to the home through either their cable provider (cable modem) or phone provider (DSL). With the appropriate wiring in place, an external modem is connected to the line provided through which the computer in the home will connect. The modem provides the interface through which the home computer can be physically connected to the Internet.

When the home user is connected to the ISP's physical connection to the Internet, the ISP must still assign the home user's computer an IP address in order for the computer to communicate over the Internet. IP addresses are assigned two ways, statically and dynamically. If static addressing was to be used, the install technician would configure the computer's network interface card (NIC) with the specific IP address during install. Static assignment by an ISP would limit the total number of customers an ISP could have by the total number of external addresses they control. Let's say that XYZ ISP had subleased a block of IP addresses from a large corporation in the amount of 1,000 unique valid addresses. If that ISP statically assigned addresses to their customers, then the total number of customers they could have on the Internet would be limited to 1,000. Leasing blocks of external IP addresses is very expensive as the demand is high compared to availability. ISPs realize that it is unlikely that all their customers will be on the Internet at the same time, so in order get the largest return on their investment, they use an addressing scheme called dynamic addressing, which allows for computers that are actively connected to the Internet to be assigned an unused IP address.

Here's how dynamic addressing works. XYZ ISP has 1,000 addresses available to their customers. They set up a server, referred to as DHCP server, which maintains a list of the available addresses. At installation, the technician sets the consumer's computer NIC to get an address assignment through DHCP. When the consumer's computer is turned on and connected to the network, the NIC puts out a broadcast requesting an IP address assignment. The DHCP server responsible for the assignment responds to the request by providing an IP address from the pool of available addresses to the computer's NIC. The length of time that the computer will use that assigned address is based upon the "lease" time set by the DHCP server. Remember that the ISP wants to have the maximum number of customers using the smallest number of addresses, so the ISP wants to ensure that any unused addresses are made available to other computers. The lease time determines how long that address will used before the NIC will be required to send out another broadcast for an IP address. The IP address returned after the reassignment could be the same address used previously or an entirely new address, depending on what's available in the server pool.

TIP

A number of details about the configuration of a computer's NIC(s) can be determined in Windows by using the `ipconfig` command at the computers command prompt—most importantly the computer's IP Address (see Figure 8.1).

Figure 8.1 *ipconfig* Command

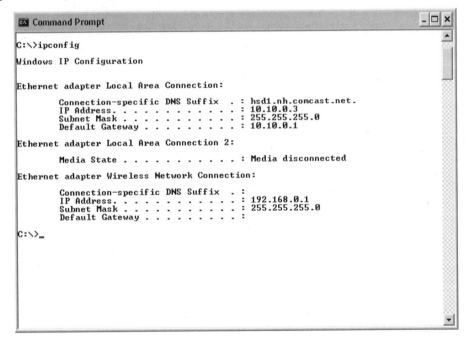

Note that this example provides details on three different NICs; two physical Ethernet ports identified by the Local Area Connection designation and one wireless network connection. Each NIC can possess a different IP address. IP addresses are important because each device that communicates over the Internet must have an address. In a computer crime investigation involving the Internet, it is very likely that the investigator will need to track an IP address to a location—preferably a person. As discussed earlier, ISPs control the assignment of IP addresses, and ISPs can provide the link between the IP address and the account holder. Understanding the distinction between static and dynamic IP assignment is very important because the investigator must record the date/time that IP address was captured. If the ISP uses DHCP, the IP address assignments can change—investigators need to be sure that the account holder identified by the ISP was actually assigned the IP address in question when the illicit activity occurred.

Let's take a moment and think about this. You're investigating an e-mail-based criminal threatening case where you were able to determine the originating IP address of the illegal communication. You were able to determine which ISP controls the address space that includes the IP address in question. If ISPs use dynamic addressing, how are you going to be able to determine which subscriber account used that address if any of a thousand or more could have been assigned to the suspect's computer? In this case, it would be extremely important for you to also record and note the date and time of the originating communication. The date/time stamp can be matched against the logs for the DHCP server to determine which subscriber account was assigned the IP address in question at that time.

The Explosion of Networking

Much like ISPs use dynamic addressing to maximize the number of customers they could have using a limited number of addresses, customers began using routers to increase the number of computers they could use in their homes that could share that IP address provided by the ISP. The router passes network traffic back and forth between the Internet and all the home computers in the residence connected to that network router. All the network traffic sent from the home computers through the router to the Internet will be seen as coming from a single IP address. The investigator who traces an IP address back to a router will need to do more case follow-up at the location to determine if there is more than one possible computer involved. Analysis of the router configuration and/or logs may provide more information about the computer requesting and receiving the illegal traffic as information, such as the computer's hostname, internal IP address, or MAC address.

Networks have become common place today as the cost and implementation of computer systems has dropped dramatically. Years ago, computer systems were very large (room size) and extremely expensive. This limited the organizations that could afford to use computers in any meaningful way. Today, computers are much more powerful and affordable. This has allowed both companies and individuals to purchase and use numerous computer systems to accomplish specific needs. The concept of networks, much like the Internet, allows multiple computers to become interconnected to each other in order to share files and resources. The computers on the network will still need to be assigned IP addresses in order to communicate with other computers on the network—but the addresses assigned within a network behind a router, *or gateway*, will fall into the category of internal IP addresses. Unlike the external address assignments required to send and received information on the Internet, internal IP addresses allow computers within a network to communicate with one another. In order for computers on these private networks to access the Internet, there is likely to be an established gateway that has been assigned a single external IP address to be used by all computers on the network.

NOTE

Internal IP addresses can also be used to set up more than one computer into a network environment. When computers are placed within a network, they will be able to see the existence of each other on the network and can be used to pass communications and share files. This is completely independent and not reliant upon having access to the Internet. However, without some type of Internet access, the communications transmitted over that internal network (most often referred to as a private network) would remain within that network and would not be accessible to other computers not physically included in its scheme. Private networks are very common in corporate environments where large numbers of employees need to access or share files with other employees, but for security purposes, no Internet connection is included in order to stop possible unauthorized access from outside the network.

Gateways become a transfer agent for computer traffic between computers on the network and the Internet. This means that the network owner is only required to assign a single external IP address to the gateway in order for one or hundreds of the computers on the network to access the Internet. This provides a challenge to investigators who have been able to trace back that IP address to the gateway owner. The IP address no longer identifies a specific computer directly, but merely identifies the gateway that handed the traffic on to the Internet on behalf of all the computers on the private network. More follow-up must be performed in order to establish the identity of the system that sent the request to the gateway initially.

A benefit of investigating a traditional wired network is that the number of devices connected often is limited to the location at hand and physical limitations of transmission over wired lines. Being able to trace an IP address back to a particular location and network greatly helps reduce the total overall number of suspects. If other identifying information such as the internal IP address, hostname, and MAC address has been determined, then the ability to narrow the suspect down to a single device is greatly increased. If the device is found, then traditional investigatory techniques can be used.

Hostname

Hostnames are the system names assigned to a computer by the system user or owner. These names are used to identify a computer in a network in a format that is easiest to understand by people. If there are multiple computers in the network, each could be given unique identifying names making them more easily recognizable, such as Receptionist PC or Dave's Laptop. The naming choice selected might help to identify the likely location or user of that system. If for example you were investigating a threatening e-mail that had originated from a computer within a network named "Jedi," you might look for people who have access to the network who are also fans of the *Star Wars* series. Keeping in mind that the names can be changed by the user at any time, the matching or nonmatching of a hostname to a suspicious communication or activity is by no means conclusive in itself.

MAC Address

MAC addresses are the identifying number assignment given to NICs that provide network connectivity. That connectivity can be wired or wireless depending on the type of NIC present. MAC addresses are unique to every NIC and would be most equivalent to a serial number. This means that if an investigator is able to determine the MAC address of the device used in the crime, then the device containing the NIC could be identified specifically. However, just like a hostname can be changed, MAC addresses can also be changed through a process called MAC spoofing. Whether or not a MAC address matches a particular communication is not in itself conclusive evidence that the computer containing the NIC was or was not responsible.

TIP

In the previous Tip we learned that the *ipconfig* command can provide some details about a computer's network interface card configuration. There is a switch that can be added to the *ipconfig* command that provides more detail about the NIC configuration. At the command prompt, *ipconfig /all* is used (see Figure 8.2).

You will notice that other details have been provided that are not seen in the *ipconfig* command, including the computer's hostname, and each of the NIC's MAC addresses.

Figure 8.2 *ipconfig/all* Command

Being able to determine the computer's MAC address is a useful skill for investigators. At one organization, network security had set alerts in their system to notify the system administrator when MAC addresses of stolen equipment appeared on the network. The systems administrator notified law enforcement that a stolen laptop had just connected to one of the organization's wireless access points, and they were able to direct the officer to the general area in range of the given access point. The officer was able to make a directed patrol of the area looking for anyone using a laptop that matched the general description of the stolen laptop. Unfortunately the officer was not aware of the `ipconfig/all` command. Knowing that command would have allowed the officer to conduct field interviews and request consented permission to check the MAC address of any of the suspected laptops against the recorded MAC address of the stolen laptop.

TIP

Once investigators have narrowed the scope of their network investigation down to one computer, they may want to consider the following lines of questioning:
Who has access to the device?
Did they have access on the date and time in question?
Did they have motive?
Is there evidence still on the device that can be retrieved?
What information does the suspect provide?

The Explosion of Wireless Networks

In the not too distant past, networks were isolated to corporate and government entities using large computer clusters and a wired infrastructure. It was less common to find homes with a computer; much less a network. All of that changed with the advent of wireless technology. Many homes and consumer establishments contain private and/or open networks providing access to the Internet, network devices, or offline storage. Cellular companies also compete within the wireless space and offer numerous Internet-enabled devices that allow consumers to stay connected. This proliferation of interconnected and overlapping wireless networks allows criminals to be more portable, creating a heightened challenge to law enforcement to first locate the origin of the action or communication.

Hotspots

Hotspots refer to locations where wireless Internet services are readily available to any user. Some are fee-based and others are offered as a free service to attract customers. In the fee-based system, the person connecting to the network is required to submit valid payment information prior to being granted access. As a service to attract customers into their establishments, many businesses now offer free Internet. This means that anybody entering the establishment, or within range of their wireless signal, can utilize their network to gain access to the Internet. These free hotspots can pose a significant problem for law enforcement since an IP address traced back to any establishment that is set up as a free network is likely to leave the investigator with a large suspect pool—basically anyone within range of the network.

In these situations, the timestamp of the illegal or suspicious activity continues to be critical to the investigation. Knowing the date and time of the alleged incident would allow you to narrow down the pool of possible suspects. A pattern of illegal activity from the address might help build a profile of the offender sufficient enough to jog the memory of employees about a "regular" who visits the location during those time frames. Of course, be careful not to exclude employees in the pool of possibilities unless they can be eliminated based on work assignments and schedule. Tracing back the IP address will provide only a lead toward where the investigator should look further. It will be traditional investigative skills that will help yield a possible suspect. Understanding IP addresses, hostnames, and MAC address assignments will be crucial to matching your suspect's device to the router configuration and/or traffic logs.

TIP

Investigators working cases involving wireless networks should consider the following lines of inquiry:

Do the employees remember anything unusual during those time periods?

Is the establishment equipped with video cameras and is there footage of the time period in question?

Does the investigator have a possible suspect photo, sketch, or other information that might help in the follow-up?

Does the router providing the service maintain activity logs? If so, what was the computer name and MAC address of the device that perpetrated the activity in question?

Wardriving

As people learn to appreciate and utilize new technologies, they can inadvertently open themselves up to an opportunist who prays on that innocent lack of understanding. Wireless technology is a perfect example. People have longed for the day when they wouldn't be forced to sit at the same desk or location in their home or office to use a computer, but could move about freely without the constraint of wires. Laptop devices have evolved to the point that they are lighter, more portable than, and just as efficient as full-size desktop computers. Most now come equipped with a wireless card as a standard device, which means that the only new device needed to achieve true portability at home or office is the installation of a wireless router.

Wireless routers are so inexpensive and easy to set up that many homes and offices are now wireless enabled. Many wireless routers come with installation CDs that automate the entire process using default settings that will work with most devices. This means that within a few quick steps of returning home with this device, the average person can have a fully functional wireless network established that will communicate with the wireless-enabled laptop they already own. Using the old adage "if it works don't fix it." many will make no attempt to secure that network from outside intrusion. They will not be aware that they have just created an open wireless network that is available to anyone within the wireless signal range.

There are those that drive through neighborhoods looking for the presence of open, unsecured wireless networks. This process is referred to as *wardriving*, and requires no special equipment other than a wireless-enabled device that is capable of detecting wireless signals. Some will record the location of these networks for their own personal use, still others might post the locations on the Internet as part of a greater hotspot map for anyone to utilize. The types of crimes that can be perpetrated using one of these locations varies. First, the intruder may use the network only as free access to the Internet with no illegal intent other than nonpermissible use of that network and Internet account.

Some people may use this opportunity to scan the network, looking for devices within the network that have known vulnerabilities that they might be able to exploit in order get account and password information. This network could be used to send threatening e-mails, launch viruses, or transfer child pornography. An investigator who has been able to trace the IP address back to the home owner account would need to use some traditional policing skills, which might include interviewing residents, consented or warranted searches of Internet-enabled devices, and review of the wireless router's configuration and log files. Computer skills will lead the investigator to the location, but traditional police work will tie everything together.

Security Alert...

Investigating Wireless Networks

There are situations where a homeowner may contact an investigator about unauthorized access of his or her wireless network. Since most routers have the ability for logging and e-mail alerts about certain activity, an investigator with consent of the network owner could set the configuration of the system to generate log files and e-mail the investigator when suspicious activity is occurring. Remember that in order for a person to use the network, he or she would have to be within range of the signal. If an investigator knew the activity was occurring in real-time, he or she might be able to locate a suspect based

Continued

www.syngress.com

on activity in the neighborhood. What other houses appear to have activity?

Are there any suspicious people or vehicles in the area?

Since the range of the signal is typically a setting within the administrative function of the router, it would also be possible to lower the signal power, reducing the overall range of the network. This in turn may pull the suspect into closer proximity to the location, making them easier to locate. Recently, I recall an investigation where a neighborhood child was suspect of stealing a laptop from a residence. The network had been secured and would allow access only to that specific laptop, so logging was enabled with e-mail alerts to notify the investigator should any activity be initiated by that laptop. That type of activity alert would notify the investigator that the stolen laptop was in range of the network, which might yield a suspect with evidence in hand.

Wireless Storage Devices

In order to keep up with demand for wireless, many manufacturers now offer remote wireless storage devices, which could pose a significant challenge to investigators trying to locate illegal material. Within the range of a wireless network, a suspect could potentially hide a storage device in an area of their residence that is not readily accessible or apparent. This poses a significant challenge to investigators during consent and search warrant execution. Investigators must always be thinking about the possibility of a remote storage device, especially if it is determined that a wireless network is in use.

Certain limitations with these remote devices can be useful in determining their existence, ultimately helping to determine their location. Even with their portability, these devices will need some type of power source and persistent connectivity to the network. This can limit their proximity to the signal area of the device they typically associate with as well as power availability. When powered, these devices will connect wirelessly to the network they're configured to associate with. This means that if an investigator is able to gain access to the gateway device establishing the network, they might very easily identify that there is another associating wireless device that they have not accounted for. The real challenge comes when these devices are not powered. Without power these devices are off and will not associate with the wireless devices, making them invisible to the entire network. Their discovery would have to come through physical observation at this point, rather then through their virtual presence.

If an investigator had the skills to recognize that a wireless network was in use within the suspect's residence, he or she might be more inclined to ask probing questions about that network, possibly getting the suspect to disclose the existence of a remote device. Physical searches of the residence could also be potentially more productive if the investigator has keyed in on the fact that there might be remote devices involved, requiring a more thorough and educated search.

Interpersonal Communication

As people look to stay connected with friends, family, and coworkers, they are likely to use one or more methods of communication, including e-mail, chat, and blogging—all of which are easily supported on today's computers and portable devices such as laptops, PDAs, and cellular phones. Investigators must be familiar with how these various systems work and how one might be able to retrieve critical case information from stored communications or fragments of previous exchanges. What makes the area of interpersonal communication so important to the investigator is that people are inherently very social; people routinely discuss their daily lives with friends and may even brag about crimes to others. Being able to capture, decipher, and trace back communications to their origin is a critical law enforcement skill.

E-mail

E-mail communication was present at the start of the Internet, and has exploded over the last decade, making it more likely that people today use e-mail in some form or another. E-mail provides another conduit through which people can communicate 24 hours a day, 7 days a week. Unlike a phone conversation that needs the recipient to answer, an active e-mail discussion can be carried out through multiple e-mails spread over time. Messages are sent and are held in a waiting inbox at the convenience of the recipient, who will choose when to read the message and how best to respond. Once an e-mail is read, it is usually up to the receiver to decide and make the conscious choice to delete or discard that communication. This provides a unique opportunity to law enforcement investigating crimes involving e-mails, since undeleted e-mails will be viewable and previously deleted e-mails might be recovered through various forensic methods.

There are countless e-mail addresses and accounts in use today. They fall into two major category types. The first are e-mails generated with e-mail programs that reside on the local user's machine. One of the most common is Outlook or Outlook Express (a Microsoft product), which runs on the user's machine and can be set up with relative ease assuming the account holder has an active Internet connection. E-mails sent and received through this type of account will be stored locally on the user's machine. If this type of e-mail program is used to generate and send illegal communications, it is likely that evidence of those communications might be recovered from the machine used.

The other popular e-mail service is free Internet-based e-mail such as Microsoft's Hotmail and Google's Gmail. These services don't require users to have any special programs in order for them to send and retrieve e-mail in their account. They are able to access mail that is stored on servers provided by the provider they use by signing into a previously created account. These services are extremely portable since they can be accessed from any computer with Internet access and a web browser. With an Internet-based account, an e-mail might be traced back to the originating ISP and it may also be possible to determine the IP address of the machine that connected when the account was created. This is, of course, all dependent on whether the service provider maintained those records for any specific period of time. Even with this type of account, remnants of Web-based e-mail may be recoverable as HTML documents in temporary Internet files or drive space that hasn't been overwritten by newer files.

With all e-mail cases, it is critical that the investigator follows up on the e-mail address associated with the active case he or she is working. Since there are countless e-mail addresses in use on the Internet, it is not uncommon to have hundreds, if not thousands of variations for the same or similar address. John_Smith@domain is entirely different than JohnSmith@domain. Be sure to match all instances of your suspected e-mail communications exactly.

Chat/Instant Messaging

Chat and instant messaging is another extremely popular method of communication. Unlike e-mail, which ends up being loaded on an e-mail server or downloaded onto the receiver computer's local e-mail program, chats and instant messages are made through direct communication between the two devices. The devices involved exchange communications back and forth in real-time for as long as that "window" is open. Conversations held in chat are not saved by the applications typically used to facilitate this method of communication. This means that for the most part, chat and instant messaging conversations are lost once that session ends.

Service providers do not log chat and instant message traffic, which can be challenging to the investigator investigating a case where chat or instant messaging might have been used. Just like with e-mails, it is extremely important that investigators trace or follow up on the correct screen name or chat id being used by the suspect(s). There are still cases where an investigator might be able to retrieve chat history, as it is possible that one or all of the parties involved may have turn on logging within the application they use. Remnants of chats might also reside on drive space that has not been overwritten by new files. This is where forensic examination can come in very handy if a suspect computer has been seized.

Social Networking and Blogging

Social networking sites, such as Myspace and Facebook, and blogging technologies allow people a conduit through which they can post their thoughts, ideas, and self-expression onto the Internet instantly. For example, within Myspace, users can create an account for themselves along with a personal Web page through which they can express themselves in any manner in which they see fit, be it through music, video, or written expression. These pages become part of a larger online community with similarly minded individuals being able to link together into what is referred to as a *friends network*. Since the information entered at account creation has no true factual verification, it is possible for people to create fictitious identities in order to pass themselves off as someone they're not. The name an investigator might obtain from a Myspace created page might not be the actual identity of the person who created and uses that space. However, it might still be possible to obtain information from the organization responsible for Myspace, such as an account holder's IP address information used during the original account creation or the IP addresses the account holder used to access the account—that type of IP information might be traced back to a suspected user account.

Even though there are no guarantees that information on Myspace pages will be completely factual, this type of online community provides a very powerful and unique service to law enforcement. If an investigator is able to positively identify an online identity as belonging to a specific suspect, the investigator might also be able to develop further leads about conspirators based on other identities contained in their friends network. It is critical to investigators that they monitor the activity of potential suspects that they identify by keeping up with the suspect's social networking and blog-related activity.

Media and Storage

Media exists in numerous configurations with varying storage capacities. Most people today are very familiar with the floppy disk, CD-ROM, and DVD—all of which can store and contain files of evidential value. DVDs started reaching capacity sizes in excess of 8 gigabytes, which meant that suspects could save illegal files that would have filled up an entire computer hard drive just years ago on one silver disk. Finding just the right DVD during a search of a suspect or residence could provide numerous evidentiary files. A smaller segment is likely to be familiar with hard drives and understand their role within the computer.

The trend now within media is that of portability. As if trying to find a CD or DVD wasn't hard enough, further technology advances have brought about flash drives and mini smart cards. Many flash drives are smaller than a pack of gum and some mini smart cards are the size of a postage stamp (only thicker) and are capable of holding gigabytes of information. Investigators must be aware of the different types of digital media that exist and be able to identify the media in the field. The variety, and more importantly the size, of media must be taken into consideration when applying for search warrants where digital evidence is suspected; the hiding places for this type of storage are countless.

Summary

What makes computer crime so fearful to some and intriguing to others is the unknown. As investigators learn to deal with and investigate crime involving computers, many are quick to label any crime with a computer presence as a computer/cyber crime. Many of these investigators, and prosecutors, believe that computer crimes are really new crimes; but criminals and "crime" have shown the ability time and time again to be able to adapt to new technologies. It is reasonable to question whether computer crime is just a generational phenomenon caused by a gap in computer understanding and acceptance by many older Americans that did not have the same opportunities to use and learn on computers as the younger generations. Is it likely that this problem will correct itself over time? In the future, computer crime, as it is viewed today, will become nonexistent—not because crime won't exist in the future, but because computer-related crimes will be viewed for what they really are, *crime*.

Solutions Fast Track

Demystifying Computer Crime

- ☑ The explosion of computer technology and acceptance has opened up a whole new world of opportunity to the criminal element that constantly looks for new ways to exploit people through time-proven scams and tactics.

- ☑ The key for investigators is to gain at least some basic computer knowledge and skills to put you ahead of the average computer user, skills that allow you to apply traditional policing skills and procedures to the case.

- ☑ There is a direct correlation between the ease of use by the end user compared to the complexity of the underlying code that is required for the application to run. The simpler the program is to the end user, the more complex the coding; the more complex the coding, the more likely that fragments of information will be left behind. These fragments can be located by law enforcement during investigations.

Understanding IP Addresses

- ☑ All law enforcement investigators need to understand the basics of IP addressing in order to trace users of the Internet to a physical location.

- ☑ In a computer crime investigation involving the Internet, it is very likely that the investigator will need to track an IP address to a location—preferably a person.

- ☑ Investigators need to record the date and time that an IP address was captured to ensure the captured IP was actually assigned to the suspect identified—dynamic addressing can cause the assigned IP addresses to change.

The Explosion of Networking

- ☑ The investigator who traces an IP address back to a network will need to do more case follow-up at the location to determine if there is more than one possible computer involved.

- ☑ Hostnames and MAC addresses can be used as investigative tools to help identify a computer on a network.

The Explosion of Wireless Networks

- ☑ The proliferation of interconnected and overlapping wireless networks allows criminals to be more portable.

- ☑ The anonymity provided by free WiFi access in hotspots and stolen WiFi, that is, wardriving, highlights the importance of good police work to mitigate the impact of the technology on the investigation.

☑ Investigators need to consider that wireless storage devices will be used by suspects, and a plan to detect and find these devices must be part of the overall search planning.

Interpersonal Communication

☑ People are inherently social and routinely discuss their daily lives with friends and may even brag about crimes to others. Being able to capture, decipher and trace back communications to their origin is a critical law enforcement skill.

Frequently Asked Questions

The following Frequently Asked Questions, answered by the authors of this book, are designed to both measure your understanding of the concepts presented in this chapter and to assist you with real-life implementation of these concepts. To have your questions about this chapter answered by the author, browse to **www.syngress.com/solutions** and click on the **"Ask the Author"** form.

Q: I'm new to cyber crime, but I really want to get involved. Should I jump right into doing forensics?

A: Although there is plethora of training available in the field of digital forensics, you may want to consider getting acclimated to crimes with a cyber component before jumping in with both feet into forensics. Much of what is discussed in this chapter reflects the belief that most cyber crime is just plain ol' crime. Where we may hold this belief to help those that dislike technology realize that they can still work computer crime cases without having a thorough knowledge of computers, we may suggest the same train of thought to you; there is plenty of crime to investigate that has a cyber component that does not require a forensic examination. Tracing e-mail harassments, responding to threats over chat, and investigating sexual solicitations over IM are but a few of the types of crimes that can be investigated without immediately requiring a forensic exam. My recommendation is to find a training course that focuses on the investigation of Internet-related crime—the skills you learn in class such as this won't be wasted if you choose to go the forensics route in the future. By the way, by focusing on crimes that you can investigate without requiring a forensic examination will make your chief a lot happier than your request to purchase $20,000 of software equipment to start processing forensics cases.

Q: I want to get involved with catching predators online. I've seen the TV shows and there doesn't appear to be anything to it. Why should I bother to learn all the technology junk if I don't need to?

A: This is a very popular question. Unfortunately, the fact that it gets asked shows that many people do not know what they do not know, and goes squarely to the heart of *application stupidity*. Agreed, there is little technical knowledge required to "chat" with a potential suspect, and if everything goes according to plan, they show up at your door and you take them into custody. But what happens when things don't go according to plan? Are you aware of the underlying software or process that makes the chatting possible? Is your machine configured correctly and appropriately protected—naming the computer DetectiveDesk22 may show up during a scan of your computer and may blow your cover. Are you knowledgeable about how the particular chatting software works? Does it use a proxy? Will it provide you a direct connection during a file transfer or webcam stream—and if yes, do you have the skills to capture the bad-guy's IP address during that exact moment of transfer? Do you have the skills to properly set up an online identity and protect it from discovery? Although the initial setup of the identity may be trivial, the long-term maintenance and believability of the profile may affect your investigations.

In principle, it sounds like a good idea to get a screen name together to begin enticing predators into the stationhouse, but obtaining basic computer investigative skills will go a long way toward conducting more successful and productive investigations. Further, these skills may prove critical one day when a predator shoots you a webcam image of a child held hostage—that exact moment is not the time to begin learning about the underlying technology—these skills need to be acquired and practiced before employed in active operations.

Chapter 9

Digital Forensics and Analyzing Data

Solutions in this chapter:

- **The Evolution of Computer Forensics**
- **Phases of Digital Forensics**

- ☑ **Summary**
- ☑ **Solutions Fast Track**
- ☑ **Frequently Asked Questions**

Introduction

Digital forensics is probably the most intricate part of the cyber crime investigation process. It is often where the strongest evidence will come from. Digital forensics is the scientific acquisition, analysis, and preservation of data contained in electronic media whose information can be used as evidence in a court of law. The practice of *Digital Forensics* can be a career all in itself, and often is. Other times it is a subset of skills for a more general security practitioner. Although the corporate digital forensic practitioner is not a law enforcement officer, it is a wise practice to follow the same procedures as law enforcement does when performing digital forensics. Even in a corporate environment, the work one performs can quickly make it to a courtroom. Regardless if the case is civil or criminal the evidence will still be presented the same.

The Evolution of Computer Forensics

Traditional digital forensics started with the seizure of a computer or some media. The drives and media were duplicated in a forensically sound manner bit by bit. Way back—if there is such a thing in computer technology—the forensic duplication would be combed through using a hex or disk editor application. Later the forensic applications and suites evolved and automated some of the processes or streamlined them. The forensic practitioner would undelete files, search for temporary files, recover e-mail, and perform other functions to try and find the evidence contained on the media.

Today there are more user-friendly programs that present data in a GUI, and automate much of the extremely technical work that used to require in-depth knowledge and expertise with a hex editor. There is also a wealth of hardware to make the practice even more conducive, but the reality is the processes thus far have not changed that much.

From the time of those first primordial seizures to today, a set of *Best Practices* has emerged; the attempt is to provide a foundation for the work performed under the heading Digital Forensics:

- Do not alter the original media in any way.
- Always work on a duplicate copy, not the original.

- The examination media must be sterile as to ensure that no residual data will interfere with the investigation data.

- The investigator must remain impartial and report the facts.

For the most part, best practices and methodology have remained unchanged since the origins of digital forensics. The system is documented; the hard drives are removed and hooked to a write-blocking device. The imaging utility of choice was used to create a forensic image, and the forensic application of choice is used for examination. The *Best Practices* were not viewed as guidelines; but as absolutes. This has worked well to date, but some elements are beginning to become dated. Although these best practices have served as a cornerstone for the current procedure, many of the elements of the best practices are beginning to fall behind the technology curve and may need to be changed or adjusted.

Unlike other forensic sciences, digital forensics subject matter continues to evolve, as do the techniques. Human fingerprints may be changing and evolve over time, but it won't be noticeable to the fingerprint specialists in their life-time. The trace chemicals in a piece of hair may change, but the hair itself is going to stay pretty much the same. The techniques may evolve, but the subject matter does not noticeably. Digital evidence on the other hand continues to change as the technology does. Operating systems and file systems will progress and change. Realistically, operating systems change nearly every five years. Storage arrays continue to grow larger and larger as the technology improves, magnetic data density increases, and the price points come down. Flash media drives continue to grow larger in capacity and smaller in form factor. The volume of devices with potential storage for evidence has grown exponentially and will continue to. Gaming systems, digital audio player, media systems, Digital Video Recorders—the list continues to grow. The boom in the digital camera market created a tremendous volume of devices and analysis need that traditionally were in the realm of photographic examiners, not the computer geek. As the assortment of potential evidence sources continues to grow, the methodologies need to expand greatly.

For example, a cellular phone normally needs to stay powered on to retain all the data. If the device stays on it may connect to a wireless network. To ensure the device is isolated from the network the investigator will need to use a Faraday device—but in reality by removing the device from the network we actually change the data on the device. The device will make a note to itself of the details of going off the network.

Terminology Alert...

Faraday Device

A Faraday device or Faraday cage is a device constructed to block radio signals from entering or exiting the protected area, creating an electromagnetic shield. It consists of a metal conductor or a mesh that prohibits the entry or escape of electromagnetic signals.

In the pages that follow I will address some of the difficulties that occur and how some of the technologies and best practices are falling behind the technology curve. These include not only technical challenges but the procedural challenges.

Phases of Digital Forensics

Traditional digital forensics can be broken down into four phases. Some of the work performed may overlap into the different phases, but they are very different:

- Collection
- Examination
- Analysis
- Reporting

Collection is the preservation of evidence for analysis. Current best practices state that digital evidence needs to be an exact copy—normally a bit stream copy or bit-for-bit duplication—of the original media. The bit stream copy is then run through a cryptographic hashing algorithm to assure it is an unaltered copy. In modern digital forensics often this is done by physically removing the hard drive from the device, connecting it to a write blocking unit, and using a piece of forensic software that makes forensic duplicates. Examination is the methodical combing of the data to find the evidence. This includes work such as document and e-mail extraction, searching for suspicious binaries, and data carving. Analysis is the process of using the evidence recovered to work to solving the crime. The analysis is the pulling together of all the bits and pieces and deciphering them into a story of what happened. Report is the phase where all the other phases are documented and explained. The report should contain the documentation of the hardware, the tools used, the techniques used, and the findings. All the individual phases have their own issues and challenges.

TIP

Here are some great resources on Computer Incident Handling and Digital Forensics:

NIST "Computer Security Incident Handling Guide" SP800-61 http://csrc.nist.gov/publications/nistpubs/800-61/sp800-61.pdf

NIST "Guide to Integrating Forensic Techniques into Incident Response"SP800-96 http://csrc.nist.gov/publications/nistpubs/800-96/sp800-96.pdf

National Institute of Justice – Forensic Examination of Digital Evidence: A Guide for Law Enforcement

www.ojp.usdoj.gov/nij/pubs-sum/199408.htm

RFC Guidelines for Evidence Collection and Archiving www.faqs.org/rfcs/rfc3227.html

---

Collection

Traditional digital forensics best practices are to make a full bit stream copy of the physical volume. This normally entails physically removing the hard drives from the suspect system, and attaching the drive to another system for forensics duplication. A forensic image is a bit-by-bit copy of the original media. It copies all the data on a storage device, including unused portions, the deleted files, and anything else that may have been on the device. The suspect hard drive should be protected from alteration (remember the procedure?) by a hardware solution, a software solution, or both. The hardware solution is normally either a write-blocker or a hardware imaging device. A write-blocker blocks the write commands from the examination system that some operating systems would normally perform. Software solutions entail mounting the suspect drive or device as read-only by the operating system.

The data must be unaltered and the chain of custody must be maintained. Where practical, all the work should be performed on a copy; the originals need to be preserved and archived. To be able to ensure the data is unaltered, the original drive and the imaged drive are hashed and the hashes are compared to ensure that an exact bit-by-bit copy has been acquired.

Terminology Alert...

Hashes

Hashes use cryptographic algorithms to create a message digest of the data and represent it as a relatively small piece of data. The hash can be used to compare a hash of the original data to the forensic copy. When the hashes match, it is accepted as proof that the data is an exact copy. Although it has not been challenged yet, the traditional hashes of CRC, MD5, and SHA1 have been cracked. Also, there are limitations in the sheer volume of 128 bit hashing algorithms such as MD5. There are only 2^{128} possible MD5 hashes. If the large multi-terabyte file server being analyzed stores $2^{128} + 1$ files, there absolutely will be two different files with unique data with the same hash. Now it is understood that 2^{128} is about 340 billion billion billion billion, and it would be an extremely large storage array of tiny files, but this fact opens the door for doubt, which could ruin a criminal prosecution. Although 2^{128} is still a huge number, as storage grows, it is not unrealistic to believe that 128 bit hashes will become an increasing issue. It will probably be an issue on large storage systems long before it becomes as big an issue on single workstations. The future appears to be the use of the SHA-256 algorithm and other 256 bit hashes. For now, the National Software Reference Library Hashes use the SHA-1 and MD5 algorithms.

Digital evidence needs to be:

- **Admissible** It must conform to certain legal rules before it can be put before a court.

- **Authentic** The data must be proven to relate to the incident. This is where additional documentation is important.

- **Complete** It must be impartial and tell the entire account.

- **Reliable** There can be nothing relative to the collection and handling of the evidence that could create any doubt. Chain of Custody procedures become crucial.

- **Believable** The reports and documentation must present everything so it is believable and understandable by a judge or jury.

Any digital evidence collected must meet these requirements. The challenge that is surfacing is the admissibility. There are the traditional rules and best practices that concentrate on data from static or powered down systems. As we will see next, there are issues where this approach is either difficult, impossible, or may leave large amounts of data behind. Challenges to collecting the data for analysis can be getting the files off the systems, and once they are off the system. Does the system have some way of connecting external storage or is there even physical access to do so? If there is no physical access, how long will it take to move the data off the system to work with it? An option may be to work with the data on the system, but is there enough storage on it to be able to duplicate and analyze it? If the system was compromised, can the use of the utilities and binaries on it be trusted? Most likely not.

The next option is to move the data off via the network connection. How large is the network link to move the data off? If the data cannot be worked onsite, do you have the storage to transport it? Do you have the storage to work with it later? Do you have systems powerful enough to comb and query through all the data? Are all the systems in the same data center, or do you have to travel or have multiple teams working simultaneously? There are a multitude of questions, and some preplanning can be essential.

Incidents at a large business or other large network can aggravate these issues, and can be extremely complex. The cyber crime responder will almost surely find a variety of systems running a multitude of operating systems. The devices can encompass nearly everything and anything. The most important step when responding to a large cyber crime incident is to take a few minutes and first figure out what kind of systems you are dealing with. It's worth the time to gather any available documentation, such as network diagrams and system configurations.

The key early on is to avoid tunnel vision. There can be a multitude of systems that need data to be recovered from them, needing possibly as many ways to get at the data. It is easy to fall into the trap of centering on the first system found to be compromised or involved, when that system may be the tip of the iceberg. If all the concentration of the investigation is centered on the first system, then all the other evidence may be missed initially. Or if the retention times of logs or volatile data are too short, then the data may be gone forever. Just like a lost hiker searching for the path, work in circles out from the point of discovery. From that initial machine of interest, begin to look outward, concentrating on access paths that lead to it. Do not forget physical paths to a system—access controls and video surveillance is present in most data centers or offices, and physical access logs definitely should be reviewed.

Preparation

An assortment of tools are needed, both hardware and software. If you have the opportunity, try and get as much information as possible before you go to the machines. If it is in your native environment, preplan what is required for a normal engagement, and for the contingencies. A few extra phone calls or extra minutes to gather extra tools can save hours later trying other acquisition methods or struggling with inadequate hand tools. It can also help you determine if you need additional resources, or if it is over your head. If you are in a corporate environment you should have the specifications for the critical systems available to assist law enforcement in working with your systems if you are not going to do the acquisitions in-house. Most likely this information should be available for disaster recovery or hardware failure issues.

Be sure to have enough drives or storage to hold all the forensic images that will be collected. The drives should be prepared beforehand. The preparation should entail wiping the drive so that there is no data that could contaminate the data collected. It also eliminates the allegation that there could be data planted or that the evidence collected was tainted. A log should be kept that documents the preparation of the storage media.

A federal law enforcement officer appears at a data center to assist in a cyber crime investigation. He states to the corporate forensics person handling the case, "I'm here to pick up the server." The corporate forensics person stares at him blankly, and then asks, "Did you bring a box truck and a few more men and maybe a few small boys to help?" "Why?" asks the officer. "Because the 'server' is seven racks if you include the storage array!"

Considering many middle of the road personal computers today are shipping with 400 GB drives, the full bit stream copying or imaging is becoming a hardware and time commitment. Something to consider: hardware-based imaging solutions such as the Logicube MD5 require a target drive larger than the evidence drive. Currently the choice would be a 500 GB or 750 GB drive. Encounter a 750 GB drive, and the collection needs to be done with a solution that allows the image to span media. One Terabyte single drives will enter the consumer market in 2007. The point is a plan B should always be considered or prepared in case the primary method just won't work. An interesting trend to watch is the growth of storage media. The concept of Moore's Law as it relates to processing power is well known. Hard drives since their introduction in 1956 took 35 years to reach 1 gigabyte. One gigabyte is routinely carried in digital cameras and cell phones today. The 500 gigabyte or half a terabyte drive took 14 more years to make it to the consumer market. It only took two more years to double and reach the one terabyte mark [PC World]. As this trend continues the volume of data to examine will explode.

When it comes to being prepared for response, a Linux machine is a must-have. Some people will like a Mac, and they work well in this situation also. A system that can perform a SMB and NFS mounts, run netcat, ftp, and scp can be invaluable. A Windows system can do these things also, but they need far more third-party software to do so. A *nix base system will also have the ability to mount a wider variety of file systems. Once the data is recovered, all the native *nix tools will be available to search and manipulate the data.

Notes from the Underground...

Suggested Tool Kit Contents

Your tool kit should contain the following components:

Hardware Target hard drives, write blocker, and cables (network, IDE, and SCSI)

Software Boot disks and drivers for both your forensic system and any system you may encounter, especially for network cards

Tools Allen keys; large and small screwdrivers (standard, Phillips, and Torx)

Other content Labels , anti-static bags, pens and markers, blank media: (CDs, DVDs), and a camera

A final consideration is that data may need to be preserved in order of volatility. The most volatile data needs to be preserved first. This applies to running systems for the most part, but the way in which we approach live systems will become more important in the near future; but more on that later. An example of an order of recovery of system data according to volatility looks like this:

- **Live system information** This includes memory, the routing table, ARP cache, and a process list. The concern with live system information is that it is difficult or impossible to image the system memory or other live data with altering the original data.

- **Virtual memory** Swap space or paging files

- **Physical disks** The physical hard disks of a system

- **Backups** Offline back-up media such as magnetic tape or other media: It is extremely possibly the data you are looking for may not be on the system today, but it was there yesterday and is on last night's backup.

The multitude of potential systems and devices that may be encountered during a cyber crime investigation requires the creation of a large and flexible toolkit. This toolkit needs to include not only the hardware and software to deal with a variety of devices, but the investigator's own toolkit of tricks and procedures to deal with them. This toolkit should include resources to turn to when the forensic practitioner is in a situation beyond their skills.

Difficulties When Collecting Evidence from Nontraditional Devices

We have witnessed an explosion in the growth of storage media, but we have also seen the continuing development of alternative storage media. The diversity of devices and storage formats continues to be a challenge. These can include, but are not limited to, the following.

Hard Drive Interfaces

The first issue, though not really new, has expanded with the popularity of SATA and other technologies. For the most part, hard drives were either IDE or SCSI. IDE was either 3 1/2 or 2 1/2 . With the marvels of technology we now have drives with the 1.8-inch interface. There is the addition of SATA, in both 3 1/2 and laptop sizes, which luckily use the same connectors. Then there are all the SCSI adapters. There is also Fiber channel, but we will save that for later. In the absence of a drive adapter, there is always network acquisition at the cost of time. Then again there are only a bazillion network cards to try and build boot disks or scrounge drivers for.

The best way to be ready for the different drive interfaces is have a selection of drive adapters on hand. The cost of most of them is relatively inexpensive. Most of the adapters allow the use of a standard IDE write-block device, or once adapted, mounted read-only. As always be sure to test and validate a configuration before using it on an actual acquisition.

If the drive cannot be adapted to a writeblock, there is always the option of a network or USB acquisition.

MP3 and Digital Entertainment Systems

MP3 players such as iPods continue to increase in storage capacity and capabilities. Many have the ability to act as a personal organizer. Most devices also have the ability to act as portable storage. In addition, malware has been created to use devices like iPods to steal data from systems.

Most of these devices can be treated like an external hard drive. Although many of them have a small hard drive and can be disassembled and the drive removed for acquisition, this can be tedious and difficult. A solid strategy is to acquire them though their interface, which is normally USB. As with an external drive they can be write-block through hardware solutions or mounting the drive, and read-only through the operating system.

Notes from the Underground...

Storing Data on Alternative Media

Why would we even care about the data on some alternative media? In addition to the sheer storage potential, the devices have become powerful enough to allow software to be run on them. Some examples:

Pod slurping Pod slurping is the use of an iPod to steal information from a system. Once the iPod is connected an application launches and copies all the files of specified types to the iPod in under a few minutes. Due to the increasing storage capacity of an iPod, multiple systems can be dumped to a single device.

MP3 players and automatic teller machines (ATMs) MP3 players with a recording function have been used to compromise certain ATMs by recording the sounds from the telephone lines. Once all the data is captured, it can be used to steal from the accounts that have used the ATM.

Phones and PDAs

Nearly everyone is carrying a cell phone today, if not several. The line between the cell phone and the PDA has blurred. Similarly, the line between a cell phone, PDA, or computer has again blurred. It is not uncommon for a device to have over 1 GB of storage, and can be a gold mine of data and evidence. Just be sure you legal process paperwork or privacy policies are addressed during seizure. The data on devices that run on battery can be extremely volatile, and they may need to be processed quickly or kept on a power supply. Special care must also be taken to avoid data corruption on wireless-enabled devices, so a Faraday device should be considered.

Mobile phones are probably one of digital forensics' biggest conundrums. The sheer volume of manufacturers, chipsets, and operating systems (many of them proprietary) makes it impossible to gather data from all the devices through the same process. It is often impossible to acquire a full physical dump of all the storage on a device. A logical dump of the information is all many software packages can provide. Some software packages require the installation of an applet or driver to provide for the acquisition. Due to the fact that connectivity to the device requires the device to be powered up, nearly all acquisitions are live acquisitions. The acquisition of the device will change the data. The volatility of the data on a mobile device also contradicts the traditional realm of digital forensics as the acquisition is similar to a network forensic capture since it is a snapshot at a specific moment in time. It is highly likely that if the device was reacquired that data would be different, and in turn the hashes of the data would be different. At least any of the memory cards in the device can be acquired in a traditional manner.

A cell phone or wireless-enabled PDA should be isolated via a Faraday device. The wireless device should also have an auxiliary power source if the batteries will not maintain the unit until it can be processed. This is especially important because some devices will panic and scan for the network when isolated, using its power reserve faster than normal. Due to the volatility issue presented by power and wireless networks the device should be processed as soon as possible. The practitioner will also find there is no silver bullet for phones and PDAs. An extensive toolbox of software and cables will be needed if a variety of devices is encountered. Lastly if all else fails, the data on the devices can be documented by manually examining them and photographing the screens as the exam progresses.

Flash Memory

Many devices use flash memory. MP3 players, digital cameras, cell phones, USB drives, and handhelds are examples. During evidence collection and seizure be sure to look carefully for pieces of media. Formats like Mini SD are extremely small. Also be sure to look for the hardware that may go with the media. Some formats like xD are used in a limited number of devices. Flash memory can be challenging as there are already many formats and more are being created. The density continues to improve as does data storage in general, so some flash media is becoming quite large.

Flash memory card readers for a variety of formats are a must. Luckily they are relatively inexpensive to keep most of the formats on hand. There are some forensic versions available that are built read-only, which helps reduce the potential issues, but a normal card reader can be used with any of the other procedures to protect the data integrity.

Notes from the Underground...

U3 Smart Drives

U3 Smart Drives are some of the latest portable storage technology solutions. Although they are extremely handy with features like portable software, they can be a challenge for the forensic practitioner. Some of the same features that make U3 drives so versatile can also make them difficult. The U3 drives by design remove all personal data when removed, therefore there is very little artifact to analyze when they are removed from a system. U3 drives also have an autorun feature similar to a CD. The autorun can be a security issue as shown by projects like the U3 USB Hacksaw from HAK.5. The USB Hacksaw, when inserted into a system, automatically executes software that locates documents on the infected machine and sends them via encrypted e-mail to the attacker (www.hak5.org/wiki/USB_Hacksaw).

U3 drives also normally have security software included that can create protected areas of the drive to protect user data. These encrypted areas can be a challenge for the forensic practitioner to access.

Gaming Machines

Modified or "modded" game consoles like an Xbox, Xbox 360, or PS2 can be a source of evidence. For example: An Xbox with a mod chip and Xbox Media center can be a powerful system used to store video, music, or other data. The system can act as a server or a client. Nonmodified systems use a proprietary file system, not supported by more forensic applications. What can make the triage of the system tricky is that it is often difficult to tell from the exterior if the machine has been modified. This is an example where some traditional investigative intelligence and triage may reduce the forensic practitioner's workload.

Gaming system should absolutely be considered during the evidence seizure process. The can be treated and handled basically as any other PC during acquisition and examination as they used the same basic hard drive busses.

GPS

Global Positioning System receivers are fairly commonplace in many vehicles or handheld units. They can provide valuable information in the form of historical locations or waypoints. Some of the more advanced units combine cellular radios to allow for tracking or other data uses. These hybrid units, like many other devices, continue to blur the lines between traditional drives classification. So for the digital forensics practitioner, what procedure should be used? An agency's GPS procedure or their cell phone procedure?

A GPS will likely require some homework before tackling. There will often be drivers or manufacturer-specific software required to interface with the device. If there is no other way to extract data from the device, like a cell phone, a manual exam taking pictures may be required.

Digital Video Recorders

From TiVo or a MythTV system to commercial camera system digital video recorder (DVR), the DVR continues to find its place in homes as part of entertainment systems, or in businesses as part of the security system. Many commercial DVRs use proprietary file systems or data formats. They may require a volume of file carving or manual analysis. A TiVo, which in addition to having Wi-Fi network capability and transferring data to other PCs, now also allows some limited Internet functions. Commercial digital video recorders may also use special codecs for playback; research your devices before attacking them.

DVRs should also be considered during the evidence seizure process. They can be treated and handled basically as any other PC during acquisition and examination since they used the same basic hard drive busses. A common issue with the examination of commercial DVRs is to ascertain the format their video files are in. Some research into the device and the codecs used should be started early when faced with one.

PBX and VoIP Systems

The line between the traditional PBX and the everyday IT sever has virtually vanished. The evolution of Voice Over Internet Protocol (VOIP) utilizing PCI-based interface cards and software designed to work on nonproprietary operating systems have made the PBX just another server. Examples are an Asterisk server running on a Linux system, or YATE on a Windows system. Voicemail servers and Interactive Voice Response systems are following suit. The trend of expanding VOIP services on commodity hardware coupled with the expansion of security research into VOIP protocols may make the telephony equipment a more prevalent target of cyber crime. The maturing of VOIP and the attention it is receiving from security researchers means it will also receive attention from blackhats and crackers. When approaching these systems, remember there can be many interfaces to communications networks beyond Ethernet such as PSTN and ISDN.

The documentation of the connections is always important, but probably even more so when dealing with a telecom device as there will likely be more than usual. Like many other systems in the nontraditional arena, a PBX will require some research to aid in making sound decisions about how to approach it. A PBX based on a traditional server can be approached like any other server, but a legacy commercial PBX can be a very specialized piece of equipment requiring special skills.

TIP

Resources for Alternative Media Forensics:
www.Multimediaforensics.comwww.Phone-forensics.com
Phone Forensics Yahoo Group

Hardware Documentation Difficulties

Documenting hardware configuration is a tedious but essential part of the forensic process. The magnitude of documentation is in direct correlation to number and type of devices being acquired. What we, as examiners, cannot afford to forget are the various aspects to documenting hardware.

Within the documentation process itself, all the system configurations need to be documented, including the installed hardware and BIOS settings, such as the boot device. Other essential aspects of hardware documentation are the time settings of the system and the system clock of each device. The system time needs to be documented and compared to the actual time. The time zone setting may also be crucial when creating timelines or other analysis. The presence of a NTP time server should be noted. Remember, a system on a Microsoft Windows domain will sync its time with the domain controller, but the time by default can be off by 20 seconds and function properly.

Traditional forensics dictates that all the identifying labels and numbers are documented. Often pictures of all sides and labels are taken as part of the documentation process. This can also be extremely difficult with large systems. It could potentially take a day to unrack and photograph all the systems in a rack. Depending on the approach taken to acquire data from a system, the complete detailed hardware documentation may need to occur after the acquisition is done. If the system is live it most likely will not be desirable to shut down a complex system to document it, and then restart it to perform an acquisition. If you have the opportunity, look at a blade server enclosure and the servers in a datacenter in one day. Consider how to document each of the blades as you would a typical PC. Then think about the fact that a typical rack can often hold six enclosures holding 16 blade servers. I would hope the IT staff has some decent documentation to work from. If you can verify from their existing documentation instead of working from scratch, you can save a lot of time.

A large storage system is probably another example of an instance where the devices will need to be documented after they are acquired unless the physical option is used. This is because it may not be practical to image each drive individually. Once the storage system's logical image is complete, the drives can be removed from the enclosure and documented. The documentation of rack after rack of hard drives can be even more daunting than even blade servers.

The network topology and any systems that directly interface with the system such as through NFS or SMB mounts should also be documented. If the investigation expands, it may be necessary to increase the documentation of the surrounding network to encompass the switches, routers, and any other network equipment. In the case of an intrusion any of these paths could be the source of the compromise.

A final item to document is the console location if one exists. Even today, not all unauthorized access happens through a network connection.

Complete and clear documentation is key to a successful investigation. If the incident leads to litigation the report created from the documentation will make a valuable reference for the examiner. Complete documentation will help to remove any doubt cast by the defense or other party in a civil matter.

Difficulties When Collecting Data from Raid Arrays, SAN, and NAS Devices

Enter the corporate or government arena and now the 500 GB hard drive becomes multiterabytes or petabytes storage systems. Faced with a 20 terabyte SAN, the complexity of obtaining a forensic image of the physical drives and reassembling the logical volume is considerable. Add the logistics of storing the forensic images or owning the storage hardware "just in case" is not always very practical.

So for sake of argument, let's say you were able to image and hold the 20 terabyte SAN array, and maybe reassemble it into a logical volume; how much computing power and time does it take to search that volume of data?

The era is approaching where a better triage process needs to occur so the evidence that is pertinent to the investigation is collected first. The adoption of more parallel operations needs to occur. The examination and analysis phases need to begin as the systems triaged as less important continue to be acquired and imaged. This in time will make the examination and analysis processes more efficient, and allows investigations to complete in a timelier manner.

Depending on the goals of the investigation, often an entire system may not be entirely necessary. If there is a single individual under investigation for financial fraud, then it may likely not be of value or necessary to image 20 terabytes of storage on a file server that affects 200 other employees. It is more efficient to triage the area where the individual had access and start with that data.

RAID

A Redundant Array of Independent Disks and Network Attacked Storage are used to hold large volumes of data and often provide some level of redundancy. A RAID uses multiple disks to provide redundancy or performance enhancements over a single disk. As it applies to forensics, the RAID appears as one logical disk, but spans multiple physical disks. If the individual physical disks are removed and imaged separately, the RAID must be reassembled using the forensic software later in order to get the useful data. It is often much simpler to perform an acquisition of the logical drive. If your organization policies require it, after the logical acquisition a physical acquisition of all the drives can be performed. A note about RAID array reassembly: Be sure to get the raid controller configuration. It can save you tremendous amounts of time later if the assembly of the physical images is performed.

SAN

Storage area networks (SAN) like NAS are challenging not only because of the size, but the technology involved. The two predominant SAN types are fiber-channel and iSCSI. The positive thing about SANs is that they are divided into logical unit numbers (LUN). If the data relevant to the investigation is restricted to a single system, then the LUN allocated to that system may be the only part of the SAN that needs to be acquired. Linux tends to be the logical choice to use as an imaging platform since there are not many fiber-channel write blocks at the time of this writing. An important point is to make sure the host bus adapter (HBA) is supported. iSCSI SANs can normally be attached via the network adapter. If time is more of an issue than budget, there are iSCSI HBAs with Linux support available to offload some of the processing from the CPU. The HBAs have an onboard SCSI Application Specific Integrated Circuit, which would provide a considerable performance gain.

The greatest challenge when working with a SAN is sheer storage to copy the data to. Vendors are building great solutions like multiterabyte portable RAID enclosures to assist with this issue. Another option is to use software that allows the spanning of target media during an acquisition.

The hardware to deal with large storage systems can be expensive. A multiterabyte portable raid and a fiber channel write-block can run well over $10,000.

NAS

Network attached storage (NAS) devices are appliances with the sole purpose of providing data storage. A NAS can be a challenge to obtain a forensic image from since they run limited services and protocols. If they can be acquired forensically through an attached system, then that may be the preferred option. Otherwise the NAS may need to be disassembled and imaged drive by drive. There are many NAS devices designed and marketed for the home or small business user. They are no longer just in the realm of the enterprise. Fortunately for the cyber crime investigator, the storage capacities are not yet that extremely large—but that will change with time.

So how do we follow the traditional best practices again when there is no real practical way to access the drives directly and take physical images? The other very real consideration with large storage systems is there is a large investment into the hardware. Since there is a large investment it would be logical to assume that system is attached to a system that is at least marginally important. For a business that needs its systems running to generate revenue, it may again become a business decision to limit the scope of work to limit the downtime.

Difficulties When Collecting Data from Virtual Machines

Virtual machines residing on a host system are commonplace for a variety reasons, from Enterprise virtual servers to nefarious purposes on a blackhat's machine. Virtualization applications have matured to the extent that reliable systems can be built for production machines, not just development and testing work as in the past. What can make virtual machines interesting is they could conceivably be a host of one operating system hosting multiple virtualization platforms, each with multiple virtual machines of different operating systems. The forensic practitioner is faced with the specter of multiple OSes, and the complexity of each of the virtualization applications on a single system. Add a RAID or external storage and one may desire a change of profession.

Luckily most of the major forensic suites support the most popular virtual disk formats, making the acquisitions a bit easier. Virtual machines can also be imaged live just like a physical system if a live system is encountered.

A static or dead acquisition depends on the tool choice. One option is to export the virtual disk file from the host machine's image and mount the virtual disk file as a drive. Another choice is to use a tool like VMware Disk mount utility. It allows the virtual disk to appear as a drive attached to the system. The virtual disk then can be imaged with the tool of choice if it is not natively supported. The reality is the virtual disk is very similar to a dd image with some additional data.

Difficulties When Conducting Memory Acquisition and Analysis

Memory analysis is becoming more needed and common on running systems. Especially as systems can be compromised without ever accessing the disk the only artifact may be in memory. Commercial products like Core Impact do it, so it is conceivable that the product or its technology can be used for nefarious purposes.

There are multiple examples of malware such as the Witty Worm that are memory resident only. This and other potentially valuable pieces of investigative data will be missed if we continue to examine only systems that have been shut down. The volume of data that is memory resident today is over a hundred times larger than the entire hard drive from the 1980s. It's another example where the accepted procedures and best practices are lagging behind the technology curve.

TIP

An excellent paper on memory acquisition and analysis by Mariusz Burdach is available on his Web site, http://forensic.seccure.net/ pdf/mburdach_digital_forensics_of_physical_memory.pdf.

Avoid calling a memory acquisition an "image." It is not a true image in the traditional forensics sense. This is because without specialized hardware it is not really possible to create a bit by image of the system memory without affecting some part of it. In a way it is similar in concept to the Heisenberg uncertainty principle: when an electron's location is measured, it is moved. When memory is acquired, it is normally changed.

Most *nixes allow the acquisition of memory fairly easily, because the system sees memory as a file like everything else. The staple *dd* or any of its forensic variants like *dcfldd* can be used to create a memory acquisition. Microsoft Windows allows access to the physical memory object but requires Administrative privileges to access it. There are tools available that allow the memory to be acquired; the versions of *dd* compiled for Windows are the most common. There are also tools and scripts available to assist in analyzing the dump.

A note: there have been security enhancements in Windows XP 64-bit, Windows 2003 Server SP1, and Windows Vista. These versions of the operating systems block all user mode access to the physical memory.

The future appears to be hardware-based devices such as a dedicated PCI card [hwmem] or through the IEEE 1394 firewire interface [fwmem], but even though the concepts and prototypes have existed for years there are no readily available commercial products. The apparent advantage of hardware solutions is the decreased impact on the running system. For this reason, the hardware solutions will most likely emerge as the favored method. There is currently a debate, and will continue to be for some time, over the practice of memory acquisitions. IT is seen by many as contaminating the evidence. Others see it as obtaining all the data and evidence available. The often-used defensive analogy is in a physical crime scene, and the crime scene unit enters the area to recover fiber and fingerprints. Their actions and movements are documented to prove they did as little contamination as possible. In the digital realm many feel if the same care is taken to document all the actions taken then the contamination is controlled and documented.

My personal opinion is I would rather have the data and have to fight to admissibility later than lose potentially key data and investigative intelligence.

Examination

Examination consists of the methodical sifting and combing of the data. It may consist of examining dates, metadata, images, document content, or anything else. Many forensic practitioners use the same step-by-step process for their examination; key word search, obtain web histories, search unallocated space, search file slack. It all depends on what the goal of your investigation consists of. Remember forensics is just an aspect of the larger investigation. Since the needs of the exam may change with the investigation I believe the traditional forensic menu used by many is becoming impractical. The Nintendo Forensics practice of running some keyword searches and some scripts written by others is probably missing lots of key evidence.

The larger volumes of data require better triage methods while streamlining the process to allow for deeper inspection of key areas like the Windows registry. The increased use of tools such as hashes to filter known files along with other tools to sort the files for focused examination can help speed the examination process when facing a huge amount of data.

Notes from the Underground...

Forensic Tools

There are many tools that can assist with forensic examination. The tool selection can be based on personal preference, or the strengths of the individual application, or sometimes budget. There are forensic packages that can cost thousands of dollars or be freeware. Regardless of the tools chosen, it is a best practice, when possible, to use multiple tools. The primary reason is to not miss a piece of evidence due to an issue inherent to the tool—when the multiple tools agree on a finding it helps remove any doubts surrounding the reliability of the tool.

Utility of Hash Sets

Hash sets are precompiled lists or databases of known file hashes. For instance all the files associated with an application install or a series of illegal images are hashed with a cryptographic algorithm and the resulting hashes are put into an indexed collection. During an examination, the hashes of the application set are compared to all the hashes of the files found on the system. A matching hash mathematically nearly guarantees the file is a file associated with the application regardless of its name. Hashes traditionally have been used to find known suspicious files such as malware, cracker tools, or illegal images.

Just as hash sets can be used to look for known bad things, through the same process they can be used to locate known good or benign files. By using hash sets to locate the files that are not related to the investigation or are unchanged operating system files, for example, they can filter out the noise. Dependant on the triage of a case, a hash set of known operating system files can quickly filter out a quantity of files that in all likelihood do not need to be examined. For instance an incident where there is not believed to be a compromise of the system would not initially need to search or examine all the driver files. The use of hashes to filter out known files known to be unaltered from the hardware vendor can greatly reduce the volume of information to be examined and in turn the time to examine a system. The files left behind are either altered or files in user space that will probably be where the real evidence or information lies.

TIP

The creation of personal hash sets as part of the preparation task can be a time saver later. Creating hash sets of all of an organization's gold or standard images of workstations and servers used for new installs necessitates only altered or added files to be analyzed. The files of internal applications can also be hashed and sets created to also help filter out files that would not be included in more mainstream hash sets.

Difficulties Associated with Examining a System with Full Disk Encryption

An increasingly common issue is full disk encryption. This will change how hard drives are acquired. As the issues of lost and stolen laptops continue to impact organizations, many IT departments are turning to full- or partial-disk encryption to protect data. For the forensic practitioner, this usually means the data of interest will be in the encrypted portions of the drive.

If all the data of interest is encrypted, traditional forensic practices will be useless. The choices are to perform a live image of the system with the encrypted storage mounted, if possible, or unencrypt the drive after acquisition.

As are many other issues in contemporary digital forensics, this is another area where the best practices and procedures are trailing the technology. Which solution you use should be evaluated and your own procedures created. In a crunch, the live system image will almost always be faster.

Trusted Platform Module (TPM)

The Trusted Platform Module is another emerging technology that will enhance existing encryption schemes. The TPM is a chipset being installed in newer machines that stores keys, passwords, and certificates. The chipset provides for hardware-based encryption functionality that may prove to be a challenge.

A suggested methodology for dealing with drives that have been encrypted with full disk encryption follows:

- Image in state traditionally
- Restore the acquired image back to a sanitized target disk
- Decrypt the target disk
- Acquire the decrypted target disk
- Analyze the decrypted disk as normal

This methodology, although significantly increasing the time required and doubling the required storage, leaves the original unaltered and maintains a forensic image of the original. It sounds simple, but the challenge is the third step. Decrypting the drive may take the a few Cray super computers and the code breakers of the NSA if the encryption is strong and the key unavailable. In lieu of those resources, the normal tricks of password cracking can be used. The requirement for complex passwords and the volume of passwords the average user must remember has rekindled the trend of written down passwords. When searching for passwords look for hiding places within an arms length. Remember to check for passwords during incident response and seizure phases. Another trick is to use the other evidence found to create a dictionary to use for a brute force attack. Remember that the hash of the original encrypted drive will not match the unencrypted drive. They are different data sets and need to be documented as such.

Alternative Forensic Processes

A newer concept, at least in name is *fast forensics*. Fast forensics is defined as "those investigative processes that are conducted within the first few hours of an investigation, that provides information used during the suspect interview phase. Due to the need for information to be obtained in a relatively short time frame, fast forensics usually involves an on site/field analysis of the computer system in question."[nw3c] The implementation of fast forensics creates a need for some additional resources and procedures to perform some examination and initial analysis functions outside of the lab. The focus is to provide some important intelligence to provide the investigators key pieces of evidence or leads to use in interviews or other searches.

Some fast forensics techniques utilize Linux or other forensic boot disks to perform on-scene searches or document extraction. The boot disks run in memory only and mount the hard drives as read only so as not to corrupt the evidence.

Analysis

Every cyber crime incident will involve at least some analysis of data retrieved from systems. Some will consist of only a few small files from a system or two, or may range to terabytes from many machines. The core of an investigation could consist of a single piece of media or it may consist of thousands of hard drives. The trick lies in the analysis that will put all the pieces together. The analysis of an entire cyber crime event can be far more complex than the analysis of any of the systems themselves; the sum of the parts is truly greater than the whole. It can be likened to a symphony. Any single instrument may be difficult to play, but to bring all the pieces together is far more complex. The cyber crime investigator needs to build a toolbox of utilities to analyze the data from a myriad of systems and be able to correlate the data into a complete, coherent picture.

The analysis of the digital forensic process is the phase where we look deeper into the data. The analysis is the sum of all the data applied toward the resolution of the incident.

An example of an analysis follows.

An intellectual property theft case didn't yield much until the data from a bunch of systems were pulled together. The file server audit logs were reviewed and the user list it provided was used to query the proxy server logs. When the log files for those uses were reviewed a short list was created by focusing on webmail and forum traffic. The short list was used to triage and prioritize the exams of the user workstations. The exams of the workstations quickly revealed the individual when the webmail messages were pulled from the internet cache, and recreated.

During the analysis phase it is imperative to tie in any other investigation intelligence that has been gathered. It is in this phase that the data from multiple systems or sources is pulled together to create as complete a picture and event reconstruction as possible. There is a difference in evidence for court and evidence to find the next piece for the investigation. A piece of evidence discovered may not be strong enough to stand on its own, but may be the item that provides the next lead.

Another factor that is a challenge is that analysis of large amounts of data takes time. In the heat of an incident or a large high profile investigation it is often difficult to manage the expectation of management. It can take huge amounts of time to import logs into various applications. It can take hours to move and copy data between storage systems. Be prepared to explain why it may take days to get some preliminary answers. It could take weeks or months to have all the data combed, all the I's dotted and the T's crossed, especially in an incident that may effect customer data and have reporting requirements.

Notes from the Underground…

Anti-forensics

Anti-forensics is the movement to exploit weaknesses in the forensic process or tools. It can also be the acts of hiding data from the forensic exam. Old techniques were as simple as running a script to perform a *touch* command on every file to alter the date and time stamps. Other traditional techniques are log and temporary file deletion. Other tools and techniques have emerged that are far more sophisticated.

Metasploit Well known for the well-integrated suite of penetration testing tools, the Metasploit Framework had branched out into a suite of anti-forensics tools.

Timestomp A tool that allows you to modify all four NTFS timestamp values: modified, accessed, created, and entry modified.

Slacker A tool that allows you to hide files within the slack space of the NTFS file system.

Transmogrify An upcoming tool to defeat forensic tools' file signaturing capabilities by masking and unmasking your files as any file type.

And not as directly an anti-forensic tool as the others,

Sam Juicer A Meterpreter module that dumps the hashes from the SAM, but does it without ever hitting disk. Tools such as pwdump access the disk and potentially leave more footprints (www.metasploit.com/projects/antiforensics/).

The Defiler's Toolkit The Defiler's Toolkit consists of a pair of tools that allow a more secure deletion of files on UNIX systems. The toolkit is made up of Necrofile and Klismafile. Both files make alterations to the file system to remove evidence of the files that once existed. Necrofile overwrites or basically wipes the inodes that no longer have a file name associated to it. Klismafile does the same to the directory table. In theory the use of Klismafile is detectable by noticing the blank space in the directory table, but it would have to be explicitly looked for. More information about the Defiler's Tookit is available at www.phrack.org/archives/59/p59-0x06.txt.

Commercial tools The anti-forensic tools are no longer only in the realm of uber-hacker. With the availability of commercial tools to per-

Continued

form secure deletion, even novice computer users can work to hide their electronic footprints.

- **Evidence Eliminator** www.evidence-eliminator.com/ Robin Hood Software
- **Window Washer** www.webroot.com/consumer/products/ windowwasher/n-Webroot Software

Although these tools are not foolproof, they can make the forensic task extremely more difficult (www.phrack.org/archives/ 59/p59-0x06.txt).

Just as the investigation of a cyber crime event can involve any of a variety of systems or devices, it can involve a single machine or thousands. The addition of multiple systems complicates the analysis process as the data from the many examinations is pulled together.

Analysis of a Single Computer

Most cyber crime investigations involve the examination of a system or device, and most start with the exam of a single computer. The focus of the exam can be as diverse as the tasks the computer can be used for.

Metadata

Metadata is data about data. Examples are the author of a Word document, or the creation date of a spreadsheet. A resource for an overview of Microsoft Office Metadata is Microsoft KB223396. Depending on the scope or type of investigation, do not discount the importance of metadata.

A case that got its big lead from document metadata was the BTK case. The BTK killer sent the Wichita TV station KSAS a floppy disk with a message contained in a document. A forensic exam of the floppy disk revealed a file and some deleted files. The file metadata of the Test Art.rtf showed the file was last saved by user Dennis and listed the name of a church. A search for the church's Web site revealed the President of the congregation was Dennis Rader, who was eventually convicted of the BTK murders. [Stone]

Exchangeable Image File Format

Exchangeable Image File Format (EXIF) is metadata contained in an image file, and though it varies among devices it can provide valuable information such as the make and model of the camera that took the image. The EXIF can also reveal if an image has been altered with a graphics program. The EXIF data can be used to tie an image back to a specific model camera or cell phone with a camera. The EXIF data also often will have a date and time stamp of when the image was taken or altered. There are several EXIF formats; therefore, the data can vary slightly. Also be aware, not all devices will propagate all the data.

Binary and Malware Analysis

Some binary and malware analysis ability is a requirement. The initial step is to identify any malware that maybe on a system. This is often achieved through either being identified by hash sets, or not filtered by a hash set. Once a file that is suspicious is identified there are two major methods for analyzing it: statically and dynamically.

Static analysis entails searching the binary for text strings or identifying if the file was packed. Packing an executable compresses the file, normally to make reverse engineering more difficult.

Dynamic analysis uses behavioral analysis to identify the malware or its actions. The file is placed in a safe environment such as a test network or virtual machine. The file is then executed and its actions observed in a zoo for software. Items like network traffic generated or files accessed are noted and used to analyze the binary.

Notes from the Underground...

Virtual Machines

Virtual machines are the crash test dummies of forensics. In addition to being useful for malware analysis, they can be useful for documenting the actions of legitimate software or even user actions. When faced with trying to find out where evidence related to certain programs may be on a system, testing in a virtual machine allows the dynamic monitoring to lead the examiner to the static artifact on the real system.

It is important to identify malware on a system when conducting computer forensics. If the presence of malware is found, all is not lost in your case.

The malware can be monitored to identify its actions. Once documented, and its actions recorded, you can determine if the actions of the malware produced the results that are in dispute. If the malware did not produce the evidence in question, you will be able to counter defense's argument that the malware produced the evidence and not the suspect. If no malware exists, the Trojan defense again can be countered.

NOTE

A Trojan defense is a tactic used to deny performing some actions on a system by blaming a piece of malware such as a virus or worm.

Deleted Items

A strength of forensic applications is the ability to recover deleted files in entirety or at least the artifact that it existed. When an operating system deletes a file it does not remove the data. It only changes the pointer to the file to tell the file system that the file no longer exists and the space is available for new data. Forensic applications then identify the deleted files that still exist or display the artifact that they once did exist. Deleted files may affect the culpability of suspects by demonstrating willful actions to hide their actions.

Data Carving

Files of different types have pieces of data at the beginnings and ends that define what the file is. These pieces of data are called the headers and footers. Using the signatures of the headers and footers the applications and tools are able recover or carve files or pieces of files out of the *cruft* that ends up on storage media. Files that contain plain text characters can have the words carved out of their remnants. Data carving can be time consuming and tedious. It can also be rewarding because evidence can be recovered that would otherwise been missed.

E-mail Analysis

The analysis of e-mail has a burden of legal process in addition to the technical challenges. For law enforcement agents, the legal process is dependent on the state of the data. For the private sector, the proper policies need to be implemented and reviewed by attorneys to address the expectation of privacy issues.

There is far more analysis that can be performed on e-mail than just header analysis. E-mail analysis can depend on whether the data are stored on the server or the client. Do not overlook the utilities included in the server or client platform for search and advanced search functions. There are also normally import and export functions included that allow the data to be analyzed in other applications. For example, a Microsoft Outlook PST can be exported to Excel for analysis. Once in Excel summary reports such as a pivot table count can be run to find trends.

TIP

A powerful commercial tool to analyze many types of e-mail formats is Paraben Forensics Email Examiner. In addition to the ability to work with many e-mail file formats, it has the ability to recover deleted e-mail, and perform advanced searches on a wide variety of e-mail formats from multiple vendors.

Analysis of an Enterprise Event

The examination of a single machine can be complex and time consuming, but it can also be the tip of the iceberg. The complexity of a single workstation exam can be multiplied hundreds or thousands of times over. The likelihood of multiple operating systems and architectures and the additional burden of potentially complex network configurations can task even highly skilled practitioners.

Additional tools are needed to help correlate the data from all the individual systems and devices into a comprehensive form where it can be digested and analyzed. A series of log files can take on a whole new meaning when presented graphically. Examples of these are system flow charts and event timelines.

System Flow Charts

A flow chart, or other graphical representation of the network, can show which systems were impacted and when based on the analyzed data (see Figure 9.1). The chart would show the data excerpt of an IP address from the firewall log. Next it could show the snippet of a directory transversal from the Apache logs, and so forth. It becomes valuable especially when explaining the incident to nontechnical individuals.

Figure 9.1 System Flow Chart

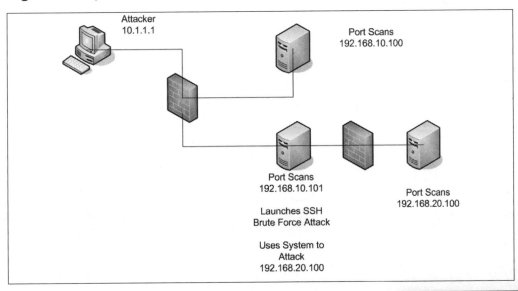

Beyond the usefulness of the graphical representation of the traffic, a system flow chart when compared to a network diagram may help point out areas that may have been affected but not yet identified. Graphical documents tend to work well when explaining results to nontechnical management or if the events lead to litigation, attorneys, and juries.

Timelines

A timeline graph of the incident or the analysis can be a valuable report. It can help display the entire progression of what analysis was done when on what system (see Figure 9.2). It is often easier to look at a chart and see the progression of an incident instead of sifting through a hundred e-mails later. Also a timeline could show what systems were impacted when based on the analysis data. The chart would show the data excerpt of an IP address from the firewall log. Next it could show the snippet of a directory transversal from the Apache logs, and so forth.

Figure 9.2 Timeline Graph

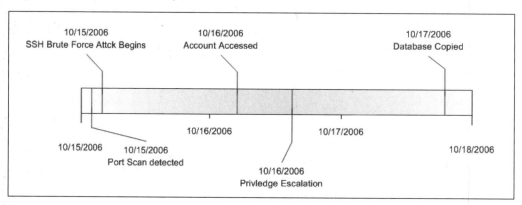

Timelines are useful to lay out the progression of events as they unfolded. They also are useful to highlight gaps in activity. These gaps in activity may be where some evidence was missed or there was activity not yet uncovered. As mentioned before graphical documents tend to work well when explaining results to nontechnical management or if the events lead to litigation, attorneys, and juries.

Tools for Data Analysis

There are as many ways to analyze the data as there are log files. There are tradeoffs to any of them, whether it is cost, performance, or complexity. Often tools that are used on a daily basis by system administrators to perform proactive troubleshooting and tuning can be the same tools used for reactive analysis.

Normally as the tolls increase in performance, they also increase in cost and/or complexity. Some of the tools are GREP, PERL scripts, Excel, SQL, and commercial network forensics tools.

GREP

GREP is an indispensable tool and an essential skill for the incident responder or forensics practitioner. The GREP command simply searches a file or files for a pattern. The power is in the flexibility of the patterns that can be created or the ability to recursively search directory structures of files. GREP is licensed under the GPL, so its cost is nothing, and GREP exists natively on virtually every *nix operating system, and has been ported to everything else. For the novice, there are many Internet sources on how to craft GREP patterns. An important limitation to remember is GREP works on text-based files, and will not be able to search every file that may be encountered. If you are dealing with large text-based log files then GREP is extremely useful.

Spreadsheets

If you are a more visual person, you are more comfortable in a graphical user interface (GUI), and your log files are relatively small, then a spreadsheet may be an option. Spreadsheets have the ability to sort, count, and manipulate your data. Another bonus is the ability to create visual graphs and charts based on you data, to explain to management, law enforcement, the prosecutor, or the jury, later. Simple functions can be created to display items like unique IP addresses or counts of IP addresses. If the log files are fairly small then the uses are limited only by your ability to create formulas or manipulate the data.

Databases

If your log files are large, another available tool is databases. Databases are used on a daily basis to store and report on data, so why not for log files involved in cyber crime incident? The database used is a matter of budget and expertise. Some issues to keep in mind are the overhead involved in the essential aspects of the database like primary keys. This additional data will add to the storage requirements.

An advantage of SQL databases is that they provide you with ways to analyze and report the data that are limited only by your creativity. Additionally the SQL database allows correlation of logs from various systems once they are loaded into tables. Load in all the systems logs and query to find everywhere an IP address has gone or attempted to go. Finally, since SQL queries are a standard, they can be easily explained to those familiar to SQL.
The disadvantages of an SQL database are that they can require huge volumes of storage if you have large log files and want to perform correlation. Complex queries of large databases can also require a lot of processing power or time. Correlation and reporting can take even larger amounts of computing power or time.

The flexibility and power of the SQL database makes it an invaluable tool to crunch through massive amounts of log files and correlate them into a comprehensive report.

Snort

Snort can be used to analyze capture files, not just real-time traffic. It is useful to parse out attack signatures from captures where an IDS system may not have been. An added benefit is that Snort can be used to parse out traffic that may not traditionally be an attack but may be valuable to an investigation such as login attempts. Since Snort is an open source application, its cost is low. Snort also has a supportive user community, and it is well documented. There are plenty of resources to assist in creating custom signatures.

Security Event Management Systems

Many organizations have begun to install Security Event Management (SEM) Systems to compile and correlate all the logs from the various systems. The SEMS may well be the future of analysis tools for the network. A SEMS can quickly correlate data from the various security appliances and systems.

SEMS are valuable in analyzing data through the correlation and reporting. A caveat to the SEMS reporting is that the logs received or displayed often are altered. The logs often are truncated or normalized so original raw logs will need to retrieved and preserved from the originating system.

Many SEMs are still plagued by performance issues as they struggle to deal with the deluge of data streaming from systems. The databases often have performance issues in large implementations.

If a SEMS is implemented well and operating in an enterprise, it is an excellent resource to assist in triaging affected systems early in an incident.

Reporting

At the end of examinations and analysis comes perhaps the most tedious but arguably the most important phase.

The report is compilation of all the documentation, evidence from the examinations, and the analysis. The report needs to contain the documentation of all the systems analyzed, the tools used, and the discoveries made. The report needs to have the dates and times of the analysis, and detailed results. It should be complete and clear so the results and content are understood perhaps years down the road.

The report may be the most important phase of digital forensics. If the report is incomplete, or does not accurately document the tools, process, and methodology, all the work may be for nothing. Reporting will vary depending on the needs of your organization, but in most cases the minimum must include the documentation of the devices that were examined, the tools used, and the factual findings. Even if a procedure was used and yielded nothing of value it should be documented not only for completeness, but to demonstrate that the examination covered all the bases.

Perhaps the greatest challenge after all the other hurdles of acquisition, examination, and analysis is how to present it all in a manner that cannot be questioned. There is a very real risk that some newer forensic techniques have not yet been challenged in a court room.

TIP

Document that all the software used was properly licensed. It may not be necessary to go into great detail about the licenses, but close that hole early.

In a corporate environment, there is often a need for multiple reports—the forensic analysis report and the report created for executive management at the minimum. A challenge is in the midst of an important or high profile investigation, management will want updates and answers. Often when the incident involves volumes of data, one is being asked for answers when it is premature to give them. A strategy may be to provide a "shiny thing" to distract them long enough to get some results. The shiny thing may be just a statistical report and a high-level overview of the occurrence such as the acquisition of 10 systems for a total of 7.5 terabytes of data that is now being examined and analyzed.

Other ways of presenting the data in reports are timelines and a flow chart of accesses. A timeline report of a forensic examination of a system would display the dates and times of file accesses. A timeline report of data from disparate systems would show the steps taken during the investigation or analysis. The flow chart would show details of the impact or interaction with a system such as the traffic through a firewall, and then the access to a server.

Summary

In the introduction, we discussed the current best practices, and how the current best practices may be negatively impacted by ever-changing technology. The greatest challenge for the forensic practitioner going forward will be at times forging ahead without best practices to back them up. The same tasks will need to be accomplished in a more diverse and volatile environment. It is becoming the norm that devices may not be completely imaged because it is sometimes impossible to take a complete physical image. It may also be impractical to take an entire physical image of a multiterabyte SAN array.

The sheer volume of diverse devices and formats will make it extremely more difficult for the forensic practitioner to be an expert on it all. It will also create an ever-increasing need for continuing education. The tool kit required to work in digital forensics is not like the handyman's toolbox; it has become the mechanic's large toolchest.

A refreshing trend is the increasing focus of academia into the research of the digital forensics field. There also has been an increase in academic programs specifically for digital forensics, bridging the gap between traditional computer science and IT degree programs and criminal justice curriculums.

The last piece of wisdom—know when to ask for help.

References

NW3C. Information on the National White Collar Crime Center's courses, including the Fast CyberForensic Triage (FCT), is available online at www.nw3c.org/ocr/courses_desc.cfm.

Penerson, Melissa, J, "Hitachi Introduces 1-TB Hard Drive," *PC World Online*, 2007. Available at: www.pcworld.com/article/id,128400-pg,1/article.html.

Carrier, B. and J. Grand, "A Hardware-Based Memory Acquisition Procedure for Digital Investigations." *Digital Investigation Journal. Vol. 1, Num. 1.* Elsevier Advanced Technology, 2004. Available online at: www.digital-evidence.org/papers/tribble-preprint.pdf

Stone, Randy. "Computer Forensics and the Arrest of BTK," 2005. PowerPoint Presentation available at: www.nlectc.org/training/nij2005/StoneMarriott1.pd

Solutions Fast Track

The Evolution of Computer Forensics

☑ The technology is changing faster than forensic best practices.

☑ The volume of data is increasing extremely rapidly.

☑ The drive diversity continues to grow.

☑ Some data are increasingly volatile.

Phases of Digital Forensics

☑ Data storage diversity requires many tools and procedures.

☑ The increased data storage requires large target storage devices.

☑ The time requirement for collection will continue to increase.

☑ More data collected equates to more data to sift through.

☑ The increased use of techniques to reduce the data of interest should be employed.

☑ The increase in the data available can simplify the final analysis, or it can just create a bigger haystack to hide the needle in.

☑ The analysis of the entire incident is far more complex than the examination of any single system.

☑ Reporting is possibly more important than ever as the techniques and procedures must be more finely documented because of potential impacts on volatile data.

☑ A poor report can make the best cyber crime investigation appear a disaster.

Frequently Asked Questions

The following Frequently Asked Questions, answered by the authors of this book, are designed to both measure your understanding of the concepts presented in this chapter and to assist you with real-life implementation of these concepts. To have your questions about this chapter answered by the author, browse to **www.syngress.com/solutions** and click on the **"Ask the Author"** form.

Q: Is specialized equipment required for proper digital forensics?

A: Yes. The debate continues as to the requirement for formal digital forensics training, but training into the proper processes and methods is required.

Q: What is the most important part of digital forensics?

A: The procedures and methodolgys are the foundation. If they are solid, the rest will follow.

Q: Will one peice of forensics software do everything I need?

A: You can never have enough tools in the toolbox. That being said, the major forensic suites should do most of the functions the average digital forensics practioner may need. It is also a best practice to back up your findings with a second tool, so more than one may well be needed.

Chapter 10

Cyber Crime Prevention

Solutions in this chapter:

- Ways to Prevent Cyber Crime Targeted at You

- Ways to Prevent Cyber Crime Targeted at the Family

- Ways to Prevent Cyber Crime Targeted at Personal Property

- Ways to Prevent Cyber Crime Targeted at a Business

- Ways to Prevent Cyber Crime Targeted at an Organization

- Ways to Prevent Cyber Crime Targeted at a Government Agency

Introduction

For many of us, using a computer for the first time was an amazing experience. We couldn't believe what we saw or what was happening inside "that machine." Today, wristwatches, sun glasses, an ordinary looking pen, cell phones, and, of course, personal digital assistants (PDAs) can do more than my Apple II computer system. We have seen remarkable technologies come to fruition and achieve a life of their own. Who would have thought that a tiny device called an iPod would change society? Or that we would witness what seems like our total assimilation with the BORG, given the digital devices now attached to our ears, mouths, and waistbands… Forget the nerd pocket holders—we go straight for the insertion point and attach devices wherever we can! Again, who would have imagined such changes? Certainly not me.

The point is, with all the remarkable and amazing technological introductions over the past 30 years, both with personal computer systems and today with handheld devices, we are still vulnerable to the frailties of human behavior. We may have the best technology devices ever introduced, and yet succumb to our "creature of habits" lifestyle, allowing portions of our lives to be exposed, manipulated, and/or destroyed. By that, I am suggesting all the governance or influences of computer-digital technology in our lives is often discarded by behavior we could have, and should have, controlled. We know better than to completely trust everything that comes over the transom with such devices, but because such information is disseminated by a cell-phone text message, e-mail, fax, phone message, or some other communication form created by the digital gods of the BORG… we don't want to be left out.

The information in this chapter is not "new" certainly, but it is nevertheless common-sense data we must review. Perhaps for some of us we only need to re-examine it once; for others, monthly; for yet others, weekly; and for some of you… every day! Just the same, we will explore methods, techniques, and call-to-action steps to help prevent cyber crime—at work, home, and play. Please understand that everything written and published about "How to Prevent Cyber Crime" is a guide for both sides. Sadly, for some this will serve as a challenge and a way for someone to show up the experts. Hopefully for you, though, you'll listen to protect your identity, your family, your job, and your country. Be confident that you can roam freely and move in and out of cyber space. Review your habits and be the safe individual you know you should be.

> ## Notes from the Underground...
>
> ### New World
> The Internet has ushered in a new world, seemingly one without borders, with few enforceable rules, and one that suggests its members have total anonymity. It is one big sandbox where the world, works, plays, learns, and watches. Beware, however, for the world is changing...

Ways to Prevent Cyber Crime Targeted at You

Anyone connected to the Internet is at risk of being targeted and could become a victim of cyber crime themselves. Some have suggested you are more likely to be threatened, bullied, assailed, or "mugged" online than on your local street corner. With this in mind, you must make active steps to prevent yourself from getting injured, either emotionally, financially, or physically. You must protect you, your identity, your reputation, and your well being. You are the one who will allow others to know information about you directly by responding, or indirectly by not following common-sense guidelines. This section identifies ways you can protect yourself and prevent cyber crime from occurring on a personal level.

Often, you will hear *cyber cops* ask the following questions:

- Why would someone want to target you?

- Who might the culprit be?

- What might you have that they want?

- How did they gain access to your computer system, PDA, or cell phone?

- When could these attacks have occurred?

Would you have any answers the preceding questions? Have you actually devoted thought to any of it? I'm not suggesting we all become paranoid techno-freaks. When I am asked why I use online banking, I respond "Why wouldn't I?" I have several bank and money accounts. Nevertheless, I have a finite amount that I place in my online account. The monies I leave in that account don't stay there long. And my other accounts are where? That's right, at totally different institutions. Sounds inconvenient to some, but it is safer in today's identity-theft climate.

Some suggest the best defense is a consideration of possible motives, and then a diligent preparation to prevent or ward off the actions of others. Review that list of questions again. Anything come to mind? There are several instances where a disgruntled teenager has downloaded pornography and gotten "Daddy" in trouble with "Mommy" to deflect attention away from other situations. Instances have occurred where marital discord has led to divorce and an upset wife has downloaded "kiddie porn," afterward alerting authorities about it to discredit her spouse in regards to custody and financial disputes.

How often have you walked into an empty office or cubicle only to notice your co-worker has failed to log out or lock their computer? How many times have you heard a co-worker share their password, or log on to a system only to have another use it? Lastly, in regards to protecting your identity, do you freely share your data with the world? Do you BLOG and tell all? Do you post personal pictures, stories, and other details online? If you answered yes to any of these, why? And what do you hope to gain?

A colleague of mine works at a prominent university in Mississippi teaching computer technologies and digital forensics. One of the assignments he tasks his students with is to purchase a used hard drive from a local pawn or thrift store and see what details remain on the drive. One student became so enamored with the data that he curiously went online and looked for the fellow using popular search engines. To the student's surprise, he not only found the previous owner of the hard drive, but discovered where he lived, his wife's name, and that he was having an affair. Using TerraServer and MapQuest, he found more information, and uncovered more sordid personal and financial details. All the while, the previous owner had no idea of this "investigation," and likely still does not know. Finally, the professor had to remind the student that the exercise was over and to leave the *cyber-stalking* to others. The point here is, have you inadvertently provided roadmaps to your home, life, and personal data—all because you wanted a personal Web site?

Back to the questions, though. *Just why would someone target you?* Did you offend anyone? Do you have poor online habits that might allow someone to quickly gain access to your bank accounts? Are you in the middle of a divorce or have you given your spouse reason to suspect something is amiss? Are your adult children looking for their supposed inheritance? Have you posted to your Web site inflammatory or inciting comments?

Who might the culprit be? We find that over 90 percent of cyber attacks come from someone you know. Often times, the attack is a result of some trivial or heated disagreement at work with a colleague, or at home with a spouse, child, or relative. Most computers that are randomly compromised are done so to utilize some zombie or peer-to-peer manipulation of your computer's processing power, not your personal data.

What might you have that they want? Again, are they looking for money? If yes, what information is on your computer that wouldn't be found on your statements in the filing cabinet? Are you taking sensitive data from your workplace home? Is this sensitive data from work on your home computer, or on a laptop, or on a portable media device like a USB thumb-drive, MP3 player, or iPod? Again, why would a complete stranger want to hack your computer system? Sadly, many times there is more information about you in your trash than on your computer.

How did they gain access to your computer system, PDA, or cell phone? Once again, we leave the cyber space for a moment and return to ordinary crime. Was the scene of the crime electronic only, or did you assist by forgetting to address some physical security issues?

- Did you lock your office?
- Did you lock your house?

- Did you leave your laptop in the backseat of your car with the windows down on a warm sunny day?

- Did the USB device fall out of your pocket on the plane or train?

- Did you leave your iPod in the wash room?

- Why was your cell phone left at your favorite restaurant, again?

By now, you must have heard of personal firewalls for your computer, as well as keypad locks for your cell phone, PDAs, and other devices that more safely secure your digital data.

When could these attacks have occurred? Do you leave your computer on and connected to the Internet at all times? Do you leave your digital information open and available? What were you doing and where were you when the attack occurred? Figure it out and plan on preventing easy access.

Make access to your personal information difficult, even if it means it will be inconvenient for you. Cynthia Heatherington, a leading expert in identity protection, suggests six steps to protect yourself in the online world.

1. Open a P.O. Box for personal correspondence and bills. Submit a change of address form to send all mail there.

2. Unlist and unpublish your telephone numbers.

3. Never put your name, number, or information on any application or form without checking to see what the policy is.

4. Mail a written request to all major information suppliers requesting your information be removed.

5. Start a corporation, trust, or dba title to conduct your personal business.

6. Stop sharing information in unnecessary scenarios.[1]

The simpler it is to store information, the easier it is for others to find. A friend relayed that his wife had been recently stalked by an old boyfriend who found information on her whereabouts on the Web. This friend lives on a private lane, has a P.O. Box, an unlisted telephone number, and should have been virtually impossible to find. However, the stalker was able to locate my friend's wife by using her Social Security number. Sadly, databases of yesteryear—from schools, to shopping stores, to financial institutions—that required a Social Security number, allowed him to find her tax returns and her address. Too much information is out there, and we all need to limit our exposure.

The following are points to consider in how to better protect yourself from being a target of cyber crime:

- Have your own personal computer log in at home and work.

- Keep your log in information private and secure from others.

- Memorize your password(s).

  Don't share it or them.

  Don't use common dictionary words.

  Don't use family names, colors, hobby data, or religious data.

- Always *LOCK* your system when you walk away from your desk.

- Avoid, or better yet, never post personal photos of you on a nonsecured Web site.

- Never post personal data.

- Never provide your password(s), PIN information, or banking details from a soliciting e-mail, or Web site.

- Install and run a personal firewall.

- Install and run antivirus software.

- Install and run antispyware software.

- Update your computer frequently with security patches, as well as operating system and application service packs.

- Use encryption for sensitive e-mail and Web transactions.

- If you are a Windows user, use the New Technology File System (NTFS), not FAT32.

- If you have a portable device for storing data, use the Encrypting File System (EFS), part of NTFS. This includes laptops, MP3 devices, and portable drives.

- Make sure your PDA and cell phone have an activation password.
- Report any cyber-harassments and/or cyber threats.
- Purchase a good shredder—a good cross-cut one!
- Don't use your computer for criminal purposes!
- Don't believe you are anonymous on the Web!

Ways to Prevent Cyber Crime Targeted at the Family

The Internet and the World Wide Web contain a wealth of valuable data and information for families. However, with all that good come unwelcome elements, too. Many activities on the Internet are, and can be, very disruptive to the family. Every family unit is unique, and as such, each family must define proper rules of Internet engagement and usage. Everything stated in the previous sections could apply, and perhaps should apply. However, you should define what is *right* and *proper* for your family.

One main issue to consider is that of *access*. Internet use and what is posted, shared, and/or accessed on the Internet is one of personal decision making. Too many try to infer *moral* obligations or arguments of good versus evil. There is one overriding issue, however, and that is the issue of access. My children and your children cannot purchase a pornographic magazine from a store, they cannot attend an NC-17 movie without being of age, and they cannot purchase products restricted for 18- or 21-year-old individuals—however, the Internet does not enforce these same rules and laws. So, you as a family unit need to identify what will be your best roadmap and guidelines for Internet usage in your home.

Notes from the Underground...

Thanks, But No Thanks Dad

After getting a new computer system, a caring Grandfather gave his computer to his daughter and her family. Upon inspection, the son-in-law found that the computer contained not only massive pornography but also child pornography. Thanks, Dad, now what do I do?

Popular suggestions for Internet access in the family, and the prevention of inappropriate or dangerous behavior include the following:

- Make sure there is an *open screen* policy—meaning the computer display faces the doorway and is exposed for all to see.

- Establish time limits on computer use and Internet access.

- Try to separate the game systems from the educational system—many families have a computer for games, and another for homework. Having an Xbox, Playstation, or similar device helps.

- Talk honestly and frankly about the good, bad, and ugly found on the Internet with your children.

- Limit your exposure, and theirs, by not posting too much personal data on the Web—especially at sites like MySpace, YouTube, and similar spots.

- Chat rooms are full of dirty old men. If you are okay with your 12-year-old communicating with degenerates posing as overly anxious pubescent friends—go for it! Or just say no to chat rooms.

- Let your children know you will read their chats and e-mails, and will contact their friends from time to time. Then, make sure you do so and review those contacts and communications that are inappropriate for your family.

- Let your spouse know you have a keylogger and to beware.

■ Do not keep child pornography a secret. It is contraband and you must report it to the authorities. In line with that idea, you should seek help for family members who use it.

■ Visit, read, and print out those items and suggestions from the following sites, as well as similar ones. These sites have great ideas, lists, and more helpful information for you and your family.

www.fbi.gov/publications/pguide/pguidee.htm

http://bob.nap.edu/html/youth_internet/

www.missingkids.com/missingkids/servlet/ResourceServlet?
    LanguageCountry=en_US&PageId=2954

www.missingkids.com/missingkids/servlet/ResourceServlet?
    LanguageCountry=en_US&PageId=2954

www.missingkids.com/missingkids/servlet/ResourceServlet?
    LanguageCountry=en_US&PageId=2954

www.ftc.gov/bcp/conline/edcams/kidzprivacy/kidz.htm

www.ala.org/ala/alsc/greatwebsites/greatsitesbrochure.pdf

www.childrenspartnership.org/

www.packet-level.com/kids/Courses/Internet%20Safety%
    20for%20Kids%20-%20Instructor%20Notes-v1.1.pdf

This list and the Web addresses will help you and your family formulate rules and guidelines for Internet usage. Recently, McGruff the Crime Dog launched a "Take a Bite out of Cyber Crime" campaign. The new Junior CyberGuards program launching in 2007 teaches middle-school students to be more mindful of their online usage, and to watch out for predators.

WARNING

What no one is telling you is that you need similar rules for cell phones and online gaming devices like the Xbox or PlayStation. Be warned that these technologies are equally as powerful and need the same attention!

Even if your computer is safe and secure, you may have forgotten about your cell phones, iPods, and Xboxes! You must the same conversations with your family regarding text messaging on your cell phones and accessing the Web from your cell phone. This preventive medicine may prove more difficult than with the computer since there are few, if any, tools to assist monitoring behavior or limiting access to sites via a cell phone or PDA.

Likewise, a whole new crop of degenerates are being found at Xbox Live, PlayStation Live, and similar online spaces, where they want to "team-up" with your kids. Don't ignore the dangers. They are the same that exist in chat rooms, e-mail conversations, and instant messaging. Your children can communicate via wireless headsets to any person wishing to join in. Do you know who they are playing with? Have you seen the games they are playing? And when their "friend" requests a face to face to share important details on how to better play the game, do you know where they are going?

Recognize that the same rules and guidelines are true for cell-phone users. Access to chat rooms, the ability to send and participate in e-mail conversations, and instant messaging exist with cell phone use, too. Do not be afraid to take your children's cell phone for review. Identify unknown or unfamiliar telephone numbers and discuss the dangers of predators in this community. Monitor cell phone use and make sure all is in line and appropriate regarding the guidelines you have established with your family.

NOTE

Most law enforcement and governmental agencies are instructed to include collecting cell phones, PDAs, MP3 players, iPods, and online gaming devices like the Xbox, as well as PlayStation when serving subpoenas and search warrants. These devices can hold vital data and information that might lead to your child or a perpetrator. Don't simply dismiss the communication abilities and data storage these devices contain.

Ways to Prevent Cyber Crime Targeted at Personal Property

It is clear problems exist and will persist in the online Internet world. Software, hardware, and Internet vendors continue to clash and blame one another when problems emerge. By now, you should understand this silly cycle and realize you hold a level of responsibility, too. It is up to you, the end user, to purchase products to help fill the holes the software and hardware vendors have failed to provide. Some of the following items have been mentioned before, but this is what you need to do to protect your digital devices and help prevent cyber crime targeted at your personal property.

Anti-Virus software

Most computer systems come with two or three 90-day trial copies of anti-virus software. This isn't an option; it is a must. Make sure you are using some tool to protect your computer system from viruses. Viruses typically cause damage, often referred to as the "payload." The role of most computer viruses is to spread like a germ from one host to another. These self-replicating viruses are typically instructed to infect as many hosts as they can, and to possibly extract, move, or delete your files or completely destroy the operating system, rendering your computer helpless. Damage to your system will occur if you do not use an anti-virus software tool. Some anti-virus products also look for spyware and/or Trojans. In the end, you will need several tools, and definitely anti-virus software.

Anti-Spyware Software

Spyware is relatively new and comes in a variety of deployed methods. The primary goal of a piece of spyware code is to get into your computer without your knowledge and/or permission. Once in, spyware instructs the computer to relay information to some other system about your internet use or redirect you to a website. Some spyware is relatively harmless, perhaps a set of marketing instructions. Other spyware is more annoying by constantly redirecting your browser and/or displaying pop-up windows. It is very unfortunate that there are people and instructions of code placing instructions on your computer without your approval. As a result of these actions, we must all have anti-spyware software on our computers.

> **WARNING**
>
> Occasionally, anti-spyware software provides false positives and other misleading data to scare you into purchasing the tool. Some anti-spyware software is actually fake and completely ineffective. For a good independent review and a list of trusted anti-spyware tools, go to www.spywarewarrior.com/rogue_anti-spyware.htm#trustworthy.

Both malware viruses and spyware tend to be installed by you, the user. Perhaps you have been guilty of the following:

- A friend sends you an e-mail with a video or sound clip, a game of some sort, or a cool desktop image, and you listen or install the attached file. The intention of your friend was pure, merely sharing some joyful or funny moment. Unfortunately, for both of you, the virus or spyware was installed simultaneously.

- A "Security Window" pops up, instructing you to download a needed file—and you blindly follow the instructions. Ironically, one of the biggest culprits of these is fake spyware information windows, which often claim to be part of Microsoft Internet Explorer, and so you install it.

- Some browsers have "add-on" functions that are really just spyware or virus executables. However, they appear to be needed, so once again you install them.

- Occasionally, you get the virus or spyware from a legitimate software vendor that has been infected and is inadvertently shipping the virus or spyware with their software.

Personal Firewall Software

This tool is intended to protect in-coming and out-going communications. The role of a personal firewall is to prevent intrusion from uninvited Internet traffic. It also serves as a facilitator in that it provides information about applications or users attempting to contact or communicate with the computer. It also acts as a personal firewall, providing information about the other computer system or server. Like the two aforementioned tools, every homeowner should have a personal firewall to protect their data and their family, and to prevent their computer from being manipulated.

The guidelines to prevent property damage to your computer are quite exhaustive. The following reviews the steps you should take to protect your computers:

- Choose one anti-virus tool. Running two such tools simultaneously is not a good idea.

- Choose one personal firewall tool. Running two such tools simultaneously is not advisable.

- Plan to have two or more anti-spyware tools. Because there are so many unknowns in this category, it is required to have at least two, or ideally three or more, installed and running on your personal computer

- Anti-virus, anti-spyware, and personal firewall software are only useful if you're using the most recent version. Get regular updates!

- Consider getting help from your ISP or online provider to supply services that include anti-virus and anti-spam software, and e-mail filtering.

- Read the end-user license agreement (affectionately known as EULA) for all of these tools, but especially for the anti-spyware software. Some of the anti-spyware licenses provide a clause for them to spy on you! Or to provide an endless stream of pop-up advertisements.

- Find the programs that best match your privacy and security needs.

- Make sure you test your tools. It is the only way to ensure your computer system is being protected.

- Use a wiping tool like WhiteCanyon's *WipeDrive* to completely erase and sanitize your used or donated hard drives, thumb drives, or cell phones.

- Delete all data from your cell phones and PDAs before donating them or throwing them away.

- Destroy CDs, DVDs, floppies, or similar storage devices before discarding. Most shredders will shred these.

The Internet is not a kind and gentle world. Too many discontent and probing users are waiting out there. Every time a fix is devised to prevent unwelcome intrusions, a new door is found. Managing these tools requires diligence on your part. Yours is not an optional role in preventing cyber crime. Updating these tools and properly maintaining them is a burdensome requirement for us all.

> **NOTE**
>
> While this section discussed tools primarily for computers, recognize that in the coming months there will be issues regarding cell phones, PDAs, MP3 players, iPods, and online gaming devices like the Xbox or PlayStation. These devices can be used to distribute malicious malware codes or have personal data extracted from them.

Ways to Prevent Cyber Crime Targeted at a Business

The next three sections are closely related. Your role in each of these will differ. Some of you will have more direct responsibilities and obligations, while others will merely be the recipients of what has been determined.

Each business, company, and/or corporation has policies or procedures, or at least they should, for installing and maintaining software to protect their intellectual data and property, the information regarding their employees, and the communications of their employees. We have discussed several of these tools, anti-virus, anti-spyware, e-mail spam filters, and firewalls. In addition, many businesses utilize some form of network intrusion detection software (NIDS). Unlike individual or family users, however, corporate users are targets of malware or malicious software. Malware is intent-driven and includes viruses, Trojans, worms, spyware, or some other type of destructive software. These unwanted and undesirable software programs are designed to penetrate and damage computer systems—in short, to bring a network or Web site server down.

One of the most infamous instances of malware was the *Slammer* virus that was released in January of 2003. The Slammer virus spread faster than any other known attack, including the Code Red or Blaster viruses and the Klez or Nimda worms. This Microsoft SQL virus started creating millions of clones, and doubled almost every 8.5 seconds. By the time the Internet world started to realize the problem, over 300,000 cable modem users in Portugal were down. South Korea's cell phone and Internet service providers were in total chaos, and many were shut down for over 24 hours. Many airlines, including Continental, had to cancel flights. The price tag estimated to recover worldwide was over $1.2 billion. It was not a "good" day for those network administrators who had failed to update their MS-SQL software. Had they followed their policies and procedures, they could have avoided and averted the entire episode.

"Dealing with viruses, spyware, PC theft, and other computer-related crimes costs U.S. businesses a staggering $67.2 billion a year, according to the FBI. The FBI calculated the price tag by extrapolating results from a survey of 2,066 organizations. The survey, released Thursday, found that 1,324 respondents, or 64 percent, suffered a financial loss from computer security incidents over a 12-month period."[2] As you can see, if your business is not protected, if you do not have policies and procedures in place, and if you do not adhere to the rules of the Internet world, you will suffer a loss in both real and unrealized opportunities and costs!

Many believe more losses exist than reported. Too many businesses choose not to report cyber crime for fear of loss of income from customers, bad press, or loss of employment. It is time for stiffer penalties to be imposed on those corporate leaders that elect to hide cyber crimes. There needs to be more attention and participation in organizations like the Association of Certified Fraud Examiners (ACFE—www.acfe.org) or the InfraGard organization (www.infragard.net) that helps protect our cyber boundaries. Make a difference. Be observant and helpful, and establish guidelines like the following:

- Understand what your business's appropriate and inappropriate use policies are, and then follow them.

- Continue to use the prevention methods discussed for individuals, families, and property.

- Follow and enforce strict password management policies.

- Clearly communicate security solutions to all employees.

- Establish proper audit policies for user accounts, computer accounts, and management tools for server communication.

- Do not possess unauthorized information or corporate intellectual property.

- Do not distribute or use *pirated* software.

- Do not provide access to your computer to any unauthorized individual.

- Stay informed about changes to your phone, Internet, intranet, and computer access.

- Report any cyber threats, intimidation, stalking, or harassment.

- Don't assume your Web use or e-mail communication is private and confidential at work. It isn't and it can be used against you. So, DO NOT commit crimes at work.

- Contact the FBI to report any type of corporate, medical, pharmaceutical, financial, or security fraud. Go to the following site to learn more about the Corporate Fraud Initiative: www.fbi.gov/aboutus/transformation/white_collar.htm.

Ways to Prevent Cyber Crime Targeted at an Organization

Like businesses, nonprofit and academic organizations need to employ policies and procedures to protect the rights of the organization, the employees, volunteers, students, and members. The best way to prevent cyber crime is to educate members on the unique rules and guidelines of your organization. Organizations need to identify potential vulnerabilities and possible exploits.

Just because you are a nonprofit or academic organization does not give you the excuse to not comply. Some years ago, while teaching computer forensic sessions at a conference, our host university was hit by the *Blaster* virus. Suddenly, we were no longer focusing on our intended topic, but attending to duties that should have been addressed by their network personnel. Since the university did not have clear-cut policies and rules of engagement to enforce updating software patches, we were all hit by the virus. We ended up spending unnecessary time correcting the problem so we could proceed with the topic at hand. All of this could, and should, have been prevented if the university had followed their own procedures.

Understand who is working for you and why. Do background checks on your volunteers, and do not provide access to any system without knowing some history about the members of your organization. Follow the guidelines as outlined in the Business section.

Ways to Prevent Cyber Crime Targeted at a Government Agency

In 2001, the U.S. Justice Department suggested that upwards of 85 percent of U.S. companies and federal agencies had been victims of hacks and intrusion attempts. Whether that figure is correct or not, the issue remains that all governments are, and will continue to be, under cyber attacks. As a result, strict policies and procedures must be enacted and enforced. These need to occur *pro*actively, not *re*actively.

The recent loss of data by the Veteran's Association is an example of how quickly sensitive data can end up in the wrong hands. Each agency is responsible for what is needed and required and most adhere to the policies defined for their specific agency. Many agencies are learning that the following devices can be used to store data. Hence, these devices are used to copy sensitive, private, or classified data. Whether you are a business, an organization, or a government agency, the items in Figure 10.1 illustrate new methods of stealing stored data.

Figure 10.1 Devices with Storage Data Capabilities

From left to right and down:

- Pocket knife with USB storage device
- USB storage device
- Wristwatch with USB storage device
- Ordinary digital camera
- Common cell phone
- MP3 player sunglasses with USB storage device
- PDA handheld device
- SanDisk 1GB storage device
- SanDisk 512MB storage device
- Personal ring with storage device
- iPod music device that stores over 60GB of data
- Identification card with information

As you can see, more abilities exist to store and steal data than ever before. Something as innocent as a pocket pen with a 20MB storage compartment could be used to download malware onto your network or steal sensitive information. Many government agencies and corporate businesses forbid the use, or bringing in, of digital cameras, MP3 players, iPods, and USB storage devices. With that in mind, we all know that storage devices will continue to get smaller and faster. The question is, "Are we ready for them?"

Summary

Each of us is confronted with cyber technologies every day. Whether it is the mapping tool in our cars, our cell phones, our PDAs, or a computer, we can't help but be active participants. The ever-changing and evolving Internet world will keep on influencing our daily lives and we must be prepared to address these changes and adjust to the evolution.

There is much to consider and much to do. However, as we start to make a conscious effort to learn more about these issues, we will be able to help thwart cyber crimes and put a dent in their impact.

Notes

1. Cynthia Heatherington, "Opt Out of the Internet: Protect Your Identity & Family Online," Dallas Crimes Against Children (ICAC) Annual Conference, August 2006.
2. Joris Evers, CNET News.com Online Broadcast, January 19, 2006.

Solutions Fast Track

Ways to Prevent Cyber Crime Targeted at You

☑ Realize that you are not anonymous on the Internet.

☑ Limit, or do not provide, any personal data to known or unknown online sources, databases, or requesting entities.

☑ Identify strategies to protect your identity and personal data.

Ways to Prevent Cyber Crime Targeted at the Family

☑ Have an open-screen or family-room computer guiding principle.

☑ Read the various publications regarding Internet safety for families, and then identify those guidelines and rules you and your family will incorporate and use.

☑ Be very cautious and extremely suspicious of Web sites or e-mail attachments requesting you to install something on your computer.

Ways to Prevent Cyber Crime Targeted at Personal Property

☑ Update all software regularly.

☑ Use anti-virus, anti-spyware, and personal firewall software.

☑ Participate in e-forums, and public and political meetings or discussions regarding personal privacy and security rights.

Ways to Prevent Cyber Crime Targeted at a Business

☑ Follow all policies and procedures as set forth by the Human Resource and IT departments.

☑ Report any suspicious behavior—either online or off.

☑ Become a member of organizations that strengthen businesses, like the ACFE and InfraGard.

Ways to Prevent Cyber Crime Targeted at an Organization

☑ Everyone who uses a computer in your organization presents a security risk. Make sure you know your co-workers.

☑ An Internet thief has access to more information that can lead to personal gain than a street thug with a gun. Protect your organization's data.

☑ Work with your local communities to support cyber crime prevention efforts.

Ways to Prevent Cyber Crime Targeted at a Government Agency

- ☑ Assist and help governmental agencies by contacting the Internet Crime Complaint Center (IC3) at www.ic3.gov/ and reporting all abuses and cyber crime–related instances.

- ☑ Recognize that cyber terrorism does exist, follow outlined procedures, and be cautious in your communications.

Frequently Asked Questions

The following Frequently Asked Questions, answered by the authors of this book, are designed to both measure your understanding of the concepts presented in his chapter and to assist you with real-life implementation of these concepts. To have your questions about this chapter answered by the author, browse to **www.syngress.com/solutions** and click on the **"Ask the Author"** form.

Q: What can I do to get involved?

A: Start slow and simple. If you are actively updating your software and applying service packs, using anti-virus, anti-spyware, and personal firewall software you are already involved. There are many organizations that discuss high-tech crime, online crime, and fraud prevention. Use a search engine to find the parent organization and then the local chapter nearest you.

Q: Are there some specific cyber-crime prevention organizations you can recommend?

A: There are many, but here are just a few: the Association of Certified Fraud Examiniers (ACFE)—www.acfe.org; the High Technology Crime Investigation Association (HTCIA)—www.htcia.org; and InfraGard—www.infragard.net.

Appendix A

Legal Principles for Information Security Evaluations[1]

Solutions in this chapter:

- **Uncle Sam Wants You: How Your Company's Information Security Can Affect U.S. National Security (and Vice Versa)**

- **Legal Standards Relevant to Information Security**

- **Selected Laws and Regulations**

- **Do It Right or Bet the Company: Tools to Mitigate Legal Liability**

- **What to Cover in IEM Contracts[2]**

- **The First Thing We Do...? Why You Want Your Lawyers Involved From Start to Finish**

☑ Solutions Fast Track

☑ Frequently Asked Questions

WARNING: THIS APPENDIX IS NOT LEGAL ADVICE

This appendix provides an overview of a number of legal issues faced by information security evaluation professionals and their customers. Hopefully, it will alert readers to the issues on which they should consult qualified legal counsel experienced in information security law. This appendix, however, does not, and cannot, provide any legal advice or counsel to its readers. Readers should not, under any circumstances, purport to rely on anything in this appendix as legal advice. Likewise, following any of the suggestions in this appendix does not create an "advice-of-counsel" defense to regulatory or law enforcement action or to civil legal claims. Readers involved in information security are strongly urged to retain qualified, experienced legal counsel.

Introduction

You have watched the scene hundreds of times. The buttoned-down, by-the-book police lieutenant and the tough-as-nails, throw-out-the-rules-to-save-lives detective debate in front of the police chief. A child is kidnapped and the clock is ticking; a murder is about to be committed and the judge will not issue a warrant. The world-weary police chief has to make a split-second decision. Is there a way to live within the law but save the child? How does the police chief balance the duty to protect the people of the city with fealty to the rulebook? Is there a creative way to do both? On television, this scene usually happens in an aging, shabby, police headquarters office furnished with Styrofoam cups of stale coffee, full ashtrays, fading green walls, and rickety metal desks. Now, imagine this same drama being performed on an entirely different stage.

Uncle Sam Wants You:
How Your Company's Information Security Can Affect U.S. National Security (and Vice Versa)

It is September 2011. As the tenth anniversary of al-Qa'ida's devastating attacks on our nation approaches, the president is faced with increasingly clear intelligence that what's left of the infamous terrorist group has fulfilled its long-standing ambition to be able to launch a devastating attack on the U.S. through cyberspace. Perhaps they will disable our air traffic control or financial exchange network. Perhaps they will penetrate Supervisory Control and Data Acquisition (SCADA) systems to attack dams or other energy facilities. Perhaps they will shut down power to hundreds of hospitals where surgery is underway. Or maybe they will directly target our heavily information systems-dependent military forces. The targets and magnitude are far from clear.

As September 11, 2011, dawns though, it becomes obvious that cyber-attacks are underway, even though the perpetrators are undetermined. What becomes increasingly clear is that the attacks are striking us directly, not from overseas; from dozens, perhaps hundreds, of university and corporate servers right here in the U.S. The scene that follows plays out in the stately, wood-paneled, electronically sophisticated confines of the Situation Room in the West Wing of the White House. Our protagonists here are The Secretary of Defense, the Director of National Intelligence, the National and Homeland Security Advisors to the president, and the Attorney General. And, of course, in this scene, the decision maker carrying the weight of the world is not a big city police chief, but the President of the United States.

In all likelihood, the president will receive conflicting advice from his senior advisors. Some will insist that U.S. law prohibits the government from disabling the servers within the U.S. from which the attacks are coming, or even trying to learn who is behind the attacks. These advisors urge caution, despite intelligence indicating that the attacks are actually coming from terrorists overseas, using the servers in the U.S. as "zombies" to carry out their plot. These advisors will further argue that the president has no option but to use the cumbersome and time-consuming criminal law process to combat these attacks. The attorney general's law enforcement officers must collect information, go to a federal judge, and get a warrant or, in this case, dozens or hundreds of warrants, to try to determine who is behind the attacks (unless emergency access without a warrant is authorized by law). Even in such emergencies, organizing and directing law enforcement control over hundreds or thousands of zombies is an overwhelming effort.

Other officials will advise the president that by the time any progress will be made going the law enforcement route, devastating damage to the critical infrastructure may already have occurred, and the overseas perpetrators disappeared, covering their tracks. These advisors will argue strenuously that the president has ample constitutional and legal authority to use any element of U.S. power (military, intelligence, or law enforcement) to defeat the attacks and defend the nation. They will argue that using the normal law enforcement route would not only be futile, but would amount to an abdication of the president's primary constitutional responsibility to protect our nation and its people from attack. Finally, they will respectfully remind the president of the sage advice of Vietnam War era U.S. Supreme Court Justice Arthur Goldberg that "While the constitution protects against invasions of individual rights, it is not a suicide pact."[3]

As a purely legal and constitutional matter, the president's more hawkish advisors will likely be correct.[4] However, that in no way will lessen the terrible moral, ethical, and political burden that will fall on the president: whether or not, in the absence of perfect information, to order counterattacks on information infrastructures inside the U.S.

While reasonable experts still disagree on the probability that such a scenario will arise in the next decade (and there are differences of opinion even among the authors of this chapter), most agree that the scenario is technically possible.[5] The U.S. National Strategy to Secure Cyberspace describes the following necessary conditions (which exist today) for "relative measures of damage to occur [to the United States] on a national level, affecting the networks and systems on which the Nation depends:

- Potential adversaries have the intent.

- Tools that support malicious activities are broadly available.

- Vulnerabilities of the Nation's systems are many and well known.[6]

Thus, even in an unclassified publication, the U.S. government has confirmed that our adversaries, whether terrorists, rogue states, or more traditional nation–state enemies, possess a classic combination for the existence of threat: intent + capability + opportunity. If September 11, 2001, taught us anything as a nation, it is that when these three are present, we had better be prepared.

More concretely, senior Federal Bureau of Investigation (FBI) officials and others have testified before Congress that terrorist groups have demonstrated a clear interest in hackers and hacking skills; the FBI predicts that, "terrorist groups will either develop or hire hackers."[7] Material found in former al-Qa'ida strongholds in Afghanistan showed al-Qa'ida's interest in developing cyber-terror skills.[8] Former U.S. government "cyberczar" Richard Clarke pointed out that a University of Idaho student, arrested by FBI agents on allegations of terror links, was seeking a PhD in cyber security. Clarke warns that, "similarly to the fact that some of the Sept. 11 hijackers had training in flight training, some of the people that we're seeing now related to [al-Qa'ida] had training in computer security."[9] Several experts, including cyber experts at Sandia National Laboratories and the U.S. Naval Postgraduate school, have bluntly asserted that adversaries could disrupt significant portions of the U.S. power grid, for time periods ranging from minutes, to days, and even longer.[10]

Cyber attacks have already been used to disrupt online elections in Canada, and attacks by terrorist groups have been launched to "crash" government computers during elections in Indonesia, Sri Lanka, and Mexico.[11] Finally, apart from terrorist groups and rogue states, a number of nations potentially adversarial to the U.S. now openly include cyber warfare as part of their existing military doctrine, including China and Russia.[12]

This scene, then, is plausible,[13] except that we will be lucky if it takes until 2011 to play out.

Many international legal experts assert that, under internationally recognized laws of armed conflict, attacks by foreign nations or international terrorists using bits and bytes through cyberspace can be acts of war just as can the use of guns or bombs or fuel-laden airliners.[14] If a nation determines that a cyber attack is an act of war against it, that determination, in turn, triggers a number of rights on the part of those attacked to take defensive or responsive action against their attackers.[15] Recognizing the threat of a cyber attack and the potential need for more than a law enforcement response, President Bush in 2003 announced a new U.S. policy with regard to such attacks:

> When a nation, terrorist group, or other adversary attacks the United States through cyberspace, the United States response need not be limited to criminal prosecution. The United States reserves the right to respond in an appropriate manner. The United States will be prepared for such contingencies.[16]

In a cyber attack (unlike in a conventional military attack), it may be difficult for decision makers to know against whom to take action to stop the attack and/or respond. Unlike a terrorist bombing, though, or even the heinous September 11, 2001 attacks, a cyber attack may continue for a long enough period of time that rapid defensive action may dramatically reduce the damage done to the critical infrastructure and economy, even where the perpetrator is still unknown.

Thus, a cyber attack in progress using "zombied" servers inside the U.S. will present decision makers with a uniquely vexing dilemma. If they do nothing in the initial minutes and hours after the attack is underway, they may allow far greater damage than if they take decisive action to stop the attack and disable the attacking machines. Taking such action, however, risks damage or destruction to the zombied servers themselves, perhaps without identifying the guilty parties. Further, doing so can destroy information that may be needed later to identify and apprehend the perpetrator(s).

Making the situation even more dangerous and complex is the fact that, "distinguishing between malicious activity originating from criminals, nation state actors, and terrorists in real time is difficult."[17] In many cases, affirmative attribution will be nearly impossible with today's technology. Thus, decision makers facing the agonizing choice of taking action to disable or destroy zombied servers inside the U.S. or risking greater damage to our nation if they wait, may not know in time to make a sound decision on whether a true attack is underway or whether what looks like the initial stages of an attack is instead other malicious activity.

What does this mean to information security evaluation professionals and their customers? First and foremost, it means that *you do not want the "zombied" servers used in a cyber attack to be yours.* When the U.S. (or another nation)[18] decides to mount an official response against the hijacked servers being used to launch an attack, it will be a very bad day for the entity whose servers are being used. Additionally, though prudent information security consultants will remain current on all potential threat vectors for purposes of protecting your customers' networks, the identity of any particular threat will be largely irrelevant, even if the origin could be determined. Custodians of sensitive information of any kind have myriad reasons to develop and maintain a reasonable information security posture: business operational needs; preventing economic loss and industrial espionage; mitigating potential litigation, regulatory, and prosecution risks; and maintaining a reputation for responsible security vis-à-vis others in the same business.

The risk of involuntarily becoming part of a cyber attack, or defending against such an attack, adds another important incentive to do what most businesses and educational institutions already recognize as the right thing to do. Unlike other motivations for information security, however, avoiding involvement in a cyber attack is important even if an organization does not maintain any "sensitive" information. Unlike "traditional" hackers, criminals, and others who might exploit information security vulnerabilities, terrorists do not ignore companies simply because they are unable to find sensitive information. Instead, terrorists care about what damage can be done using your servers as proxies. And governments (ours or others) also will not care what information you have or do not have, if it is determined that your servers are involved in an attack and must be neutralized (or worse).

Second, understanding the way governments see information security provides a context for understanding how policy statements contribute to the development of a legal "duty" for individuals and organizations to secure their portions of cyberspace (discussed in greater detail below). In a nutshell, the actual knowledge or constructive knowledge (i.e., information in the public domain) of public policy mandating private "owners" of cyberspace to secure their components, may create a legal "duty" to do so, which could be the subject of future litigation. Likewise, emerging federal policy on potential cyber attacks could well contribute to the movement, already gathering steam, to further regulate private information security at the federal level.

Legal Standards Relevant to Information Security

Laws are made by politicians and politicians are driven by public and media reaction to specific incidents. Laws, therefore, are made piecemeal, at least until a critical mass is reached, which then leads lawmakers to conclude that an emerging patchwork of related, but often inconsistent, laws and regulations require an omnibus law to create consistency and greater predictability. In the absence of such a unifying federal law, particular industries or sectors are targeted for regulation as perceived problems in those industries become public. Laws and regulations covering targeted industries are gradually expanded through civil litigation and regulatory action that is limited only by the patience of judges and the imagination of plaintiffs' lawyers, prosecutors, and regulators.

This is the current situation in the law of information security. As discussed in "Selected Federal Laws" below, federal law regulates information security for, among other things, personally identifiable health care information, financial information of individuals, and, to an increasing degree, financial information in the hands of publicly traded companies. Though there is no "omnibus" federal statute governing all information security, the standards of care being created for these specific economic sectors are being "exported" to other business areas through civil litigation, including by regulators and state attorneys general.[19]

For information security practitioners, this is a good news/bad news story. Often, attempts at "comprehensive" regulation turn out to be a jumbled mess, particularly when multiple economic sectors with differing operational environments and needs are being regulated. Such regulation can be particularly ineffective (or worse) when promulgated before the private sector, which has developed solid, time-tested best practices, implements a workable solution. On the other hand, a patchwork of different federal, state, and international laws and regulations (as is the current state of information security law), can be confusing and puts a premium on careful, case-specific legal analysis and advice from qualified and experienced counsel

Selected Federal Laws

To illustrate the array of laws that impact information security, the following provides a general survey of statutes, regulations, and other laws that may govern information security consultants and their customers. This list is not exhaustive, but may help identify issues in working with customers and in understanding which "best practices" have actually been adopted in law.

Gramm–Leach–Bliley Act

One of the earliest U.S. government forays into mandating information security standards was the Gramm–Leach–Bliley Act (GLBA).[20] Section 501(b) requires each covered financial institution to establish "appropriate safeguards" to: (1) ensure the security and confidentiality of customer records and information; (2) protect against anticipated threats or hazards to the security or integrity of those records; and (3) protect against unauthorized access to, or use of, such records or information which could result in substantial harm or inconvenience to any customer.[21] GLBA required standards to be set by regulation for safeguarding customer information.[22] This task was accomplished with the promulgation of the Interagency Guidelines Establishing Standards for Safeguarding Customer Information (the "Guidelines").[23]

The Guidelines apply to Customer Information maintained by covered "financial institutions," both of which terms are broadly defined under applicable law and regulations. The Guidelines require a written security program specifically tailored to the size and complexity of each individual covered financial institution, and to the nature and scope of its activities.[24]

Under the Guidelines, covered institutions must conduct risk assessments to customer information and implement policies, procedures, training, and testing appropriate to manage reasonably foreseeable internal and external threats.[25] Institutions must also ensure that their board of directors (or a committee thereof) oversees the institution's information security measures.[26] Further, institutions must exercise due diligence in selecting and overseeing, on an ongoing basis, "service providers" (entities that maintain, process, or otherwise are permitted access to customer information through providing services to a covered institution).[27] Institutions also must ensure, by written agreement, that service providers maintain appropriate security measures.[28]

Health Insurance Portability and Accountability Act

The Health Insurance Portability and Accountability Act of 1996 (HIPAA) became law in August 1996. Section 1173(d) of HIPAA required the secretary of Health and Human Services (HHS) to adopt security standards for protection of all Electronic Protected Health Information (EPHI).[29] Development of these security standards was left to the HHS secretary, who promulgated the HIPAA Security Final Rule (the "Security Rule") in February 2003.[30] All covered entities, with the exception of small health plans, must now comply with the Security Rule.[31]

Because HIPAA has, in some ways, the most elaborate and detailed guidance available in the realm of federal law and regulation with regard to information security, we focus more on the HIPAA Security Rule than any other single federal legal provision. In addition, many of the general principles articulated in the Security Rule are common to other legal regimes dealing with information security. As a general framework, the HIPAA Security Rule: (a) mandates specific outcomes; and (b) specifies process and procedural requirements, rather than specifically mandated technical standards. The mandated outcomes for covered entities are:

- Ensuring the confidentiality, integrity, and availability of EPHI created, received, maintained, or transmitted by a covered entity[32]

- Protecting against reasonably anticipated threats or hazards to the security or integrity of such information[33]

- Protecting against reasonably anticipated uses or disclosures of EPHI not permitted by the HIPAA Privacy Rule[34] and

- Ensuring compliance with the Security Rule by its employees.[35]

Beyond these general, mandated outcomes, the Security Rule contains process and procedural requirements broken into several general categories[36]:

- **Administrative Safeguards**[37] Key required processes in this area include: conducting a comprehensive analysis of reasonably anticipated risks; matrixing identified risks against a covered entity's unique mix of information requiring safeguarding; employee training, awareness, testing and sanctions; individual accountability for information security; access authorization, management, and monitoring controls; contingency and disaster recovery planning; and ongoing technical and non-technical evaluation of Security Rule compliance.

- **Physical Safeguards**[38] Physical security safeguard measures include: mandated facilities access controls; workstation use and workstation security requirements; device and media controls; restricting access to sensitive information; and maintaining offsite computer backups.

- **Technical Safeguards**[39] Without specifying technological mechanisms, the HIPAA Security Rule mandates automated technical processes intended to protect information and control and record access to such information. Mandated processes include authentication controls for persons accessing EPHI, encryption/decryption requirements, audit controls, and mechanisms for ensuring data integrity.

The Security Rule contains other requirements beyond these general categories, including: ensuring, by written agreement, that entities with whom a covered entity exchanges EPHI, maintain reasonable and appropriate security measures, and holding those entities to the agreed-upon standards; developing written procedures and policies to implement the Security Rule's requirements, disseminating such procedures, and reviewing and updating them periodically in response to changing threats, vulnerabilities, and operational circumstances.

Sarbanes-Oxley

The Sarbanes–Oxley Act of 2002 (SOX) creates legal liability for senior executives of publicly traded companies, potentially including stiff prison sentences and fines of up to $5,000,000 per violation, for willfully certifying financial statements that do not meet the requirements of the statute.[40] Section 404 of SOX requires senior management, pursuant to rules promulgated by the Securities and Exchange Commission (SEC), to attest to: "(1) the responsibility of management for establishing and maintaining an adequate internal control structure and procedures for financial reporting; and (2) …the effectiveness of the internal control structure and procedures of the issuer for financial reporting." [41] Section 302, also requires that pursuant to SEC regulations, officers signing company financial reports certify that they are "responsible for establishing and maintaining internal controls," and "have evaluated the effectiveness" of those controls and reported their conclusions as to the same.[42]

Federal Information Security and Management Act

The Federal Information Security and Management Act of 2002, as amended, (FISMA) does not directly create liability for private sector information security professionals or their customers.[43] Information security professionals should be aware of this law, however, because the law:

- Legally mandates the process by which information security requirements for federal government departments and agencies must be developed and implemented

- Directs the federal government to look to the private sector for applicable "best practices" and to provide assistance to the private sector (if requested) with regard to information security

- Contributes to the developing "standard of care" for information security by mandating a number of specific procedures and policies

FERPA and the TEACH Act

The Family Educational Right to Privacy Act (FERPA) prohibits educational agencies and programs, at risk of losing federal funds, from having a policy or practice of "permitting the release of" specified educational records.[44] FERPA does not state whether or not the prohibition places affirmative requirements on educational institutions to protect against unauthorized access to these records through the use of information security measures. It is certainly possible that a court could conclude in the future that an educational institution, which fails to take reasonable information security measures to prevent unauthorized access to protected information, is liable under FERPA for "permitting the release" of such information. The 2002 Technology, Education and Copyright Harmonization Act (the "TEACH Act") explicitly requires educational institutions to take "technologically feasible" measures to prevent unauthorized sharing of copyrighted information beyond the students specifically requiring the information for their studies, and, thus, may create newly enforceable legal duties on educational institutions with regard to information security.[45]

Electronic Communications Privacy Act and Computer Fraud and Abuse Act

These two federal statutes, while not mandating information security procedures, create serious criminal penalties for any persons who gain unauthorized access to electronic records. Unlike laws such as HIPAA and GLB, these two statues broadly apply, regardless of the type of electronic records that are involved. The Electronic Communications Privacy Act (ECPA) makes it a federal felony to, without authorization, use or intercept the contents of electronic communications.[46] Likewise, the Computer Fraud and Abuse Act of 1984 (CFAA) makes the unauthorized access to a very wide range of computer systems (including financial institutions, the federal government, and any protected computer system used in interstate commerce) a federal felony.[47] As a result, information security professionals must take great care—and rely on qualified and experienced legal professionals—to ensure that the authorizations they receive from their customers are broad and specific enough to mitigate potential criminal liability under ECPA and CFAA.[48]

State Laws

In addition to federal statutes and regulations implicating information security, there are numerous state laws that, depending on an entity's location and the places in which it does business, can also create legal requirements related to the work of information security professionals.

Unauthorized Access

In Colorado (and in other states), it is a crime to access, use, or exceed authorized access to, or use of, a computer, computer network, or any part of a computer system.[49] It is a crime to take action against a computer system to cause damage, to commit a theft, or for other nefarious purposes. However, it is particularly important for information security professionals to be aware that it is also a crime to knowingly access a computer system without authorization or to exceed authorized access. This is one reason it is critical for information security professionals, with the advice of qualified and experienced counsel, to negotiate a comprehensive, carefully worded, Letter of Authorization (LOA) with each and every customer (discussed in detail below).

Deceptive Trade Practices

Deceptive trade practices are unlawful and may potentially subject anyone committing them to civil penalties and damages.[50] In Colorado (as in many other states), "deceptive trade practices" include:

- "Knowingly mak[ing] a false representation as to the characteristics... [or] benefits of goods, ...services, or property"[51]

- "Fail[ing] to disclose material information concerning goods, services, or property which information was known at the time of an advertisement or sale if such failure to disclose such information was intended to induce the consumer to enter into a transaction"[52]

Deceptive trade practices laws have been used by regulators to impose (through lawsuits) information security requirements on entities in industries not otherwise subject to statutory or regulatory standards.

These are only two of the many types of state laws potentially applicable to information security professionals and their customers. In addition, common law negligence doctrines in every state can create civil legal liability for information security professionals and their customers (discussed below in "Do it Right or Bet the Company: Tools to Mitigate Legal Liability").

Understanding the myriad state laws that apply to information security, and to any particular entity, and how such laws overlap and interact with federal laws, is complex and constantly evolving. Information security professionals and their customers should consult qualified and experienced legal counsel to navigate this challenging legal environment.

Enforcement Actions

What constitutes the "reasonable standard of care" in information security, as in all areas of the law, will continue to evolve, and not only through new statutes and regulations. Prosecutors and regulators will not be content to wait for such formal, legal developments. In lawsuits, and enforcement actions against entities not directly covered by any specific federal or state law or regulation, prosecutors and regulators have demonstrated the clear intent to extend "reasonable" information security measures even to those entities not clearly covered by specific existing laws. This is being done through legal actions leading to settlements, often including consent decrees (agreements entered into to end litigation or regulatory action) wherein a company agrees to "voluntarily" allow regulators to monitor (e.g., for 20 years) the company's information security program.[53]

Since these agreements are publicly available, they are adding to the "standard of care" to which entities will be held, in addition to providing added impetus for similar enforcement actions in the future. Thus, customers of information security professionals should take scant comfort in the fact that there are not yet specific laws explicitly targeted at their economic sectors or industries.

Three Fatal Fallacies

Conventional wisdom is a powerful and dangerous thing, as is a little knowledge. Unfortunately, many entities realizing they have legal and other requirements for information security have come to believe some specific fallacies that sometimes govern their information security decisions. More disturbingly, a significant number of information security providers, who should know better, also are falling victim to these fallacies. Herewith, then, let the debunking begin.

The "Single Law" Fallacy

Many information security professionals, both within commercial and educational entities, and among the burgeoning world of consultants, subscribe to the "single law" fallacy. That is, they identify a statute or set of regulations that clearly apply to a particular institution and assume that, by complying with that single standard, they have ended all legal risk. This assumption may be true, but in many cases is not. Making such an assumption could be a very expensive error, absent the advice of qualified and experienced legal counsel.

Take, for example, a mid-sized college or university. Information security professionals may conclude that, since FERPA clearly applies to educational records, following guidance tailored to colleges and universities based on what they conclude are the appropriate Department of Education standards, is sufficient to mitigate any potential legal liability. Worse yet, they may decide to gamble that, given current ambiguity about whether FERPA requires affirmative action to prevent unauthorized access to such records, they need not take any affirmative steps to try and prevent such access. This could be an expensive gamble, particularly if the educational institution does not ask itself the following questions:

- Does the school grant financial aid or extend other forms of credit? If so, it could be subject to GLBA.

- Does it operate hospitals, provide psychiatric counseling services, or run a student health service? If so, it could be subject to HIPAA.

- Does the school's Web site contain any representations about the security of the site and/or university-held information? If so, it could be subject to lawsuits under one or more (depending on whether it has campuses in multiple states) state deceptive trade practices laws.

The Private Entity Fallacy

Focusing on SOX and the resulting preoccupation with publicly traded companies, some institutions take solace in being private and in the fact that, so the argument goes, they are not subject to SOX and/or that they can somehow "fly under the radar" of federal regulators and civil litigants. Again, a dangerous bet. First, the likelihood of comprehensive federal information security regulation reaching well beyond publicly traded companies grows daily. Second, anyone who believes that lawyers for future plaintiffs (students, faculty, victims of attack or identity theft) will be deterred by the literal terms of SOX is misguided. The argument (potentially a winning one) will be that the appropriate "standard of care" for information security was publicly available and well known. The fact that one particular statute may not apply, by its plain terms, does not relieve entities of awareness of the standard of care and duty not to be negligent. Third, and most importantly, a myopic focus on SOX (or any other single law or regulation) to the exclusion of the numerous other potential sources of liability, will not relieve entities of the responsibility to learn about, and follow, the dictates of all other sources of law, including, but not limited to, HIPAA, GLBA, state statutes, and common law theories and, depending on where an entity does business, international and foreign law, such as the complex and burdensome European Union Privacy Directive.[54]

The "Pen Test Only" Fallacy

Every information security professional has dealt with the "pen test only" customer, probably more than once. This customer is either certain that their information security posture is so good that they just need an outside party to try and "break in" (do a penetration test) to prove how good they are, or feels an internal bureaucratic need to prove to others in the company how insecure their systems are. Generally, the customer has a limited budget or simply does not want to spend much money and wants a "quick hit" by the information security professional to prove a bureaucratic point. One variation on this theme is the customer who wants the penetration test as a first step, before deciding how far down the Information Security Assessment/Evaluation road to walk.

There is no way to say this too strongly: **starting with a penetration test is a disaster**, particularly if there is no way to protect the results from disclosure (see "Attorney-client Privilege" below). At least as important are the horrendous legal consequences that can flow from starting with a penetration test without establishing a more comprehensive, longer-term relationship with qualified and experienced lawyers and, through them, information security technical consultants. Not only will the customer almost certainly "fail" the penetration test, particularly if done as the first step without proper assessment, evaluation, and mid-stream remediation, but this failure will *be documented in a report not subject to any type of attorney-client privilege or other protection from disclosure.*

In short, testing done at the worst possible time in the process in terms of exposing vulnerabilities will be wide open to discovery and disclosure by your customers' future adversaries. From the standpoint of the information security technical professional, this also could lead to your being required later to testify, publicly and under oath, as to the minutest of details of your work for the customer, your methodology and "trade secrets," and your work product.[55]

Do It Right or Bet the Company: Tools to Mitigate Legal Liability

In recent years, numerous articles have been written on how to protect your network from a technical perspective,[56] but, at least throughout mid-2005, the headlines swelled with examples of companies that have lost critical information due to inadequate security. Choice Point, DSW Shoes, several universities, financial institutions including Bank of America and Wachovia, MasterCard and other credit providers, and even the FBI have been named in recent news articles for having lost critical information. As one example, ChoicePoint was sued in 2005 in actions brought in states ranging from California to New York and in its home state of Georgia. Allegations in the lawsuits included that ChoicePoint failed to "secure and maintain confidential the personal, financial and other information entrusted to ChoicePoint by consumers"[57]; failed to maintain adequate procedures to avoid disclosing some private credit and financial information to unauthorized third parties; and acted "willfully, recklessly, and/or in conscious disregard" of its customers rights to privacy.[58] Legal theories used in future information security-related lawsuits will be limited only by the imagination of the attorneys filing the suits.

It is hardly a distant possibility that every major player in information security will be sued sooner or later, whether a particular suit is frivolous or not. It is a fact of business life. So, how can information security consultants help their customers reduce their litigation "target profile?"

We Did Our Best; What's the Problem?

Many companies feel that their internal information technology and security staffs are putting forth their best efforts to maintain and secure their networks. They may even be getting periodic penetration tests and trying to make sense out of the hundreds of single-spaced pages of "vulnerabilities" identified in the resulting reports. So why isn't that good enough? The answer is that "doing one's best" to secure and maintain a network system will not be enough unless it is grounded in complying with external legal standards (discussed above). Penetration tests alone are likely not enough to demonstrate reasonable efforts at meeting the standard of care for information security. In ChoicePoint's case, at least based on what has been made public as of mid-2005, penetration tests would not have helped. ChoicePoint appears to have fallen victim to individuals who fraudulently posed as businessmen and conned people into giving them what may have been otherwise secure information.

Ameliorating any one particular potential point of failure will almost never be enough. Companies today must understand the potential sources of liability that apply to all commercial entities, as well as those specific to their industry. Only through understanding the legal environment and adopting and implementing policies to assure a high level of compliance with prevailing legal requirements can a company minimize the risk of liability. Of course, this system approach cannot be not static. It requires ongoing review and implementation to assure compliance in an ever-changing legal environment.

The Basis for Liability

A company's legal liability can arise as a result of: (a) standards and penalties imposed by federal, state, or local governments; (b) breach of contractual agreements; or (c) other non-contractual civil wrongs (torts) ranging from fraud, invasion of privacy, and conversion to deceptive trade practices and negligence. Avoiding liability for criminal misconduct also involves an understanding of the statutes and regulations applicable to your business and adhering to those requirements. Federal and state statutes may impose both criminal penalties as well as form the basis for private lawsuits.

Negligence and the "Standard of Care"

The combination of facts and events that can give rise to civil claims when information security is breached and the specific impact on business operations, are too numerous to discuss in detail. Understanding the basis for liability and conducting business in a manner designed to avoid liability is the best defense. In many cases, the claim of liability is based in a charge that the company and its officers and directors acted "negligently." In law, "negligence" arises when a party owes a legal duty to another, that duty is breached, and the breach causes damages to the injured party. Generally speaking, acting "reasonably" under the circumstances will prevent information security consultants or their customers from being found "negligent."[59] The rub is that what is "reasonable" both: (1) depends on the particular circumstances of individual situations; and (2) is constantly evolving as new laws and regulations are promulgated and new vulnerabilities, attack vectors, and available counter-measures become known.

Certainly, when a company maintains personal or confidential customer information, or has agreed to maintain as confidential the trade secret information of another business, its minimum duty is to use reasonable care in securing its computer systems to avoid theft or inadvertent disclosure of the information entrusted to it. Reasonable care may range from an extremely high standard when trust and confidence are reposed in a company to secure sensitive information, to a standard of care no more than that generally employed by others in the industry.

A reasonable "standard of care" is what the law defines as the minimum efforts a company must take not to have acted negligently (or, put another way, to have acted reasonably). A strong foundation to avoid liability for most civil claims begins with conducting the company's affairs up to the known standard of care that will avoid liability for negligence.

The appropriate, reasonable standard of care in any given industry and situation can arise from several sources, including statutes, regulations, common law duties, organizational policies, and contractual obligations. Courts look to the foreseeability of particular types of harm to help determine an industry standard of care. In other words, a business must exercise reasonable care to prevent an economic loss that should have been anticipated. As a result of ongoing public disclosure of new types of harm from breaches in information security, it is increasingly "foreseeable" that critical information may be lost through unauthorized access, and the policies and practices used to protect that information will take center stage in any negligence action.

What Can Be Done?

Fully understanding the risks, as assessed by qualified and experienced counsel, is an essential first step. Taking action that either avoids liability or minimizes the consequences when things go wrong is the next stride. The following are some suggestions that will help in the journey.

Understand Your Legal Environment

Mitigating legal liability begins with understanding the laws applicable to a company's business. (A variety of potentially applicable legal requirements are outlined in the "Legal Standards Relevant to Information Security" section above.) Ignorance of the law is no excuse, and failure to keep pace with statutory requirements is a first source of liability. Working with professionals, whether inside or outside of the company, to track changes in legislation and tailor your information security policies is the first line of defense. Careful compliance with laws not only helps reduce the potential for criminal liability or administrative fines, but also evidences a standard of care that may mitigate civil liability.

Comprehensive and Ongoing Security Assessments, Evaluations, and Implementation

Working with qualified and experienced legal counsel and technical consultants, a company must identify and prioritize the information it controls that may require protection, and catalogue the specific legal requirements applicable to such information and to the type of business the company is in. Next, policies must be developed to assure that the information is properly maintained and administered and that the company's personnel conduct themselves in accordance with those policies. Policy evaluations must include the applicable legal requirements, as well as reasonable procedures for testing and maintaining the security of information systems.

Critically, the cycle of using outside, neutral, third-party assessments/evaluations, implementation and improvement, and further assessment, must be ongoing. A static assessment/evaluation sitting on your shelf is worse than none at all. Almost equally bad is actually implementing the results of assessments/evaluations, but never reassessing or modifying them or insufficiently training employees on them, or evaluating those employees on their understanding and implementation of such results.

Use Contracts to Define
Rights and Protect Information

Most businesses understand the process of entering into contracts and following the terms of those contracts to avoid claims of breach. What is not so easily identified is how contractual obligations impact the potential of civil liability based on how information is secured and managed within a particular business? Many areas within a company's business require contracts to be developed and tailored to avoid liability and preserve the integrity of the business. One example is the Uniform Trade Secrets Act (UTSA), adopted in nearly all states and intended to protect confidential information of value to a company's business. Under the UTSA, confidential information may include formulas, patterns, compilations, programs, devices, methods, techniques, or processes that derive independent economic value from not being generally known to the public and for which the company has made reasonable efforts to maintain confidentiality. Almost every company has trade secrets—from its customer lists to its business methodologies afford a competitive advantage. Any protection for these valuable assets will be lost if a company fails to make reasonable efforts to maintain the information as confidential.

At a minimum, contracts must be developed that commit employees not to disclose the trade secrets of the company, or any information legally mandated to be protected (e.g., individual health care or financial information). These agreements are often most effective if entered into at the time of, and as a condition to, employment. This is because most contracts require value to support enforceability and because a delay in requiring a non-disclosure agreement may allow sensitive information to be disclosed before the contract is in place.

Employment policies should reinforce the employee's obligation to maintain confidentiality. These policies should also provide clear guidance on procedures to use and maintain passwords and to responsibly use the information secured on the network. Regular interviews and employee training should be implemented to reinforce the notion that these requirements are mandatory and taken seriously by management. Vendors and service providers that may need to review confidential information should only be permitted access to such information under an agreement limiting the use of that information and agreeing to maintain its confidentiality. Hiring a consultant to perform a network security evaluation without a proper confidentiality agreement could later be found to be sufficient evidence that a company failed to take reasonable efforts to maintain information as confidential, with the result that the information is not longer a trade secret entitled to protection.

Use Qualified Third-Party Professionals

Working with qualified information security professionals to implement proper hardware and software solutions to minimize a security breach is critical, but never enough. These functions need to be performed in conjunction with a system of evaluation testing and retesting that integrates legal considerations, and under the supervision and guidance of qualified and experienced legal counsel.

In addition, working with qualified and experienced outside counsel can substantially improve success in the event that claims of negligence are asserted (using attorneys and technical professionals trained to conduct comprehensive and ongoing systems assessments and evaluations is evidence of the reasonableness of the efforts to prevent the loss). Companies' internal staff may be equally competent to develop and implement the strategies of information security, but regulators, courts, and juries will look to whether or not a company retained qualified and experienced outside counsel and technical consultants before a problem arose. Working with these experts increases the probability that best practices are being followed and independent review is the best way to mitigate against foreseeable loss of sensitive information.

As discussed in more detail below, retaining outside professionals in a way that creates an attorney-client privilege may offer protection (in the event of civil litigation, regulatory, or even criminal, action) from disclosure of system vulnerabilities discovered in the information security assessment and evaluation processes. The privilege is not absolute, however, and may have different practical applications in the civil and criminal contexts and, in particular, when a customer elects to assert an "advice-of-counsel" defense.

A key requirement emerging as a critical part of the evolving information security standards of care is the requirement to get an external review by qualified, neutral parties.[60] These requirements are based on the sound theory that, no matter how qualified, expert, and well intentioned an entity's information technology and information security staff is, it is impossible for them to be truly objective. Moreover, the "fox in the hen house" problem arises, leaving senior management to wonder whether those charged with creating and maintaining information security can and will fairly and impartially assess the effectiveness of such security. Finally, qualified and experienced outside legal counsel and technical consultants bring perspective, breadth of experience, and currency with the latest technical and legal developments that in-house staff normally cannot provide cost-effectively.

Making Sure Your Standards-of-Care Assessments Keep Up with Evolving Law

As suggested above, the legal definition of a "reasonable" standard of care is constantly evolving. Policymakers take seriously the threats and the substantial economic loss caused by cyber-attacks. New laws are continually being enacted to punish attackers and to shift liability to companies that have failed to take reasonable information security measures. Contractual obligations can now be formed instantly and automatically simply by new customers accessing your customer's Web sites and using their services, all over the Internet and, thus, all over the world. As new vulnerabilities, attacks, and countermeasures come to public attention, new duties emerge. In short, what was "reasonable" last month may not be reasonable this month.

Information security assessments and evaluations provide a tool to evaluate, and enhance compliance with, best practices in protecting critical information; however, they are, at best, only snapshots unless they are made regular, ongoing events. Best practices begin with understanding and complying with applicable laws, but can only be maintained through tracking and implementing evolving statutory requirements. Working with qualified and experienced counsel to follow new legal developments in this fast-moving area of the law and advise on the proper interpretation and implementation of legislative requirements is becoming essential to navigate through this ever-changing landscape.

Plan for the Worst

Despite all best efforts, nothing can completely immunize a company from liability. Failing to plan a crisis management and communications strategy in the
event of lost or compromised information can invite lawsuits and create liability
despite a track record showing your company exercised a reasonable standard of
care in trying to protect information. Avoiding liability involves planning for
problems. For example, one class action filed against ChoicePoint alleges that
shareholders were misled when the company failed to disclose (for several
months) the existence of its security breach and the true extent of the information that was compromised. Having had policies in place to provide guidance to
executives in communicating with customers and prospective shareholders may
well have avoided these allegations. California currently has a Notice of
Security Breach law that was enacted in 2002.[61] As of May 2005, Arkansas,
Georgia, Indiana, Montana, North Dakota, and Washington have followed suit
by enacting some form of legislation requiring disclosure relating to breaches of
security, and bills have been introduced in not less than 34 other states to regulate in this area.[62] As of mid-2005, there was no similar federal regulation,
although, several disclosure bills have been introduced in Congress.

A strategic policy to deal with crisis management must take into account
disclosure laws in all states in which a company operates. Making disclosures
that comply with multiple laws and that minimize the adverse impact of information security breaches and disclosures of them must be planned far in
advance of a crisis. Again, this is a constantly changing landscape, and these policies need to be reviewed and updated on a regular basis. It is critical that these
policies and plans are developed and carried out with the assistance of qualified
and experienced counsel.

Insurance

As more information security breaches occur and are disclosed, the cost to
businesses and individuals will continue to rise. In 2002, the Federal Trade
Commission (FTC) estimated that 10 million people were victims of identity
theft. According to Gartner, Inc., 9.4 million online users in the U.S. were
victimized between April 2003 and April 2004 with losses amounting to
$11.7 billion.[63] Costs to business from these losses will likely grow to stag-

gering levels in the coming years, and this trend is capturing the attention of some of the more sophisticated insurance companies. Some companies are developing products to provide coverage for losses resulting from breaches of information security. Companies should contact their carriers and do their own independent research to determine what coverage, if any, is or will become, available.

Customers of information security consultants, with the advice of qualified and experienced counsel, must take into account all of these issues in determining how best to mitigate their legal risk. A key component of mitigating that risk is the relationships established with information security consultants, including qualified and experienced counsel and skilled and respected technical consultants. Those relationships, of course, must be established and governed by written contracts (discussed in the next section).

What to Cover
in Security Evaluation Contracts[64]

The contract is the single most important tool used to define and regulate the legal relationship between the information security consultant and the customer. It protects both parties from misunderstandings and should clearly allocate liability in case of unforeseen or unintended consequences, such as a system crash, access to protected, proprietary, or otherwise sensitive information thought secure, and damage to the network or information residing on the network. The contract also serves as a roadmap through the security evaluation cycle for both parties. A LOA (described in the next section) serves a different purpose from a contract and often augments the subject matter covered in a contract or deals with relationships with third parties not part of the original service contract. In most evaluations, both will be required.

The contract should spell out each and every action the customer wants the provider to perform. Information security consultants should have a standard contract for a packages of services, but should be flexible enough for negotiation in order to meet the specific needs of the customer. What is, or is not, covered in the contract, and how the provisions should be worded, are decisions both parties must make only with the advice of qualified and experienced counsel familiar with this field. As with any other legal agreement between parties, both signatories should fully understand all the terms in the contract, or ask for clarification or re-drafting of ambiguous, vague, or overly technical language. Contract disputes often arise in situations where two parties can read the same language in different ways. Understand what you are signing.

What, Who, When, Where, How, and How Much

The following paragraphs provide an overview of what should be included in security evaluation and information security service contracts. They include checklists of questions that the contract should answer for both parties; however, remember that each assessment is different because customer's needs and the facts of each evaluation process will differ. Make sure the contract you sign clearly covers each of the topics suggested here, but keep in mind that this is not an exhaustive list and cannot replace the specific advice of your own legal counsel for your specific circumstances.

What

The first general requirement for a contract for information security evaluation services is to address the basic services the consultant will perform. What are the expectations of both parties in performing the non-technical aspects of the business relationship, such as payment, reporting, and documentation? What services does the contract cover? What does the customer want? What can the information security consultant provide? A number of categories of information should appear in this first section.

Description of the Security Evaluation and Business Model

In the initial part of the contract, the information security consultant should describe the services to be provided and, generally, how its business is conducted. This information provides background on the type of contract that is to be used by the parties (e.g., a contract for services or a contract for services followed by the purchase and installation of software to remediate any identified vulnerabilities). This initial section should also identify the customer and describe its business model. For example, is the customer a financial organization, a healthcare organization, an organization with multiple geographic locations under evaluation, or subject to specific legal requirements and/or industry regulations?

Definitions Used in the Contract

Each contract uses terms that will need further explanation so that the meaning is clear to both parties. Technical terms such as "vulnerability" and "penetration" should be spelled out. Executives sign contracts. Attorneys advise executives whether or not to sign the contracts. Both must understand what the contract means.

Description of the Project

The contract should provide a general statement of the scope of the project. If the project is a long-term endeavor or a continuing relationship between the two parties, this section should also include a description of how each part of the project or phase in the relationship should progress and what additional documents will cover each phase or part of the project. This section also clearly defines what the information security consultant will and will not do throughout the evaluation. Also, in the description of the project, the customer should clearly define the objectives it wants the information security consultant to accomplish. Are all the entity's networks included? What types of testing are required? This section should also include the types of vulnerabilities that the information security consultant is not likely to discover based on the types of testing, the networks tested, and the scope of the overall evaluation, as permitted by the customer.

Assumptions, Representations, and Warranties

In every assessment, the parties must provide or assume some basic information. These assumptions should appear in the contract. Assumptions are factual statements, not a description of conversations the parties have had (e.g., "The schedule in this contract is based on the assumption that all members of the evaluation team will work from 8:30 A.M. to 5:30 P.M. for five days per week for the full contract period."). With regard to the network assumptions, the customer should provide basic information on network topology upon which the assessment team can base assumptions for the types of vulnerabilities they will look for and testing methodologies that will successfully achieve the customer's objectives (e.g., "The evaluation methodology applied to the customer network under this contract relies on the assumption that the customer maintains servers in a single geographic location, physically secured, and logically segregated from other networks and from the Internet.")[65] The language in this section should also address responsive actions should the assumptions prove false: Under what circumstances is the contract voided? What can make the price go up or down? In the event of unexpected security or integrity problems being created during an evaluation, when should the testing be stopped? Who decides? When should the customers' management be informed? At what levels?

IEM contracts should include "representations and warranties" by the customer spelling out certain critical information that the customer "warrants" to be true such as: descriptions of the customer's business operations and information they hold within their systems; what agreements the customer has with third-party vendors and/or holders of their information; what information systems external to those controlled by the customer, if any, could be impacted by the evaluation and testing to be done, and what measures the customer has taken to eliminate the possibilities of such impact; and the degree to which the customer exclusively owns and controls information and systems to be evaluated and/or tested or has secured written agreements explicitly authorizing evaluation and testing by others that do own or control such information and systems.[66]

Boundaries and Limitations

In addition to stating what the evaluation will cover, this initial section should also address what the assessment will not cover in terms of timing, location, data, and other variables. The general goal of the evaluation cycle is to provide a level of safety and security to the customer in the confidence, integrity, and availability of its networks. However, some areas of the network are more sensitive than others. Additionally, each customer will have varying levels of trust in the evaluation methodology and personnel. Not all evaluation and testing methodologies are appropriate for all areas of a network. The customer should give careful consideration to what is tested, when and how, as well as what the evaluators should do in the event of data contamination or disclosure.

If a customer runs a particular type of report on a specific date to meet payroll, accounting, regulatory, or other obligations, that date is not a very good time to engage in network testing. Even if the testing methodology is sound and the personnel perform at peak efficiency and responsibility levels, human nature will attribute any network glitch on that date to the testing team. Sensitive data requires an increased level of scrutiny for any measure taken that could damage or disclose the information, or make the use of the information impossible for some period of time. Such actions could result in administrative or regulatory penalties and expensive remediation efforts.

Data privacy standards vary by industry, state, country, and category of information. A single network infrastructure may encompass personnel records, internal audits or investigations, proprietary or trade secret information, financial information, and individual and corporate information records and databases. The network could also store data subject to attorney-client or other legal privilege. Additionally, customers should consider where and how their employees store data. Does the customer representative negotiating the scope of the project know where all the sensitive data in his/her enterprise are stored, and with what degree of certainty? Does the customer have a contingency plan for data contamination or unauthorized access? How does the security evaluation account for the possibility that testing personnel will come into contact with sensitive data (see Non-Disclosure and Secrecy Agreements section below)? In this portion of the contract, the customer should specify any areas of the network where testing personnel may not conduct evaluations, either for a period of time or during specific phases.

Both parties should be sensitive to the fact that the customer may not own and control all areas of the network. A customer can only consent to testing those portions of the network it owns and controls.

NOTE

Evaluation of other portions of a larger corporate network or where the evaluation proceeds through the Internet, requires additional levels of authorization from third parties outside the contractual relationship, and should never be carried out without explicit agreements negotiated and reviewed by qualified and experienced counsel.

In some cases, the evaluation can continue through these larger networks, but will require additional documentation, such as a LOA (see " Where the Rubber Meets the Road: the Letter of Authorization as Liability Protection" below).

Identification of Deliverables

Without feedback to the customer presented in a usable format, evaluating and testing the network is a waste of resources. The contract should state with a high degree of specificity what deliverables the customer requires and for what level of audience. For example, a 300-page technical report presented to a board of directors is of little use. A ten-slide presentation for the officers of a customer company that focuses on prioritizing the vulnerabilities in terms of levels of risk is far more valuable. Conversely, showing those same ten slides to the network engineering team will not help them. The key in this section of the contract is to manage expectations for the various levels of review within the customer's structure.

Who

The second general requirement for a contract for security evaluation services is to spell out the parties to the agreement and specify the roles and responsibilities of each (including specific names and titles of responsible individuals) for successfully completing the evaluation. This identity and role information is critical for reducing the likelihood of contract disputes due to unmet expectations.

Statement of Parties to the Contractual Agreement

Each party should be clearly identified in the contract by name, location, and principal point of contact for subsequent communications. Often, the official of record for signature is not the same person who will be managing the contract or engaged in day-to-day liaison activities with the evaluation personnel. Additionally, this section should spell out the procedures for changing the personnel of record for each type of contact.

Authority of Signatories to the Contractual Agreement

Ideally, the level of signatory to the contract should be equal, and, in any event, the signing official must be high enough to bind the entities to all obligations arising out of the contractual relationship. It is often also helpful for the customer signatory to be a person empowered to make changes based on recommendations resulting from the evaluation.

Roles and Responsibilities of Each Party to the Contractual Agreement

Spelling out the levels of staffing, location of resources, who will provide those resources, and the precise nature of other logistical, personnel, and financial obligations is critical. It allows both sides to proceed through the evaluation cycle with a focus on the objectives, rather than a daily complication of negotiating who is responsible for additional, unforeseen administrative issues. Some common areas of inclusion in this section are:

- Who provides facilities and administrative support?
- Who is responsible for backing up critical data before the evaluation begins?
- Who is responsible for initiating communication for project status reports. Does the customer call for an update, or does the evaluation team provide regular reporting? Must status reports be written or can they be oral and memorialized only in the information security consultants' records?
- Who is responsible for approving deviations from the contract or evaluation plan and how will decisions about these be recorded?

- Who will perform each aspect of each phase of the evaluation (will the customer provide any technical personnel)?

- Who is responsible for mapping the network before evaluation begins (and will those maps be provided to the evaluation team, or kept in reserve for comparison after the evaluation ends)?

- Who is responsible for briefing senior officers in the customer organization?

- Who is responsible for reporting discrepancies from the agreed project plan to evaluation POCs and executives?

- Who is responsible for reporting violations of policies, regulations, or laws discovered during the evaluation?

- Who has the authority to terminate the evaluation should network irregularities arise?

- Who bears the risk for unforeseen consequences or circumstances that arise during the evaluation period?

Non-disclosure and Secrecy Agreements

Many documents and other information pertaining to information security evaluations contain critical information that could damage one or both parties if improperly disclosed. Both parties bear responsibility to protect tools, techniques, vulnerabilities, and information from disclosure beyond the terms specified by a written agreement. Non-disclosure agreements should be narrowly drawn to protect sensitive information, yet allow both parties to function effectively. Specific areas to consider including are: ownership and use of the evaluation reports and results; use of the testing methodology in customer documentation; disclosures required under law; and the time period of disclosure restrictions. It is often preferable to have non-disclosure/secrecy agreements be separate, stand-alone documents so that, if they must be litigated later in public, as few details as possible of the larger agreement must be publicly exposed.

Assessment Personnel

A security evaluation team is composed of a variety of expert personnel, whether from the customer organization or supplied by the contractor. The contract should spell out the personnel requirements to complete each phase of the assessment successfully and efficiently. Both parties should have a solid understanding of each team member's skills and background. Where possible, the contract should include information on the personnel conducting the assessment. Both parties should also consider who would fund and who would perform any background investigations necessary for personnel assigned to evaluate sensitive networks.

Crisis Management and Public Communications

Network security evaluations can be messy. No network is 100 percent secure. The assessment team will inevitably find flaws. The assessment team will usually stumble across unexpected dangers, or take actions that result in unanticipated results that could impact the network or the data residing on the network. Do not make the mistake of compounding a bad situation with a poor response to the crisis. Implementing notification procedures at the contract phase often saves the integrity of an evaluation should something go wrong. The parties also should clearly articulate who has the lead role in determining the timing, content, and delivery mechanism for providing information to the customer's employees, customers, shareholders, and so forth. This section should also spell out what role, if any, the customer wants the assessment team or leader to play in the public relations efforts. A procedure for managing crisis situations is also prudent. Qualified and experienced legal counsel must be involved in these processes.

Indemnification, Hold Harmless, and Duty to Defend

Even more so than in many other types of contracts for services, the security evaluation contract should include detailed provisions explicitly protecting the information security consultants from various types of contract dispute claims. In addition to standard contract language, these sections should specifically spell out the responsibilities (and their limits) of both the customer and the information security consultants to defend claims of damage to external systems or information and intellectual property or licensing infringement for software, if any, developed by the information security consultant for purposes of the evaluation.

Ownership and Control of Information

The information contained in the final report and executive level briefings can be extremely sensitive. Both parties must understand who owns and controls the disclosure and dissemination of the information, as well as what both parties may do with the information following the review process. Any proprietary information or processes, including trade secrets, should be marked as such, and covered by a separate section of the contract. Key topics to cover include: use of evaluation results in either party's marketing or sales brochures; release of results to management or regulatory bodies; and disclosure of statistics in industry surveys, among other uses. The customer should spell out any internal corporate controls for the information in this section. If the customer requires encryption of the evaluation data, this section should clearly spell out those requirements and who is responsible for creating or providing keys.

One important ownership area that must be specifically covered in information security evaluation contracts is how reports and other resulting documentation from the evaluation are to be handled. May the information security consultants keep copies of the documents, at least for a reasonable period of time following the conclusion of the evaluation (e.g., in case the customer takes legal action against the consultant)? Who is responsible for destroying any excess copies of such information? May the information security consultant use properly sanitized versions of the reports as samples of work product?

Intellectual Property Concerns

Ownership and use of intellectual property is a complicated area of the law. However, clear guidance in the prior section on the ownership and use of evaluation information will help the parties avoid intellectual property disputes. The key to a smooth legal relationship between the parties is to clearly define expectations.

Licenses

The evaluation team must ensure that they have valid licenses for each piece of software used in the evaluation. The customer should verify valid licensing.

When

The third general requirement for a security evaluation services contract is to create a schedule for conducting the evaluation that includes all of the phases and contingency clauses to cover changes to that schedule. At a minimum, the contract should state a timeline for the overall evaluation and for each phase, including:

- A timeline for completing deliverables in draft and final formats
- Estimated dates of executive briefings, if requested
- A timeline for any follow-up work anticipated

Actions or Events that Affect Schedule

Inevitably, something will happen to affect the schedule. Personnel move, network topography changes a variety of unforeseen factors can arise. While the contract team cannot control those factors, it can draft language in the contract to allow rapid adaptation of the schedule, depending on various factors. Brief interruptions in assessments can mean long-term impacts if the team is at a sensitive point in the assessment. At the contracting phase, both sides should consult with other elements in their companies to determine what events could affect the schedule. Failure to plan adequately for scheduling conflicts or disruptions could result in one party breaching the contract. Both parties should agree on a contingency plan if the evaluation must terminate prematurely. Contingency plans could include resuming the evaluation at a later time or adjusting the total amount of the contract cost based on the phases completed.

Where

The fourth general requirement for a contract for security evaluation services is to define the location(s), both geographic and logical, subject to the evaluation. Where, precisely, are you testing? To create boundaries for the evaluation and prevent significant misunderstandings on the scope of the assessment or evaluation, list each facility, the physical address and/or logical location, including the Internet Protocol (IP) address range. Make sure that each machine attached to that IP space is within the legal and physical control of the customer. If any of the locations are outside the U.S., seek the immediate advice of counsel on this specific point. While covering the rapid developments in overseas law of this field is beyond the scope of this section, understand that many countries are implementing computer crime laws and standing up both civil and criminal response mechanisms to combat computer crime. Various elements of a network security evaluation can look like unauthorized access to a protected computer. Both the evaluation provider and the customer need to take additional cautionary measures and implement greater notification procedures when considering an evaluation of a system located even partially abroad. Additionally, this section should cover the location the evaluation team will use as their base of operations. If the two locations are separate geographically, the parties must address the electronic access needed for the evaluation.

Exercise an extra level of caution if the evaluation traverses the Internet. Use of the Internet to conduct evaluations carries an additional level of risk and legal liability because neither party owns or controls all of the intermediate network structures.

WARNING

Do not act where your evaluation and testing must traverse the Internet without the advice of qualified and experienced counsel.

How

The fifth general requirement for a contract for security evaluation services is to map out a methodology for completing the evaluation. This section should identify and describe each phase of the evaluation and/or the overall testing cycle if the contract will cover a business relationship that will span multiple assessments. The key is to prevent surprises for either party. Breaking complex assessments and/or evaluations up into phases in the contract allows the reviewing officials to understand what they are paying for and when they can expect results. State with precise language what the evaluator will be doing at each phase, the goals and objectives of each phase, each activity the evaluation team will complete during that phase, and the deliverables expected. Do not use technical slang. A separate background document on evaluation and testing methodology (i.e., NSA/IAM, IEM, ISO 17799, and so on) is often more useful than cluttering the contract with unnecessary technical detail. This section should also state and describe the standards the evaluation team will use for measuring the evaluation results. Testing should bear results on a measurement scale that allows for comparisons over time and between locations.

How Much

The sixth, and final, general requirement for a contract for security evaluation services is to spell out the costs of the evaluation and other associated payment terms. This section is similar to any other business service contract. At a minimum, it should include the following five elements.

Fees and Cost

The parties should discuss and agree to a fee structure that meets the needs of both parties, which in most cases will call for multiple payments based on phase completion. A helpful analogy is the construction of a house. At what phases will the homeowner pay the general contractor: excavation and clearing the lot; completion of the foundation; framing; walls and fixtures; or final walkthrough? Also, consider the level of customer management that must approve phase completion and payment. In most cases, the final payment on the contract will be tied in some way to the delivery of a final report. Both parties should also carefully discuss the costs for which the customer is responsible. If evaluation teams must travel to the customer's location, who pays for the travel, food, lodging, and other non-salary costs for those personnel, and what level of documentation will be needed to process payment? Do the costs include airfare, lodging, mileage, subsistence (meals and incidentals), and other expenses? Does the customer require that the expenses be "reasonable" or must a customer representative authorize the expenses in advance? To avoid disputes that detract the team's attention from the assessment, spell out the parties' expectations in the contract. The parties should also cover who pays for extraordinary unanticipated expenses such as equipment failure. In some circumstances, the best method for dealing with truly unexpected expenses is to state affirmatively in the contract that the parties will negotiate such costs as they arise.

Billing Methodology

In order for the customer's accounting mechanisms to adequately prepare for the obligations in the contract, the billing or invoicing requirements should be spelled out. If the customer requires a specific type of information to appear on the invoice, that information should be provided to the contractor in writing, preferably in the contract. The types of fees and costs that will appear on the invoice should also be discussed, and the customer should provide guidance on the level of detail they need, while the contractor should explain the nature of their billing capabilities.

Payment Expectations and Schedule

The contract should clearly represent both parties' expectations for prompt payment. Will the contractor provide invoices at each phase or on a monthly cycle? Are invoices due upon receipt or on a specific day of the month? Where does the contractor send the invoice and to whom within the customer's structure? Does the contractor require electronic payment of invoices, and if so, to what account? What penalties will the contractor assess for late payments or returned checks? Again, the key factor is to address both parties' expectations to prevent surprises.

Rights and Procedures to Collect Payment

In the event of problems in the contractual relationship or changes in management that affect the contract, what are the parties' rights? As with other commercial contracts, articulating the rights and remedies is essential to minimize or avoid altogether the expense of disputes.

Insurance for Potential Damage During Evaluation

Which party, if either, will carry insurance against damage to the customer's systems and information as well as to those of third parties?

Murphy's Law (When Something Goes Wrong)

The final standard set of clauses for the contract deals with the potential for conflict between the parties or modifications to the contract.

Governing Law

Where both parties are in the same state, and the evaluation is limited to those facilities, this clause may not be necessary. However, in most cases, the activities will cross state borders. The parties should agree on which state's law applies to the contract and under which court's jurisdiction parties can file lawsuits. Determining venue for disputes before they arise can reduce legal costs.

Acts of God, Terror Attacks, and other Unforeseeable Even

Attorneys and network engineers share at least one common trait; neither can predict with any certainty when things will go wrong, but all agree that something will eventually happen that you did not expect. Natural disasters, system glitches, power interruptions, military coups, and a thousand other events can affect a project. Where the disruption is the fault of neither party, both sides should decide in advance on the appropriate course of action.

When Agreement Is Breached and Remedies

When one party decides not to fulfill or becomes incapable in some way of performing, the terms of the contract, or believes the other party has not met its contractual obligations, a party can claim a breach (breaking) of the agreement and demand a remedy from the opposing party. Many types of remedies exist for breach of a contract. Either party can also take the matter to court, which can be very messy and extremely expensive. Anticipating situations such as these and inserting language in the contract to deal with potential breaches could save thousands of dollars in attorney fees and court costs. Both parties should discuss the following options with counsel before negotiating a contract for security evaluation services. First, are arbitration or mediation options appropriate or desirable? Second, should the matter proceed to court, one party will inevitably claim attorney's fees as part of the damages. Anticipate this claim and include language that specifies what fees are part of the remedy and whether the party who loses the dispute will reimburse attorney's fees, or whether each side will be responsible for its own attorney's fees.

Liquidated Damages

Liquidated damages are an agreed, or "liquidated," amount that one party is required to pay the other in the event of a breach or early termination of a contract. Liquidated damages are valuable to bring certainty to a failed relationship but are not appropriate if used to create a windfall or punish a party for not completing their contractual obligations. Instead, to be legally enforceable, a liquidated damages clause must estimate the parties' reasonably anticipated damages in the event of a breach or early termination of the contract. Liquidated damages cannot be a penalty and are not appropriate if actual damages can be readily determined.[67] Courts in Colorado, for example, generally will enforce a liquidated damages clause in a contract if: (1) at the time contract was entered into, anticipated damages in case of breach were difficult to ascertain; (2) parties mutually intended to liquidate them in advance; and (3) the amount of liquidated damages, when viewed as of the time the contract was made, was a reasonable estimate of potential actual damages a breach would cause.[68] If these factors apply to your transaction, liquidated damages should be considered to avoid protracted debates regarding the parties' harm when a breach occurs.

Limitations on Liability

Limitations on liability should always be considered and, if possible, incorporated in any contract for evaluation services. Typical clauses might state that liability is limited to an amount equal to the total amount paid by the customer under the contract. Other limitations on damages may require the customer to waive incidental or consequential damages or preclude recovery arising from certain conduct by the information security consultant. Like liquidated damages, however, the ability to limit or waive damages may be restricted by both statute and court decisions. For example, in some states, contractual provisions that purport to limit liability for gross negligence or for willful or wanton conduct are not enforceable.[69] In most states, limitations of liability are acceptable and will be enforced if the agreement was properly executed and the parties dealt at arms length.[70] Accordingly, you should try to limit the customer's right to recover consequential damages, punitive damages, and lost profits. Working with qualified counsel will assist in determining what limitations are enforceable in each specific transaction.

Survival of Obligations

This section makes clear what happens to specific contractual obligations, such as duties of non-disclosure and payment of funds owed, following the expiration of the contract.

Waiver and Severability

This section of the contract describes what happens if either party wants to waive the application of a portion of the contract, and allows for each section of the contract to be severable from the contract as a whole should a court rule that one clause or section is not enforceable. This section is also standard contract language and should be supplied by the attorney for the party drafting the contract.

Amendments to the Contract

For contracts that span significant periods of time, it is likely that one or both parties may require modifications to the contract. To avoid disputes, the original contract should spell out the format for any amendments. Amendments should be in writing and signed by authorized representatives of both parties. The parties should also discuss the financial arrangements surrounding a change to the contract. Proposed amendments to the contract must be accepted by the receiving party.

Where the Rubber Meets the Road: The LOA as Liability Protection

The contract functions as the overall agreement between the organization performing the security assessment and the company or network that will be tested or assessed. A LOA should be used between any two parties, whether party to the same original evaluation contract or not, to document consent to specific activities and protect against different types of adverse liability. For example, Widgets-R-Us contracts with Secure-Test to test the security of a new online shipping management network linked to Widgets' warehouses. ISP-anywhere provides the bandwidth for Widgets' east coast warehouses. Widgets should provide a LOA to Secure-Test consenting to specific network traffic that could trigger ISP-anywhere guards or intrusion detection systems. A copy of the letter should be provided to ISP-anywhere, in advance of the testing, as notice of the activity and a record of Widgets' consent. Additionally, depending on the language of the service agreement between Widgets and ISP-anywhere, Widgets may need to ask ISP-anywhere to provide a LOA for any of Secure-Test's activities that could impact their network infrastructure or otherwise void the bandwidth service agreement. ISP-anywhere was not a party to the original information security evaluation contract and, therefore, Secure-Test needs this additional form of agreement for the activities.

It is an unusual case in which a customer is the sole user of a third-party network system. Accordingly, the network hosts information for businesses and individuals that may maintain confidential information or information not owned by the customer. Merely accessing this information without proper authorization can result in both criminal and civil penalties. In addition, agreements between the customer and the network host may prohibit such access to the system altogether. You, along with your counsel, must always review these relationships with your customer, comply with contractual limitations, and obtain appropriate authorizations.

In many cases, the LOA will turn out to be the single most important document you sign. In addition to the potential civil liability for any damage to your customer's or third parties' systems that occur during periods when you arguably exceed your authorized access, failing to obtain adequate authorization may result in the commission of a crime. As discussed in "Legal Standards Relevant to Information Security" above, the federal Computer Fraud and Abuse Act imposes criminal liability for unauthorized access to computer systems and for exceeding the scope of authorization for accessing certain computers. Every state has passed some form of law that prohibits access to computer systems without proper authority.[71] Working with qualified and experienced legal counsel is vital to assure that your work avoids violation of law and the potential for criminal liability.

Another typical use of a LOA is augmentation of a part of the evaluation or correction of unforeseen technical challenges during the course of the contract (e.g., Widgets-R-Us acquires a warehouse on the west coast after the security evaluation begins, and wants to add this warehouse to the list of facilities Secure-Test will review). Widgets-R-Us does not need a new contract, and most likely does not need to amend the current contract, so long as both parties will accept a LOA to expand the scope of the security assessment. Whether or not to allow LOA amendments to a standing contract should be a term written into the original contract itself.

An important section of a LOA (similar to the overall contract itself) is a comprehensive and detailed statement of what a customer is not authorizing (i.e., certain systems or databases that are off limits, specific times that testing is not to be done, the tools the information security consultant will, and will not use, security measures that the customer will not permit the consultant to take, and so forth). This is equally important for the customer and the information security consultant.

LOAs should be signed by officials for each party with sufficient authority to agree to all specified terms. Importantly, LOAs between a customer and information security consultant should identify any and all types of information or specific systems for which the customer does not have the authority to authorize access. While LOA provisions can be part of the basic contract itself, as with non-disclosure agreements, it is often preferable to have the LOA be a separate, stand-alone agreement so that, if the LOA must be litigated later in public, as few details as possible of the larger agreement must be publicly exposed.

Beyond You and Your Customer

Simply obtaining your customer's consent to access their computer systems is necessary, but it is not always enough. Your customer has obligations to its customers, licensors, and other third parties. Honoring these commitments will avoid potential liability for both you and your customer.

Software License Agreements

Typically, software used by the customer will be subject to a license agreement that governs the relationship between the customer and the software provider. It is not uncommon for software license agreements to prohibit decompilation, disassembly, or reverse engineering of the software code, and to limit access to the software.

The use of tools to penetrate computer systems can constitute the use, access, and running of executable software using the computer's operating system and other programs in a manner that may violate the license agreement. To avoid civil liability, the consultant should have qualified and experienced legal counsel review applicable license agreements and, where appropriate, obtain authorization from the licensor prior to conducting tests of the customer's system.

Your Customer's Customer

To avoid creating liability for your customer, you need to understand your customer's customers and their expectations. Your customer should be able to identify their customer's confidential information and any specific contractual requirements. Understanding the source of third-party information (how it is stored and where appropriate or required), and obtaining consent to access their information is essential. To maintain the integrity of your work, you must respect the confidentiality of your customer and third party-information available to your customer. This is true even if no formal demand is made or no written agreement is entered into. You will be perceived as an agent of your customer; professionalism requires discretion and maintaining privacy.

Similarly, you need to recognize and honor intellectual property rights of your customer and its customers. In general, to protect your customer, you must also protect its customers with the high standards of respect for information privacy and security you provide to your customer.

The First Thing We Do…?
Why You Want Your Lawyers
Involved From Start to Finish

Few of Shakespeare's words have been more often quoted (and misquoted) than the immortal words of "Dick the Butcher": "The first thing we do, let's kill all the lawyers."[72] What generally is left out by modern lawyer bashers cheering Dick on in his quest is that Dick, and the band of rogues to which he belonged, were planning to overthrow the English government when this battle plan was suggested. The group followed up the lawyer killing idea shortly thereafter by hanging the town clerk of court.

The most reasonable reading of this passage is that Shakespeare intended to demonstrate that those who helped people interpret and litigate the law were, in fact, necessary to the orderly functioning of society. This interpretation is not without fierce challenge, however. In fact, a cottage industry emerges from time-to-time on the Internet debating whether Shakespeare was pro- or anti-lawyer. One prolific Internet lawyer-basher even suggests that the fact that lawyers use Shakespeare to justify our existence is conclusive evidence both of our ignorance and, to put it more charitably than the author, willingness to twist the facts to our own ends.[73]

Two things are certain. First, lots of people hate lawyers, some with very good reason. Second, the only thing worse than your own lawyer is the other guy's lawyer.

Having litigated numerous cases, and advised information security professionals inside and outside the federal government, we can assure information security professionals and their customers that, if and when you are sued by victims of attack or identify theft, or find yourselves in the sights of regulators or prosecutors, you will look to your lawyer as, if not a friend, at least a most necessary evil. And you will wish you had consulted that lawyer much, much sooner. Here's why.

It would seem obvious that, when the task is to determine how an entity may most effectively come into compliance with the numerous and complex legal requirements for information security, a qualified and experienced attorney should be involved. Surprisingly, this often does not appear to be the case today with information security evaluations. Most assessments and evaluations are conducted by computer engineers, accounting, and consulting firms. To be sure, that each of these professional competencies plays a necessary role in information security evaluations. However, since a key question is how to best comply with the current standards of care and, thus, mitigate potential legal liability, experienced and qualified counsel should be quarterbacking this team, much as a surgeon runs an operating room, even though nurses, anesthesiologists, and other competent professionals are crucial parts of the operating team.

WARNING: DO NOT PRACTICE LAW WITHOUT A LICENSE

In virtually every U.S. state, individuals are legally prohibited from practicing law without a license. For example, in Colorado, "practicing law" is defined, by law, to include, "counseling, advising and assisting [another] in connection with" legal rights and duties.[74] Penalties for the unauthorized practice of law in Colorado can include fines or imprisonment.[75] Information security consultants should not, under any circumstances, purport to advise customers as to the legal implications of statutes such as the HIPAA, Gramm-Leach-Bliley financial information privacy provisions, or other federal, state, or local laws or regulations. First, the consultants risk legal action against them by doing so. Second, they do their customers a grave disservice by leading them to believe that the customers can take any legal comfort from advice given them by non-lawyers.

Beyond this seemingly obvious reason for including the services and expertise of experienced and qualified legal counsel in conducting information security evaluations, a number of other factors also support doing so.

Attorney-Client Privilege

The so-called attorney-client privilege is one of the oldest protections for confidential information known to the law, and it is quite powerful. In every state, though with varying degrees of ease in establishing the privilege and differing degrees of exception to it, communications of legal advice from legal counsel to a client are "privileged," that is, protected, from compelled disclosure, including in civil lawsuits.[76] Information given by the client to the lawyer for the purpose of seeking legal advice is similarly protected.[77] In many, but not all jurisdictions, at least in civil litigation, once a court finds that the privilege applies, no amount of need for the privileged information claimed by a legal adversary cannot outweigh the protection created by the privilege.[78] This near-absolute protection is less certain, however, in at least some jurisdictions, in the criminal context.[79]

Further, courts in many states appear to apply a heightened level of scrutiny to corporate counsel and other "in-house" attorneys than they do to outside law firms retained by a corporation to perform particular legal services.[80] That is, courts force corporations to jump through more evidentiary "hoops" before allowing the attorney-client privilege for communications with in-house counsel than they do to communications with outside law firms.[81]

Importantly for information security consultants, courts have held (albeit in contexts analogous, but not identical, to information security, such as work with environmental consultants and accountants) that technical work performed by expert consultants can also enjoy attorney-client privilege protection.[82] Critically, though, this protection can attach to the consultant's work if, and only if, the client hires the attorney to perform a legal service (i.e., advising the client on how best to comply with HIPAA and/or other laws, and then the attorney hires the consultant to provide the attorney with technical information needed to provide accurate legal advice).[83] And this chain of employment cannot be a sham or mere pass-through used by the client to get the technical information but improperly cloak that data improperly with the privilege protection.[84]

The potential for the technical aspects of information security evaluations to enjoy enhanced protection from disclosure has obvious implications for information security evaluation results. If done honestly and correctly, the "chain of employment" (the hiring of a lawyer to provide legal advice which, in turn, requires assessment/evaluation work by technical experts) can protect all of the work. The legal advice, as well as, for example, technical reports showing identified potential vulnerabilities in the client's information security, may be protected under the attorney-client privilege.

It is important to recognize that, like information security measures, the attorney-client privilege is never "bullet proof." It is not absolute and there are, in every jurisdiction, well-recognized exceptions and ways to waive the protection (e.g., information provided to an attorney for the purpose of perpetrating a crime or fraud is not protected).[85] The protected nature of appropriately privileged information may disappear if the client or the attorney reveals that information to third parties outside the communication between the attorney (and consultants hired by the attorney) and certain company personnel (or in the presence of such third parties, even if the attorney is also present).[86] There are also times when it is appropriate to waive the privilege (e.g., a business or educational institution may choose to waive the privilege in order to assert an "advice-of-counsel" defense.) Also, the so-called Thompson Memorandum, issued by U.S Deputy Attorney General Larry Thompson in January 2003,[87] encourages companies to cooperate with the government in investigations by setting forth factors that are used to determine whether the government will pursue criminal prosecution. One important factor is whether the company is willing to waive the attorney-client and other privileges. Still, it is better to have these privileges to waive in an effort to encourage the government not to prosecute than not to have the privileges at all.

Courts have concluded that the societal benefit of not discouraging entities from conducting their own assessments of their compliance with applicable law outweighs any potential downside of the privilege, such as preventing all relevant information from coming out at trial.[88] This also makes good common sense. Entities will be far more likely to initiate their own compliance assessments/evaluations in information security, as in numerous other areas, if they are confident the results will be protected.[89]

Advice of Counsel Defense

Unfortunately, many information security consultants, auditors, and others attempt to advise customers about how to comply with laws and regulations they believe are applicable. This is problematic for several important reasons. First, generally speaking, experienced and qualified attorneys will be better able than others to accurately interpret and advise concerning the law.

Second, as noted several times already, non-attorneys may run afoul of state law by purporting to provide legal advice.

In addition to these reasons, following the advice of non-lawyers as to how to comply with the law does not provide the same level of legal defense in future lawsuits, regulatory proceedings, or prosecutions as following an attorney's advice. In general, a client who provides full and accurate information to an attorney in the course of seeking advice on how to comply with information security law, and makes a good faith effort to follow that advice, can enjoy what is known as the "advice of counsel" defense.[90] This defense is a significant protection against legal liability. Following an attorney's advice on information security legal compliance can protect the client, even if that advice turns out to have been in error.[91]

Establishment and Enforcement of Rigorous Assessment, Interview, and Report-Writing Standards

Important components of information security evaluations and assessments are the interviews of key customer personnel and reviews of their documents. While this work can be, and often is, performed exclusively by engineers or other consultants, interviewing and document review are skills in which lawyers tend to be particularly proficient. These two tasks form major portions of the daily work of many lawyers. As important as actually conducting interviews and reviewing documents is making certain that the right people are interviewed and that all relevant documents are located and carefully reviewed. These tasks, in turn, require the evaluation team to be flexible and alert to new avenues of inquiry that arise during the course of an evaluation (as well as during preparation for, and follow up to, the evaluation). Again, these skills are ones that lawyers exercise virtually every day in their ordinary practices.

Regardless of how much information is collected, it is useless to the customer until it is put into a form that is clear, understandable, and placed in its appropriate context. Extraneous information must be removed. Simple, declarative language must be used. The implications of each piece of information included in the report must be clearly identified. Here again, clear, understandable writing is the stock-in-trade of good lawyers. Attorney involvement in the drafting, or at least reviewing and editing, of information security evaluation reports can add significantly to the benefit of the process, and the final product, to the customer.

Creating a Good Record for Future Litigation

Many qualified and experienced lawyers also know how to write for judges and juries. There is a flip side of the coin of attorney-client privilege to help protect confidential results of information security evaluations from compelled disclosure in court. That is, the benefit of managing the process so that the resulting reports will work well in court in the event that the privilege fails for some reason (inadvertent waiver of it by the client, for example) and a report must be disclosed, *or* a report ends up being helpful in litigation and you *want* to disclose it. In such circumstances, two things will be important. First, the evaluation process and resulting report(s) must stand up under the evidentiary standards imposed by the civil litigation rules. For example, good records of interviews and document reviews should be kept in such a way as to prove a defensible "paper trail" that will convince the court that the information is reliable enough to be allowed into evidence in a trial. Second, reports should be written in a way to clearly describe threats and vulnerabilities, but not overstate them or speak of them in catastrophic terms when such verbiage is not warranted.

Lawyers, and especially experienced trial lawyers, tend to be skilled at both tasks.

Maximizing Ability to Defend Litigation

In a real sense, all of the benefits of involving qualified and experienced counsel previously discussed will help information security professionals and their customers defend against future litigation and, as important, deter would-be litigants from suing in the first place. There is an additional benefit for defense of potential litigation, often phrased as "in on the takeoff, in on the landing." Particularly in business areas with a significant inherent risk of litigation or enforcement action, having qualified and experienced trial lawyers involved early in the business process and throughout that process, will help maximize the ability of the work of information security consultants and their customers stand up to future litigation.

Dealing with Regulators, Law Enforcement, Intelligence, and Homeland Security Officials

Your meeting with Uncle Sam could happen in at least two ways: you may call him, or he may call you. The first is preferable.

The first scenario may unfold in several ways. Your customer may believe it is a victim of an attack on its information systems, terrorism-related or otherwise, and either not be able to stop the attack as it unfolds, not be able to ascertain its origin after it is over, or not be able to determine whether the attackers left behind surprises for further attack at a later time. Or your customer may simply believe contacting the authorities is the right thing to do. In any event, those authorities may want to talk with you—and potentially subpoena you to testify in court—as part of their investigation. Alternatively, an attack may take place while you are working on the customer's systems, making you, in effect, the "first responder."

The second scenario, Uncle Sam reaching out affirmatively to you and/or your customers, also may unfold in multiple ways, but two things are fairly constant. One, the government will be looking at your customer's systems well before they contact your customer. Two, when they come, they generally will get the information they need, even if a subpoena or warrant is necessary. As demonstrated by the National Strategy to Secure Cyberspace, and, particularly since 9/11, the existence of some type of "cyber unit" at many national law enforcement, intelligence, and homeland security organizations, Uncle Sam is keenly interested in any breaches of cyber security that could threaten our national security. This interest, and the government's aggressiveness in pursuing it, is likely only to increase.

In either scenario (voluntary or involuntary contact with the government, including state law enforcement agencies), what you and/or your customers do in the first few hours may be critical to how intact their information systems and sensitive information are when the process is complete. Who has the authority to speak to government authorities? What can and cannot be said to them? How much legal authority (request vs. search warrant vs. subpoena) will be required before allowing them in? Is there any information that they should not be allowed to review? What is the potential legal liability for sharing too much information? Too little? Obviously, your customers (and you, if you are involved) will want to cooperate with legitimate requests and, in fact, may have requested the government's help, but all businesses, educational institutions, and information security consultants must take care not to create civil or criminal liability for themselves by how they conduct their contacts with governmental authorities.

Here again, the keys are: (1) immediately gain the assistance of qualified legal counsel experienced both in information security law and in dealing with law enforcement, intelligence, and homeland security officers; and (2) have a plan in place beforehand for how such authorities will be dealt with, including having legal counsel retained and ready to go.

Notes from the Underground...

What to Look For in Your Attorneys

There are a number of obvious characteristics one should seek in any attorney retained for any purpose. These include integrity, a good reputation in the legal community, and general competence. You also want to consider an attorney with a strong background in corporate and business transactions who is familiar with the contracting process. One useful tool for evaluating these qualities as you attempt to narrow your list of potential attorneys to interview is a company called Martindale Hubbell (*www.martindale.com*). Look for lawyers with an "AV" rating (Martindale's highest).

(Note: Never hire any attorney without at least one face-to-face meeting to learn what your gut tells you about whether you could work with him or her.)

In the area of information security evaluation, you will want to look for attorneys with deep and broad expertise in the field. The best way to do so is to look for external, independently verifiable criteria demonstrating an attorney or law firm's tested credentials (e.g., is the lawyer you seek to retain listed on the National Security Agency Web site as including individuals certified as having been trained in NSA's

Continued

Information Security Assurance Methodology (IAM)? If so, on the appropriate NSA Web page (e.g., www.iatrp.com/indivu2.cfm#C), you will find a listing similar to this: Cunningham, Bryan, 03/15/05, (303) 743-0003, bc@morgancunningham.net)

Has an attorney you are considering authored any published works in the area of information security law? Has he or she held positions, in the government or elsewhere, related to information security? Finally, there's the gut check. How does your potential lawyer make you feel? Are you comfortable working with him or her? Does he or she communicate clearly and concisely? Does he or she seem more interested in covering their own backside than in providing you with legal counsel to protect your interests?

The Ethics of Information Security Evaluation[92]

The eighteenth century philosopher, Immanuel Kant, observed, "[i]*n law a man is guilty when he violates the rights of others. In ethics he is guilty if he only thinks of doing so.*"[93] To think and act ethically requires more than just strict compliance with the law. It requires an understanding of your customer, their business environment, and the duties your customer owes to others, under statutory requirements as well as private contracts. The reward is an increased likelihood of compliance with laws and establishing credibility in the community that will reduce the likelihood of disputes with customers and increase your marketability. Ethics relate to your conduct and not to the conduct of those with whom you are transacting business. However, it is not unethical to be alert to the possibility that others with whom you are dealing are themselves unethical. Do not be naive. Pursuit of an ethical practice does not replace the need to protect yourself through reliable processes, consistent methodologies, and properly drafted contracts that include defined work, limitations on liability, and indemnifications.

Do not think of violating the rights of others. Do not take short cuts. Do not assume that you can conduct your work without understanding the needs and rights of others and acting to protect them. Failing to understand the rights of customers you have been retained to help, or of those involved with your customers is tantamount to thinking of violating their rights. Ethical business, therefore, requires you understand the players and whose rights are at stake.

Finally, though it sounds obvious, do your job well. Martin Van Buren counseled that "[i]t is easier to do a job right than to explain why you didn't." Customers often insist on short cuts and reject proposals that require time delays to document the relationship and obtain the appropriate consents before the work begins. Customers soon forget their front-end demands for cost savings and expedience in completing the project. Hold firm. Do the job right and avoid having to explain to an angry customer, a prosecutor, a judge, or a jury why you did not.

Solutions Fast Track

Uncle Sam Wants You: How Your Company's Information Security Can Affect U.S. National Security (and Vice Versa)

☑ The U.S. Government has announced both the possibility of a significant information security attack on our U.S. critical infrastructure, and its intent to respond forcefully to such an attack if necessary, and the duty of the private sector to better secure its portion of cyberspace.

☑ Although no one can predict when and how severe such an attack may be, prudent commercial and educational entities, after the attacks of September 11, 2001, also should assume it will happen and act accordingly.

☑ This is an additional reason, beyond business operational needs, legal and regulatory requirements, and customer confidence, why commercial and educational entities should engage qualified and experienced legal counsel and technical information security providers sooner rather than later.

Legal Standards Relevant to Information Security

- ☑ A complex web of federal, state, and international statutes, regulations, and common law is evolving to create legal duties for commercial and educational entities in the area of information security.

- ☑ Non-lawyer consultants, even knowledgeable ones, cannot lawfully give advice on compliance with these laws, and commercial and educational entities should not rely on them to do so.

- ☑ This chapter cannot provide commercial and educational entities (or anyone else) with legal advice. Only qualified, licensed, and experienced legal counsel in a direct relationship with individual corporate and educational clients can do so.

Selected Laws and Regulations

- ☑ At the U.S. federal level, HIPAA, GLBA, SOX, the Computer Fraud and Abuse Act, and other statutes and the regulations under them, as well as new ones yet to emerge, are constantly creating new information security legal obligations.

- ☑ State laws and "common law" theories such as negligence also may result in liability for failing to follow emerging "standards of care."

- ☑ Civil damages, regulatory action and, in some cases, even criminal liability, may result from failure, on the part of commercial and educational entities and the information security consultants who provide services to them, to seek (and follow) the advice of qualified and experienced legal counsel concerning these many emerging legal obligations.

Do It Right or Bet the Company: Tools to Mitigate Legal Liability

- ☑ Hire qualified, outside, legal and technical professionals.

☑ Effectively manage your contractual relationships to minimize liability.

What to Cover in IEM Contracts[94]

☑ Information security consultants must ensure that their legal obligations and rights, and those of their customers, are clearly spelled out in detailed written agreements.

☑ At a minimum, these should cover the topics discussed in the body of the chapter.

☑ In most cases LOAs, which are separate documents appended to an overall contract, should be used to clearly establish the authority, and any limitations on it, of information security consultants, to access and conduct testing on all types of information, systems, and portions of the Internet necessary to carry out the requested work.

The First Thing We Do...? Why You Want Your Lawyers Involved from Start to Finish

☑ Lawyers are a necessary evil to all information security consultants and their customers.

☑ Lawyers add value by, among other things: (1) helping to establish protection from disclosure, both for discovered customer information security vulnerabilities and the trade secrets and working methodology of information security consultants; (2) creating additional legal defenses against future liability.

☑ Lawyers (and only lawyers) may lawfully advise clients as to how best to comply with HIPAA, GLBA, SOX, and other federal and state statutory, regulatory, and common law legal requirements.

Frequently Asked Questions

The following Frequently Asked Questions, answered by the authors of this book, are designed to both measure your understanding of the concepts presented in this chapter and to assist you with real-life implementation of these concepts. To have your questions about this chapter answered by the author, browse to **www.syngress.com/solutions** and click on the **"Ask the Author"** form.

Q: Why can't I advise customers about compliance with HIPAA or SOX information security requirements if I'm a knowledgeable information security consultant?

A: Doing so would not only put you at risk for violating state law prohibitions against the unauthorized practice of law, but also fail to provide your customers either with attorney-client privilege protection against disclosure of vulnerabilities information or an "advice of counsel" defense.

Q: Why doesn't my in-house lawyer's involvement give me sufficient attorney-client privilege protection?

A: Contracting information security evaluations through in-house counsel is better than not having that involvement. However, as discussed, courts in multiple jurisdictions impose a higher standard for allowing attorney-client privilege for in-house counsel than for outside, retained lawyers.

Q: How often do I need to have information security evaluations?

A: Courts and regulators will apply a "reasonability" determination on this question, and it will be fact-specific, depending on the industry you are in, the types and amount of sensitive information you hold, and the then-current status of legal and regulatory requirements applicable to your business. In general, however, they should probably be no less frequently than once a year and, in many cases, more often.

Q: How much does having a lawyer involved add to the cost of information security evaluations?

A: Assuming you locate qualified and experienced counsel working with equally qualified technical consultants, and those two groups, in partnership, provide an integrated product that is priced in a reasonable and packaged way, your costs may well be less than using large, expensive, hourly rate-based consulting companies alone.

Q: How likely is a catastrophic information attack on our country?

A: There is a great deal of disagreement on this question, including among the authors of this chapter. However, the U.S. government has based a publicly stated policy on the possibility of such an attack and, post-9/11, it is prudent to assume such an attack could take place. Perhaps most importantly, assuming such an attack could occur only supports the myriad other business reasons to take reasonable information security measures, including one that lawyers rarely talk about: it is the right thing to do.

Q: Why are scientists now using lawyers more than rats for experiments?

A: (1) There are now more lawyers available than there are rats;(2) it is possible for scientists to get emotionally attached to the rats; and (3) there are some things you just can't get a rat to do.

References

[1] This chapter was written jointly by: Bryan Cunningham, Principal at Morgan & Cunningham LLC, a Denver-based homeland security consulting and law firm, and formerly Deputy Legal Adviser to the U.S. National Security Council and Assistant General Counsel, Central Intelligence Agency; C. Forrest Morgan, Principal at Morgan & Cunningham LLC, and Amanda Hubbard, Trial Attorney, U.S. Department of Justice with extensive experience in the U.S. Intelligence Community. The authors also gratefully acknowledge the research and analysis assistance of Nir D. Yarden. The views expressed herein are solely those of the authors and do not necessarily represent the views of the publisher or the U.S. government.

[2] This section drew, in part, from portions of pages 7–11 of *Security Assessment: Case Studies for Implementing the NSA IAM*, used by permission of Syngress Publishing, Inc.

[3] *Kennedy v. Mendoza-Martinez, 372 U.S. 144, 160 (1963).*

[4] *See, e.g.,* the 1993 opinion of the U.S. Department of Justice Office of Legal Counsel: "The concept of 'enforcement' is a broad one, and a given statute may be 'enforced' by means other than criminal prosecutions brought directly under it. " *Admissibility of Alien Amnesty Application Information in Prosecutions of Third Parties,* 17 Op. O.L.C. (1993); *see also* the 1898 opinion of Acting Attorney General John K. Richards:

> The preservation of our territorial integrity and the protection of our foreign interests is intrusted, in the first instance, to the President. . . . In the protection of these fundamental rights, which are based upon the Constitution and grow out of the jurisdiction of this nation over its own territory and its international rights and obligations as a distinct sovereignty, the President is not limited to the enforcement of specific acts of Congress. [The President] must preserve, protect, and defend those fundamental rights which flow from the Constitution itself and belong to the sovereignty it created.

> *Foreign Cables,* 22 Op. Att'y Gen. 13, 25-26 (1898); *see also Cunningham v. Neagle,* 135 U.S. 1, 64 (1890).

[5] As Discussed in FN 13.

[6] United States National Strategy to Secure Cyberspace, February 14, 2003 (hereinafter "National Strategy") at 10. The National Strategy is available at: *http://www.whitehouse.gov/pcipb/*.

[7] See Testimony of Keith Lourdeau, Deputy Assistant Director, Cyber Division, FBI Before the Senate Judiciary Subcommittee on Terrorism, Technology, and Homeland Security, February 24, 2004 ("The FBI assesses the cyberterrorism threat to the U.S. to be rapidly expanding, as the number of actors with the ability to utilize computers for illegal, harmful, and possibly devastating purposes is on the rise. Terrorist groups have shown a clear interest in developing basic hacking tools and the FBI predicts that terrorist groups will either develop or hire hackers, particularly for the purpose of complimenting large physical attacks with cyber attacks."); Robert Lenzner and Nathan Vardi, Cyber-nightmare, http://protectia.co.uk/html/cybernightmare.html.

[8] *Id.*

[9] *Frontline* interview conducted March 18, 2003, at

http://www.pbs.org/wgbh/pages/frontline/shows/cyberwar/interviews/clarke.html.

[10] *http://www.pbs.org/wgbh/pages/frontline/shows/cyberwar/interviews/clarke.html.*

[11] *http://www.pbs.org/wgbh/pages/frontline/shows/cyberwar/interviews/clarke.html;* Hildreth, CRS
Report for Congress, *Cyberwarfare,* Updated June 19, 2001, at 18, at
http://www.fas.org/irp/crs/RL30735.pdf

[12] *Cyberwarfare.* at 2.

[13] The idea of a catastrophic cyber attack against the U.S. by terrorist groups is far from univer-
sally accepted. *See, e.g.,* James A. Lewis, *Assessing the Risks of Cyber Terrorism, Cyber War and Other
Cyber Threats,* Center for Strategic and International Studies, December 2002, at
http://www.csis.org/tech/0211_lewis.pdf. Indeed, as noted above, one of the three authors of this
chapter believes that, while technically possible, this threat is often overstated, at least as a near-
term possibility. For information security professionals and their customers, however, the prudent
course—given our adversaries' capability, intent, and opportunity and the stated U.S. Government
policy of being prepared to respond to cyber attack—is to assume the possibility of such an
attack. In addition, the plethora of known active threats to information security, including extor-
tionists, identity thieves, gangs attempting to amass and sell financial and other valuable personal
information, malicious hackers, and others, provide precisely the same incentive to secure information systems' as do would-be cyber-terrorists.

[14] *See, e.g., Law of Armed Conflict and Information Warfare—How Does the Rule Regarding Reprisals
Apply to an Information Warfare, Attack?,* Major Daniel M. Vadnais, March 1997, at 25 ("To the
extent that information warfare is manifested by traditionally understood damage to sovereign
integrity, the law of armed conflict should apply, and proportional reprisals may be justified. On
the other hand, to the extent that damage to a sovereign's integrity is not physical, there is a gap
in the law."). *http://www.fas.org/irp/threat/cyber/97-0116.pdf.*

[15] *Id.*

[16] National Strategy at p. 59 (A/R 5-4).

[17] National Strategy at p. 49 (Priority V: National Security and International Cyberspace Security
Cooperation).

[18] Nearly as dangerous for our Nation as attacks from within the U.S. directed *at* us, would be if zombied servers here were being used to launch an attack *against another nation*. Imagine the reaction of China or Iran if servers inside the U.S. were being used to damage their infrastructure or harm their people. First, they likely would not believe denials by our government that these acts of war were being carried out deliberately by our government. Second, even if they did believe such denials, they still might feel compelled to respond with force to disable or destroy the systems of, and/or punish, those they perceived to be their attackers.

[19] Particularly in the wake of the 2005 publicity surrounding security breaches at ChoicePoint, LexisNexis, MasterCard, major banks, other commercial entities, and universities, a number of pieces of legislation requiring disclosure of information security breaches and/or enhanced information security measures were working their way through the U.S. Congress, or were threatened in the near future. *See* Roy Mark, *Data Brokers Step Into Senate Panel's Fire*, e-Security Planet.com, http://66.102.7.104/search?q=cache:REXdffBCvEYJ:www.esecurityplanet.com/trends/article.php/3497591+specter+and+information+security+and+disclosure&hl=en.

[20] 15 U.S.C. §§ 6801, et. seq.

[21] 15 U.S.C. § 6801(b).

[22] 15 U.S.C. §§ 6804 – 6805.

[23] Available at *http://www.ffiec.gov/ffiecinfobase/resources/elect_bank/ frb-12_cfr_225_appx_f_bank_holding_non-bank_affiliates.pdf.*

[24] *Guidelines.*

[25] *Id.*

[26] *Id.*

[27] *Id.*

[28] *Id.*

[29] EPHI is defined in the law as individually identifiable health information that is transmitted by, or maintained in, electronic media, except several narrow categories of educational, employment, and other records. 45 C.F.R. part 106.103. Note, however, that the separate HIPAA Privacy Rule also requires "appropriate security" for all PHI, even if it is not in electronic form.

[30] 45 C.F.R. part 164.

[31] Compliance with the Security Rule became mandatory for all but small health care plans in April 2005. "Small" health care plans have until April 2006 to comply.

[32] 45 C.F.R. part 164.

[33] *Id.* One reason it is crucial for information security professionals to retain, on an ongoing basis, qualified, experienced counsel is that "reasonably anticipated" is essentially a legal standard best understood and explained by legal counsel and because what is "reasonably anticipated" is constantly evolving as new threats are discovered and publicized, and information security programs

must evolve with it in order to mitigate legal liability,

[34] *Id.*

[35] *Id.*

[36] It is worth remembering that a significant majority of the process and procedural requirements are *not* technical. This, among other considerations, counsels the use of multidisciplinary teams, of which technical experts are only one part, to conduct and document information security evaluations.

[37] 45 C.F.R. Part 164.308.

[38] 45 C.F.R. Part 164.310.

[39] 45 C.F.R. Part 164.312.

[40] 18 U.S.C. § 1350.

[41] SOX § 404.

[42] SOX § 302.

[43] FISMA, Title III of the E-Government Act of 2002, Public Law No. 107-347.

[44] FN: 20 U.S.C § 1232g

[45] As enacted, the TEACH Act amended Section 110 of the Copyright Act. 17 U.S.C. §110.

[46] 18 U.S.C. § 2510, *et. seq.*

[47] 18 U.S.C. § 1030, *et. seq.*

[48] Other federal laws and regulations potentially relevant to the work of information security professionals and their customers include, but are not limited to, the Children's Online Privacy Protection Act of 1998, information security standards promulgated by the National Institute of Standards, Presidential Decision Directive 63 (May 22, 1998), and Homeland Security Presidential Directive 7 (December 17, 2003). In addition, numerous state laws, including provisions of the Uniform Commercial Code and Uniform Financial Transactions Act, as enacted in the various states, implicate information security requirements for specific economic sectors and/or types of transactions.

[49] Colorado Revised Statutes § 18-5.5-102.

[50] Colorado Revised Statutes § 6-1-105.

[51] Colorado Revised Statutes § 6-1-105(e).

[52] Colorado Revised Statutes § 6-1-105(u).

[53] Between 2001 and 2005 such actions included those against: Microsoft Corporation, Victoria's Secret, Eli Lilly, and Ziff Davis Media, Inc., among others. *See, e.g.,* *http//www.ftc.gov/os/2002/08/microsoftagree.pdf;* *http://www.oag.state.ny.us/press/2002/aug/aug28a_02_attach.pdf.*

[54] *Directive 95/46/EC of the European Parliament and of the Council of 24 October 1995 on the protection of individuals with regard to the processing of personal data and on the free movement of such data, Official Journal of the European Communities of 23 November 1995 No L. 281,* 31, *available at* *http://www.cdt.org/privacy/eudirective/EU_Directive_.html.*

[55] *See, e.g.,* Transcript of Hearing Before U.S. District Judge Royce Lamberth, in which an information security consultant is examined and cross-examined under oath, in public, for multiple days, concerning penetration test work done for the U.S. Bureau of Indian Affairs. http://66.102.7.104/search?q=cache:d30x73ieDSwJ:www.indiantrust.com/_pdfs/3am.pdf+lamberth+and+cobell+and+transcript+and+miles&hl=en

[56] For example, B. Grimes *The Right Ways to Protect Your Net* PC World Magazine, September 2001, offers tips for tightening your security and protecting your enterprise from backdoor hackers and thieves.

[57] *http://wsbradio.com/news/0223choicepointsuit.html.*

[58] *Harrington v. ChoicePoint Inc.,* C.D. Cal., No. CV 05-1294 (SJO) (JWJx), 2/22/05.

[59] Generally, a post-hoc calculation of "reasonability" will be based on balancing such factors as: (1) the probability of reasonably anticipated damage occurring; (2) the expected severity of the damage if it does occur; (3) reasonably available risk mitigation measures; and (4) the cost of implementing such measures.

[60] *See, e.g., Assurance of Discontinuance, In the Matter of Ziff Davis Media Inc.,* at 7, available at *http://www.oag.state.ny.us/press/2002/aug/aug28a_02_attach.pdf.; Agreement Containing Consent Order, In the Matter of Microsoft Corporation,* at 5, available at *http://www.ftc.gov/os/2002/08/microsoftagree.pdf.*

[61] California Civil Code Sections 1798.29 and 1798.82 accessible at *http://www.leginfo.ca.gov/calaw.html.*

[62] 2005 Breach of Information Legislation. http://www.ncsl.org/programs/lis/CIP/priv/breach.htm.

[63] P. Britt, *Protecting Private Information* Information Today (Vo. 22 No. 5 May, 2005) *http://www.infotoday.com/it/may05/britt.shtml.*

[64] This section drew, in part, from portions of pages 7-11 of *Security Assessment: Case Studies for Implementing the NSA IAM,* used by permission of Syngress Publishing, Inc.

[65] Assuming the NSA IAM is used, of course, much of this critical work will already have been documented prior to initiation of the IEM.

[66] The issue of securing complete authorization for all types of information and systems (internal and external) that may be impacted by evaluation and testing, is intentionally covered in multiple parts of this section. It is absolutely critical to the legal well being of both the consultant and the customer to ensure clarity of responsibility for these, which is why this section provides multiple different avenues for addressing this problem. Equally critical is a clear understanding of the "divi-

sion of liability" for any damage that, notwithstanding best efforts of both sides, may result to external systems. This should be taken care of through a combination of indemnification (described below), clear statements of responsibility in the contract, written agreements with third parties, and insurance.

[67] *See, e.g., Management Recruiters, Inc. v. Miller, 762 P.2d 763, 766 (Colo.App.1988).*

[68] *Board of County Commissioners of Adams County v. City and County of Denver, 40 P.3d 25 (Colo.App.,2001).*

[69] *See, e.g., Butler Manufacturing Co. v. Americold Corp., 835 F.Supp. 1274 (D.Kan. 1993).*

[70] *See, e.g., Elsken v. Network Multi-Family Sec. Corp., 838 P.2d 1007 (Okla.1992)*

[71] National Conference of State Legislatures information page accessible at *http://www.ncsl.org/programs/lis/cip/hacklaw.htm.*

[72] *Henry VI*, Part 2, act iv, scene ii.

[73] *See, e.g.,* Seth Finkelstein, "The first thing we do, let's kill all the lawyers" – It's a Lawyer Joke, *The Ethical Spectator,* July 1997., available at: *http://www.sethf.com/essays/major/killlawyers.php.*

[74] *Koscove v. Bolte, 30 P.3d 784* (Colo.App. 2001*).*

[75] *See, e.g.* Rule 238(c), Colorado Court Rules (2004).

[76] *See, e.g., Pacamor Bearings, Inc. v. Minebea Co., Ltd.,* 918 F.Supp. 491, 509-510 (D. N.H. 1996).

[77] *Id.*

[78] *See, e.g., Diversified Indus., Inc. v. Meredith, 572 F.2d 596, 602 (8th Cir. 1978).*

[79] *See, e.g., People v. Benney, 757 P.2d 1078 (Colo.App. 1987).*

[80] *See, e.g., Southern Bell Telephone & Telegraph Co. v. Deason,* 632 So. 2d 1377 (Fla. 1994); *McCaugherty v. Sifferman,* 132 F.R.D. 234 (N.D. Cal. 1990). *United States v. Davis* 132 F.R.D. 12 (S.D.N.Y. 1990).

[81] *See, e.g., United States v. Chevron,* No. C-94-1885 SBA, 1996 WL 264769 (N.D. Cal. Mar. 13, 1996).

[82] *See, e.g., Gerrits v. Brannen Banks of Florida* 138 F.R.D. 574, 577 (D. Colo. 1991).

[83] *See, e.g., id.*

[84] *See, e.g., Sneider v. Kimberly-Clark Corp.,* 91 F.R.D. 1, 5 (N.D. Ill. 1980)

[85] *See, e.g., In re Grand Jury Proceedings,* 857 F.2d 710, 712 (10th Cir. 1988).

[86] *See, e.g., Winchester Capital Management Co. vs. Manufacturers Hanover Trust Co.,* 144 F.R.D.170, 174 (D. Mass. 1992).

[87] U.S. Department of Justice, *Federal Prosecution of Business Organizations* in *Criminal Resource Manual* No. 162 (2003) available at *http://www.usdoj.gov/usao/eousa/foia_reading_room/usam/title9/crm00162.html* and amended and available at *http://www.usdoj.gov/dag/cftf/corporate_guidelines.html.*

[88] *See, e.g., Union Carbide Corp. v. Dow Chem. Co.,* 619 F. Supp. 1036, 1046 (D. Del. 1985)

[89] A related protection to that of the attorney-client privilege is the so-called "work product" doctrine. This protection for materials that might tend to show the strategies or other "mental impressions" of attorneys when such materials are prepared "in anticipation of litigation" would cover the work of information security consultants assisting attorneys in preparing materials for use at a trial or to deal with regulators or law enforcement officials. Work-product protection is significantly more susceptible to being held inapplicable by the court, upon a sufficiently high showing of need by your adversary, than is the attorney-client privilege.

[90] *See, e.g., United States v. Gonzales*, 58 F.3d 506, 512 (10th Cir. 1995).

[91] *Id.*

[92] Entire books could be written on this topic, and some have, at least on the broader topic of IT ethics. *See, e.g., IT Ethics Handbook: Right and Wrong for IT Professionals*, Syngress Publishing, Inc. A comprehensive discussion of Information Security Evaluation ethics is beyond the scope of this book. This discussion is simply to remind us all of some things we learned from our parents that translate into our business relationships.

[93] Available at

http://en.thinkexist.com/quotation/in_law_a_man_is_guilty_when_he_violates_the/7854.html.

[94] This section drew, in part,, from portions of pages 7-11 of Security Assessment: Case Studies for Implementing the NSA IAM, used by permission of Syngress Publishing, Inc.

Investigating Insider Threat Using Enterprise Security Management

Solutions in this appendix

- What Is ESM?

- What Is a Chinese Wall?

- Data Sources

- Bridging the Chinese Wall: Detection through Convergence

- Conclusion

What Is ESM?

Enterprise security management (ESM) is a general term that has been applied to security event monitoring and analysis software. There have been plenty of acronyms thrown around over the years to describe these solutions such as:

- **SIM** Security Information Management
- **SEM** Security Event Management
- **SIEM** Security Information and Event Management
- And many others

Regardless of the acronym, the focus of ESM solutions is to allow an analyst to monitor an organization's infrastructure in real-time regardless of product, vender and version. The vendor agnostic approach helps simplify tasks related to analysis, reporting, response and other facets of event morning. ESMs have traditionally been applied to IT security, insider threats and compliance, but there extensibility has stretched far beyond these areas in the last few years to include a wider set of solutions. However, it all starts by first collection events. These events can come from any number of sources including:

- Traditional security products
  - Firewalls
  - Intrusion Detection and Prevention Systems
  - VPNs
  - Anti-virus
  - Identity Management Systems
- Network Devices
  - Routers
  - Switches
  - Wireless Access Points (WAP)
- Mainframe, Server and Workstation Information
  - Operating Systems
  - Applications

- Physical Security Solutions
  - Badge Readers
  - Video Cameras
  - Heating Ventilation and Air Conditioning (HVAC)
- Various Others
  - Vulnerability Scanners
  - Policy Managers
  - Asset Managers
  - Proprietary and Legacy Solutions
  - Mobile Devices
  - Telephony Systems
  - RFID
  - Point Of Sale (POS) Systems
  - GPS
  - Timesheets
  - Etc.

Essentially, if an asset creates an event and that event can be captured by the ESM, it can be used. Once the ESM has collected the events it will use real-time, automated techniques such as correlation, anomaly detection, pattern discovery, and visualization to reduce false positives, prioritize critical events, and alert an analyst to a potential issue. ESM also facilitates a framework for security analysts to apply human intuition to issues through interactive charts, visual tools, and investigation techniques. This powerful combination of automated and human-driven analysis makes the identification of risks more efficient and effective.

ESMs can also offer a number of forensic analysis and incident management features. From a forensic investigation perspective, ESMs support advanced discovery techniques, reporting and analysis applied against data that is stored with the ESM's database. In terms of response, ESMs generally have integrated case management and integration with third party ticketing systems such as Remedy. Additionally, they have alerting and escalation that can be configured to work in parity with organizational processes such as change management procedures. Another capability for response is the ability to actually make modifications to devices with or without human intervention in order to stop an attack. Some examples of these responses are:

- Disabling user accounts

- Filtering IPs on firewalls, layer-3 switches and routers

- Terminating sessions on VPNs, wireless access points, intrusion prevention systems and other network devices

- Quarantining devices to separated and controlled VLANS

- Stopping access at layer-2 by applying MAC address filters or disabling a physical port on a switch

From a business operations perspective, the ESM can also help communicate risk and compliance. Senior managers and executives alike commonly rely on output to make them aware of their organization's security posture. Armed with this information more educated decisions can be made about risk acceptance, risk remediation and risk management. Compliance is also an important part of the ESM's capabilities with the ability to develop clear reports, aid in analysis, and assist in tracking assets that are associated with IT Governance and forms of regulatory compliance such as Sarbanes-Oxley, PCI, GLBA and HIPAA.

ESM at the Center of Physical and Logical Security Convergence

Logical security is becoming more tightly integrated with physical security every year. Digital solutions and IP-based protocols are becoming the standard for physical security and they are cheaper. For example, the cost to deploy digital surveillance cameras, and store their compressed data has greatly reduced. And as the technologies become more integrated, they can provide checks and balances such as comparing video surveillance and badge reader information with VPNs and other forms of logical access. From an operational perspective, a view into each discipline will become a requirement for incident prevention, detection and management. Having a central location for investigation, analysis, correlation and prioritization – across the board just makes sense. All this feeds into better controls for compliance and enforcement of policy and ultimately a faster, more effective method for reducing risk while increasing operational efficiencies. ESM helps with this by providing several critical features to facilitate this.

By aggregating physical and logical events into a central location, an organization can get a holistic perspective of its security posture. Having all the information within a central repository allows for more thorough investigation and analysis. Information can be correlated, prioritized and yield actionable results for the analysts.

Since most ESMs have an integrated case management system and bidirectional connectivity with third party ticketing systems, the physical and logical security teams can collaborate more effectively with each other by using features like alerting, escalation and case management. This helps to cut down on confusion around job responsibilities during an incident.

Since access controls are built into ESMs the types of features and types of events that a physical and logical security group can access will be tightly controlled. This is an important point for reporting because a daily report might need to be generated for each security team lead. Many of the issues that they are concerned with will be quite different while others are shared. It makes sense to limit the information to just that which the respective security teams require.

An interesting example of disparate teams converging is a fusion center. Fusion centers are collaborations between local, state and federal governments to address a wide range of issues including terrorist attacks. Obviously each group has information that they are concerned with that they don't need to share with others. However, each group also has access to information that the other may not, but would prove useful. They are not just consumers of information, but also collectors. This information may be human intelligence, physical security and logical security data. Thus just like physical and logical security teams cooperating, fusion centers are becoming more common in hopes of increasing efficiencies and reducing risk. There are several cities and states that have begun building fusion centers to work with national agencies. For example, LA, Arizona, Colorado, Illinois, Massachusetts, Virginia, New Jersey and New York either already fusion centers are investigating them. New York for example has its own foreign intelligence agency focused on information gathering with office in around twenty-six countries.

Clearly there is some overlap between local, state and federal agencies, but there is also a great deal of information that doesn't need to be shared between agencies. The same holds true for physical and logical security teams. While they may want to share case management, reporting, alerting, escalation, and investigation frameworks, they don't need to share all portions exclusively. Consider that many ESM solutions have both an administrative console and a thin web client. In practice, most logical security teams will leverage the administrative console on a regular basis, while the physical security team utilizes the thin client for more general tasks such as managing cases, viewing reports, and viewing events.

The net of physical and logical security convergence through ESM is that convergence of these groups is no longer an opaque topic. Security is more than firewalls; it's more than badge readers. Understanding this, today's organizations are demanding a truly holistic view of their security posture and ESM can provide it. With a suite of tools for event collection, analysis, collaboration and response, ESM has been making convergence a reality. Before we get into the ESM architecture, let's outline a few short, examples of where ESM has integrated with physical security solutions for truly unique and effective converged security strategies.

By using CAC (Common Access Cards) the Department of Defense has begun implementing a system where physical and logical identification and access control is associated with a singe card. These CACs offer the same features as a traditional physical access card complete with photo ID and descriptive information about the carrier. However, they also have the ability to log the holder of the card onto a logical network. For example, after scanning their CAC in a CAC reader by the door to enter a building, an individual could swipe the card in a CAC reader that is connected to their workstation to authenticate themselves on the network. Further, they could use the CAC to encrypt information, access secured websites and other mechanisms used for secured logical access. CACs are slowly replacing military IDs and will eventually be carried by most DoD employees and contractors. There are discussions to make CAC the standard for authentication for the TSA Registered Traveler Program and the Guest Worker Program. From a convergence perspective, CAC is a great leap forward because now a user's physical and logical identity are associated with a common key, instead of a physical access ID being something like 10010011 and a logical ID being bsmith, both will be bsmith. This also makes issues around provisioning new employees or revoking access much easier. Since all access is associated with one CAC, if you provision or revoke the CAC, you can more quickly and effectively provision or revoke the individual's access in its entirety. No longer is there a need to work through multiple groups to manage all forms of access. CAC makes the job of the ESM that much more efficient because the ESM doesn't have to map bsmith to 10010011, and potentially many other IDs. Now bsmith is a common key that the ESM can associate with all that user's identities.

Some organizations have even brought traditionally outsourced security monitoring services in-house to better their response time to incidents, thus reducing risk and even saving money. For example, fire alarms, burglar alarms, facility access and video surveillance can be monitored by an in-house physical security organization. By pulling these services in-house, they now have the option to more easily integrate these services with their overall risk monitoring capabilities within ESM.

Many banks are finding that getting their physical and logical security teams to work together can be invaluable – especially during fraud investigations. Since each team has their own key competencies they can leverage one another during investigations, for example, by having the security teams work with internal and external auditors. The bank's corporate security department will work the case from a financial perspective as well as working with law enforcement agencies, while the logical security departments provides the IT details that are needed to support the case.

ESM as the core of such a system allows for seamless communication and documentation of the investigation, and provides a complete audit trail of everything that was done. There is no need to document events after the fact, because it is happening in real-time. Nobody wants to take time out of an investigation to write down everything they are doing. Unfortunately, this is an important and often overlooked step. With a shared case management system, and complete audit trails of the network-centric portions of the investigation, physical and logical, the jobs of the investigators become more streamlined.

ESM Deployment Strategies

This section will explore several ESM deployment strategies. Each component of the ESM architecture will be discussed. ESMs can be deployed in standard, high availability, and geographically dispersed configurations. Additionally, there are additional components within the ESM architecture that can be used as a standalone solution or in conjunction with a more robust ESM strategy that expands to network response and network configuration. To begin with, we'll look at one example of an ESM deployment starting with Figure B.1.

Figure B.1 Basic ESM Deployment

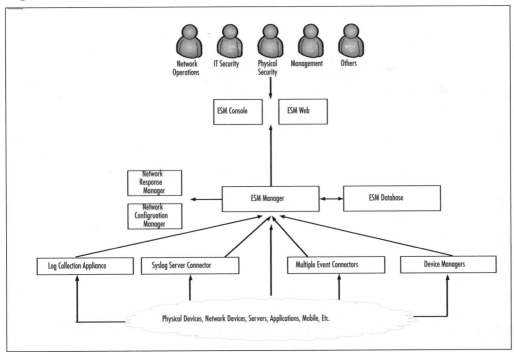

The components of Figure B.1 will be explored starting from the bottom and working up.

As mentioned earlier, regardless of the logs being generated – those from physical devices, network devices, servers and so on, ESMs are designed to receive and process them. Between the point devices and the ESM manager, there are a number of ways to transport the logs.

On the far left of the diagram is a log collection appliance. These types of appliances can be used as standalone solutions, or as part of a broader ESM solution. As a standalone solution, they are designed to collect logs at very high volumes – tens of thousands of logs every second and provide long term storage. This storage can be many years of data in some cases because of compression capabilities. Figure B.2 shows a high level view from a log collection appliance.

Figure B.2 Log Collection Appliance – System Status View

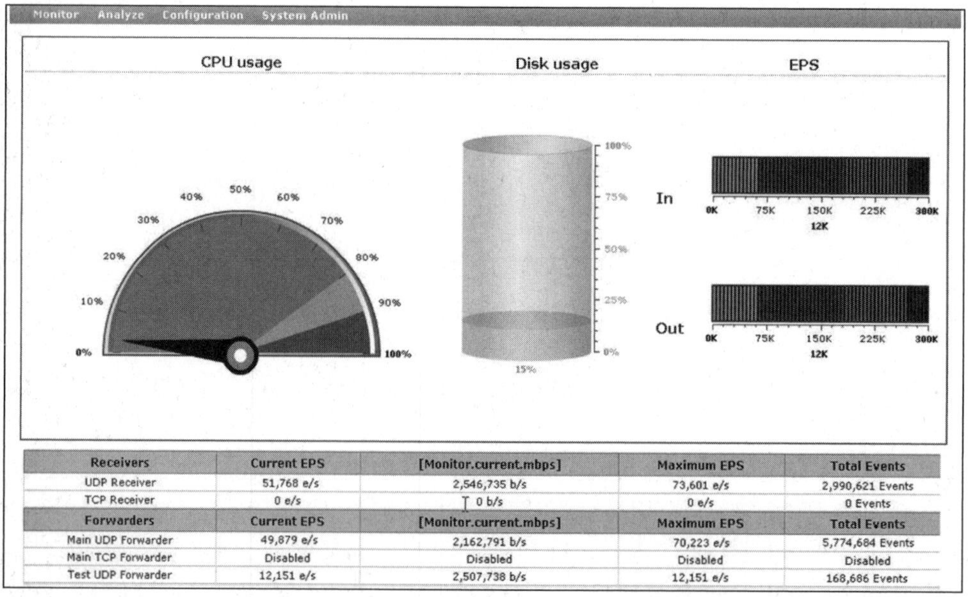

Receivers	Current EPS	[Monitor.current.mbps]	Maximum EPS	Total Events
UDP Receiver	51,768 e/s	2,546,735 b/s	73,601 e/s	2,990,621 Events
TCP Receiver	0 e/s	↑ 0 b/s	0 e/s	0 Events
Forwarders	**Current EPS**	**[Monitor.current.mbps]**	**Maximum EPS**	**Total Events**
Main UDP Forwarder	49,879 e/s	2,162,791 b/s	70,223 e/s	5,774,684 Events
Main TCP Forwarder	Disabled	Disabled	Disabled	Disabled
Test UDP Forwarder	12,151 e/s	2,507,738 b/s	12,151 e/s	168,686 Events

Source: ArcSight Logger v1.0

Figure B.2 is an interactive web session with the log collection appliance. Since these devices are designed to collect and store massive amounts of information, it is helpful to have a dashboard to evaluate its status. For example, form left to right the CPU usage, disk usage and number of events per second received and transported (to the ESM manager for example) are shown. Using this type of dashboard it is a fast and easy to get an understanding of what is happening within the appliance. The next figure, B.3, shows another view within the log collection appliance focused on analysis.

Figure B.3 Log Collection Appliance – Analysis View

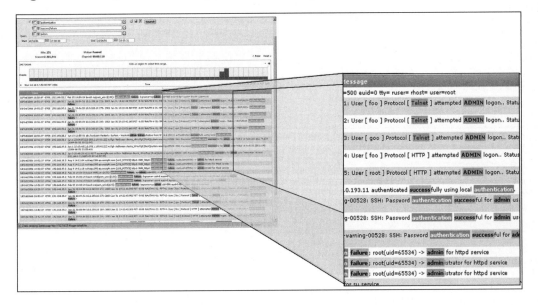

Source: ArcSight Logger v1.0

In Figure B.3 there is an exploded view in the appliance's analysis grid. This grid displays the events that are flowing into the appliance based on certain criteria such as time, protocols, source IPs, destination IPs and other key variables. This particular image shows telnet access for the admin account where there were failures and successes. Search criteria like this may be valuable in an audit when researching historical data stored within the appliance for the use of non approved protocols like telnet where sensitive information and passwords are transmitted in clear text.

Log collection appliances provide a solid solution for organizations that what an easy to deploy appliance that allows rapid analysis along with high-speed log collection and inexpensive long term storage. If the appliance is used as part of a broader ESM strategy, it can then forward all or a subset of the data to the ESM manager for more advanced analysis. In these scenarios, it might be likely to have multiple log collection appliances deployed a key locations within the organization. For example, they may be divided up by geography or business unit. Many organizations do have management silos. If this is the case, it may be desired to keep all logs separated at operational levels, but the global security team may require a more holistic view. Figure B.4 illustrates such a case and shows how an organization might deploy the log collection appliances to consider business and geographical boundaries and still maintain global oversight.

Figure B.4 Distributed Log Collection Appliance Architecture

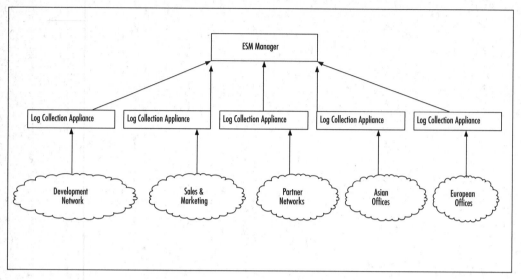

Back to Figure B.1, the next log collection capability utilizes an organization's existing log management strategies. This is most commonly syslog servers. Syslog servers can collect syslog messages from a number of devices. Residing on the server would be software commonly called event connectors. These connectors come in many forms – syslog, SNMP, proprietary formats like Check Points OPSEC or Cisco's RDEP and many others. In general, if an organization already has central locations where logs are being collected, it is a simple task to install a collector on each of the aggregation points. The connectors will in turn do some pre-processing on the logs and send them to the ESM manager.

While it is somewhat unusual these days for a large organization to not have any type of log aggregation strategy that can be leveraged by ESM, it does occur, at least in some small subsets of the network. In these cases, it is possible to simply send logs directly from the point devices to the ESM manager. This type of design doesn't allow for pre-processing capabilities such as encryption, compression, filtering, aggregation and other features that will be covered later, but it will at least move the logs into the ESM so they can be analyzed.

A more common strategy for an organization that doesn't have a log aggregation strategy is to use existing servers to deploy a large number of event connectors on them. This is somewhat similar to the log collection appliance, but only from the perspective of being able to receive, pre-process, and relay events to the ESM manager. These systems with multiple versions of event connectors installed don't allow for the high event capture, long term storage or rapid analysis at the same level of an appliance.

The final strategy for moving logs from point devices to the ESM manager is to deploy event connectors any natural aggregation points such as device managers. These are commonly firewall managers, IDS managers, access control databases and so on. Many organizations will utilize several strategies with the intention of being able to collect all the mission-critical logs while at the same time reducing the number of point devices that have to be altered. By using connectors at aggregation points such as a syslog server or a device manager, using event collection appliances, or a server built with multiple connectors installed, an organization can easily deploy a log management strategy that feeds the ESM with only a handful of collection points even though logs from thousands of systems are being analyzed. This low touch approach is one reason why many organizations find that a holistic ESM strategy is really quite practical as it doesn't require manipulation of the point systems generating the logs. Nobody would use ESM in a large environment if they had to make changes to every system being monitored; these solutions make it possible.

The next stages of the diagram have to do with the ESM manager and database. Essentially, the ESM manager is the brains of the architecture. It is a central location for everything from correlation and analysis through case management and alerting. It also leverages the ESM database which is typically an enterprise-level database such as Oracle for forensic analysis. That is, all the events entering the ESM are processed in memory, in real-time, however, if historical analysis and reporting on past events is desired, instead of receiving events from the various collection points, the ESM will retrieve the events from the database. Real-time and forensic analysis within the ESM manager is generally seamless, with the same tools available to each.

ESMs generally allow several forms of interaction including a console and a web interface. The console is software that is loaded on a laptop or workstation. Consoles are usually more feature-rich and allow for the administrative tasks such as creating original content like rules, reports, dashboards, and define user access privileges. Consoles connect directly to the ESM manager. The web interface is a slimmed down version of the console that simply requires a web browser to connect to the ESM manager, or in some cases, as standalone web server that in turn communicates with the ESM manager. Regardless of the console or the web interface, these solutions will usually provide 128-bit encryption with 1024-bit key exchange by leveraging HTTPS. This same level of encryption is also used between the log collection appliance and event collectors to the ESM manager.

Regardless of the web interface or console interface, both solutions can provide granular access controls for the users. In most cases these access controls can be tied to standard user names and passwords, LDAP, PKI, RADIUS, two factor authentication and similar access control systems. In most situations an organization will have several groups that want access to ESM components, and each group will have one or many users. In this format, it is a simple task to add and remove privileges across various disciplines. Consider the following privileges based on groups.

- Members of the network operations team can either use the console or web interface to access events that are specific to routers, switches and other network gear. They may want to use the ESM's case management system, reporting and visualization features. However, they don't need access to other features nor do they need access to events that are not directly related to their group.

- Members of the IT security team may want to look at everything across all groups, and may require the most advanced ESM analysis capabilities to be at their disposal. However, there may be members within this group that are more concerned with compliance issues. As such, they are only privy to events related to those assets associated with regulatory compliance as defined in the ESM's asset database.

- Physical security teams and management alike may only require access through the web interface. They may both want to see graphical dashboards and the case management system. They may also want report access and maybe even daily reports for their respective areas. For example, the physical security team may want to see a report that documents entry into a particularly sensitive area of the facility. Managers may want to see high-level reports regarding how efficiently cases are being addressed and what the overall risk posture is in comparison to previous weeks and quarters.

As ESM capabilities have been maturing over the years, there has been growth in their core capabilities. We've already addressed the log collection appliance which allows for a standalone or an integrated technology to collect, store, and rapidly analyze massive event flows. Other areas are related to network response and network configuration. As organizations have grown, they've found the need to not only detect, but to also as Figure B.1 shows, respond in the case of the network response manager (NRM) and prevent through a pragmatic approach to network device configuration with the network configuration manager (NCM). These systems integrate well with traditional ESM capabilities similarly to physical security solutions. However, by use of comparison to physical and logical security convergence later in this Appendix we will explore network operation center and security operation center convergence through enhanced coloration and communication.

Security has steadily become a part of an organization's critical path. There was a time where operations could still be up with no security, but those days are all but gone. To address this, security vendors have developed high availability architectures for their solutions; ESM vendors are no different. Figure B.5 illustrates a high availability design for the ESM manager and the ESM database.

Figure B.5 High Availability ESM Architecture

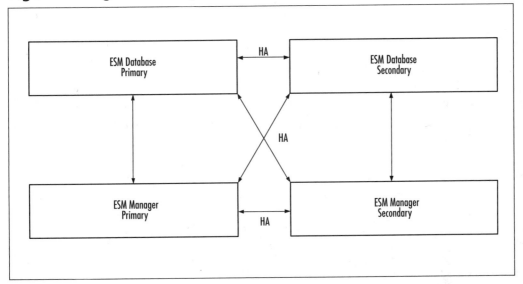

Most ESMs can use a number of high availability options such as Legato, Veritas and Oracle RAC. In Figure B.5 events are received by the primary ESM manager for real-time processing. That manager sends events to the primary ESM database for storage and forensic analysis. Should the primary manager suffer an outage, or be taken off line for maintenance, the secondary ESM Manager will start collecting the events and can still use the primary ESM database. Once the primary ESM manager comes back online events will be sent to it instead of the secondary.

Should the same scenario be applied to the primary database, the process would be the same. The communication between the primary and secondary ESM databases will re-sync once the primary database comes back online.

This architecture can also survive an outage of any one ESM manager and any one ESM database at once. That is, if the primary ESM manager is up, but the primary ESM database goes down, the ESM architecture will run between the primary ESM manager and the secondary ESM database. Also, if the secondary ESM

Manager is running, and communicating with the primary ESM database, it can switch over to the secondary ESM database if there is yet another outage.

The managers and the databases are always in sync during operation up until the point where one of the devices goes down. Once connectivity is reestablished, they will begin the process of resynchronization. This design allows for a very stable ESM architecture.

In addition to high availability designs, there is often a need to be a hierarchy. ESM in this sense is like computer science 101. If you want to make something scalable, you build a hierarchy – much like DNS. With this type of architecture the ESM manager and database pairs can be infinitely wide and deep. However in practices, the hierarchy tree is rarely more than a few layers deep, although they can be relatively wide based on the organization's desire to segment operations. Figure B.6 explores a hierarchical ESM architecture.

Figure B.6 Hierarchal ESM Architecture

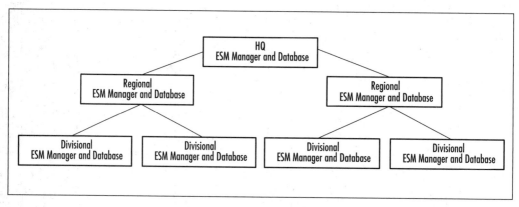

Figure B.6 shows how an organization can have various divisions. Each division can house its own ESM deployment. These divisions are only responsible for what happens within their division. At the regional level there is a similar deployment to that in the division. However, a key difference is that the regional ESM manager does not receive events from event connectors or a log collection appliance, but rather from the divisional manager. From the perspective of the regional ESM manager, the divisional managers are simply another event feed. Based on organizational policies all or a subset of the divisional data will be sent to the regional managers for analysis. If a subset is desired, the regional teams may only send events that are considered to be of a high level of severity or impacting mission-critical assets for example. Finally, the same process can be applied to the ESM manager at the organization's head quarters. Additionally, the analysts at head quarters can access any of the regional and divisional ESM managers directly as long as they have access privileges to do so. This may allow them to conduct more detailed investigations if there are events that haven't been forwarded to their ESM manager.

These are essentially the major components of an ESM architecture. However, as stated earlier in the Appendix, there are certain relationships in regards to network response and network configuration that fit within this architecture too. In the following section, we will explore the concept of a *Chinese Wall* and show in detail how a calculated insider-trading scam between an investment banker and a stock broker working for a large Wall Street financial firm could be foiled by combining physical and logical event data through Enterprise Security Management (ESM).

What Is a Chinese Wall?

In the security world, there is a term known as *the Chinese wall*. A Chinese wall is intended to prevent certain users with compartmentalized knowledge from communicating. In this Appendix, we will examine what this means and how organizations implement it to protect information from becoming available that could lead to an insider committing fraud. The solution we present in this Appendix encompasses a security team empowered by advanced analytic tools and an understanding of the benefits that come from analyzing data beyond the typical firewall and intrusion detection system. We will cover how the analysis process and eventual detection mechanism utilize data sources that focus far more on the activity of users than on just network traffic. These sources include both Voice over IP (VoIP) call detail records (CDRs), and e-mail transaction logs that can tell us about communication among individuals within an organization.

These devices are considered to be nontraditional sources, and the idea of collecting data from these systems has not appeared on the radar of most security teams. They comprise some very advanced (and rare) operations in which all user activity is monitored and tracked, including call records, documents printed, and building and room access. Because these are nontraditional data sources, new challenges are associated with collecting data from these devices. We will address those challenges, and their solutions, in this Appendix.

A Chinese wall in this context is obviously not the massive 6,700-kilometer wall built by the Ming Dynasty back in the 1300s to keep out the attacking Mongols. The term was recoined after the United States stock market crash of 1929. The expression comes from laws that Congress passed designating that policies needed to be in place to create a logical separation between different groups of commercial and investment bankers. One of the main drivers for this mandate was that the stock market crash was largely blamed on overinflated stock prices due to insider trading and price manipulation. The law Congress passed in 1933, called the Glass-Steagall Act, initially banned commercial banks from having anything to do with brokerages. Since then, the rule has become less strict, and now large financial organizations are involved in investment banking, stock trading, and numerous other financial activities.

The Chinese wall is also known as the *Brewer-Nash model*, which is designed to prevent conflict-of-interest situations from arising, and to prevent information from being leaked. The model classifies data as conflict-of-interest categories. Once the data is categorized, users, as well as processes that run on behalf of a user, are broken up into what's known as a *subject*. Rules are then put into place to describe which subjects can access or read and write which objects. The following excerpt is from "The Chinese Wall Security Policy," written by Dr. David F.C. Brewer and Dr. Michael J. Nash of Gamma Secure Systems Limited (Surrey, United Kingdom):

> Access is only granted if the object requested:
>
> a) is in the same company dataset as an object already accessed by that subject, i.e. within the Wall, or
>
> b) belongs to an entirely different conflict of interest class.
>
> Write access is only permitted if:
>
> a) access is permitted by the simple security rule, and
>
> b) no object can be read which is in a different company dataset to the one for which write access is requested and contains unsanitized information.

The preceding rules explain how the Brewer-Nash model defines data read and write permissions. The read rule is attempting to ensure that a user reads only the data he has already read, other data that is similarly classified, or data that is totally unrelated to the data he previously read. The write rule is attempting to ensure that users who want to write data must have already had previous access to that data, and that the data is on their computers. This is known as *the simple security rule*. The user also cannot read any object in a different conflict of interest, and the data must be unsanitized, meaning that it hasn't been obfuscated. "The Chinese Wall Security Policy" is interesting reading; you can read it at *www.gammassl.co.uk/topics/chwall.pdf.*

Some refer to this as separation of duties. Most organizations have accounts payable and accounts receivable departments that share a common application, such as SAP, to enter new accounts and pay accounts. Employees who have the ability to enter a new account should *never* have permission to pay the account as well. The conflict of interest is apparent: An employee may add a dummy account that is really a front company, and slowly, over time, he may use this account to embezzle money from his employer.

Over the past 40 years, the Federal Reserve Board, which is responsible for regulating banks, has been allowing banks to create subsidiaries that can be involved in mergers and acquisitions and the selling and underwriting of securities. This is where the problem presents itself. You now have a large company with thousands of employees that may or may not know each other and can benefit from the information that others within the organization possess.

Let's look at a very simple example. Joe, who works in the Mergers and Acquisitions department, knows that a company he has been working with will soon be sold to a much larger company, and he knows the sale will yield a profit. Larry works for the same organization as Joe, except he works in the Investment Banking sector. If Joe happens to have an "innocent" conversation with Larry over a weekend golf game, and lets Larry in on a little secret that a particular company will soon be sold, Larry can advise all his clients to invest in this company, which will undoubtedly turn a large profit for his clients, in turn fattening his pockets based on his commission. This is one definition of *insider trading*. Figure B.7 depicts the scenario.

Figure B.7 The Flow of a Data Leak

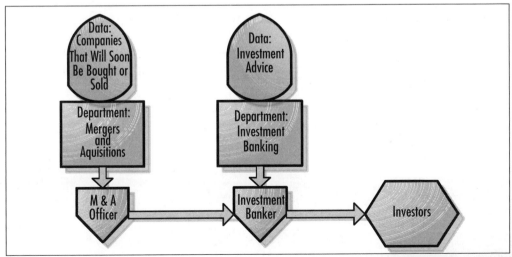

Figure B.7 shows the way the investment data would leak between the Mergers and Acquisitions department and the Investment Banking department. The boxes in the middle show the departments and the shields above the departments show the data that each department knows about that the other does not. The information leaks from the Mergers and Acquisitions department, via a department officer, to an investment banker. Now the conflict of interest arises because the investment banker has knowledge of a company that will soon be sold, which, depending on the price, can drive that company's stock prices up or down. If the investment banker leaks this information to his clients, you have a classic case of insider trading.

Since the relaxation of the Glass–Steagall Act, no law says an organization can't have both a Mergers and Acquisitions and an Investment Banking department, and no law says that if an organization does have both departments, the departments have to be physically separated. Rather, corporations tend to operate under an inferred *logical separation* that's really based on the honor system, and we all know how well that works. Although the examples in this Appendix focus on financial institutions, the same principles apply to other types of organizations. The intelligence community, for example, has a level of clearance known as *compartmentalization*. The idea behind compartmentalized clearance is that no one person knows all the details of a mission. In the case of foreign intelligence, one team knows the identities of the operatives, another group knows the targets, and a third knows what information is trying to be collected. This means that if one person was leaking information, he wouldn't be able to compromise the entire mission.

What can we do about this? Keeping people who want to communicate apart from each other is an extremely difficult task. We can put measures into place using physical access systems, or place restrictions on phone numbers that people can dial from office lines. However, almost everyone has a cell phone, and in most organizations, you can't stop people from having lunch together inside the office, much less outside the office. And you certainly can't control what people do on weekends. We've seen extreme examples in which CIA employees are monitored and will be followed by surveillance teams to ensure that they are not communicating with others. Typically this occurs after there is reason to believe that these employees are committing treason. As we mentioned earlier, the "new" Chinese wall is based on an honor system, so putting restrictions in place really just causes users to become more evasive. If you alleviate the restrictions put on users and passively monitor their behavior, they will typically make a mistake and bring their activities to light, especially if they don't know you're watching them. By looking at patterns of activity and communications, and by using advanced correlation tools, we can make sense of the masses of log data and draw direct conclusions. In the next section, we will look at some of the challenges involved with collecting data from new devices, such as e-mail and telephone call logs.

Data Sources

In this section, we will discuss the technologies we will be working with in this Appendix. We call these *new data sources* because they veer away from the traditional security event. In order to detect fraudulent activity and anomalies in users' behavior, you will need to analyze more than just intrusion detection system data. We are not aware of any signature that you can write in any intrusion detection system that will tell you that two "trusted" employees are committing insider trading. Such a system looks for an attack pattern that is traversing the network and targeting computer systems. In this case, we are not dealing with a logical attack per se, although an attack is taking place. The users here have legitimate access to the systems and the data they are accessing, but the problem arises when they share the information with other users who are not privy to it.

This is a classic example of an insider threat. Internal threats are very difficult to spot and can cost corporations millions of dollars. Insider threats deal with users who are internal to the organization and have access to systems and data. How can you catch someone that doesn't appear to be doing anything wrong? The book *Insider Threat*, by Dr. Eric Cole, discusses many examples of actual cases of insider threat. Another book we recommend is *Enemy by the Water Cooler*, by Brian Contos, which details how to address the insider threat problem from an ESM perspective. Experience shows that to detect an internal threat, an early warning system must be in place. Most internal compromises are preceded by reconnaissance activity and can be detected early if an early warning system is being used. One of the main drivers of an early warning system is data sources that refer to actual users, not just Internet Protocol (IP) addresses. In the next two sections, we will look at some of these technologies.

E-mail

Everyone has heard of e-mail. It's been around for ages, and almost every corporation uses it in one way or another to conduct day-to-day business and communicate both internally and outside the company. Organizations offer e-mail as a service to their employees, and the employees typically connect to a corporate mail server via a client such as Microsoft Outlook. Risks are associated with corporate mail, and far greater risks are associated with Web mail. In corporate mail environments, a user who intends to sneak data out of the company can attach a file to her outgoing message and send the file to any number of people, including competitors, ex-coworkers, or even foreign nationals. Fortunately for us, we can track such activity via the corporate mail server.

Typically when an employee is being investigated, all of her past e-mail will be investigated to determine any wrongdoing or to build a case against her. The difficulty arises when users begin to access Web mail servers such as Yahoo! and Hotmail. These sites allow users to connect from within an organization, and attach the same file and mail it to the same people—but without leaving any sort of record of what they've done. Now, when an investigation is underway, the analyst or legal team cannot go back to the mail server and pull up records of that person's activities. An emerging field known as *information leak prevention* (ILP) tries to address these types of threats. ILP products look at content as it crosses the network, similar to intrusion detection systems; however, so far, they have experienced problems concerning false positives, similar to what intrusion detection system vendors faced years ago.

Investigators and legal teams have been using e-mail transactions as evidence of wrongdoing for years, so why is this considered a "new" data source? E-mail is considered to be a new data source because it falls outside the realm of what the typical security organization usually monitors. E-mail transactions generally have not been analyzed in real time; they have been used as part of forensic investigations. Once an employee is suspected of wrongdoing, any e-mails she has sent are questioned. Now we are trying to draw conclusions and detect early warning indicators of a potential data leakage *before* it happens, not after the fact. The information that you can gain from examining e-mail messages may surprise you.

Benefits of Integration

Several use cases come to mind. One is information on the sender and recipient, which allows you to build "top talkers" charts that let you determine who talks to whom, what domains are receiving information from your company, and what domains are sending information to your employees. E-mail messages are also useful for human resources (HR) investigations of employees. Someone from HR or the legal department will typically request all the e-mails a particular employee has sent as part of collecting evidence for some wrongdoing. Further, there is the message or the subject, which allows for some insight as to what is actually being communicated. And when a file is attached to an e-mail, the filename can appear in the subject line, which enables some monitoring of attachments that are being sent. Other use cases involve the size of e-mail messages that are being sent, and the times the user sent the messages. It may arouse suspicions if a user is always sending large e-mail messages in the middle of the night; this could represent some type of information leak or other activity which may be a concern to the organization.

Encryption is another great example. Even though an encrypted message cannot be read based on the frequency and recipient, you could infer what is happening.

Since we mentioned HR, it's also worth mentioning the legal issues regarding monitoring employees' e-mail transactions. When employment begins at most organizations, the new employee and the employer sign a policy that usually states that all communications using company equipment are subject to monitoring. The policies typically in place are not always quite as specific as they should be, however, and in many privacy cases, such policies have been questioned in court.

To avoid confusion, the policy should clearly state that e-mails can and will be monitored. In cases in which policies clearly state the companies are monitoring e-mail, courts have found in favor of the companies. One such case is *Bourke v. Nissan*. Nissan fired Bourke when he was accused of receiving and sending sexually explicit e-mails. Bourke took Nissan to court for violation of privacy, and the court ruled in favor of Nissan because its policy clearly stated that e-mails were being monitored. We have also seen discrimination cases in which an employee claims he is being "picked on" because his e-mails are being monitored, but not those of other employees. In these cases, it is important to be able to prove that everyone is treated in the same way, and that in cases of suspected wrongdoing, the investigation process is the same.

Challenges of Integration

Because e-mail has been around for so long and e-mail messages contain so much useful information, why isn't e-mail collection and analysis more widespread? Challenges exist when it comes to collecting this type of information. Let's look at one of the most common e-mail messaging systems in the world, Microsoft Exchange Server.

Distributed Logging

The first challenge with collecting data from Exchange is that organizations usually have more than one Exchange server. A large bank, for example, may have upward of 600,000 employees, and to accommodate that many accounts and the large volume of e-mail transactions that occur daily, the company may use several Exchange servers per location. Microsoft doesn't provide any centralized logging mechanism, so collection and configuration must be done on a per-server basis. Figure B.8 depicts the configuration section of the Exchange Server Admin console. Two options are available: enable message tracking and enable subject logging.

Figure B.8 The Exchange Server Admin Console

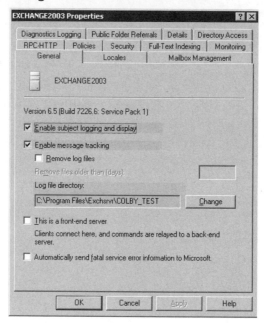

In order for Exchange to write a tracking log, you must enable the message tracking option. To ensure 100 percent data collection, subject line tracking should be enabled as well.

To further the Exchange collection challenge, each server writes to a specified directory. As we said, Microsoft does not provide centralized logging, so any collection needs to occur from each server, or the logs must be written to a shared directory. When using shared directories, problems may arise, such as security issues, access, and bandwidth utilization, due to the high volume of messages that are being logged.

In addition, a collection mechanism is required that understands and follows the log rotation facility that is configured as part of Exchange message tracking. If an automated process is collecting the logs that are being written, it must be able to deal with the filename changing and a new file being written to, as part of the log rotation.

Event Volume

Exchange message tracking generates upward of eight messages per e-mail sent. Because this log can be used as a debugging facility, a message is logged for each step in the process of a mail delivery. Table B.1 provides a sample of some of the events that are generated. For more information regarding the events that Exchange can generate, visit the Microsoft TechNet Web site, *http://support.microsoft.com/kb/821905*.

Table B.1 Events Generated during E-mail Delivery

Event ID	Event Name	Event Description
1019	SMTP submit message to AQ	A new message is submitted to Advanced Queuing.
1020	SMTP begin outbound transfer	The Simple Mail Transfer Protocol (SMTP) is about to send a message over the wire.
1021	SMTP bad mail	The message was transferred to the Badmail folder.
1022	SMTP AQ failure	A fatal Advanced Queuing error occurred.
1023	SMTP local delivery	A store drive successfully delivered a message.
1024	SMTP submit message to cat	Advanced Queuing submitted a message to the categorizer.
1025	SMTP begin submit message	A new message was submitted to Advanced Queuing.
1026	SMTP AQ failed message	Advanced Queuing could not process the message.
1027	SMTP submit message to SD	The Mail Transfer Agent (MTA) submitted a message to the store driver.
1028	SMTP SD local delivery	The store driver successfully delivered a message (logged by the store driver).
1029	SMTP SD gateway delivery	The store driver transferred the message to the MTA.
1030	SMTP NDR all	All recipients were sent an NDR.
1031	SMTP end outbound transfer	The outgoing message was successfully transferred.

The high volume of events generated per e-mail is not the only factor that contributes to the number of events Exchange generates. If you have multiple Exchange servers deployed, as most organizations do, each server the message passes through will generate the same number of events. In order to reduce some of the event volume, your collection mechanism needs to be able to filter out some of the noise. When analyzing Exchange events, it is typically sufficient to filter out all events except for event ID 1028, which is the event generated when an e-mail message has been delivered. Filtering down to this event ID reduces the noise by a factor of at least eight. This doesn't apply only to Exchange. In the Sendmail world, at least two events are written per server for each e-mail that is sent or received. This is not quite as extreme as eight messages per e-mail, but it still lends itself to filtering.

Log Format

Once the collection is in order, the message needs to be parsed and the values need to be mapped to their respective normalized fields. For detailed information regarding normalization. The following log shows the events written when one e-mail message is sent through Exchange in raw format:

```
# Message Tracking Log File
# Exchange System Attendant Version 6.5.7226.0
--Headers--
# Date Time   client-ip      Client-hostname       Partner-Name  Server-
hostname      server-IP      Recipient-Address      Event-ID      MSGID
Priority      Recipient-Report-Status       total-bytes   Number-Recipients
Origination-Time      Encryption     service-Version      Linked-MSGID
Message-Subject       Sender-Address


— SMTP submit message: user1 -> user2 Subject: hello this is the subject
2006-3-28     0:0:0 GMT      192.168.10.53 company14.company.com-
SERVER7192.168.1.4    user1@company.com      1019
4482DA7C4F42034FA368EB309567E38D172E90@company14.company.com    0        0
4715   1      2006-3-28 0:0:0 GMT   0      Version: 6.0.3790.1830      -
hello this is the subject   user2@company.com      -


— SMTP begin submit message: user1 -> user2 Subject: hello this is the
subject
2006-3-28     0:0:0 GMT      192.168.10.53 company14.company.com-
SERVER7192.168.1.4    user1@company.com      1025
4482DA7C4F42034FA368EB309567E38D172E90@company14.company.com    0        0
4715   1      2006-3-28 0:0:0 GMT   0      Version: 6.0.3790.1830      -
hello this is the subject   user2@company.com      -
— SMTP submit message: user1 -> user2 Subject: hello this is the subject
2006-3-28     0:0:0 GMT      192.168.10.53 company14.company.com-
SERVER7192.168.1.4    user1@company.com      1024
4482DA7C4F42034FA368EB309567E38D172E90@company14.company.com    0        0
```

```
4715    1      2006-3-28 0:0:0 GMT   0       Version: 6.0.3790.1830      -
hello this is the subject    user2@company.com    -
```

— SMTP message categorized and queued for routing: user1 -> user2 Subject: hello this is the subject

```
2006-3-28     0:0:0 GMT    192.168.10.53 company14.company.com-
SERVER7192.168.1.4    user1@company.com    1033
4482DA7C4F42034FA368EB309567E38D172E90@company14.company.com    0      0
4715    1      2006-3-28 0:0:0 GMT   0       Version: 6.0.3790.1830      -
hello this is the subject    user2@company.com    -
```

— SMTP message queued for local delivery: user1 -> user2 Subject: hello this is the subject

```
2006-3-28     0:0:0 GMT    192.168.10.53 company14.company.com-
SERVER7192.168.1.4    user1@company.com    1036
4482DA7C4F42034FA368EB309567E38D172E90@company14.company.com    0      0
4715    1      2006-3-28 0:0:0 GMT   0       Version: 6.0.3790.1830      -
hello this is the subject    user2@company.com    -
```

— SMTP local delivery: user1 -> user2 Subject: hello this is the subject

```
2006-3-28     0:0:0 GMT    192.168.10.53 company14.company.com-
SERVER7192.168.1.4    user1@company.com    1023
4482DA7C4F42034FA368EB309567E38D172E90@company14.company.com    0      0
4715    1      2006-3-28 0:0:0 GMT   0       Version: 6.0.3790.1830      -
hello this is the subject    user2@company.com    -
```

Message transfer in: user1 -> user2 Subject: hello this is the subject

```
2006-3-28     0:0:0 GMT    -      -      -       SERVER7-
user1@company.com    1028
4482DA7C4F42034FA368EB309567E38D172E90@company14.company.com    0      0
4715    1      2006-3-28 0:0:0 GMT   0       -      -       hello this is the
subjectuser2@company.com
```

Each message in the preceding log contains information that needs to be mapped to a normalized schema. It is common practice to refer to vendor documentation to obtain a description for the nonobvious event fields. Table B.2 gives some examples of brief descriptions for these fields, as provided by Microsoft.

Table B.2 Event Fields and Descriptions

Field	Description
date-time	The date and time of the message tracking event. The value is formatted as *yyyy-mm-ddhh:mm:ss.fffZ*, where *yyyy* = year, *mm* = month, *dd* = day, *hh* = hour, *mm* = minute, *ss* = second, *fff* = fractions of a second, and *Z* signifies Zulu, which is another way to denote UTC.

Continued

Table B.2 continued Event Fields and Descriptions

Field	Description
server-ip	The Transmission Control Protocol/Internet Protocol (TCP/IP) address of the source or destination Exchange server.
server-hostname	The name of the Exchange server that created the message tracking log entry. This is typically the name of the Exchange server holding the message tracking logfiles.
recipient-address	The e-mail addresses of the message's recipients. Multiple e-mail addresses are separated by a semicolon.
total-bytes	The size of the message that includes attachments, in bytes.
recipient-count	The number of recipients in the message.
message-subject	The message's subject, found in the Subject: P2 header field.
sender-address	The e-mail address specified in the **Sender:** P2 header field, or the **From:** P2 header field if **Sender:** is not present.

From Logs to ESM

Once the data has been successfully collected, normalized, and passed to the ESM platform, it is available for analysis and correlation. Figure B.9 shows Exchange message tracking events once they have been processed and presented to a security analyst via the ArcSight Console.

E-mail events are a great source of information. Not only are they useful as a way of tracking who is talking to whom and what information is leaving an organization, but they also lend themselves to visual analysis. By creating event graphs showing sender-to-recipient traffic, with the subject of the e-mail message as the connecting node, it is very easy to see who a particular user is communicating with and how many people have received the communication.

Figure B.9 Exchange Message Tracking Events after Processing, As Shown in the ArcSight Console

	End	↓ 1	Name		Message		Attacker User Name		Target User Name		Priority		Device Vendor		Device Product
	8/15 22:33:59		Email Message		what time		sender@company.com		manager@company.c...		2		Microsoft		Exchange Server
	8/15 22:33:58		Email Message		Tonight		sender@company.com		girl@yahoo.com		2		Microsoft		Exchange Server
	8/15 22:33:57		Email Message		New Project		sender@company.com		user@dest4.com		2		Microsoft		Exchange Server
	8/15 22:33:56		Email Message		New Project		sender@company.com		user@dest3.com		2		Microsoft		Exchange Server
	8/15 22:33:54		Email Message		New Project		sender@company.com		user@dest2.com		2		Microsoft		Exchange Server
	8/15 22:33:53		Email Message		New Project		sender@company.com		user@dest1.com		2		Microsoft		Exchange Server
	8/15 22:33:50		Email Message		New Project		sender@company.com		user@dest.com		2		Microsoft		Exchange Server

Source: ArcSight ESM v4.0

However, because most organizations' e-mail traffic usually is in the millions of e-mails per day, it would be inefficient to try to manually look at the messages as they scroll by in a channel-type view, as shown in Figure B.9. It is much easier to view these events in a visual representation. Figure B.10 shows an event graph of one user's e-mail traffic. The dark box in the middle is the sender, the gray connecting circles are the e-mail subjects, and the white boxes are the recipients. The user is sending an e-mail with a subject of "new project" to five other users; an e-mail to his manager; and an e-mail to a friend at Yahoo.com. One of the most interesting use cases is to watch all traffic destined for Web mail accounts and examine the size for possible information leaks.

Figure B.11 shows a detailed view of the e-mail event. The fields that are typically the most used are the message field, where the e-mail subject is mapped; and the bytes in/out field, where we can look at the size of the message. As we mentioned earlier, the size of an e-mail is very useful in terms of analysis. If you continuously put message sizes through a statistical analysis engine you can determine the average e-mail size per user as well as overall. This allows you to monitor and investigate large deviations. In the figure, the sender and recipient are mapped to the attacker and target username fields, and these are required to do any analysis on a per-user basis. Finally, the number of recipients allows you to track e-mails that have been sent to a large audience.

Figure B.10 Event Graph of One User's E-mail

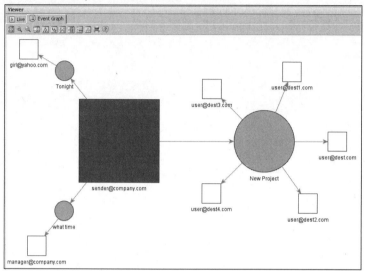

Source: ArcSight ESM v4.0

Figure B.11 A Detailed View of the E-mail Event

Name	Value
Event	
Name	Email Message
Message	New Project
End Time	15 Aug 2006 22:33:50 PDT
Bytes In	6021
Bytes Out	6021
Agent	
Agent Type	exchange_trackinglog
Device	
Device Severity	0
Device Host Name	EXCHANGE1
Device Address	192.168.1.4
Device Vendor	Microsoft
Device Product	Exchange Server
Attacker	
Attacker Dns Domain	company.com
Attacker User Name	sender@company.com
Target	
Target Dns Domain	dest.com
Target User Name	user@dest.com
Device Custom	
Device Custom Date1.Origination-Time	15 Aug 2006 03:14:35 PDT
Device Custom Number1.Encryption	0
Device Custom Number3.Number-Recipientss	5
Device Custom String2.MSGID	F3AF005DED40E940AFE4F2DADB.

Source: ArcSight ESM v4.0

Room for Improvement

Microsoft probably did not intend for security teams to collect and analyze Exchange message tracking logs, so ease of collection and parsing was not part of the product criteria because these logs were meant for debugging purposes. With that in mind, Microsoft could make improvements in several areas. One improvement could be the addition of a consolidated logging mechanism. A centralized log collector would eliminate the scenario of connecting to each Exchange server to collect messages, and getting duplicate events as a message passes through each server. This would also alleviate the need to open network shares or install connectors on each Exchange server. It also would be nice to have different levels of logging. If all you had to do was track e-mails sent and received, it would be nice to turn off logging for all the other components. The most important improvement, however, would be the ability to log attachment names. It would be nice to see the actual attachment that was being sent with an e-mail. This is where the Exchange logs are lacking. If this functionality existed, it would be possible to see what types of documents were leaving the organization and being sent among groups. If we can write a signature on our intrusion detection system that will parse out the attachment name, it should be a trivial addition for Microsoft.

In addition to Exchange, Sendmail does not log attachment names either. We have not been able to find a statement from either vendor indicating that they will include this capability in later releases of their products, nor that they are even considering doing so. Everyone should call the vendor of their mail server and relay the message that this is important information and should be a requirement for future releases. As noted earlier, ILP systems are available that monitor e-mail as it crosses the network. Such products will provide the attachment names from e-mails that have been sent, but they come with their own sets of problems. Also, it's fairly easy to change the name of an attachment, thus requiring deep inspection where the actual content of the attachment is analyzed. In large organizations, dealing with the massive amounts of traffic that need to be inspected can get expensive from a device perspective.

E-mail is a great technology for communication. It allows users within organizations to communicate efficiently across time zones, and it allows friends to stay in touch. Just imagine if every time you sent an e-mail you actually had to pick up the phone to get the same message delivered. You would never get anything done. As with all conveniences, we pay a price; a security risk is associated, and therefore, we must take precautions, such as monitoring.

Voice over IP

Now we will walk through the collection of VoIP logs. VoIP is a way to send voice over a standard IP network. Voice coders and decoders are used to convert voice into IP packets that can be sent over the network. The Session Initiation Protocol (SIP) takes care of the routing and management of VoIP transactions. VoIP phone systems are becoming more and more prevalent. They are in most large organizations and have even started to hit the hotel and consumer markets. VoIP systems generate what is known as a call detail record (CDR), which is really just a log entry stating that a call was made or received. Tracking phone calls has been a hot topic in recent times, with the collection of CDRs from the major phone companies being considered an invasion of privacy, but in the private and public sectors, usually an agreement is signed stating that all IP-related activity can and will be monitored for misuse. It's hard to say whether CDRs should be considered to be logical security or physical security, but it seems that it could be considered either or neither. We consider phone records as a combination of the two.

To understand VoIP logging let's start with a simple example of how a call takes place. Figure B.12 depicts a typical VoIP topology. The call starts from the originator and is routed to the phone's default gateway, which in the VoIP world is known as the *signaling server*. The signaling server is responsible for the setup and teardown of calls. The signaling server then routes the call to a call server, which runs software that performs call control functions such as accounting and administration, protocol conversion, and authorization. The call server then passes the call to the VoIP switch, which either sends the call out or routes it back to another internal phone.

In VoIP, the sound from your voice is treated as data. The sound is converted into packets and traverses the network just as normal IP packets would. There are routers and switches, but the difference here is that a simple latency issue doesn't make your download slow; it makes your VoIP service unusable, a condition known as the *jitters*. You may have experienced this before, where the person you are talking to sounds as though he is on another planet. A VoIP network consists of other components, such as media gateways that handle protocol conversions or components that convert text to voice. For further information on the inner workings of VoIP visit *www.protocols.com/pbook/VoIPFamily.htm*, where you'll find a great introduction to the components and protocols involved.

Figure B.12 Simple VoIP Topology

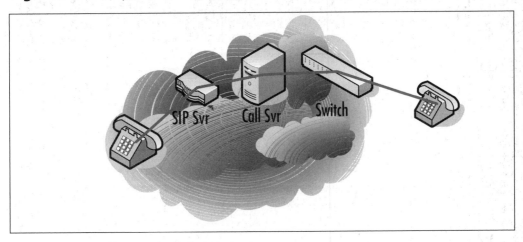

Benefits of Integration

As with tracking any type of communications, monitoring VoIP logs provides basic session information similar to monitoring e-mail traffic. The information typically provided in a CDR is the call initiator, the recipient, and the duration of the call. If we compare CDRs to e-mail events, we can consider the duration to be the size of the message or how much information was communicated. Basic use cases would be to monitor top talkers, or monitoring who is talking to whom and what time of day calls are being placed. An interesting application for VoIP logs is to monitor off-hour usage, meaning who comes into the office on the weekends or in the middle of the night to make long-distance personal calls.

More advanced use cases would be to build relationship charts that show all the people from different groups that are communicating with each other. For example, in the intelligence community, there are people with compartmentalized knowledge who should not share this information with other people who have different compartmentalized knowledge. It seems as though monitoring phone calls among people would be very appealing to some of the more classified segments of the industry. In the use case we are discussing in this Appendix, VoIP logs play a key component to the detection mechanism that is proposed. Monitoring phone calls between users who should not be communicating on a regular basis will uncover anomalies such as high volumes of calls between users and long call duration. This type of behavior, although it may be normal and may not be malicious, can indicate that a user should be investigated further.

Challenges of Integration

VoIP systems have been designed from the beginning with CDR logging in mind. Most, if not all, call servers have the capability to log the calls made and received. This logging was not designed with the security analyst in mind; its main driver is billing. If there was no logging, it would be impossible for service providers to charge for calls that are placed or received.

Call servers write CDRs to local text files, but this is not the ideal place to collect them. The call servers usually have a management software package available that connects directly to a Transmission Control Protocol (TCP) port on each switch where these logs are constantly being streamed out (similar to syslog). Once they are collected, they are put into a database where they can be analyzed for billing and usage information. This works great for integration with ESM, because log aggregators are our friends. Because the logs are already being aggregated and collected, all that's needed is one connector to connect to one system to obtain all the call records from all the switches managed by the telephony manager application.

The next step for integration with VoIP products is configuration, which is by no means a difficult task. Enabling CDRs for external-to-internal calls and internal-to-external calls is typically the default on most systems. On the Nortel system depicted in Table B.3, you can easily show the configuration of the trunks and see that CDR logging is enabled.

Table B.3 Trunk Configuration on a Nortel System

Default Configuration	CDR Logging Enabled
...snip...	
TYPE CDR_DATA	
CUST 00	
CDR NO	
IMPH NO	
OMPH NO	
AXID NO	
TRCR NO	
...snip...	
...snip...	
TYPE CDR_DATA	
CUST 00	
CDR YES	
IMPH NO	

Continued

Table B.3 continued Trunk Configuration on a Nortel System

Default Configuration	CDR Logging Enabled

```
 OMPH NO
 AXID NO
 TRCR NO
...snip...



...snip...
TYPE CDR_DATA
CUST 00
```

CDR YES

```
 IMPH NO
 OMPH NO
 AXID NO
 TRCR NO
...snip...
```

Granted, that's not very challenging. The challenging part is configuring the logging of internal-to-internal calling. Most phone systems do not log this by default, because it's not relevant to billing. In order to log this data, internal call detail (ICD) needs to be enabled. On Nortel systems, this setting is set to **ICDD (Internal Call Detail Disabled)** by default. Table B.4 shows how the configuration should look on a Nortel system if ICD is enabled.

Table B.4 Configuration on a Nortel System When ICD Is Enabled

Default Configuration	ICDA Enabled

```
...snip...
CLS
CTD FBA WTA LPR MTD FNA HTA TDD HFA CRPA
MWA LMPN RMMD SMWD AAD IMD XHD IRA NID OLD VCE DRG1
POD DSX VMD CMSD SLKD CCSD SWD LNA CNDA
CFTD SFD MRD DDV CNID CDCA MSID DAPA BFED RCBD
CDMD LLCN MCTD CLBD AUTU
GPUD DPUD DNDD CFXD ARHD CLTD ASCD
CPFA CPTA ABDD CFHD FICD NAID BUZZ AGRD MOAD AHD
```

Continued

Table B.4 Configuration on a Nortel System When ICD Is Enabled

Default Configuration	ICDA Enabled
DDGA NAMA	
...snip...	
...snip...	
CLS	
CTD FBA WTA LPR MTD FNA HTA TDD HFA CRPA	
MWA LMPN RMMD SMWD AAD IMD XHD IRA NID OLD VCE DRG1	
POD DSX VMD CMSD SLKD CCSD SWD LNA CNDA	
CFTD SFD MRD DDV CNID CDCA MSID DAPA BFED RCBD	
ICDA CDMD LLCN MCTD CLBD AUTU	
GPUD DPUD DNDD CFXD ARHD CLTD ASCD	
CPFA CPTA ABDD CFHD FICD NAID BUZZ AGRD MOAD AHD	
DDGA NAMA	
...snip...	

Log Format

The logging format from VoIP systems is generally very simple and doesn't contain too many fields that are relevant to ESM. The fields that are interesting for analysis are the call initiator, the recipient, and the call duration fields. The following log example is from a Nortel system:

```
N 025 00 2600     T001023 08/16 17:34 00:03:18 A 14155551212 & 0000 0000
N 027 00 T001002 2600     08/16 17:38 00:00:06 A 14155551212 & 0000 0000
N 029 00 2600 2669     08/16 17:38 00:01:02 & 0000 0000
```

The first line shows an internal-to-external call, placed from extension 2600 to the number 415-555-1212, at 17:34, with a duration of 3 minutes and 18 seconds. The second line shows a call originating from an external number going to extension 2600 with a 2-second duration. The third line shows an internal-to-internal call from extension 2600 to extension 2611 lasting 6 seconds.

The relevant fields in the preceding log are the source of the call, the destination, the duration, and the trunk the call went through. The trunk the call went through is not important in the actual analysis, but as far as understanding whether a call was inbound or outbound, the location of the trunk in the log line is important. In the preceding example, the trunk is the value that starts with a **T** and is in bold. If the trunk appears before the extension, as in line two, it is an incoming call; if the trunk appears after the extension, it is an outbound call; and if no trunk is specified, the call was placed between two internal phones. It is also important to note that these logs are from a call server that serves only one prefix. If you have a server that serves multiple prefixes, the extension numbers will be five digits rather than four.

From Logs to ESM

After parsing the logs and sending the events to the ESM platform, they are ready to be analyzed and compared with other event feeds. As part of VoIP log processing, a process needed to be put in place to map the values to the appropriate fields. This can be especially challenging when placement of the values changes the meaning of the events, as is the case with the position of the trunk value. Furthermore, because this is a new event source, the schema does not always contain a field that can deal with a value such as a phone number. This requires that we add a new field to the system, or that we use a field that may be reserved for different types of values.

In this case, it's best not to abuse a field used for an IP address or a username; rather, we should use a field that is reserved for custom values for devices such as this. Figure B.13 shows how the events would look to an analyst as they come into the ArcSight ESM v4 console. Notice the direction associated with each event. The internal-to-internal calls have no direction because they stay within the same system. This will be important in our analysis process later.

Figure B.13 ArcSight ESM v4

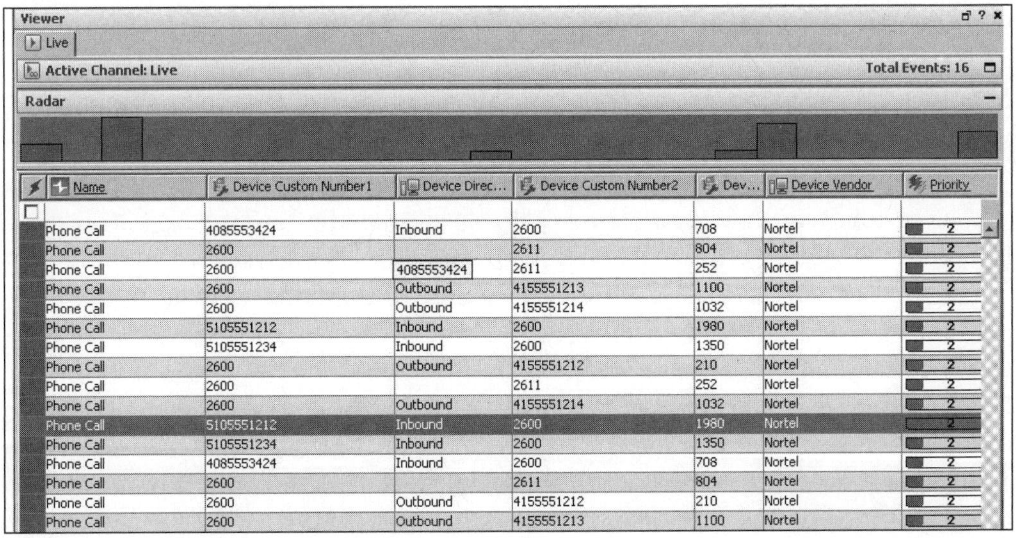

Name	Device Custom Number1	Device Direc...	Device Custom Number2	Dev...	Device Vendor	Priority
Phone Call	4085553424	Inbound	2600	708	Nortel	2
Phone Call	2600		2611	804	Nortel	2
Phone Call	2600	4085553424	2611	252	Nortel	2
Phone Call	2600	Outbound	4155551213	1100	Nortel	2
Phone Call	2600	Outbound	4155551214	1032	Nortel	2
Phone Call	5105551212	Inbound	2600	1980	Nortel	2
Phone Call	5105551234	Inbound	2600	1350	Nortel	2
Phone Call	2600	Outbound	4155551212	210	Nortel	2
Phone Call	2600		2611	252	Nortel	2
Phone Call	2600	Outbound	4155551214	1032	Nortel	2
Phone Call	5105551212	Inbound	2600	1980	Nortel	2
Phone Call	5105551234	Inbound	2600	1350	Nortel	2
Phone Call	4085553424	Inbound	2600	708	Nortel	2
Phone Call	2600		2611	804	Nortel	2
Phone Call	2600	Outbound	4155551212	210	Nortel	2
Phone Call	2600	Outbound	4155551213	1100	Nortel	2

Source: ArcSight ESM v4.0

Figure B.13 shows several calls being made and the fields as they map to the ESM schema. In the highlighted event, an inbound call was placed from 510-555-1212 to extension 2600. The call's duration was 1,980 seconds or 33 minutes. Figure B.14 shows a detailed event view of this phone call.

Figure B.14 Detailed Event View of Call Shown in Figure B.13

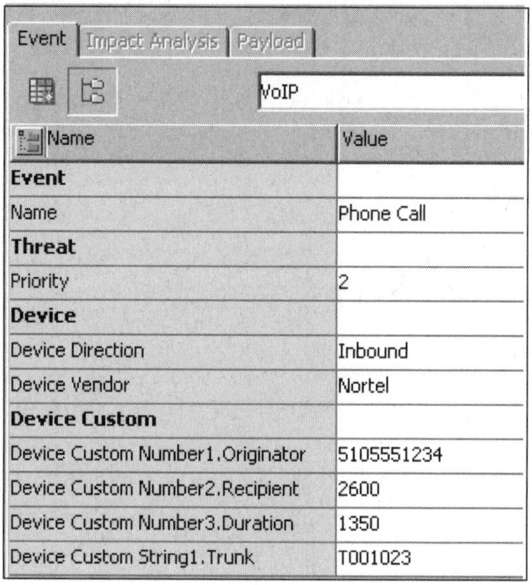

Event	Impact Analysis	Payload	

VoIP

Name	Value
Event	
Name	Phone Call
Threat	
Priority	2
Device	
Device Direction	Inbound
Device Vendor	Nortel
Device Custom	
Device Custom Number1.Originator	5105551234
Device Custom Number2.Recipient	2600
Device Custom Number3.Duration	1350
Device Custom String1.Trunk	T001023

Source: ArcSight ESM v4.0

The fields displayed are the event name; the priority of the event, which in this case is 2 because this is a normal event similar to a firewall accept; the direction of the call; the product vendor that generated the event; the originator; the recipient; the duration; and the trunk over which the call came. The biggest challenge here is the duration. This is a very important field in terms of analysis, as it allows you to compute top talkers, top talker pairs, and the most expensive phone calls. If you recall from the raw logs, the duration was in a time format whereby the call in this detailed view would have had a value of 22:30, or 22 minutes and 30 seconds. The raw value is very difficult to do any computation on, so the number must be converted into seconds to allow for functions to be run. In this example, 22:30 is converted into decimal notation as 22.5 minutes and then multiplied by 60 to get the total number of seconds that the call lasted.

Figure B.15 is a visual analysis of these phone calls. The call originator is represented by the small dark boxes; the call direction is represented by the gray circles; and the destination or call recipient is represented by the white boxes. The figure shows several transactions. On the left, you can see that three inbound calls are placed to extension 2600. The graph on the right shows all the calls placed from extension 2600: three outbound calls and one internal-to-internal call.

Figure B.15 Visual Analysis of the Preceding Phone Calls

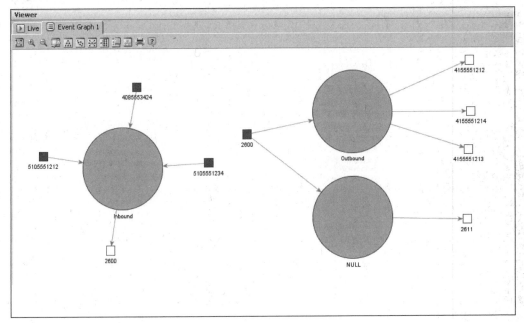

Source: ArcSight ESM v4.0

Visualization of event data always lends itself to speeding up the analysis process. It has been said that a picture is worth a thousand loglines, and seeing a visualization of phone calls made and received validates that statement. The number of phone calls made and received by large organizations per day can be in the millions (or, at least, hundreds of thousands). Trying to make any sense of those calls in a text-based log-file in the format shown previously would be a nightmare. With a visual representation of the same messages, we can quickly separate inbound and outbound calls as well as determine the caller and recipient.

Although the examples in this Appendix include a detailed explanation of VoIP CDRs and how we can collect them, similar logging mechanisms exist on most, if not all, private branch exchange (PBX) phone systems. PBX phone systems are beginning to be phased out by more advanced VoIP systems that are considered more reliable as well as more cost-effective. The events that a PBX system writes are known as call state events (CSEs) and again are written after a phone call has been completed. PBX state events contain much of the same information that a VoIP system will write to a CDR—typically the caller, recipient, and call duration.

Logical security typically deals with events generated from devices that are tied into the IP network of an organization. In the past, the phone system was completely separated from the IP network, so if it was even considered, it was more in the communication or physical monitoring realm. Now with the introduction of IP-enabled phones, it tends to be a gray area where the collection of CDRs could be considered either physical or logical. As we move to the next section, it's important to remember the information that we can obtain through the collection of CDRs. These events are not security events per se, and they don't indicate any wrongdoing, but the statistics they provide give analysts another data point in their detection of an insider trading attempt.

Bridging the Chinese Wall: Detection through Convergence

Now that we have an understanding of what a Chinese wall is and some of the benefits and challenges of the collection of new data sources for analysis, we will walk through a simple scenario of two employees working for a large investment bank and how their plan to trade insider knowledge is detected. Several advanced correlation techniques will be addressed in the eventual detection, such as role-based correlation and statistical anomaly detection. The example we are using in this Appendix involves two users in an investment bank, but the theory and detection mechanism could be applied to any type of organization where silos of information need to be separated. Government agencies currently use these principles and data sources to monitor the communications of their internal employees. In such an example, it is not investment information that is considered compartmentalized; it is much more serious—the data could be the location of agents, agents' identities, or upcoming missions, where a compromise wouldn't have a dollar price tag. This technology currently is applied across vertical markets because the underlying principles are good security practices and prevent the compromise of information among departments where the combination of compartmentalized knowledge leads to compromise.

The Plot

David and Maxwell work for a large financial institution, Finance123. They work in different departments: David works in the Mergers and Acquisitions department and Maxwell works in the Brokerage and Investment Banking department. Because communication between these two departments represents a conflict of interest and violates compliance regulations, strict policies are in place prohibiting communication between the departments. The policies even go so far as to restrict the employees from entering the building through the same entrance. The policies are verbally communicated, but there are no restrictions on who you can call, what e-mail addresses you can send or receive, or who you can meet for lunch down the street. Unfortunately, for Finance123, the technology and policies are not in sync. Not all policies can be implemented with technology; sometimes there are staff and procurement limitations, and as the old saying goes, "where there is a will, there is a way." This is especially true of how humans behave when they are trying to get around the "system." The best you can hope for in this situation is an early detection mechanism through warning signs, anomaly detection, and analysis, finding and stopping the problem before it occurs.

Maxwell and David, our conspirators, know that the information they hold is valuable to one another. If David clues Maxwell in on an upcoming acquisition Maxwell can recommend to all of his clients to invest in the company that is going to be bought. This is good for both Maxwell and David; their commissions increase and they look like financial superstars. This activity is exactly what the Chinese wall was designed to prevent. The scenario shows how David and Maxwell's communication behavior is brought to the attention of security analysts, preventing what would be considered a breach of the set policies of Finance123 and an insider trading attempt.

Detection

Finance123 uses an advanced ESM system set up to monitor external threats and detect internal abuse. By collecting events from these nontraditional data sources, the company is able to monitor internal communications as well as detect anomalous behavior by employees. The setup is fairly typical of an ESM deployment. It consists of several components. Figure B.16 shows (from left to right) the devices generating the data, the ArcSight connectors that are collecting the data and forwarding it to the ESM system, the ArcSight Manager, and analyst consoles.

Figure B.16 Components of an ESM System

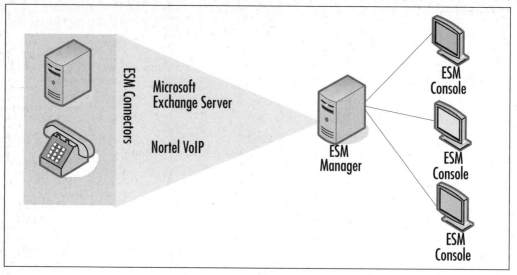

Building the Chinese Wall

The first important step for eventual detection is for the ESM platform to under-stand the users in each department. We can refer to this as *role-based correlation*. Without an understanding of which users are in each department, analysis would be extremely difficult and would require an analyst to remember the different users and their departments. Furthermore, it wouldn't be possible for the ESM platform to detect anomalous communications among groups without having an understanding of what the groups are. Because cross-departmental communications are being mon-itored between two departments, the setup is simple. All that is needed for the ESM platform to understand the user organization is a list of user attributes in each department. A *user attribute* is any value that identifies a particular user, such as a domain logon, extension, or e-mail address.

Once we know the attributes of a particular user, we can correlate events and attribute events back to that user. Using Active List technology within ESM, we can easily track these attributes and correlate events against these lists, specifically checking for a particular event value as being in one of the lists. An example would be an event sent to ESM where the source username, maxwellj@finance123.com, is checked against the Active List to validate whether maxwellj@finance123.com is a member of the Brokerage department. Figure B.17 shows the two role-based active lists.

Figure B.17 Role-Based Active Lists

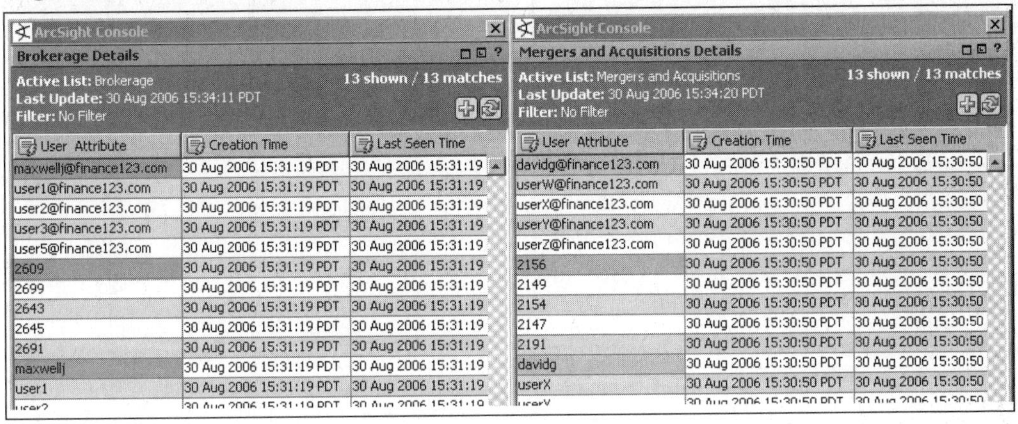

Source: ArcSight ESM v4.0

In these two active lists, we have set up a virtual Chinese wall where we are keeping track of the user attributes from each department. In the Brokerage Active List, notice that there are several entries for Maxwell. We can see his e-mail address, his phone extension, and his Windows domain account logon username. In the Mergers and Acquisitions list to the right, there are similar attributes for David.

Bridging the Chinese Wall

As David and Maxwell continue to share information with each other, they communicate using standard channels, not considering that they could be monitored. However, they are being monitored. All of their communications are being tracked, and because they have been corresponding quite a bit, their behavior sets off alerts in the ESM system because their patterns are anomalous. The setup used to detect these anomalies is a series of moving average data monitors. Data monitors sit in the real-time event flow and collect stats on the events that are coming into the ESM platform. The data monitors used in this scenario are designed to collect information on the communications that are occurring between departments. ESM is tracking all forms of communication between users in the two previously described active lists. If the e-mail sender is in the Brokerage Active List and the recipient is in the Mergers and Acquisitions Active List, or vice versa, the communication will be tracked. Similarly for phone calls, if the caller is in one list and the destination extension is in the other, the call will be tracked.

So, why not alert on all communications between departments? There may be valid business reasons for some forms of communications, but if you look at every e-mail that is sent between the departments or every phone call made, you would need a team of hundreds of analysts. This is why we are looking for anomalies; either users who have never communicated before or users who demonstrate behavior patterns that fall outside those of normal communications.

Four different data monitors are being used in this scenario. The first is tracking the number of e-mails sent between users in the two departments. Figure B.18 shows several groups of sender/recipient pairs that are communicating across departments. The number of e-mails from Maxwell to David and David to Maxwell is far higher than those from most users in the organization. They are not the only users communicating between the departments, but they are the only two who seem to be replying to each other's e-mail, as both show up as a sender and as a recipient. The other two nodes on the data monitor have only sent e-mail to the other department.

Figure B.18 Groups of Sender/Recipient Pairs Communicating across Departments

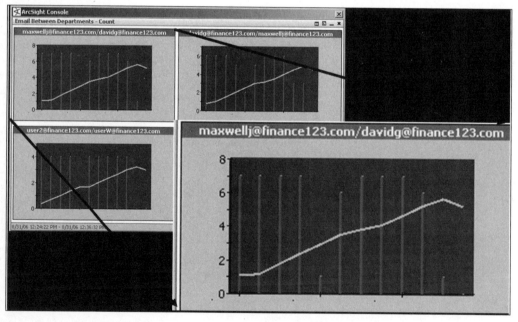

Source: ArcSight ESM v4.0

The data monitor in the preceding figure shows the number of e-mails between a given sender and recipient pair from different departments over time. Each time slice is 24 hours. The x-axis represents time—in this case, days—and the y-axis represents the number of e-mails. The expanded section shows that Maxwell has been sending David an average of eight e-mails per day for the past 11 days. This is quite a bit of communicating back and forth for two users who really don't have any business communicating. The line in the middle of the chart shows the moving average.

From the chart, one can conclude that prior e-mails sent from Maxwell to David were less than eight per day because the average is going up, and the number of e-mails sent from Maxwell to David has declined in the past two days; thus, the average begins to taper down. The node on the top right shows the number of e-mails David has sent Maxwell and the average is also going up. This is most likely because when the e-mails from Maxwell to David go up, David replies more often to Maxwell, or vice versa. The bottom-left portion shows the next highest sender recipient pair in the organization. This is user2 sending to userW.

As we continue to monitor e-mail traffic between the departments, not only do we want to look for anomalies in the number of e-mails sent, but we also want to see the size of the e-mails sent. If two users are trying to hide their communication or just not communicating via e-mail, but one sends the other a large attachment containing details on all upcoming mergers and acquisitions, that communication needs to be caught, even though the message count would be only 1, meaning that it probably wouldn't show up on an analyst's radar using the previous data monitor. Figure B.19 shows a data monitor looking for anomalies in the size of messages between users from different departments. It is apparent from the graph that Maxwell and David have been sending far more information back and forth than any other users in the two departments. We achieve this statistic by running a sum function on the bytes out field of the e-mail events that the Exchange server is generating.

As mentioned, the preceding data monitor is doing a sum function on the size of all of the e-mail messages that have been sent between users in different departments. Again, this is set up as size over a given time slice, which in this case is a 24-hour period. The y-axis is represented in bytes and the x-axis is represented in days. In the callout, you can see that Maxwell has sent David nearly 12 million bytes per day. This is nearly 1.15 MB. E-mail messages are typically very small. A large e-mail containing several paragraphs of text is typically around .5 MB. This would indicate more than the average "Hey what's up?" e-mail going back and forth, and in fact would indicate that attachments probably are being sent or that data is being pasted into the body of the e-mail.

Figure B.19 Data Monitor Looking for Anomalies in Size of Messages

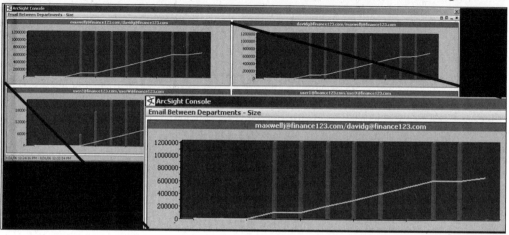

Source: ArcSight ESM v4.0

David and Maxwell have been showing up all over the e-mail anomaly data monitors, and similar data monitors are tracking the usage of the VoIP system. With the VoIP events, we can track almost the same information as with e-mail if we think about the duration of the call as the bytes sent in the e-mail message. Figure B.20 shows the sum of the duration of calls that have taken place between users in the different departments—namely, David at extension 2156 and Maxwell at extension 2609. Remember that the duration has been converted to seconds, so the numbers in the legend represent seconds.

Figure B.20 Sum of Duration of Calls between David and Maxwell

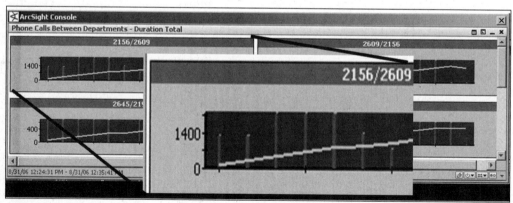

Source: ArcSight ESM v4.0

The data monitor in the figure is tracking the sum or total time spent on the phone between two extensions that are in different departments. The x-axis again represents the time slices, which are 12 hours, and the y-axis represents the total time spent on the phone per day, in seconds. The chart that is called out suggests that extension 2156 (David) has spent nearly 23 minutes per day on the phone with extension 2609 (Max). From the average marker in the middle of the graph, we can see that the average talk time between the two is steadily increasing.

Figure B.21 shows the data monitors used in this scenario, displayed on a dashboard. Although we covered only one type of data monitor in this Appendix, there are different ways to present the data monitors, including event graphs, top values, and geographic event mapping, to name a few. We will use some of these data monitor types for analysis in other use case examples in this book.

Figure B.21 Data Monitors Displayed on a Dashboard

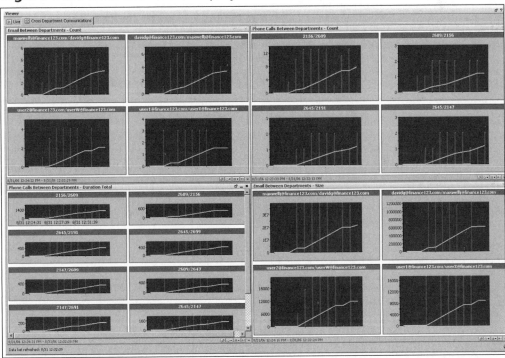

Source: ArcSight ESM v4.0

Data monitors don't just create a nice visual representation of event traffic; they also serve a much greater purpose. They actually perform statistical correlation. If an analyst wasn't watching these visual representations all day long, the communication between Maxwell and David may have gone unnoticed. However, because data monitors are doing real-time analysis, they generate correlation events which can have actions associated with them. The correlation event is based on certain conditions that are configured as part of the data monitor, such as the percent deviation that you want to trigger an alarm or have an action take place. In this case, we are alerting whenever we see a spike in communications between departments that is greater than 10 percent. This means that the analyst a Finance123 received several notifications telling her that there was a spike in traffic between these two users. Figure B.22 shows the correlation events generated by these data monitors in the analyst's console.

Figure B.22 Correlation Events Generated by These Data Monitors in the ArcSight ESM Console

End Time	Name	Device Vendor	Priority	Device Product
		ArcSight		
8/31 12:37:16	Email Between Departments - Size	ArcSight	3	ArcSight
8/31 12:37:16	Email Between Departments - Size	ArcSight	3	ArcSight
8/31 12:36:39	Phone Calls Between Departments - Count	ArcSight	3	ArcSight
8/31 12:36:39	Phone Calls Between Departments - Count	ArcSight	3	ArcSight
8/31 12:36:39	Phone Calls Between Departments - Count	ArcSight	3	ArcSight
8/31 12:36:39	Phone Calls Between Departments - Count	ArcSight	3	ArcSight
8/31 12:36:31	Phone Calls Between Departments - Duration Total	ArcSight	3	ArcSight
8/31 12:35:39	Phone Calls Between Departments - Count	ArcSight	3	ArcSight

Source: ArcSight ESM v4.0

Because the analyst has received these notifications, it's time to do some investigation. The first step the analyst must take is to look at the details of the notifications and determine who is involved and what other events may be coming from those users. The best way to do this is to run an investigative report where the username is used as a filter condition. The analyst runs several reports to show calls made between Maxwell and David, the duration of the calls, and e-mail traffic between the two users. These reports can be presented to management, legal, or HR as evidence that these users have been displaying some questionable behavior. The report in

Figure B.23 is an example of a user investigation report based on e-mail traffic between Maxwell and David.

Figure B.23 User Investigation Report Based on E-mail Traffic between Maxwell and David

	User Investigation		
Parameter Name	**Parameter Value**		
TimeZone	America/Los_Angeles		
Attacker_User	maxwellj@finance123.com		
Target_User	maxwellj@finance123.com		
Start	Aug 30 2006 12:46:10		
End	Aug 31 2006 12:46:10		

Name	Attacker User Name	Message	Target User Name
Email Message	maxwellj@finance123.com	FW: upcoming plans.xls	davidg@finance123.com
Email Message	maxwellj@finance123.com	Lunch?	davidg@finance123.com
Email Message	maxwellj@finance123.com	RE: we should use webmail	davidg@finance123.com
Email Message	maxwellj@finance123.com	Upcoming	davidg@finance123.com
Email Message	maxwellj@finance123.com	call me	davidg@finance123.com
Email Message	maxwellj@finance123.com	golf staurday?	davidg@finance123.com
Email Message	maxwellj@finance123.com	whats up?	davidg@finance123.com
Email Message	davidg@finance123.com	RE: Lunch?	maxwellj@finance123.com
Email Message	davidg@finance123.com	RE: we should use webmail	maxwellj@finance123.com
Email Message	davidg@finance123.com	clients love it	maxwellj@finance123.com
Email Message	davidg@finance123.com	re: golf Saturday	maxwellj@finance123.com
Email Message	davidg@finance123.com	seems good	maxwellj@finance123.com
Email Message	davidg@finance123.com	we should use webmail	maxwellj@finance123.com

Source: ArcSight ESM v4.0

Just by reading the message field of the e-mail alone, the analyst is very suspicious and decides that an investigation is warranted. The report is given to management, and further investigation into the contents of the e-mails, the different accounts that David has been involved with, and the investments that Maxwell has been advising on reveals too many coincidences to say they were not conducting fraudulent activities.

Conclusion

The type of fraud we discussed in this Appendix would result not only in the loss of a job, but also in legal ramifications. The employees and the company in this case are fictitious, but this type of thing happens every day and is very hard to detect. If you consider all the information that is floating around your organization, imagine having to track where it is going externally, let alone internally. These are the types of processes that we can streamline and automate through ESM and the convergence of new data sources. Although these data sources do present some challenges, such as the collection of the e-mail messages and some of the parsing of the VoIP CDRs, these are things that will only improve over time as companies tell their vendors that they need manageable logs and the ability to collect those logs in a convenient manner. Once they are collected, there are worlds of possibilities for analysis.

Index

E